Recovery in Christ

Recovering from Compulsions, Obsessions, and Addictions

Volume 1
Recovery and the Restoration of the One New Man

Floyd L. Kelley Jr.

Copyright © 2012 by Floyd L. Kelley Jr.

Recovery in Christ: Recovering from Compulsions, Obsessions and Addictions.
Volume One: Recovery and the Restoration of the One New Man.
by Floyd L. Kelley Jr.

Printed in the United States of America

ISBN 9781624195976

All rights reserved solely by the author. The author guarantees all contents are original and do not infringe upon the legal rights of any other person or work. No part of this book may be reproduced in any form without the permission of the author. The views expressed in this book are not necessarily those of the publisher.

Unless otherwise indicated, Scripture quotations are from the King James Version of the Hebrew-Greek Key Word Study Bible. Copyright © 1984, 1991 by AMG International, Inc.

www.xulonpress.com

To
My wife Stephanie,
My best friend and closest companion

My mom Floette,
My inspiration and hero

My dad Floyd,
My strength

My children and Grandchildren,
Ryan, Brandy, Nick, Kole, Dru, Hayden, Kylie, and Isabella,
My joy

A special thanks to John and Susan Lowery of Lowery International Ministries for allowing Stephanie and me to be part of their ministry team

A Note from the Author

We are fallen creatures. Fallen creatures have to recover from their fallenness in order to live the abundant life. This book lays out the theological foundation of Yahweh's recovery plan. In Yahweh's recovery plan, He places us "in Christ" so that Christ can empower us to break free from the compulsions, obsessions, and addictions that enslave us. Quantum physics gives us insight into how Yah places us in Christ and empowers us to change. So make no mistake; the title *Recovery in Christ* is not a play on words or an otherworldly concept. It is a reality that we can experience, right here, right now.

An important part of Yah's recovery plan is the renewal of our mind. We must change the way we think. Yah has given us the Bible to help us abandon our old thinking and think like Him. This is not an overnight process, however. It takes time to change the way we think about God, the universe, others, and ourselves.

If you will study this book along with its supporting scriptures, Yahweh's Word will transform your mind, and you will look at God, the universe, others, and yourself differently. What will this accomplish? Well, on the spiritual level, it will heal many of your deepest wounds and tear down many of your most fortified strongholds. On the natural level, renewing your mind will change your *perceptions* of God, the universe, others, and yourself. This will change your *attitudes* towards God, the universe, others, and yourself. In turn, this will change your *relationship* with God, the universe, others, and yourself, which will transform your life.

Now, Yahweh revealed Himself to Hebrews who lived in a Hebrew culture, so I examine the Bible from a Hebraic perspective. I have included a glossary that defines some of the terms I use in this book. So if you encounter a term that you are not familiar with, check the glossary.

This book focuses on what Yahweh has said, not on tradition and religion. This book will challenge the worldly; it will also challenge the spiritual. A worldly person focuses on earthly, natural, and material things; a spiritual person focuses on heavenly, supernatural, and spiritual things. This book will challenge the worldly to shift their focus to spiritual things. It will challenge the spiritual to shift their focus from tradition and religion to relationship.

The Bible indicates that in the last days, Yah will bring Jews and Gentiles together to form the *one new man*. Yeshua will manifest Himself through the one new man, glorify His bride, and return for her. It is time for us to set Christian and Jewish tradition and religion aside so we can become one in Christ. This book will encourage Christians to embrace their Hebraic roots; it will encourage Jews to return to the *ekklesia*; it will encourage us all to believe Yahweh.

In this volume, we will take a journey from the Garden of Eden to the city of Rome and examine the theology of recovery that Yahweh gave to the apostle Paul. During our journey, we will uncover the Hebrew roots of the Christian faith, and learn about the one new man. Long ago, the one new man (a Hebrew named Joshua and a gentile named Caleb) followed Yahweh's instructions and entered the Promise Land. Consequently, we must forsake the traditions of Rome and Jerusalem, and follow Yahweh's instructions to take our place in the one new man and enter our promise land to experience the fullness of the abundant life here on the earth.

In volume 2, we will examine the spiritual, cognitive, and neurological dimensions of compulsion, obsession, and addiction. In volume 3, we will put Yah's recovery plan into action and tear down the Adamic soul structure and also begin to build a messianic soul structure that will put an end to compulsions, obsessions, and addictions. All three volumes will bring healing, but if you are struggling with an obsession, compulsion, or addiction and all three volumes are available, begin with volume 3. I hope you enjoy the *Recovery in Christ* series and cooperate with Yahweh's recovery plan so He can transform you and equip you to live the abundant life!

Contents

Foreword xiii

Introduction xix

Part 1

An Overview of Man's Problem, Yahweh's Solution, and HaSatan's Counterfeit Solution

Chapter 1. In the Beginning 37

Chapter 2. The Beginning of Sorrows 42

Chapter 3. De-Evolution 47

Chapter 4. Searching for Fig Leaves..52

Chapter 5. The Emerging Worldview 57

Part 2

Yahweh's Plan

Chapter 6. Yahweh Rolls Out His Plan 69

Chapter 7. Abraham's Seed..75

Chapter 8.	The Congregation of Moses	80
Chapter 9.	Yahweh Renews His Covenant	85

Part 3

The Phases of Yahweh's Plan

Chapter 10.	A Deeper Look	93
Chapter 11.	From the Garden to the Mountain	98
Chapter 12.	The Dispensation of the Written Torah	105

Part 4

Israel

Chapter 13.	Darkness Overtakes the Earth	115
Chapter 14.	A Bright Light Breaks Forth	120
Chapter 15.	Who Is Israel	125
Chapter 16.	The Abrahamic Covenant	130
Chapter 17.	The Redeemed	135
Chapter 18.	Life in the Older Covenants	140

Part 5

From Religion to Relationship

Chapter 19.	Religion Takes Over	147
Chapter 20.	The Spiritual Exodus	152

Chapter 21.	A Change in the Ekklesia's Government	157
Chapter 22.	Rebuilding the Tabernacle of David	162

Part 6

The Apostle Paul

Chapter 23.	The Apostle Paul	169
Chapter 24.	The Book of Galatians	174
Chapter 25.	Divine Bookends	179

Part 7

Establishing the Context of Romans

Chapter 26.	Rome	187
Chapter 27.	The Rise of the Roman Empire	192
Chapter 28.	The Empire of Augustus	197
Chapter 29.	The Religion of Romulus and Remus	202
Chapter 30.	The Context of Romans	208

Part 8

Repositioning the Bookends

Chapter 31.	Repositioning the Bookend of Galatians	217
Chapter 32.	Repositioning the Bookend of Romans	223

Part 9

A Survey of Romans: We All Have Fallen

Chapter 33.	Romans 1:1–3:20	231
Chapter 34.	Romans 3:21–31	236

Part 10

A Survey of Romans: Inheriting Yeshua's Nature

Chapter 35.	Romans 4:1–25	241
Chapter 36.	Romans 5:1–21	246
Chapter 37.	Romans 6:1–13	250
Chapter 38.	Romans 6:14	255
Chapter 39.	Romans 6:15–23	260

Part 11

A Survey of Romans: Putting the Law in Its Place

Chapter 40.	The Debate Over Romans 7	267
Chapter 41.	Romans 7:1–14	273
Chapter 42.	Romans 7:14–25	276

Part 12

A Survey of Romans: Life in the Spirit

Chapter 43.	Romans 8:1–2	283

Chapter 44.　Romans 8:3–17..288

Chapter 45.　Romans 8:18–39..293

Part 13

A Survey of Romans: The Crown Jewel

Chapter 46.　Romans 9 and 10..301

Chapter 47.　Romans 11...307

Part 14

A Survey of Romans: Walking It Out

Chapter 48.　Applied Theology..315

Chapter 49.　Romans 12 and 13..321

Chapter 50.　Romans 14:1–20..326

Chapter 51.　Romans 14:21–16:27...332

Chapter 52.　Keeping It Between the Bookends.....................................337

Part 15

The Final Analysis

Summary..347

Conclusion...369

Bibliography..371

Scripture Index...383

Subject Index..391

Glossary 403

Figures and Tables 407

Endnotes 411

Foreword

Foreword

What the One New Man Is Saying About *Recovery in Christ*

Rabbi Curt Landry

Through the words of *Recovery in Christ*, Floyd Kelley has brought unique and insightful teaching on the mysteries of deliverance and healing. The ability to reach inside his own personal experience gives Floyd a unique gift and perspective to break down biblical truths in these areas. He is able to take a vast subject and walk readers through comprehensible steps to understanding healing and spiritual deliverance.

This book will become invaluable to those who desire to walk in the freedom of personal deliverance or as a tool to minister deliverance to others who are struggling with addictions or demonically controlled behavior.

Floyd Kelley's years of studying the Hebraic roots of the Christian faith have given him a unique biblical perspective, and through *Recovery in Christ*, his teaching enlightens the readers to their true inheritance in Abraham. He also brings a new level of understanding and compassion regarding the heart of Father God to send His only Son, Yeshua, to the cross at Calvary.

Through Floyd's personal testimony, one cannot deny the evidence that there is power in the blood of the Lamb. There is power to walk in healing, there is power to walk in deliverance, and there is power to recover all!

—Rabbi Curt Landry
Founder and CEO
House of David Ministries
Fairland, OK
www.houseofdavid.us

Dr. Dwain Miller

As Floyd's pastor for the past seven years, I can tell you that if ever there was a man who understands the supernatural power of the cross of Christ, if ever there was a man who knows the sure and certain ability of the Word of God and the enabling ministry of the Holy Spirit, Floyd Kelley is that man.

If ever there was a book that is essential to the Christian walk, the book of Romans is it. Many times the book of Romans is referred to as the constitution of Christianity. A constitution is a legal document that guarantees one's personal freedom and rights. However, if an individual does not know what his rights are, the constitution has become void of power in that person's life.

That is why the Scripture exclaims in Hosea 4:6, "My people are destroyed for a lack of knowledge."

Floyd has taken the most important document to our Christian walk and made it applicable to all of us, whether Jew or Gentile, in a way that we can understand and appropriate so that our identity in Christ as the seed of Abraham becomes our legal right to total freedom in Christ—freedom to operate as those who are either complete or who have been grafted into Yeshua.

The book of Romans is the most helpful book in all the Bible to us as Gentiles because it establishes our roots in Christ and the fact that through Abraham, we, being his seed, lack nothing.

Floyd's understanding of Hebraic roots, along with his personal testimony and background as a Gentile, has given him the perfect vantage point from which to write this powerful and practical book that is sure to establish all of us in Yeshua.

I can assure you, as a student of the Word for the past twenty-six years, I plan to incorporate this tremendous treatise on the book of Romans into all my future teaching. This is a great tool that no pastor, teacher, or serious Bible student can be without.

—Dr. Dwain Miller, Senior Pastor
Cross Life Church,
El Dorado, AR
www.crosslifechurch.net

John Lowery

Floyd and Stephanie Kelley have been a part of Lowery International Ministries for eight years. The Kelley's have an anointed calling to lead people through spiritual and emotional healing. Floyd, through his experience and supernatural insight, has a unique ability to go deep into the word of God and to communicate revelation that imparts understanding and transformation.

Every believer needs, not just a knowledge of the word of God, but also an understanding of it. When we understand the word of God, we acquire wisdom. Wisdom is the ability to apply the word of God in our lives. It is this understanding and wisdom that transforms us into "overcomers".

The book of Romans is an essential book to those of us who have been "grafted in." Until we understand our Hebraic heritage, we cannot fully understand our heritage in Christ Jesus. As "deep calls to deep", Floyd leads us into a deeper understanding of our inheritance "in Christ".

Recovery in Christ is a must-read for anyone who is struggling with a compulsion, obsession or addiction and wants to be set free. It is also an excellent tool for anyone who is in the ministry or for anyone who has a loved one who is struggling in his or her Christian walk.

— John Lowery
Former Arkansas State Representative and
the President of Lowery International Ministries

Mark Day

I graduated Bible College and entered the ministry with a view of God that held me in bondage, guilt, and discouragement. I misunderstood how God related to people in the Old Testament. I saw a God who required the people in the Old Testament to keep the law perfectly, and if they could not keep the law perfectly, well too bad, they should have tried harder. Consequently, I carried this erroneous perception over into my New Testament understanding of God.

After reading Recovery in Christ, my view of God has changed tremendously. What Floyd Kelley made clear in his book is that God's redemptive plan has never changed. The God of the Old Testament was not a God who required people to follow rules in order to become righteous, rather God required people to put their faith in the Promised Seed so that He could declare them righteous, and out of that righteousness flowed a desire to love and obey Him.

In the Church, many believe that you must earn God's love and keep a "clean record" in order to have God's fullness. I have actually seen people keep calendars that denoted when they last committed a particular sin that they were trying to overcome. As the days went by, they began to feel better about themselves because they had not committed that sin. Satan wants you to believe that your identity, worth, and success as a Christian is based on walking the straight and narrow, earning your own righteousness. If you believe Satan, you will separate yourself from the love of God and give him the power to hold you in bondage, guilt and discouragement!

Here is the good news: you do not have to wait until you overcome a certain sin pattern to put off the guilt, shame and condemnation that make it possible for Satan to hold you in bondage. No, you just need to take your position "in Christ" and realize who you are "in Him." Once you know who you are "in Christ," then Satan will not be able to separate you from the love of God, and consequently, he will lose his power over you. God does not wait for you to overcome a particular sin pattern before He loves, accepts and blesses you; He loves, accepts and blesses you so that you can draw near to Him without fear and overcome that particular sin pattern.

As for me and my house, we will not put our faith in the things that we can do for God; we will put our faith in who we are "in Christ" so that we can stay close to God without fear. For as it is written, "There is no fear in love. But perfect love drives out fear, because fear has to do with punishment. The one who fears is not made perfect in love. We love because he first loved us." 1 John 4:18-19

—Mark Day, Administrative Pastor
Cross Life Church, EL Dorado, AR
www.crosslifechurch.net

Introduction

Introduction

It is humbling to write about the Bible. The Bible has been studied, discussed, debated, and written about more than any other book in history. It is also a little frightening. The Bible reveals the Creator's thoughts about Himself, the universe, and its creatures. If I distort my Creator's thoughts and lead people astray or hurt them, I will have to give an account for my actions when I stand before His *bema* seat. This is a frightening prospect. Therefore, every morning I humbly ask my Creator for wisdom, revelation, understanding, and knowledge.

The Bible is our Creator's thoughts, words, and actions recorded on paper. A person can read the words on the pages of a Bible, but Yah's Spirit has to bring those words to life before he can understand them and they can do their creative work in his life. Now obviously, the Spirit brings different verses to life for different people at different times. Spiritually, we are all in different places. Yah relates to us this way because it helps us realize that we need each other.

Yah's Spirit reveals truth to our spirit, and our spirit reveals it to our mind. This means that we grow by grace because we are not in control of what we learn or when we learn it. The things I write about today reflect where I am today, but since the Spirit never stops revealing truth, next year I will be at a different place. Thus the material in this book will be complex to some, infantile to others, and just right for a few. I pray that this book is just right for where you are today. However, if this book seems too complex, please do not get intimidated and put it down. On the other hand, if it seems too simplistic, please do not get bored and skim it, because regardless of where you are today, the Holy Spirit will use this book to move you to a new place.

I tremble at the thought of standing before Yeshua's bema seat and Him asking me to explain why I distorted the truth to support my pet theology. So I endeavor to tell the truth, the whole truth, and nothing but the truth. Yah's Spirit reveals His thoughts to my spirit, and my spirit reveals them to my mind so that I can write them down. There is a problem, however. My worldview affects how I interpret and express the Spirit's thoughts.

Yahweh tells us to minimize this distortion by rebuilding our worldview (renewing our mind), lining it up with His.

For us to accurately discern and express the Spirit's thoughts and intents, our worldview has to line up with Yah's worldview, which means that we must view Yah, others, the universe, and ourselves as Yah views Himself, others, the universe, and us. However, no one's worldview perfectly matches Yah's worldview, which means that we all inadvertently distort some of the Spirit's thoughts as they pass through our worldview. So I want to disclose some of the primary presuppositions (primary planks) that form the foundation of my worldview. Here are a few of my primary planks: "Hear, O Israel: the Lord our God is one Lord."[1] "For I am the Lord, I change not; therefore ye sons of Jacob are not consumed."[2] "In the beginning was the Word, and the Word was with God, and the Word was God."[3] "Jesus Christ the same yesterday, and today, and forever."[4] "The Lamb slain from the foundation of the world."[5] "Think not that I am come to destroy the law, or the prophets: I am not come to destroy, but to fulfill."[6]

I know this is a little technical, but please bear with me as I differentiate between the brain and the mind. The brain is not the mind. The mind is the thoughts and intents of man's spirit. Man's spirit materializes his thoughts and intents in the brain so that he can express himself on the earth. The brain has about a hundred billion neurons in it. When our spirit focuses on something and interacts with it, our spirit's energy field connects the brain's neurons together, recording its observations, reactions, thoughts, and intents. As we focus on something new and interact with it, we relate and associate the new stimuli to the information that we have already stored in our memory circuits; and over time, this process of relation, association, and integration constructs a biological filter that we screen reality through, which shapes our perceptions of it.

We call this biological filter a *worldview*. The foundational planks in a person's worldview act as data points. The human spirit uses these data points to measure corporeal stimuli. The human spirit relates and associates new stimuli to these data points in order to determine if it should accept or reject them. The human spirit rejects the stimuli that are incongruent with its biological filter and prevents them from passing through it, relating, associating, and integrating into it. These stimuli have no impact on us. The human spirit accepts the stimuli that are congruent with its biological filter and allows these stimuli to

---

[1] *The Hebrew-Greek Key Word Study Bible*, KJV, Chattanooga, TN, AMG International, Inc., 1991, Deuteronomy 6:4.

[2] Ibid., Malachi 3:6.

[3] Ibid., John 1:1.

[4] Ibid., Hebrews 13:8.

[5] Ibid., Revelation 13:8.

[6] Ibid., Matthew 5:17.

Introduction

pass through it, relating, associating, and integrating into it. These stimuli have the potential to change us. The biological filter also screens stimuli from the spirit realm. Therefore, it is imperative that we reprogram our biological filter with the Scriptures, which are Yah's thoughts, so we can accurately discern His Spirit's communications and express them to others in the earth realm.

I have revealed some of the data points that I use to gauge the communications that I receive from the spirit realm. Now let me describe the worldview these data points have built. In my worldview, the Father, Son, and Spirit are one. It is impossible for Yahweh to change or to violate His Word because He and His Word are one. Yah completed the work of redemption before He created the earth. After Adam introduced corruption into the earth, Yahweh began manifesting His finished work in space-time. Since Yahweh finished the work of redemption prior to creating the earth and is simply manifesting it in space-time, there is only one plan.

In my worldview, the Scripture is a progressive revelation of Yahweh's plan. Yahweh implements His plan in phases using mechanisms that prepare us for eternity. Each phase builds on the previous one and sets the stage for the next. In the initial phase, Yah draws a sketch of His plan. In each later phase, Yah's revelation of His plan gets more detailed, and He puts new mechanisms that are more precise in place to implement it. At the end of each phase, there are two groups: the saved and the dammed. The thing that determines which group a person is in is how he responded to the revelation that Yah gave him. There are no inconsistencies between the Old and New Testaments. The specificity of the revelations and the mechanisms that implement them are different, but the revelations and mechanisms are not inconsistent or contradictory, which is why Yeshua said that He came to fulfill the law, not do away with it.

Each person will measure the information in this book against his own data points. If your primary planks are similar to mine, you will have no problem accepting the information in this book and relating, associating, and integrating it into your worldview. Then, if you act on the information, it will change your life. However, if your primary planks do not resemble mine, you will be tempted to label the information in this book as error and reject it. Now obviously, if you reject the information in this book, it will have no impact on your life. Before you reject the information in this book, I ask you to look at the condition of your life. If there is addiction, compulsion, or obsession in your life and you want to get free, then please consider tearing out some of your primary planks and replacing them with primary planks that are similar to mine.

I know that because of the way the brain operates, no two people agree on everything. Hence I am not asking you to agree with me on everything. The only thing that you must agree with is the *golden plank*. The golden plank is the belief that Yeshua is Yahweh clothed in flesh, that He offered Himself for our sins before He created the earth, and that He came to earth in order to bring His finished work into space-time. Since Yeshua finished

His redemptive work prior to creating the earth and is now bringing it into space-time, we cannot add to it. In other words, we cannot help Yeshua save us. The only thing that we can do is choose to believe that Yeshua has finished the work of redemption. Yeshua provides the grace, and He gives us the faith to receive His grace. Thus each person must *choose* to trust Him or to reject Him.

If your worldview rests on the golden plank, the information in this book will help you. However, if your worldview does not rest on the golden plank, this book will not help you unless you are willing to pull up your primary plank and replace it with the golden plank. Once the golden plank is in place, then you will have a firm foundation to build on, and every other plank that you select will determine the quality of your life. In order for our lives to change, we have to change. In order for us to change, we have to change the way we think. Please think about accepting the golden plank as the foundational plank in your worldview and measuring all your other planks to see if they line up with it, pulling up and replacing those that do not.

Around 1953 BC, Yahweh cut a covenant with the first Hebrew. Yahweh allowed the Gentiles to attach themselves to the Hebrews, and the one new man came into being. Over time the Hebrews formed a religion that separated them from the Gentiles and destroyed the one new man. Around AD 30, a Jewish Messiah created an institution to expand Israel's righteous remnant into a global commonwealth. After the fullness of that generation of Jews came into Israel's righteous remnant, the Jewish disciples of the Jewish Messiah shared the gospel of the kingdom with the Gentiles in order to bring them back into Israel's righteous remnant, which re-created the one new man who was supposed to manifest Yahweh's glory to the whole world.

Around AD 321, the Gentiles drove the Hebrews out of the institution they had founded. The Gentiles took over and formed their own theologies, dogmas, traditions, and holy days by filtering the Bible through a Greco-Roman worldview. The Gentiles should have filtered the Bible through an ancient Hebraic worldview, but since they had become proud and drove the Hebrews out, they strayed from the faith that was once delivered unto the saints and rebuilt the middle wall of separation that Yeshua had torn down, thus destroying the one new man.

In 1967, Yahweh began removing the scales from the eyes of the Jews. The Jews began returning to the institution that their Messiah created and their ancestors built, reuniting with the Gentiles in order to rebuild the one new man and manifest the glory of Messiah to the whole world. This is Yah's plan. So, as Gentiles, we need to humble ourselves and listen to the insights that the level-headed, born-again, Spirit-filled Jews have about the ancient Hebraic worldview and make the necessary adjustments to our theology, dogmas, and traditions.[7] The adjustments will not affect the golden plank; it is eternal and unchanging. The

---

[7] Ibid., Zechariah 8:23.

Introduction

adjustments will affect the secondary planks that we attach to the golden plank in order to build our worldview and life.

The secondary planks that we choose affect our witness, our quality of life, our review at the bema seat, and our rewards in heaven, the millennial kingdom, and the new earth. Sincere believers often disagree on secondary issues, but that does not prevent them from learning from one another. My readers may disagree with me on a particular secondary issue, but I pray that they will learn something in my book that will move them to a new spiritual place, change the quality of their lives, enhance their review at the bema seat, and increase their eternal reward.

My Struggle

Voices in the Wilderness

It was 1976. America was planning to celebrate two hundred years of freedom, but without realizing it, I was planning a slow, steady descent into the bondage of addiction. I was fifteen, and I started smoking pot, drinking alcohol, and popping pills so that I could be in the "cool" crowd. The school that I attended made sure that I heard the addicts, homeless, prison inmates, and terminally ill who were crying out from the wilderness of addiction, prophesying of my future, pleading with me to turn back; but I ignored their pleas. I ignored the pleas because I was under a sorcerer's spell that soothed my emotions and covered my insecurities so that I could hang out with the cool kids, and besides, I was smarter than those pitiful wretches!

Twenty-six years later, I woke up to learn that the cool kids were either in prison, bankrupt, diseased, or dead. I also learned that the prophecies of the pitiful wretches had come to pass. The drugs that had once allowed me to fit into society were now shutting me out of it, but I could not stop. A force compelled me to consume large quantities of pills, pot, crack, and heroin just so that I could feel normal. The price of this normality, however, was loneliness, poverty, and hopelessness. I had joined the ranks of the pitiful wretches. I was destined to cry out from the wilderness to warn wayward teens of the dangers of using drugs. I was now a prophet—a prophet who would plead with the sorcerer's younger victims in the hope of turning them back from following him, only to have them mock me and scorn my prophecies. I recalled how I had mocked and scorned the prophets who had spoken to me twenty-six years earlier, and it sickened me.

Rock Bottom

I awoke from the sorcerer's spell on August 13, 2001. On this day, I emerged from an imaginary universe, which revolved around me, to enter a universe that did not. Now, it was obvious that this new universe did not revolve around me, because in this universe, I was alone, friendless, family-less, homeless, and penniless. In this universe, I had pawned my possessions and driven everyone out of my life, including my own mother! In this universe, I had reached the much anticipated but greatly feared destination of rock bottom. Just as a salmon obeys its instincts and fights against river currents as it swims upstream to return to its birthplace as a worn-out shell of its former self in order to die, I had obeyed the sorcerer's voice and fought against society's currents, swimming upstream to return to my birthplace as a shell of my former self in order to die.

I had run out of options. I had conned, manipulated, and used up everyone in my life. I had used up my energies and resources. I had no more aces in the hole to play. I was done. I had to commit suicide or find a way to change. Addiction had become too painful for me. It was then that I realized that I had never actually lived. Waves of regret washed over me. It was as if a cold shower had opened my eyes so that I could see how tragic it would be to die before living. At that moment, I decided that somehow, someway, I was going to squirm out of the trap of addiction. Paradoxically, the icy waters of regret ignited a beacon of hope in my soul, but then I felt a monster drawing near. I had felt this ominous presence a million times. The hairs on my body stood erect to warn me that a horrifying creature was about to pounce on me, and fear smothered the flickering flame of hope, and the cold steel jaws of addiction clamped tighter.

The Hideous Monster

As I pondered the overwhelming complexities of this situation in the face of the alluring simplicity of surrender, I became increasingly aware of the monster that was closing in on me. The beast that was about to seize me and make it impossible for me to escape from the trap of addiction was *dope sickness*. When a person ingests chemicals for a long time, every organ in his body adjusts to these chemicals, and his adjusted state becomes his normal state. Once a person's adjusted state becomes his normal state, then he has no option; he has to ingest the chemicals that his organs and bodily systems are accustomed to, or else they will go into shock.

As dope sickness seizes a person, his breathing becomes shallow and difficult. The person becomes disoriented and dizzy, and his heart races. Sweat drenches the bed sheets, and the person's energy evaporates. He finds it hard to talk, listen, see, think, walk, or eat. He begins to have severe headaches, and sharp phantom pains shoot through his body. The person begins to experience severe flu-like symptoms. Dope sickness can inflict this physical torture on a person for weeks, but the worst part of dope sickness is the psychological torment of knowing that one dose of chemicals would instantly end the hellish torment and take away all the pain. This is why all a person thinks about when he is dope sick is obtaining a hit of dope.

As I languished in this place called rock bottom, vainly searching for one last ace in the hole, I was becoming increasingly anxious because I could feel the breath of the hideous beast condensing on the back of my neck. As the stench of the beast's breath filled my nostrils, the pressure to choose between suicide and change reached an apex. I knew that if I waited much longer, the beast would seize me and torture me until I abandoned all hope and acquiesced to a fate worse than death; that is, a life without hope, slowly wasting away in the trap of addiction.

I was terrified. I knew that if the serpent of dope sickness coiled around my body and began to squeeze the air out of my lungs, my survival instincts would take over. This terrified me because my survival instincts would override the desire to change or reason, override morals and social constraint, and morph me into a person who would lie, cheat, steal, rob, prostitute himself, and hurt his loved ones in a desperate bid to escape from the serpent's constricting coils and live.

Hope

What I feared the most came upon me. I felt the serpent's powerful coils slowly constricting around me. I heard the serpent whisper, "Give up. Kill yourself, because you will never change." The serpent skillfully siphoned the hope from my soul, and it looked as if he would win this struggle. Then, inexplicably, the veil of deception vanished, and I realized that rock bottom was a foundation that I could build a new life on, and hope welled up in my spirit.

As the living waters of hope refreshed my spirit, suicide lost its appeal, and the prospect of returning to addiction sickened me even more. The supernatural waters of hope refreshed my spirit and gave it the strength it needed to reject suicide and addiction and believe that recovery was actually possible. The time that I spent between a rock and a hard place; that is, between the serpent and rock bottom, was filled with unimaginable pain, but I was allowed to experience this pain so that rock bottom could work its perfect work in my heart. Rock bottom forced me to become willing to change, and it created a thirst in my spirit for the living water that would make change possible. I wish that I could tell you that I chose to change, but I cannot. The consequences of my behavior brought me to rock bottom, and it forced me to either change or die.

A Declaration of War

I did not know it, but I had arrived at an appointed time. Yah's special forces (His Spirit) came on me and gave me hope, but when I acted on that hope, it triggered a spiritual war. Yah sent His special forces to free me, but HaSatan's (see glossary) prison guards went on red alert. I had to choose to cooperate with either the special forces or with the prison guards. Sadly, my body wanted to cooperate with the prison guards because it needed the chemicals to survive. My soul was used to being in prison, and it wanted to stay, but at the same time, it wanted to escape. My spirit, however, was sick and tired of being a prisoner and wanted to cooperate with the special forces. The special forces infiltrated the prison and gave my spirit the power it needed to force my soul to speak out the words that placed my body in a chemical isolation unit (a rehab).

It took a month to flush the chemicals out of my body. The rehab unit was a safe place where my body could go through shock and reach a new state of normalcy. This was extremely painful, but when it was over, my body was a neutral party in the war for freedom. The war was now between my spirit and my soul. My soul was trying to cope with the pain of the past and its encounter with rock bottom. My soul was willing to go along with my spirit and change, but it saw everyone and everything through its wounds, and this created a lot of pain it needed to kill. On one hand, my soul wanted to change, but on the other, it wanted to kill its pain with drugs.

Yah's Spirit had freed my spirit. The rehab unit had freed my body. Now my soul needed to get free. After rehab, I kept reminding my soul of how painful rock bottom and rehab were. I avoided the people, places, and things that could activate a dangerous memory circuit. If I activated the wrong memory circuit in my soul, it could trigger a strong psychobiological response that would cause my body to abandon its position of neutrality and jump back into the fight with both feet and join my soul, and together they would drag my spirit back into prison.

I had to keep my body out of the fight. My spirit was weak, and my soul was still in chains. I avoided chemicals and any person, any thing, or any place that could activate a memory trace that could reestablish a transient chemical craving in my body. I knew that if my body got back into the fight, I would find myself behind prison walls and headed for another showdown with the serpent at rock bottom, and this scared the hell out of me; so I changed friends, routines, routes, stores, music, TV programs, and books. This was not enough, however; if I were to remain free, I had to root out the enemy strongholds in my soul, or eventually a crafty prison guard would use one of these strongholds to lure me back into the prison of addiction.

A Critical Juncture

I was at a critical juncture where most people fail. I was not doing drugs, but my soul saw the universe through its wounds, and so I still thought like a prisoner. This is dangerous. If you think like a prisoner, a part of you is comfortable being a prisoner, and it will not be long before a sly guard coaxes you back into the prison of addiction. I had to stop thinking like a prisoner and start thinking like a free man.

I started studying the Bible and listening to teachings during the day, and at night I played teaching tapes that fed my spirit as my soul slept. I sought advice from people who had gotten out of the trap of addiction so that I could learn from their experiences. I was on shaky ground for about six months, but Yah's Word took root in my heart, and my spirit grew and my worldview changed. Submitting to Yah's Word and fellowshiping with His Spirit slowly healed my soul so that I could accept my new identity as a free man.

An Illusion of Freedom

After Yahweh's Spirit had healed the wounds in my soul, I started to perceive reality differently. I endeavored to perceive everything and everyone as Yah said to perceive them and to interact with them as He said to interact with them. This meant that the pain I generated never rose to a level that made me want to kill it with chemicals. Therefore, my soul stopped craving chemicals. After the cravings were gone, then all I had to do was to continue to perceive Yah, others, and myself correctly and keep interacting with Him, others, and myself correctly. Yah will help us deal with the pain that comes from living in a fallen world, but we have a choice. We can trust Yahweh and deal with the pain His way, or we can trust ourselves and do it our way.

Most people think that recovery is abstaining from chemicals. Therefore, they grit their teeth and abstain from chemicals without changing the way that they interact with Yah, others, and themselves. Since these people have not changed the way they think, they continue to generate pain that they have to anesthetize. If these people do somehow manage to abstain from their chemical of choice, they have to find some other way to anesthetize the pain. Sadly, these people suppress the pain and continually nurse and rehearse the horrible things that happened to them when they were in their addiction in the hope that their remembrance of the pain they experienced will fortify their will so that they can continue to avoid their chemical of choice. Invariably, however, this leads to substitute addictions and a relapse into chemical bondage.

Here is the problem. These people have not submitted to Yah and allowed Him to heal their soul, so they continue to perceive everything and everyone through their wounds and generate pain that they have to kill. They run to food, sex, work, religion, ministry, meetings, porn, antidepressants, relationships, or anything else that will kill the pain so that they can abstain from their chemical of choice. These people sincerely believe that they are free, but in reality, their freedom is an illusion, because they are not free; they are merely chemical free.

The Way, the Truth, and the Life

Yah knows that we are fallen creatures who have to interact with other fallen creatures. Yah knows that we live in a fallen world and that the situations and circumstances that we face create spiritual and emotional pain in us. Yah knows that a vile spirit who wants to destroy us has tricked us into chemically anesthetizing the pain. Yah is not mad at us. Yah loves us. Our Creator wants to help us deal with the pain that comes from living in a fallen world so that we can enjoy life and be free to serve Him, but we have to humble ourselves and do it His way.

How do we recover Yah's way? The Scriptures tell us that if we will walk in the Spirit, then we will not fulfill the lust of the flesh. This means that if we will listen to the Holy Spirit and obey His voice, He will show us how to deal with the spiritual and emotional pain; and this will eliminate the need to anesthetize the soul, which will eliminate the desire to abuse drugs.

In order to walk in the Spirit, we have to be able to hear His voice and obey it. *Recovery in Christ* shows us how to reposition the human spirit so we can hear the Holy Spirit's voice. Once we recognize the Spirit's voice, then we have to obey it in order to benefit from hearing it. *Recovery in Christ* shows us how to remove the chains from the soul so that when we hear the Spirit's voice, we can obey it. If we will humble ourselves and start doing things Yahweh's way, and listen carefully for His voice and obey it when we hear it, then the abundant life is ours.

A Cure for Addiction

Is there a cure for addiction? Yes, there is! Okay, all of you who attend secular recovery groups, just relax, take a deep breath, and continue reading. I know I contradicted one of your cardinal dogmas by saying that there is a cure for addiction, but this is what Yah has said. Yah says that He will cure people, not just patch them up so that they can enjoy a temporary reprieve that is contingent on their continual meeting attendance. Yah will re-create people and change their desires, but man's recovery programs cannot do this; so for them, there is no cure.

HaSatan lures people into chemical bondage, and when they realize they are about to be destroyed and try to escape, he lures them into his recovery program and enslaves them in his proxy bondage. Under the guise of recovery, HaSatan's proxy bondage keeps people separated from Yeshua so that they will end up in the lake of fire with him. The recovery program looks biblical, but it is not. The recovery program promotes HaSatan's end-time New Age ecumenical agenda. In order to keep up the recovery façade, HaSatan grants a temporary reprieve from the torment of addiction to a few; but if they do not believe Yah

Introduction

and submit to His Son, when they die, the temporary reprieve will end, and the torment will resume and continue forever.

The Purpose of this Book

I went to two recovery groups for a few years and worked the program thoroughly. I wrote a 139-page inventory, confessed my wrongs and defects, made amends, and sought God. However, I grew tired of the meetings in which I had to listen to people nurse and rehearse their painful experiences in their addictions. I soon realized that these meetings kept the prisoner in me alive and that if I allowed him to live, I would eventually relapse. I reached out for help, and Yeshua filled me with His Spirit. I began to study the Scriptures and fellowship with Yeshua's Spirit. The leaders of the groups told me that I could not talk about Yeshua and pray for those who wanted to know Him and receive an infilling of His Spirit. This proved that there was an anti-Messiah spirit at work, so I left and asked Yahweh to teach me about real recovery.

One night I had a dream. In the dream, I saw the foundation of a house with the word *Romans* written in the middle of it. The Lord told me that He had explained His recovery plan in Romans. The next morning, I set out to understand Romans and help people recover "in Christ." I have never looked back or returned to recovery meetings, except to make amends to the groups for creating a negative attitude towards them. Yahweh's Spirit prompted me to go make amends to the groups so that I could disconnect from them, see the truth about them, and prevent the darkness of resentment from falling on me. Let me be clear: I do not resent recovery groups or anyone in them, but I must be truthful about the recovery movement and its unholy roots.

Recovery in Christ takes us on a trip from the Garden of Eden to the city of Rome. After we arrive in Rome, we will examine the book of Romans and discover the principles of real recovery. *Recovery in Christ* explains what the Holy Scriptures say about the origins of compulsions, obsessions, and addictions, and recovery from them. Once we understand what the Scriptures have to say about compulsions, obsessions, and addictions; that is, what they are, where they come from, and how to recover from them, then we can lift the veil to see who is behind the recovery movement. Once we see who is really behind the recovery movement, then we will understand its real agenda. Once we see the recovery movement's real agenda, then we will see its shortcomings and consequences that have far-reaching temporal and eternal repercussions.

The recovery movement offers a temporary reprieve that is contingent upon a person's incessant involvement in the program and his efforts to ensnare others in it. The recovery program offers little more than an idolatrous lifestyle, diminished potentials, and both temporal and eternal consequences. So get a copy of the Bible, and then read *Recovery in Christ* and verify its message. Yahweh wrote the Bible, so if anything in this book conflicts with what the Bible says, reject it. After you read *Recovery in Christ* and are convinced that it lines up with the Bible and promotes Yah's recovery plan, you will have to decide if you are going to recover His way or man's way.

In 1934, Bill Wilson saw a bright light that he assumed was God while he was withdrawing from alcohol and taking a cocktail of powerful drugs.[8] After this spiritual experience, Bill held séances and played with Ouija boards to obtain guidance. A few years later, the guidance came. One night Bill asked for guidance and the *Twelve Steps* tumbled out of his mouth with astonishing speed. The recovery movement revolves around these well-known Twelve Steps, but these steps say nothing about Yeshua, the execution stake, the blood, or the Holy Spirit. In fact, the recovery movement focuses on the self and trying to control the self with a set of universal religious principles. The universal religious principles of forgiving and making amends work for people who are not in a relationship with Yah, just as they work for people who are in a relationship with Him. So the fact that a person forgives and makes amends does not mean he is in a relationship with Yah.

In contrast, Yah's recovery plan revolves around Yeshua, and His Spirit implements it through regeneration and sanctification. Addiction is a product of the sin nature. To recover, we have to admit that we have a sin nature, believe Yeshua's gospel, and bow our knee to Him as Lord so that His Spirit can give us a new nature and slowly straighten out our life. As we conform our life to the Scriptures and follow the promptings of Yeshua's Spirit, our soul is healed and restructured and conformed to His soul; and so our defects are removed, and our character changes. During this process, the chemical cravings cease, and we are set free from addiction.

Recovery in Christ shows us how to establish and maintain a relationship with Yahweh. *Recovery in Christ* shows us how to draw upon Yah's wisdom and power to heal our soul. After Yah heals our soul, then we will perceive Him, others, and ourselves correctly and will interact with Him, others, and ourselves rightly. This will help us keep the pain that comes from living in a fallen world at a manageable level without chemicals. Life will still be painful, but we will be equipped to rise above the pain. Yah's Spirit will help us avoid addiction, proxy bondages, and anesthetizing behaviors so that we can become who we were created to be, discover the plan for our life, acquire the resources to fulfill that plan, and help others recover in Christ too.

---

[8] *Pass It On: The Story of Bill Wilson and How the A.A. Message Reached the World*, New York, NY, Alcoholics Anonymous World Services, Inc., 1984, p. 121.

Prayer

Please pray this prayer aloud and from your heart when you are ready:

My Creator, I am seeking You. Please reveal Yourself to me and lead me to truth. Please show me how to escape from the trap that I have gotten myself into so that I can worship and serve You by serving others and dying to myself so that I can live the abundant life. I ask You to heal my soul and help me understand the Scriptures and see You, others, and myself the way that You want me to so that the pain will stop and the craving will leave me. I ask these things in the name of Jesus, the Christ. Amen.

Part 1

An Overview of Man's Problem, Yahweh's Solution, and HaSatan's Counterfeit Solution

Chapter 1

In The Beginning

Questions

*W*hy is life difficult? Why do pain, emotional torment, sickness, disease, toil, poverty, lack, compulsion, obsession, addiction, accidents, and death exist? Why do we work hard, grow old, and die? If there is a deity who loves us and has the power to rescue us from suffering, then why does He let us suffer? If we love this deity and believe that He has blessed us, then why do the people who reject and ridicule Him prosper as much or perhaps even more than we do?

Questions like these can confuse, overwhelm, torment, and even destroy us. Questions like these demand answers, but more to the point, they demand the correct answers. It is very important for us to uncover the correct answers to the questions that trouble us and to govern our lives and guard our minds by what we find so that HaSatan cannot torment and destroy us. A lack of understanding or a wrong belief gives HaSatan access to our minds, and he will do his best to convince us that Yahweh does not love us and to torment us until we grow bitter towards Yah.

A lack of understanding has led millions of people into a bottomless pit of despair, where they wallow in self-pity until they grow indifferent towards any concept of a loving deity. In many cases, these people continue to spiral downward until they reject Yeshua and deny Yahweh's existence and eventually burst hell wide open. Charles Darwin was one such person. Darwin studied to be a pastor, but he ended up rejecting Yeshua and publishing the theory of evolution.

Darwin's experiences with suffering and death did not fit inside his theological box, so he built a theological box that accommodated his experiences. The theology of evolution eliminated Yah's role in creation and paved the way for a pseudoscientific system of behavioral change that eliminated Yeshua's role in delivering man from his soul or, more accurately, in delivering the human spirit from its bondage to the self, the world, and HaSatan. Yeshua came to empower us to put the self to death, but psychology (man's self-help religion) tries to fix the self.

If we wish to avoid the pit that Darwin fell into, then we will have to avoid thinking as he thought. Darwin thought that we evolved from slime, lizards, and apes. Darwin believed that man is an animal that is motivated by evolutionary instincts and that man is incapable of being moral. In Darwin's theology, there is no moral absolute, and pain, suffering, and death are merely natural mechanisms that have no spiritual cause and no spiritual solution. Therefore, Darwin's theology says to eat, drink, and be merry, for tomorrow we die and cease to exist.

Yeshua says that an eternal, omnipotent, omniscient Spirit created us. Yeshua says this Spirit created us in His image to equip us to have a love affair with Him. Yeshua says that one day we will stand before the Creator and give an account of our lives. Yeshua says that the spirit realm gave birth to the material realm, and we are eternal spirits who have the ability to love our Creator and our fellows. Yeshua says that the Creator wants us to live the abundant life and has made a way for us to do so, but there is only one problem: we have to believe it in order to receive it.

Essentially, Darwin says that we have to cope with our problems until we die, but Yeshua says that we can overcome our problems and never die because our problems are just residual manifestations of a spiritual problem that He has already solved. So choose your worldview, but do it wisely because the worldview that you choose will ultimately become your reality!

The Uncaused Cause

Yah has always existed; He is the uncaused cause. This statement does not make sense, so some people refuse to believe that Yah exists. The human mind is not able to understand an eternal being, however, because it arranges things in a space-time-mass-energy continuum, and eternal beings exist outside of that continuum. Yah is holy; that is, He is not a part of His creation. Consequently, man has no experiential information about Yah's continuum. Therefore, do not require your finite mind to understand the infinite one before you choose to believe in Him. Yahweh has given all people a measure of faith so that they can choose to believe in Him, and if they will use this measure of faith, Yah will manifest Himself to them by changing their lives.

Yahweh created time. Yahweh created heaven and the angels who inhabit it. The angels worshiped and served Yahweh, but one day the worship leader got a big head. The worship leader, Lucifer, was a very wise and very beautiful angel, but his wisdom and beauty went to his head. Lucifer decided that he was going to sit on Yahweh's throne to rule heaven and receive worship. Lucifer assembled a coalition of angels to overthrow Yahweh, but this did not work out very well because He cast Lucifer and the rest of the rebellious angels out of heaven.

Lucifer means "light bearer." This suggests that Lucifer bore Yah's glory. After the rebellion, Yah changed Lucifer's name to *HaSatan*, which means "the adversary." After Yah cast HaSatan and the other rebellious angels out of heaven, they fell to earth, where they set up a kingdom. True to form, HaSatan enthroned himself as the king of the kingdom and appointed principalities and powers to carry out his orders. After Lucifer set up the kingdom of darkness in the earth realm, Yah appeared on the earth and created a creature in His own image and likeness. Yah created man and gave him dominion. King Yahweh made man His vice regent on the earth. HaSatan was outraged! Yah had dashed his plans for a kingdom both in heaven and on earth.

The Worship Junkie

Yah put the earth and everything in it under man's authority. This meant that HaSatan and the other fallen angels were now outlaws and alien spirits. HaSatan, however, is a junkie who is addicted to receiving worship, and he will do anything to get his next fix. HaSatan's obsession to receive worship drove him to come up with a plan to overcome man.

How could HaSatan possibly overcome man? Yahweh and man were close. Yahweh's Spirit and man's spirit were in perfect fellowship with each other. In fact, Yahweh's glory clothed man in a robe of righteousness that protected him. Moreover, Yahweh's glory crowned man's head, and this crown was man's badge of authority that gave him the authority to rule over the whole earth.

HaSatan had a big problem. Yah stood behind man's authority. HaSatan would have to overpower Yah to overpower man, but this was impossible. HaSatan had to come up with a plan to separate Yah and man. How did HaSatan know that this was the solution? Well, HaSatan rebelled and lost the right to bear Yah's glory and suffered the consequences, so he knew what the consequences would be if man rebelled. HaSatan knew that if he could get man to break his communion with Yah, the glory cloud would dissipate from his body and the divine badge of authority (his crown) would evaporate. HaSatan knew that if man lost his divine badge of authority and his robe of righteousness, he would be powerless. Therefore, HaSatan set out to separate Yah and man so that he could overpower man and make him a slave. If HaSatan could enslave man, then he could force him to build up his kingdom and worship him, and thus he would get his fix.

A Mechanism of Testing

Yahweh put Adam and Eve in the Garden of Eden, literally, "the garden of pleasures." Yah met Adam and Eve's spiritual and earthly needs in this garden of pleasures. The garden of pleasures overflowed with trees that produced all kinds of fruit for Adam and Eve to eat, but two trees produced spiritual fruit. One of these special trees was the Tree of Life, which produced the fruit of eternal life, and the other was the Tree of the Knowledge of Good and Evil, which produced the fruit of the knowledge of good and evil. Yah gave Adam permission to eat the fruit of eternal life but warned him not to eat the fruit of the knowledge of good and evil because it would kill him.

Yahweh gave Adam a choice between life and death. This was HaSatan's opening. HaSatan knew that when he had a spiritual union with Yah, he was alive, but when he broke that union, he died. Therefore, HaSatan knew that if he could get Adam to eat the illicit fruit, he would die spiritually, and then he could enslave him. HaSatan's tactics were brilliant. HaSatan knew that Yah had not given Eve His Torah (teachings and instructions). Yah gave His Torah to Adam, and he instructed Eve. Eve was also more sensitive spiritually and emotionally. This is why HaSatan targeted Eve. HaSatan knew that he could get Eve to question Yah's word and that she had a lot of influence over Adam. HaSatan tricked Eve, and then they both went after Adam.

The Test Results

Adam ignored Yah's Torah and rebelled against Him by eating the forbidden fruit. The knowledge of good and evil infused Adam's spirit. Adam's newfound knowledge of good and evil reacted with his knowledge of Yah's prescribed penalty for sin, and together these two forces gave birth to the fear of punishment, which is the root of guilt. The newborn bastard child (guilt) advised Adam's spirit to avoid punishment by separating from Yah's Spirit. Foolishly Adam's spirit severed its connection with Yah's Spirit, disconnecting from its life source to die. Spiritual death interrupted the glory flowing between Yah and Adam. His robe and crown, which were his protection and authority, vanished, and he was naked; that is, he was powerless and vulnerable.

Adam's nakedness proclaimed his guilt, so he covered his body with fig leaves. Adam hoped that the fig leaves would silence the nagging voice of his conscience so that he could fellowship with Yahweh. However, Adam's conscience was not indebted to him; it was indebted to Yahweh. Therefore, it was impossible for Adam to resolve his guilt and silence his conscience. Adam's guilty spirit interacted with its biological house (the body) and generated emotions that clouded his judgment. Yah's presence filled the garden, and Adam ran and hid. Yah confronted Adam and Eve about their nakedness, and they blamed each other, the serpent, and even Him! Yah could have taken their lives for their crimes, but He took the life of an innocent animal and used its fur to cover their nakedness to reveal the principle of atonement to them.

Yah gives life, and His laws are the terms and conditions of life. If a life violates Yah's terms and conditions, it must forfeit itself back to Him. In atonement, however, Yah accepts an innocent life that is willing to forfeit itself for a guilty life. Atonement allows a guilty life to be reconciled to Yah. In atonement, Yah releases the guilty life from its obligation to surrender itself back to Him. The life of the flesh is in the blood, so the animal blood temporarily satisfied Yah's righteousness. Adam was reconciled to Yah, but he was still naked and did not have the confidence to approach Him. Graciously Yah clothed Adam. The innocent blood reconciled Adam, but the innocent covering gave him the confidence to enjoy his reconciliation.

Chapter 2

The Beginning Of Sorrows

The Primitive Atonement

The penalty for sin is death. What is death? Death occurs when the spirit leaves the body and the body returns to dust. Where does the spirit go? A spirit's relationship with Yah determines its destination. If a spirit is in a relationship with Yah at the time it leaves the body, angels gently escort the spirit to Him; but if a spirit is not in a relationship with Yah at the time it leaves the body, demons seize the spirit and take it to hell. Hell is a jail that holds spirits who are at war with Yah until He can sentence and separate them from creation in the lake of fire.

Adam sinned. Yah's righteousness insisted that he surrender his life for his crime. Yah's righteousness demanded Adam's blood, which meant that his body would return to dust and the demons would take his spirit to hell, but Yah's grace stepped between His righteousness and man's sin to allow a substitute to die so that Adam could reconcile with Yah and avoid hell.

I call this the *primitive atonement*. Yahweh limited the effectiveness of the primitive atonement because the spirit that owed itself to Him for the crime of rebellion bore His image, but the spirit of the substitute did not. The blood of the substitute could not balance the scales of justice because it did not carry the same weight as the offending blood. Hence it was incapable of perfectly satisfying Yah's righteousness. So periodically Adam had to offer more blood in an effort to keep the scales balanced, but Yah's righteousness still had an outstanding claim on him. The death of the substitute did not set aside Adam's death penalty; it postponed the enforcement of the penalty of physical death in order to give Adam a chance to reconcile with Yahweh before HaSatan carried it out so that his spirit would not have to go to hell and the lake of fire.

Yahweh's righteousness had to enforce the sentence of physical death, but His mercy wanted to give Adam a chance to be reconciled to Him before it was done. Yahweh spared Adam's life, released the curses, and kicked him out of the place of blessing. Yahweh's righteousness released the curses so that they could slowly carry out the death penalty, but Yahweh's mercy kicked Adam out of Eden. Wait a minute! How was it merciful to kick Adam out of Eden? Well, if Yahweh had allowed Adam to stay in the garden, he would have never realized that he had fallen. Adam would have eaten the fruit of eternal life and been eternally fallen, which means that he and all his descendants would have been separated from Yahweh forever.

Yah is love, and love is merciful. Yah is righteous, and righteousness demands justice. Justice and mercy are opposing forces. In Yah, however, there is a dynamic tension between these two opposing forces that yields judgments that are perfectly just and perfectly merciful. Thus, when Yah released the curses and kicked man out of the garden, His actions were perfectly just and perfectly merciful. In the end, Yah's decision will work out for our good, but in the meantime, it will cause us to suffer.

The primitive atonement did not perfectly reconcile man's spirit to Yah's Spirit, but it did make a way for man to commune with Him over a bloody altar and obtain relief from the curses. Did everyone in the Old Testament go to hell? No. If they met with Yah at a bloody altar while looking forward with the eyes of faith to the day the Seed would crush the head of the serpent, their spirits went to paradise to await the Seed's atonement.

Left Behind

The King of the universe set up His kingdom in Eden and commissioned man to rule it. The King allowed man to enjoy the kingdom's spiritual and material blessings. Man rebelled against the King, however. The King kicked man out of His kingdom, so he could no longer enjoy the spiritual blessing of unhindered communion with the King or freely partake of the kingdom's material provisions. After Yah had kicked man out of His kingdom, He placed two angels with flaming swords at its entrance so that man could not eat the fruit of eternal life.

Yah returned to heaven, taking the kingdom and the Tree of Life with Him. Why did Yah kick us out of the kingdom and return to heaven? This objectified spiritual death and its consequences, which are the cessation of communion and the loss of protection and provision.

Adam sided with HaSatan and surrendered his dominion to him. Yah left Adam behind so that he could reap the fruit of his decision. HaSatan tormented Adam and made his life hard, but since his spirit had disconnected from Yah's Spirit, he had no way to call on Him for help. Luckily, Adam remembered the primitive atonement and built an altar. He cut the throat of an innocent animal, and its warm, sticky, smelly, coagulating blood covered the stones of the altar. Adam called on Yah, and He met with him, blessing him with strength, wisdom, and provision.

Here is the bottom line: Adam's spirit disconnected from Yah's Spirit. Adam's spirit owed a debt to Yah's righteousness that he could not pay. If Adam had attempted to enter Yah's presence without a covering of innocent blood that temporarily satisfied His righteousness, Yah's righteousness would have sprung forth and consumed him in order to collect on his debt! Thankfully, however, the innocent blood of the primitive atonement permitted Adam to approach Yahweh.

Kings Become Slaves

Yahweh filled His kingdom with peace and prosperity. Adam and Eve rejected Yah and His kingdom and chose HaSatan and his kingdom. Adam and Eve submitted to a cruel master who fills his kingdom with terror and lack. This cruel spiritual creature quickly overpowered Adam and Eve's spirits and bound them in chains. Adam and Eve became this creature's slaves. Adam and Eve's new lord overruled their wills and forced them to do his will on the earth.

HaSatan forced his slaves to build a kingdom on the earth that glorified him. HaSatan's kingdom endeavored to keep his slaves separated from Yahweh. Yah's Spirit, however, invited HaSatan's slaves to have a relationship with Him through the primitive atonement and to cooperate with Him as He reestablished His kingdom on the earth.

This ignited a war between Yahweh's kingdom and HaSatan's kingdom. Yah's kingdom will prevail, and He will cast HaSatan into the fiery lake. HaSatan keeps fighting, however. HaSatan fights to obtain souls. HaSatan wants to take as many people as he can with him to the fiery lake. HaSatan uses many weapons to keep man separated from Yah, but his favorites are compulsions, obsessions, and addictions.

In sum, man sinned and his guilty conscience altered his spirit's disposition. Man's altered spiritual disposition interacted with his biology, and this created *negative emotions*. Yahweh expelled man from His kingdom and returned to heaven. HaSatan took man captive and controlled him with *compulsions, obsessions,* and *addictions*. Yah's Spirit tried to get people to meet with Him at an altar with innocent blood. Yah met with those who came to an altar with innocent blood and gave them relief from the curses, their fallen nature, and compulsions, obsessions, and addictions so that He could use them to reestablish His kingdom on the earth.

Life Gets Harder

Yahweh spoke to the ground and commanded it to produce thorns and thistles. Yahweh spoke to man and sentenced him to a life of fighting thorns and thistles to provide for his family. As man fought with these thorns and thistles, they pricked and pierced his flesh, causing blood loss and pain. The life of the flesh is in the blood. Therefore, the blood loss symbolized the unrelenting force that slowly diminished man's life force, and the pain symbolized the harmful emotions that emerged from life's struggles, both of which lead to physical death. The days of leisurely enjoying the fruit in the garden of pleasures were over. Man would now have to work himself to death in order to survive, and *poverty* and *lack* were now unpleasant realities.

Before the rebellion, there was a perfect spiritual union between Yahweh and man. This perfect spiritual union channeled Yah's glory into man's spirit, and man's spirit channeled it into his body. As Yah's glory infused man's body, it supercharged his blood with Yah's life. Yah's glory nourished man's body, and the fresh fruit he ate was strictly for his pleasure. As man rebelled against Yah, his actions severed the perfect spiritual union between Yah and him. Yah's glory stopped flowing into man's body, which meant that some other energy source had to fuel man's biological systems now. Man's spirit started to coordinate the assimilation of nutrients from food via the bloodstream in order to acquire the energy that it needed to sustain the body.

Now, if man could have grown his food in the kingdom's ground, this development, while less than optimal, would not have been disastrous. As it turned out, however, it was disastrous. Yah expelled man from the garden. This was disastrous because man's blood had to draw nutrients from the food that he managed to grow in cursed ground, which meant that the curse nourished his body now. Man's body slowly assimilated the curse into itself and began to transition from a state of order to a state of disorder, which meant that the performance of his body's energy conversion, distribution, and utilization systems began to deteriorate with each passing moment. In other words, man's body began to age, and aging led to *disease* and *death*.

Yah decreed that a woman would experience pain and anguish in childbirth. Yah also decreed that the man would rule over his wife. Finally, Yah decreed that the serpent would eat dust all the days of its life. Since man's body is made of dust, this means that Yah gave HaSatan the power of death. Yah allows HaSatan to use sin and its by-products to carry out the sentence of physical death, which explains accidents and premature deaths. HaSatan acquired the ability to control the weather, which explains natural disasters. So it looks like man planted the seeds that grew into a bumper crop of pain, suffering, sickness, disease, addictions, poverty, and death!

Yah wanted Adam to resist temptation and eat the fruit of eternal life. Adam, however, wanted to please his wife. Adam ate the illicit fruit and committed spiritual suicide and brought sickness, disease, addiction, poverty, and death into the earth. If Adam had obeyed Yahweh, we would live in a world without sickness, disease, addiction, poverty, or death. Now, before we get mad at Adam and blame him, we need to remember that Yahweh is righteous, which means that if He gave us the same choice under the same conditions, we would rebel too. Adam was man's representative. Adam's failure was our failure, and hence his punishment was our punishment.

If that is too much to stomach, then look at it this way: We came from Adam's loins; that is, we are Adam's children, and children inherit their parent's assets. Adam's assets were spiritual death, pain, suffering, poverty, addiction, disease, and death. Most of us try to avoid taking possession of that inheritance, but the executor of the estate locates us and forces us to take possession of it. So do not blame Yah for your problems; blame the person in the mirror.

Chapter 3

De-Evolution

Order to Chaos

After Yah created man, He said, "Let them have dominion over all the earth." With these words, Yah transferred the title deed of the earth to Adam and Eve. Adam and Eve became Yah's vice regents, and their power to rule came from their spiritual union with Him. Yah set up everything in the universe so that He and man could work in a symbiotic partnership that would bring His will to pass on the earth, and this tells us a lot about man's purpose.

Man's purpose is to love Yah. Yah could have compelled us to love Him, but He did not. Yah wants us to choose to love Him. If Yah forced us to love Him, our "love" would have no meaning. Yah created us in His image, which gave us the capacity to receive His love and return it to Him in the form of obedience. Yah tests every human spirit to see if it will reject His love and rebel, or embrace His love and obey Him in order to bring His will to pass on the earth. A spirit's response to Yah's love determines its eternal destiny and its rewards or punishments.

Yah revealed His love for Adam and Eve by letting them live in the garden of pleasures. At first, Adam and Eve responded with obedience. Obedience is the highest form of submission. The word *submission* means "to place under." As Adam and Eve obeyed Yahweh, they put themselves in a position to receive from Him, and His Spirit flowed through them, giving them the power to do His will. Adam and Eve were passing the test. Yah was blessing Adam and Eve, but then they turned away from His Spirit and entered a dark world of chaos, curses, and death.

The serpent tricked Eve into disobeying Yah. No one likes to be alone in his sin, so Eve got her husband to join her. HaSatan deceived Eve, but Adam chose to disobey Yah. Adam and Eve submitted to HaSatan, and his spirit overpowered them. HaSatan took control of their wills and forced them to bring his will to pass on earth. This is quite a contrast. Yah loves us, in the hope that we will submit to Him and allow His Spirit to bring His will to pass on the earth through us, blessing us in the process. HaSatan tricks us into submitting to him, holds us in bondage, and forces us to bring his will to pass on the earth, destroying us in the process.

Sin is rebellion. Rebellion is a departure from order. Hence Adam's choice introduced disorder into the creation. Before the fall, life, peace, and cooperation ruled the animal kingdom, but now death, fear, and competition rule it. Before the fall, the earth's ecosystem promoted life and prosperity, but now it promotes death and lack. Before the fall, man was a supernatural being who was in unity with Yah, but now he is a natural being who has estranged himself from Yah. Before the fall, HaSatan was an illegal alien, but now he is the god of the earth realm.

Before the fall, the universe was increasing in glory, but now its glory is decreasing; that is, it is moving from a high-energy level to a low one, or from a state of order to a state of disorder. The second law of thermodynamics describes this relentless journey from order to disorder. Everything in the universe is subject to entropy, which ensures that everything decays and nature does not add new information to living systems. Bacteria, however, have defied the law of entropy. Bacteria have acquired enough new information to evolve from one of the simplest states to the most complex state in the whole universe. Bacteria originated in a cesspool, but now it walks, talks, thinks, builds space shuttles, starts wars and governs the earth!

Jumping into the Cesspool

Science says something like this: A billion years ago, it rained on a rock. The rain leached minerals out of the rock, and these minerals collected in a pool. The chemicals combined to form an amoeba. The amoeba grew into bacteria. The bacteria grew into a fish. The fish grew legs and jumped out of the cesspool. The walking fish grew into a reptile. The reptile grew into a bird. The bird grew into a monkey. The monkey grew into you!

Yah says that He created man as the highest form of life by virtue of his spiritual union with Him, but man broke that union and took on the image of the lower life forms. Yahweh says that we did not jump out of a cesspool millions of years ago; we jumped into one six thousand years ago! Yahweh says that man de-evolved.

Adam and Eve were on probation. Yah was testing Adam and Eve to see if they would respond to His love and submit to Him by obeying Him. Yah told Adam not to eat the fruit of the knowledge of good and evil because it would kill him. The serpent told Eve that Yah was keeping the best fruit from her, and she believed him. HaSatan tricked Eve into obeying him (submitting to him) so that his spirit could flow through her and persuade Adam to rebel.

Adam and Eve sinned, and their spirits de-evolved. Spiritual de-evolution opened the door to pain, lack, bondage, religion, addiction, sickness, disease, aging, and death. Theologians call spiritual de-evolution and its consequences the *fall of man*. Man fell from the position of vice regent to the position of slave. HaSatan tricked Eve into taking off her robe of glory, but Adam willingly disrobed in order to please his wife, which tells us a lot about the two sexes.

The creation witnessed a radical change in Adam, but he refused to accept it. Adam denied the obvious and clothed himself in the fig leaves of religion. Yah intervened, and Adam took off the fig leaves so that Yah could clothe him in animal fur. On one level, this told Adam that his nature had changed. Adam had been a partaker of the divine nature, and his thoughts and desires had flowed from his communion with Yah; but he now took on an animalistic nature, and his thoughts and desires began to flow from his preoccupation with growing food, satisfying his flesh, and gathering information from his senses. Man's focus shifted from Yahweh to himself.

Spiritual Evolution

Spiritual de-evolution manifests itself as self-centeredness, selfishness, depravity, perversion, disease, poverty, compulsions, obsessions, addictions, and death. Yah's recovery plan reverses spiritual de-evolution and its consequences. The primitive atonement redeemed man's spirit from HaSatan's kingdom, but it did not regenerate him. The primitive atonement pointed to Yeshua. Yeshua came to earth to bring the fullness of His eternal sacrifice into the dimension of space-time. Yeshua's atonement redeems man from HaSatan's kingdom and regenerates his spirit. Yeshua's Spirit regenerates man's spirit and slowly transforms his soul. Most pastors do a good job explaining the regeneration event, but a poor job explaining the sanctification process, so their congregants do not know how to deal with drug addicts.

It is hard to solve a problem when you do not know what the problem is. Understanding is the key to recovery. Let no one deceive you: addiction is a product of spiritual de-evolution, and spiritual re-evolution is its *only* remedy. We need to understand the *event* of spiritual re-evolution and understand how to cooperate with the *process* that actualizes it in our lives. Deep down we all know that we need to re-evolve spiritually, but HaSatan has deceived some of us into believing that we can re-evolve without submitting to Yahweh, His Spirit, and His Word.

The State of the Union

Adam and Eve ate the forbidden fruit, and the disposition of their spirits shifted from a state of righteousness, boldness, and peace to a state of guilt, shame, and fear, which caused their bodies to release chemicals that corresponded to guilt, shame, and fear. The chemicals circulated in their bloodstreams and lodged in their synaptic clefts, drastically altering their perceptions and igniting physiological processes that manifested their spirits' disposition in the material realm. HaSatan took advantage of this phenomenon and got them to cover themselves with fig leaves.

Adam and Eve tried to pretend as if nothing had happened; but Yahweh's presence filled the garden, and like the explosion of a million neutron bombs, His holiness penetrated everything in the garden. The X-rays of Yahweh's holiness penetrated the fig leaves and exposed Adam and Eve's nakedness. Adam and Eve's spirits recoiled in fear, which caused their bodies to release chemicals to manifest that fear in the earth realm, and they hid. Adam and Eve deserved to die, but Yahweh spared them and killed an innocent animal. The blood temporarily satisfied Yah's righteousness, and He clothed Adam and Eve in its fur to cover their shame and give them the confidence to approach Him. Yah's communion with man was now on a shallow level because when man rebelled, he took on the nature of HaSatan, and animal blood could not fix that. The blood, however, did temporarily propitiate Yah's wrath so that man could commune with Him.

A Fig-Leaf Suit

A fallen man's spirit knows that he has estranged himself from Yahweh, but a fallen man's prideful soul will not confess this so he can be reconciled to Him. A fallen man refuses to admit that he is a treasonous criminal and to accept the substitute's innocent blood. A fallen man refuses to put on the covering of an innocent substitute because that would wound his pride. A fallen man wants to fix himself up by picking some fig leaves to make a covering that will allow him to fellowship with Yah without repenting, submitting, and obeying. Fallen man has searched for six thousand years for a fig-leaf suit that will resolve his guilt, silence his conscience, and cover his nakedness so that he can fellowship with Yahweh. So has fallen man found such a suit? No.

Today billions of people will wake up and put on fig-leaf suits that promise to reunite them with God without repentance, submission, and obedience. These people will put on their favorite worldview, religion, psychological principle, recovery principle, or moral principle. If they manage to find a fig-leaf suit that drowns out their conscience so that they can deceive themselves into believing that they know Yahweh, they will be dismayed when they die. After such persons die, the neutron bomb of Yahweh's holiness will detonate, and the X-rays of His righteousness will vaporize their fig-leaf suits, expose their sins, and blow them into hell!

Is there any good news? Yes, because after the fall, Yahweh said, "And I will put enmity between thee and the woman, and between thy seed and her seed; it shall bruise thy head, and thou shalt bruise his heal."[9] With these words, Yah doomed HaSatan and announced that His kingdom would return to earth. Man lost the kingdom, but Yah promised that a woman would give birth to the Seed who would defeat HaSatan and redeem man, free him from slavery and clothe his nakedness, and restore his inheritance of peace, wholeness, health, prosperity, and eternal life. Here is the good news: Yahweh preached the gospel of the kingdom to Adam and Eve!

---

[9] *The Hebrew-Greek Key Word Study Bible*, KJV, Genesis 3:15.

Chapter 4

Searching For Fig Leaves

The Human System Configuration

In the *Recovery in Christ* series, we will look at how the will of Yahweh and the will of HaSatan are communicated to the human spirit. We will look at how the human spirit uses the soul and the body to implement its will on the earth. We will look at the forces in a human that determine whether he does Yahweh's will or HaSatan's will. After this, we will look at how man's rebellion affected his spirit, soul, and body, with an emphasis on how it formed the *self* and how the structure of the self predisposes us to addiction. Last of all, we will look at what the Scriptures say about addiction and explore Yah's recovery plan. However, before we can delve into these topics, we must look at the *human system configuration* (HSC).

The HSC is a conceptual schematic of the spirit, soul, and body. Figure 1 (page 408) depicts the original HSC. I use the dynamics of the HSC to describe the study of how the spirit, soul, and body interact to create our lives on the earth. The dynamics of the HSC will be explored in the *Recovery in Christ* series, but the subject matter in this chapter requires us to have an understanding of the HSC. What follows is an introduction to the HSC.

The Birth of the Self

The human spirit lives inside a body.[10] The spirit flows through the body in order to express itself on the earth, and this configures the soul. The soul is a logical, emotive, creative, biological interface organism that connects the spirit to the material realm and the material realm to the spirit. Yah designed the soul to be an *unbiased mediator* that

---

[10] *The Hebrew-Greek Key Word Study Bible*, KJV, Job 4:19; 10:11.

manifests the thoughts and intents of the spirit on the earth; that is, it is supposed to be a biological representation of the spirit.

This is how the HSC operates: The human spirit flows through the soul to express its thoughts and intents in the earth realm. The spirit polls the soul's sensory devices in order to collect information about the earth realm. After the human spirit has collected information about the earth realm, it reacts to this information and expresses its reaction on the earth via the soul.

In the garden, Yah told the spirit what reality was and how to react to it, but the serpent told the soul that Yah was wrong and offered it his version of reality. The spirit believed Yah, but the soul sided with the serpent. The spirit was in conflict with the soul. In a sense, the serpent planted his seed (his word) in Eve's soul, where it grew into the self, and she gave birth to it. The self is HaSatan's proxy personality operating in man, and its name is telling because it comes from the Greek word *autos*, as in *autonomy*, which means "self-governing."

The spirit was at war with the soul, and the victor won the right to manifest its will on earth. At first, the spirit held its ground, but it got weary and turned away from Yah's Spirit to consider the soul's view. The spirit embraced the soul's view and broke its connection with Yah's Spirit. The spirit lost the authority and the power to rule over the soul, and the soul took control of the HSC.

The Self Tries to Silence the Conscience

Yahweh is the King of the universe. As long as the human spirit remained submitted to Yahweh's Spirit, it had the authority and the power to rule over the soul and body. This was the hallmark of the HSC's original configuration: the human spirit's unity with the Holy Spirit gave the human spirit the authority and power to rule over the soul and body so that man could do Yahweh's will on the earth. However, when Adam saw that Eve did not die after she ate the illicit fruit, Adam doubted Yah's word, and his spirit rose up out of submission to Yah's Spirit. Adam's spirit lost the authority and power to rule over his soul and body, which was tragic, because Adam's soul embraced the serpent's view of reality and believed that it could follow Eve without suffering any negative consequences. Adam's soul commanded his body to eat the fruit, and his spirit was powerless to stop his soul and his body from making this error.

Up to this point, Adam's spirit had never questioned Yah's Spirit. Adam's spirit loyally submitted to Yah's Spirit, and this empowered it to rule over his soul and body. Adam's spirit simply obeyed Yah's Spirit, so his spirit did not need to know the difference between good and evil. Adam's conscience had been inactive, but when he chose not to believe Yah, his spirit rose up out of submission to Yah's Spirit and no longer had a "North Star" to look to for guidance. Adam's spirit looked inward and discovered its own moral compass.

Adam's moral compass began to inform him of good and evil; that is, his conscience came to life to guide him.

Adam's conscience told his spirit that its actions were evil, and the disposition of his spirit transitioned from a state of peace to a state of fear, releasing a load of powerful chemicals into his bloodstream. As Adam's neurotransmitters flooded into his bloodstream, they lodged in his synaptic clefts and turned on neuronal circuits that altered his view of reality and ignited powerful physiological processes to manifest his spirit's fear in the material realm. After this, HaSatan injected his thoughts into Adam's soul to fortify it so that it could rule over the HSC. HaSatan could now use Adam's HSC to bring his will to pass on the earth. Adam's soul began to rule over the HSC, and he therefore became self-conscious and realized that he was naked.

Adam's soul took the reins of power and began ruling the HSC. Adam's spirit knew the difference between good and evil, and it heaped condemnation on the soul for being out of the created order. Instead of surrendering authority back to the spirit, however, the soul rationalized its sin. The rebellious soul refused to humble itself and surrender authority back to the spirit. The soul's refusal to repent opened a door for HaSatan. HaSatan injected some vain thoughts and imaginations into the soul and got it to fabricate intellectual arguments (fig leaves) that muffled the spirit's voice, which caused the psychological and physiological reactions to abate.

Adam's fig leaves seemed to work, but then Yah drew near to fellowship with him. His spirit's fear of punishment rebounded, and so did the volume of its voice. The voice of Adam's conscience pierced the intellectual shield that his soul had put up, and the psychological and physiological reactions intensified. Adam realized that his intellectual shield and its placebo effect did not satisfy Yah's righteousness or release him from punishment, so he ran and hid.

There are many kinds of fig leaves, but the most dangerous one is the *worldview fig leaf*. This fig leaf is very dangerous because it drowns out the voice of conscience while sanctioning aberrant behavior under the guise of intellectual progress, and in most cases, it even promises to reconcile the soul with some deity or supernatural creative force. The worldview fig leaf gives the soul an inordinate amount of power to keep the spirit separated from Yah until it leaves the body, which ensures that He will have to imprison it in hell and throw it into the lake of fire.

Worldview

A worldview is what we choose to believe about reality and man's position in it. The worldview we choose is important because we filter our experiences and observations through it, and it silently shapes our intellectual and emotional development, which is important because our intellect and emotions influence our decisions, and decisions create our lives. If our worldview differs from Yahweh's, the discontinuities between the reality that we perceive and the reality that truly exists generate cognitive and emotional breaches in our soul that HaSatan exploits.

All people need to examine their worldview and seal up the breaches in their soul to ensure that they do not end up like Darwin. Darwin's theology birthed a worldview that says that man evolved from a rock. In this worldview, man is still evolving, but he has reached the apex of his biological evolutionary potential. The forces of evolution have now shifted their attention to man's spirit in order to bring it up to the apex of its spiritual evolutionary potential. This is a very old lie, but now that genetics and quantum physics point to the reality of an immaterial realm that governs the material realm, this old lie has become much more believable.

Naturalistic Spiritual Evolution

Over the course of the last two hundred years, the theory of spiritual evolution has struggled to emerge from its academic cocoon and grow into a prominent worldview, but the atheists and materialists have prevented it. However, recent discoveries reveal serious flaws in the atheistic and materialistic worldviews. Therefore, it is time for HaSatan to slay the contrarian dogmatists on globalism's altar and bury them in shallow intellectual graves. As HaSatan slays these intellectuals, their blood will reconcile the academic world to the concept of spiritual evolution, and it will emerge from its cocoon and fly to the ends of the earth, depositing its poisonous pollen in reprobate minds where it will blossom into a fresh crop of the illicit fruit. Sadly, billions of people will believe the lie, eat this illicit fruit, and seal their own fate in the lake of fire.

Today academia is embracing the theory of spiritual evolution. Invariably, like a moth to a flame, the intellectuals in academia find themselves drawn to religions that offer a self-directed spiritual evolution that brings the fallen soul up to its fullest potential (the Eastern religions). However, much like the hidden force that causes the north pole of a magnet to repel the north pole of another magnet, a hidden force repels these same intellectuals from the religion that offers a Yahweh-directed spiritual evolution that puts the fallen soul to death (Christianity). The unholy intercourse between academia and Eastern religion has birthed a self-directed spiritual evolution that is supposed to bring the fallen soul up to the apex of its potential and produce a new species of man. This new species, *Homo noeticus*, will build a global egalitarian society, solve the world's problems, and usher in a new age of global peace and prosperity.

The Scriptures say that in the last days, people will believe "the lie." The people who do not have a love for the truth will put their trust in a ruler who will promise the nations of the earth peace and prosperity by building a global government, economy, and religion.[11] Is this a new concept we have arrived at through naturalistic spiritual evolution and intellectualism, or an age-old lie repackaged in modern jargon? In the next chapter, we will look a little deeper into this and listen for the whisperer who says subtly, "Yea, hath Yahweh said, 'Ye shall be as gods'?"

---

[11] Ibid., 2 Thessalonians 2:8–12; Daniel 8:24–25; Revelation 13:7, 15–18.

Chapter 5

The Emerging Worldview

The Age of Aquarius

As I write this chapter, it is 2009. The global economic system is writhing in pain, but this is not ordinary pain. It is labor pain. HaSatan is getting ready to birth his final kingdom that will unite the world and solve its economic woes. The elite liberal intellectuals are hard at work creating crises in order to produce the change they promised. The elites use this change to promote a gospel that will birth the child. What is their gospel? The elite's gospel says a global egalitarian society is our only answer because the Bible is not true; the Bible, they say, is just a collection of stories written by simple people who attempted to explain how the earth and man came into being by creating a mythical god. Therefore, we can disregard Yah and His rules. We can direct our own spiritual evolution and become one with the real god, and then actualize the divinity within us and become one with each other to form a global egalitarian society.

The theologies behind the elite liberal intellectual's gospel are evolution, humanism, and psychology. What root produced the poisonous belief systems of evolution, humanism, and psychology? Around 2200 BC, the ancient Babylonians invented astrology, which charts the positions of the celestial bodies and explains how their energy-gravitational fields affect us. Then, astrology led to evolution, evolution led to humanism, and humanism led to psychology. Finally, these belief systems merged to produce the religion of the New Age[i] (see endnote).

Here is a simplified view of the New Age movement: The cosmic field that bathes the earth changes, and pagans called these periodic changes in the cosmic field *astrological ages*. An astrological age is 2,150 years. Every 2,150 years, the cosmic field that bombards the earth changes, and thus we enter a new age. (We have just moved out of the Piscean Age into the Age of Aquarius.) Over the eons, the changing cosmic field modulated the energy bombarding the earth, producing information that transformed inorganic matter into organic matter. More specifically, as the earth moved through the astrological ages, the changes in the sources, wavelengths, and amplitudes of the cosmic field produced information that living organisms assimilated into their biological memory cells. In other words, the cosmic field generated new information, and the plants and animals stored it in their genes. The flow of information and energy fueled the process of evolution, producing the complexity and diversity found in nature.

Much like a sunbathing reptile, primitive life crawled out of the primordial cesspool and positioned itself to absorb the cosmic field. Slowly but surely, primitive life climbed the evolutionary ladder until it reached the highest rung. After the primitive life form evolved into the human body, it continued to absorb all the cosmic energy and information that bombarded it. None of the cosmic energy and information that bombarded man's body was able to pass through it to reach his spirit. Hence man's spirit could not evolve. Luckily, man's body has just recently reached its fullest biological evolutionary potential and stopped absorbing the cosmic energy and information. The cosmic field is now able to pass through man's body to reach his famished soul and spirit. There is a problem, however. Each person's soul blocks a certain percentage of the cosmic energy and information, preventing it from reaching the spirit. Nevertheless, man's spirit is finally evolving and becoming one with its creator (the cosmic field). Man is becoming a god!

According to this theory, it took the human body millions of years to evolve. During this time, the human spirit suffered from a lack of energy and information, which explains why man sought "God," wrote the Scriptures, and concocted all the different religions. However, man's effort to grow spiritually, before the universe was ready for him to grow spiritually, backfired. The religions we invented separated nations and ignited wars that killed hundreds of millions, but thankfully, this is ending because we have entered the Age of Aquarius. In this new age, the cosmic field is nourishing man's spirit, bringing it up to its evolutionary potential. Hence it is now time to put the divisive religions and their intolerant writings away. Now we can evolve spiritually and self-actualize into gods and come together to form a global egalitarian utopia.

This theory has many disturbing implications, but the most disturbing one is that we become gods and redeem ourselves from the fall, thus negating the work of Messiah. Another disturbing implication of this theory is that the cosmic field created everything and sustains everything, and so it is the omnipresent, omnipotent, omniscient creative being (it is God).[12] The belief that God is everything is called *pantheism*. In pantheism, everything is God, and so all roads lead to God. Ironically, though, it takes another worldview called *polytheism*, which is the worship of many gods, to express pantheism fully. A worldview built around the polytheistic expression of a pantheistic god is the ideal belief

---

[12] Marilyn Ferguson, *The Aquarian Conspiracy*, Los Angeles, CA, T. P. Tarcher, Inc., 1980, p. 382.

system to implement HaSatan's end-time plan because it invalidates monotheism. A global egalitarian society that relies upon polytheism to express the attributes of a pantheistic god cannot incorporate monotheists. Consequently, the people who refuse to abandon monotheism prevent the global egalitarian society from forming.

The New Age system is a polytheistic system that communicates the will of a pantheistic god through a network of lesser gods, like the cosmic Christ (the New Age Jesus) and Buddha. The lesser gods express the will of a most high god in different ways to different cultures. This ensures that people have "a god of their own understanding" that they can serve and by doing so enjoy a relationship with the most high god. Hence, if a person joins a New Age group and promotes the idea that people must believe that Yeshua died on an execution stake and rose from the dead, and that they must bow their knee to Him before they can know God and inherit eternal life, that person is condemned for being ignorant or intolerant and is minimized or removed. Soon HaSatan will remove or minimize the monotheists and send the great mother (the most high god) who gave birth to the lesser gods to gather her children and explain that all roads have always led to her.

The Lesser Gods

Emergents do not care what we believe about God. The emergents teach that we must remove things like intolerance, unforgiveness, resentment, and hatred from our souls so that the cosmic field can pass through our souls and reach our spirits. If we are diligent in removing the things in our souls that block the flow of the cosmic field, then we will evolve spiritually, self-actualize, and become one with God, man, and nature. The emergents say that the lesser gods are merely spirit guides who show us how to purify our souls and guide us as we evolve spiritually. The emergents say that if we take the advice of psychology and live a moral life, we will not need a spirit guide like Jesus or Buddha to help us evolve spiritually and self-actualize, which means that we can shun church and proudly proclaim that we are spiritual and not religious. Paradoxically, though, a person can be an atheist and still evolve spiritually and self-actualize.

The emergents teach that we need to confess the things that are on our conscience, express our suppressed emotions, and release resentment. Emergents say that these things block the flow of the cosmic field and prevent us from evolving spiritually and self-actualizing so that we can become one with God and man and overcome our behavioral problems[ii] (see endnote). In the recovery field, emergents say we must express our emotions, release resentment, confess our wrongdoings, and make amends and restitution so that we can grow spiritually and become one with God and actualize our relationship with God in order to become one with our peers and overcome our behavioral problems. The emergents cloak their New Age teachings in Christian garb by saying that we must search our souls and take a fearless moral inventory of ourselves, and then we must remove the things that are blocking us from the sunlight of the Spirit so that we can have a spiritual awakening and a change in consciousness sufficient enough to overcome addiction.

Emergent theology encourages us to reject the doctrines of Messiah. To emergents, Christian doctrine is divisive and intolerant; Christian doctrine blocks the cosmic field; Christian doctrine hinders spiritual growth, self-actualization, and recovery from addiction. So under the guise of recovery, the recovery movement (a vast network of small egalitarian groups) is busy preparing the way for the global egalitarian society.[13] After the rapture, the Queen of Heaven (the great mother) will send her eldest son (the anti-Messiah) to gather her children and explain that Islam, Judaism, and Christianity were all pointing to her. Anti-Messiah will say that his mother knew that the people who took the Bible literally would never surrender to him, so she took them. Most people will believe the lie and embrace the anti-Messiah and his egalitarian society.

HaSatan cultivates an environment that promotes addiction because he wants to keep people separated from Yah and prevent them from doing His will on the earth. Addictions, compulsions, and obsessions are ideally suited to accomplish HaSatan's objectives. To those who attempt to escape from HaSatan's trap of addiction, he offers his recovery plan. HaSatan's recovery plan looks biblical because he sprinkled it with biblical concepts. However, HaSatan's plan is a perversion of Yahweh's plan, and it actually encourages people to reject His plan.

Nothing New Under the Sun

In Eden, the human spirit disconnected from Yah and lost the authority and power to rule over the soul. HaSatan planted vain imaginations and thoughts in man's soul and got him to start thinking wrong so his body would release chemicals that would skew his perceptions. HaSatan fortified the strongholds in the soul so that he could rule over it, rule the HSC, enslave man, and force him to build his kingdom on earth. Man's spirit took on HaSatan's nature, and Yah's glory lifted from his body. Man's new nature revealed itself as he picked fig leaves *to improve himself so he could have a relationship with Yah*. HaSatan inspired man to invent the first self-help religion, but Yah told man that the Seed would come to redeem him, restore the earth, and reestablish the kingdom. Yahweh showed man how he could have a relationship with Him via the primitive atonement. Man now had to choose between religion and relationship.

Cain perverted Yah's plan, built a city, and invented a religion of works that caused the flood. After the flood, Nimrod gathered the people of the earth together on the plains of Shinar, built the city that became Babylon the Great, and invented a religion of works that

---

[13] Marilyn Ferguson, *The Aquarian Conspiracy*, Los Angeles, CA, T. P. Tarcher, Inc., 1980, p. 218.

revolved around a counterfeit seed. Yah came down and scattered these people to the ends of the earth.

In 2247 BC, Babylon birthed the nations and their religions.[14] In 933 BC, Israel split. Israel's king perverted Yah's plan by mixing it with paganism, thus inventing a religion of works. Israel refused to listen to the prophets and to repent. In 722 BC, Yah scattered Israel to the ends of the earth. In 300 BC, the sages took control of Moses' ekklesia. The sages perverted Yah's plan by teaching people that they could keep the Torah to fix themselves and earn salvation. Finally, the Seed came to Judah, but the sages refused to listen to Him and repent. In AD 70, Yah sent the Romans to tear down the temple and scatter Judah to the ends of the earth. In AD 321, the Romans (Esau's allies) took control of Yeshua's ekklesia, tried to steal the birthright from Israel (Jacob), and mixed Yahweh's plan with paganism, thus inventing a religion of works.

In 1350, the Renaissance began, and intellectuals, philosophers, and theologians frantically sought to explain away their Creator and make sense of the immaterial part of man. Intellectuals, philosophers, and theologians were desperate to learn how they could manipulate the immaterial part of man and fix his behavioral problems without having to submit to the Roman Church or its heavy-handed God. In 1859, Charles Darwin systematized an ancient theology and called it *evolution*. Darwin became the father of evolutionary psychology, which is the foundation that all modern psychologies are built on.[15] Psychology hoped to change people without Yah, His Spirit, or His Word. Today "psychology has become a competing religion, in particular, a form of secular humanism based on the worship of self."[16]

Spiritual, Not Religious

In 1921, Frank Buchman, a Lutheran pastor, started the Oxford Group (O.G.). The Oxford Group met in private homes or in other neutral locations and avoided biblical doctrine. "Instead of biblical doctrine, the Oxford Group Movement majored in personal experience, group sharing, channeled guidance and testimonies."[17] Paradoxically, this pastor said that he avoided talking about biblical doctrines because he did not want to upset or offend anyone.[18]

---

[14] *The Hebrew-Greek Key Word Study Bible*, KJV, Jeremiah 51:7.

[15] Gregory Kimble and Michael Wertheimer, *Portraits of Pioneers in Psychology*, volume 3, American Psychological Association, 1998, pp. 23–24.

[16] Paul C. Vitz, *Psychology as Religion*, Grand Rapids, MI, Eerdmans Publishing Co., 1977, p. 9.

[17] Martin and Deidre Bobgan, *12 Steps to Destruction*, Santa Barbara, CA, EastGate Publishers, 1991, p. 101.

[18] William Irvine, *Heresies Exposed*, Neptune, New Jersey, Loizeaux Brothers, Inc., 1980, p. 54.

In 1933, the World's Christian Fundamentals Association passed a resolution declaring that the O.G. was a false religious cult because it substituted human and natural psychological laws for the supernatural working of the Holy Spirit and the new birth, and put experience ahead of doctrine, thus denying the necessity of true belief as essential to Christian life.[19]

The O.G. perverted Yah's plan by mixing it with psychology and invented a religion that looked biblical because it was sprinkled with biblical concepts. However, it was nothing more than a New Age religion that sought to remove the hindrances to spiritual evolution and self-actualization. The O.G. used "sharing" (Carl Rogers' listening therapy that allows people to express their emotions so they are not expressed in bad behavior), confessing failures and faults, and making amends and restitution. The O.G. was an ecumenical cult that tried to improve man so that he could have a relationship with God. The O.G. did not share Yeshua with people and encourage them to surrender to Him so that He would empower them to overcome sin.

The Oxford Group used psychology to help people have a moral conversion. The O.G. consisted of many small groups, and each group had a collective conscience. Members of a group were empowered by their frequent interactions with their group's conscience. This helped the people in the O.G. comply with a set of moral standards, some of which were biblical, and their compliance changed their lives. The O.G. encouraged its members to seek guidance from God by stilling their minds so they could receive instructions from Him, but this is foolish. There are many spirits, and there is no way to tell which one is speaking to us unless the Holy Spirit has regenerated and indwelt us and we have renewed our minds with the Scriptures. HaSatan gave these people instructions and deceived them into believing that they knew Yahweh without submitting to the Scriptures, believing the gospel, and bowing their knee to His Son. HaSatan smiled every time a person who was in the O.G. boasted about being spiritual, but not religious.

The Recovery Movement

In 1934, Bill Wilson joined the Oxford Group and claimed to meet God in a hospital while tripping on a cocktail of barbiturates, morphine, belladonna, and henbane. By 1935, Bill W. and Dr. Bob Smith formed a sect in the Oxford Group known as the alcoholic squad and began holding meetings in their homes with a bunch of anonymous alcoholics, but this did not sit well with the founder of the O.G. (Buchman). Bill left the Oxford Group, and Dr. Bob soon followed. Bill W. and Dr. Bob started an organization that eventually became Alcoholics Anonymous (AA).

---

[19] Ibid., p. 60.

Bill looked to Carl Jung and William James to make sense of his believed encounter with God. Bill said that these men were the philosophical fathers of AA, which is telling because Jung was an occultist-psychologist whose teachings have been instrumental in the New Age movement,[20] and James was a philosopher-psychologist who said that God was a ubiquitous field and who exalted spiritual experience over doctrine. Bill took the teachings of these men and combined it with the teachings of the O.G. to come up with AA's Twelve Steps. (At the end of his life, Bill said the first two steps came from his spiritual experience, and the other steps came from the O.G.).[21] Bill also said that the spirit of an eleventh-century bishop named Boniface helped him write the steps.[22]

Bill and Bob were necromancers who consulted with spirits and sinners to put together the religion of AA. Yah forbids us from communicating with spirits who masquerade as dead people because they are demons sent to deceive and destroy us. Like the Oxford Group, AA is an ecumenical organization that replaces Yeshua's execution stake with psychology and spiritual experiences. Hence, when a person works the Twelve Steps, Yahweh *does not* take away his fallen nature and give him His Spirit to empower him to overcome sin and live the abundant life.

The New Age cure relies on its belief in a force that emanates from people that can influence others. If people adopt the same beliefs, meet together, and focus on a common goal, the force that emanates from the group influences each member of the group and empowers all of them to reach their common goal. The New Agers call this force the *collective consciousness*, or the *collective conscience*. AA says that God expresses Himself through the group conscience.[23] In AA, the collective conscience of a group of fallen people guides and empowers the individuals in a group, which is why attending AA meetings are so important to them and why most people do not get sober.

The religion of AA deceives people into believing that they are in conscious contact with Yah without confessing that they are sinners, repenting, and bowing their knee to His Son. In AA, people do not submit to Yeshua and make Him their Lord, which means that these fallen people are under the influence of a deceiving spirit who works through the collective conscience of the group. Strangely, the deceiving spirit encourages these people to take moral inventory of their lives. The moral inventory identifies their shortcomings and faults so they can confess them and make amends and restitution to those they have hurt. This removes resentment from their souls so that the "sunlight of the Spirit" can reach their

---

[20] Caryl Matrisciana, *Gods of the New Age*, Eugene, OR, Harvest House Publishers, 1985, p. 175.

[21] William (Bill) Wilson, *The Language of the Heart*, published posthumously, 1988, p. 298.

[22] Robert Fitzgerald, "The Soul of Sponsorship," Center City, MN, Hazelden, 1995, p. 81.

[23] *Alcoholics Anonymous*, large print ed., New York, NY, Alcoholics Anonymous World Services, Inc., 1976, p. 565.

spirits and produce a spiritual awakening and a change in consciousness, thus granting them a temporary reprieve from the disease of alcoholism.

If we do not know that the New Agers teach people to remove the things in their souls that block the flow of the cosmic field so that they can evolve spiritually, self-actualize, and experience a change in consciousness in order to overcome addiction, then we will assume that AA is a biblical program that is spiritual, not religious. Nothing could be further from the truth.

In AA, a deceiving spirit that expresses itself through the Twelve Steps and the group conscience encourages people to pray and meditate to know God's will, but Yah's Spirit has not regenerated these people; therefore, unless they are praying the sinner's prayer, He does not hear them. Any response that these people get is from a deceiving spirit, but since they are not born again and do not meet together to study the Bible, they have no way of knowing this. The people in AA meet to study a book that was inspired by the bright light that filled Bill's room as he was tripping on drugs. *The Big Book* promotes psychology, spiritual experiences, and the New Age agenda; and it does not lift up Yeshua, which can only mean that the bright light that filled Bill's room was a fallen angel named Lucifer. Lucifer (the light bearer) showed Bill Wilson how to cope with alcoholism without submitting to Yeshua so that he would end up in the fiery lake.

In sum, AA is a New Age end-times ecumenical religion that is dressed in biblical garb. AA contains a few biblical concepts, but it is antibiblical because it is a religion of works that uses psychology and a set of moral standards to produce a spiritual awakening without bowing to Yeshua and receiving His Spirit and Word. So can believers go to AA? If believers go to AA, they should go to share the gospel, but they must guard against adopting New Age ecumenical ideas that will cause them to be less dogmatic about the necessity of Yah's gospel.[iii]

The religions that Adam, Cain, Nimrod, Jeroboam, the sages, the Romans, the Oxford Group, and Alcoholics Anonymous invented all have one thing in common: they are carefully crafted counterfeits of Yahweh's plan in which people attempt to improve themselves so that they can have a relationship with Him. These religions tell us that we have to do something to improve ourselves so that we can have a relationship with Yah; but Yah says that He has already made a way for us to have a relationship with Him, and if we will believe that, then He will change our lives. Bill W. tells us to work the steps and live a moral life so that we can have a spiritual awakening, but Yah tells us to have a spiritual awakening so that we can live morally.

In chapters 1 through 5, we learned that spiritual de-evolution causes addiction and that the *only* cure for addiction is spiritual re-evolution. We learned that in Yahweh's recovery plan, He regenerates our spirit (instantly re-evolves it), and after He regenerates our spirit, His Spirit begins the process of sanctification, which changes us by putting the self to death. We learned that HaSatan's recovery plan is a perversion of Yah's plan and that in

HaSatan's plan, works lead to a spiritual re-evolution and the actualization of the true self. Finally, we learned that on the surface, the recovery plans look compatible, but they are not. In chapters 6 through 52, we will take a trip from the Garden of Eden to the city of Rome and discover Yahweh's recovery plan.[24]

---

[24] Note: In volume 3 of this series, we will talk more about AA and how it opposes Yah's recovery plan.

Part 2
Yahweh's Plan

Chapter 6

Yahweh Rolls Out His Plan

Stopping the Promised Seed

Man rebelled against Yahweh, and the self came to life. HaSatan used the self to rule over man. HaSatan deceived the self into thinking that it could make the fallen man acceptable to Yah. In a sense, HaSatan planted his seed in the self, and it gave birth to religion. The self thought that the fig-leaf religion would repair man's relationship with Yah, but Yah killed an animal to demonstrate the atonement and promised that He would send the Seed to redeem man, restore the earth, and reestablish His kingdom. If a fallen man wanted to have a relationship with Yahweh, he had to put his faith in His promise and meet with Him at a bloody altar.

The people who responded to the wooing of Yah's Spirit, believed His promise, and put their faith in the Seed were taken out of HaSatan's kingdom and put into Yahweh's spiritual kingdom. It did not take long for HaSatan to figure out that Yah would use these people to bring forth the Seed and reestablish His kingdom on the earth. HaSatan targeted these people, and they soon discovered that they had a potent adversary. HaSatan could not bear the thought of Yahweh dethroning him again, so he set out to destroy His saints. HaSatan thought the Seed would come through Abel, so he killed him. Next, HaSatan figured the Seed would come through Enoch, but before he could kill him, Yah raptured him. After this, HaSatan corrupted man's gene pool so that Yah could not keep His promise to Eve. HaSatan accomplished this by telling his angels to transfigure into men and have sex with women in order to corrupt their genetic information.

The people with the corrupted DNA multiplied and filled the earth. These people acted very wickedly and refused to repent. Nevertheless, Yah kept His promise to Eve by giving Noah grace and protecting his bloodline. Noah believed Yahweh, put his faith in the Seed, and met with Him at a bloody altar. Yah declared Noah righteous, judged the earth, and sent the flood to destroy it. Yahweh's wrath fell on the earth and destroyed the wicked. Noah and his family rose above the waters of wrath in an ark sealed with pitch (the Hebrew word *kaphar*, which means "atonement," translates into English as *pitch*). Thus the primitive atonement, which prefigured and drew upon the Seed's finished work, saved Noah and his family from Yahweh's wrath.

Babylon

Yahweh tested Noah's sons. Shem proved that his faith was real, and Yahweh blessed his line with the honor of bringing forth the Seed. Ham proved that his faith was not real, and Yah cursed his line. Later HaSatan would try to use Ham's line to prevent Shem's line from bringing forth the Seed. Nimrod, Ham's grandson, gathered the earth's inhabitants on the plains of Shinar and built a religious-political-economic system that was a counterfeit of Yah's plan and deceived people into putting their faith in a counterfeit seed. Still, Yah kept His promise to Eve by pouring out His grace on a remnant of Shem's line to keep them out of the false system. Eventually Yahweh scattered Babylon: Ham's line went west to Canaan and south to settle the southern lands, Japheth's line went north to settle the northern lands, and Shem's line stayed put.

The Infection Spreads

Human beings are biological conduits that connect the spirit realm to the material realm. These biological conduits configure themselves by what they choose to believe. If a lot of people come together and believe in a particular spiritual reality, that spiritual reality will flow into the material realm with great force and change it. Coming together in unity is a powerful force that we can use for good or evil. HaSatan deceived the Babylonians into believing his version of spiritual reality, and this allowed it to flow into the earth realm. Yah had to break up this toxic unity, so He confused their speech and scattered them to the ends of the earth.

The *Babylonian mystery religion* was a counterfeit of Yah's plan that appealed to the fallen nature; hence fallen man accepted this false system and its counterfeit seed. This system bound people to HaSatan and kept them separated from Yah and destined for the lake of fire. This fig-leaf religion clothed people in a worldview that covered their guilt and repelled the Spirit's wooing. Yahweh scattered the Babylonians to the ends of the earth so that one day they would have a chance to yield to His Spirit, believe Him, put their faith in the Seed, and meet with Him at an altar. Now, it is wonderful that Yah loved the Babylonians enough to scatter them to the ends of the earth, but unfortunately, He scattered their religion to the ends of the earth too.

The Babylonians split up, repopulated the whole earth, and formed the nations. The rulers of these nations built upon the only thing they knew: the old Babylonian religious-political-economic system. This means that every nation on the earth developed its own version of the old Babylonian religious-political-economic system, which means that every nation on earth developed its own version of the Babylonian mystery religion. Each nation adopted the elements of the Babylonian mystery religion that appealed to it. This means that the earth's inhabitants now suffered from a systemic infection that would result in their death and eternal separation from Yah. Yah had to make these people realize that they were sick and offer them a cure. The whole world was in rebellion towards Yahweh, but He had to keep His promise to Eve and Shem, so He called one of Shem's descendants out of Babylon and offered him the cure.

Yahweh Preaches the Gospel

Most of the people in Shem's line started worshiping Babylonian idols. Nonetheless, this did not nullify the promise that Yahweh had made to Shem, so He poured out His grace on a remnant of his line to empower them to remain faithful to Him. Yahweh had His eye on one of Shem's descendants, and He wanted to bring this man into the righteous remnant and use him to expand it. This man's name was Abram.

Yah promised Abram some land and told him that He would make a great nation out of him and give him a Seed who would bless the nations. Abram realized that Yah wanted to use him to fulfill the prophecy of the Seed because Shem had been telling him about this prophecy for seventy years.[25] Abram believed the good news and crossed over the Euphrates River to become a Hebrew (the word *Hebrew* means, "to cross over"). Abram believed the gospel and confessed Yah as Lord (repented from being his own lord and submitted to Him). Yah declared Abram righteous because, by faith, he looked into the future and partook of Yeshua's finished work.[26] After Abram arrived in Canaan, Yahweh cut a covenant with him.

Yah asked Abram to cut some animals in half and position the halves on the banks of a ravine so that the blood flowed into the ravine. Abram divided the animals and prepared to walk through the blood with Yahweh and exchange covenant vows, but then something incredible happened. Yah put Abram into a deep sleep. Yah knew that Abram would not be able to keep his end of the bargain, so He put him to sleep so that he would not have to walk through the pieces. This is grace.

As Abram slept, Yahweh walked through the blood alone and committed Himself to upholding both sides of the covenant. If Yah failed to give Abram the Promised Land or

---

[25] *The Tanach*, Stone Edition, Brooklyn NY, Mesorah Publications, 1996, p. 2,024.
[26] *The Hebrew-Greek Key Word Study Bible*, KJV, Galatians 3:8; John 8:56.

bring the promised Seed through his loins, then He would have to surrender His life, like the animals that had surrendered their lives to establish the covenant. If Abram failed to keep his end of the bargain, which was to obey Yah's teachings and instructions so that He could bring His plan to pass, then Yah would have to shed His blood and forgive Abram in order to uphold the covenant!

The covenant that Yah cut with Abram did not depend on Abram's performance; it depended on Yah's ability to empower him to carry out his end of the bargain and to forgive him when he failed so that the covenant promises would come to pass. In sum, Yah's covenant with Abram depended on one thing: Yah's ability to keep His promises. Thus Yah's covenant with Abram was an unconditional, unilateral covenant of grace that gave Canaan to Abram's seed forever.

Yahweh's Firstborn Sons

Yah promised to bring forth a host of children from Abram's loins. So in the spirit of cooperation, Abram and his wife started having sex, but as the years passed, they remained childless. Sarai tried to help Yah keep His promise by asking Abram to have sex with a beautiful slave girl. So (reluctantly, I am sure) Abram had sex with Hagar, and she gave birth to Ishmael.

Ishmael grew strong, and Abram and Sarai thought that their fleshly efforts to bring about Yah's plan had pleased Him, but Yah appeared to Abram and told him that the Seed who would save the world would not come through Ishmael. This revelation devastated Abram and Sarai. Abram and Sarai had done everything that they knew to do to bring forth the Promised Seed, but sadly, all their efforts were in vain. Yahweh had Abram and Sarai right where He wanted them.

After Yahweh had convinced Abram and Sarai that they could not do anything to bring forth the Promised Seed, He anointed them with His Spirit. Yahweh wanted Abram and Sarai to realize that while they had to cooperate with Him in order to bring forth the Promised Seed who would redeem man, restore the earth to a garden state, and reestablish the kingdom, their trust had to be in Him and not in their own abilities. Yahweh wanted to make sure they never forgot this lesson, so He changed their names. Yah changed Abram's name to Abraham, and He changed Sarai's name to Sarah.

Please note that Yahweh added an *h* to each of their names. The addition of the *h* may not seem significant, but it is. The tetragrammaton (a Greek word that means "the four letters") of God's name is YHWH. *Yahweh* comes from YHWH. The *yod* (*Y*) represents the Father; the *waw* (*W*) represents the Son; and the *heh* (*H*) represents the Spirit. The addition of the *h* to Abram and Sarai's names tells us that Yah put His Spirit on them.[27]

---

[27] John D. Garr, Ph.D., Th.D., *Bless You!* Atlanta, GA, Restoration Foundation, 2003, p. 60.

After Yah anointed Abram, He told him to circumcise the men in his camp. Of course, the men who followed Abram without truly believing Yah refused to be circumcised, which meant that they rejected the covenant and had to be cut off from the camp; however, the men who believed Yahweh and trusted Him willingly submitted to the ritual of circumcision.

The Mark of the Covenant

The people who did not believe Yah's promises left Abraham's camp, but the people who believed Him and put their faith in His promises stayed in Abraham's camp. Yah had elected Abraham's camp, so those who remained in it were in the Abrahamic covenant. Abraham cut off the flesh on the end of the men's penises to signify that they were in the covenant. At some point after Abraham circumcised the men in his camp, they had sex with their wives, and as their seed passed through the sign of the covenant, the covenant sanctified it. The covenant sanctified a man's seed as he implanted it in his wife's womb. This means that the children who were born in Abraham's camp were born into the covenant and were clean. This is why Abraham's camp routinely circumcised the male children when they were eight days old.

The Abrahamic covenant set the children apart for Yah. In other words, the children in Abraham's camp were clean, but when these children reached the age of accountability, they had to decide for themselves whether they wanted to remain in the covenant or go their own way. The girls made their decision at age twelve in a ceremony called a bat mitzvah, and the boys made their decision at age thirteen in a ceremony called a bar mitzvah. If a child decided to remain in the Abrahamic covenant and believed Yahweh and put his or her faith in His promises, then naturally that child would cooperate with Him by striving to obey His teachings and instructions so that he or she could enjoy the blessings of the covenant. This child would also wait expectantly for the Promised Seed who would redeem man, restore the earth, and reestablish the kingdom.[iv]

The Spirit and the Flesh

Why did Yah choose circumcision as the mark of the covenant? Well, by definition, circumcision involves cutting off the flesh, and this communicates two fundamental truths. First, Yah wanted to remind Abraham, all those born in his camp, and all who joined themselves to his camp by putting their faith in Yah and submitting to circumcision that He would fulfill His promises, not through the power of their flesh, but through the power of His Spirit. Second, Yah also wanted circumcision to remind His people that they were not to live according to the lusts of their flesh; His people were to live by every word that came out of His mouth.[28]

---

[28] *The Hebrew-Greek Key Word Study Bible*, KJV, Deuteronomy 8:3; Luke 4:4.

Normally, the world did not see the mark of the covenant. So what was the outward sign of a covenant member? A person who was in covenant with Yahweh believed His promises, trusted Him to bring His promises to pass, put no confidence in the flesh, and obeyed Him. Yahweh said that His words were spirit and life,[29] so in the older covenants, when His people obeyed His teachings and instructions, they were allowing His Spirit to lead them. Those who were in covenant with Yah did not depend on their understanding or indulge the flesh. Those who were in covenant with Yah obeyed His teachings and instructions so that His Spirit could help them subdue the lusts of the flesh and do His will. Yah said that those who bore the mark of the covenant in their flesh *and in their lives* were His sons, and those who merely bore the mark of the covenant in their flesh without the corresponding mark in their lives were not.[30] Let no one deceive you: a person who is really in Yahweh's covenant will strive to obey Him.

---

[29] Ibid., John 6:63.

[30] Ibid., Romans 2:25–29.

Chapter 7

Abraham's Seed

The Land of Canaan

Canaan was a beautiful land that flowed with milk and honey. A race of people called the Amorites lived in Canaan, but Yah promised their land to Abraham's children. Yah brought Abraham's children to Canaan, and the inhabitants of the land seduced them into forsaking His ways. Because of this, Yahweh took Abraham's children to Egypt to knit them into a nation. Yahweh kept Abraham's children in Egypt until He had to judge and punish the Amorites' sin and Abraham's children were strong enough to execute this punishment and take possession of Canaan. This may seem unfair, but it is not. Yahweh promised Canaan to Abraham's seed because He knew the Amorites would not repent, believe Him, and come into the covenant.

Egypt was the strongest and the most prosperous nation on the face of the earth. Yahweh's blessing was on Abraham's children, so they prospered in Egypt; but this alarmed the Egyptians because Abraham's children would not participate in their state religion. The Egyptians were afraid that this prospering sect would side with their enemies and overthrow the government. Hence the Egyptians enslaved Abraham's children. Abraham's children stayed in Egypt for four hundred years, and the Amorites never repented. Yahweh was going to judge the Amorites, but before He did, He was going to judge Egypt so that they would release His sons.

The Oven of Affliction

The ancient Babylonians worshiped the sun, moon, stars, trees, animals, fertility gods, and the counterfeit seed. Yah scattered these people to the ends of the earth, and a group of them founded Egypt. Not surprisingly, the Egyptians worshiped some of the same gods that the ancient Babylonians had worshiped, and their political-economic-religious systems were alike. In the Babylonian system, Marduk was the sun god, who ruled over a pantheon of lesser gods. Marduk's son Tammuz sat in the office of *pater* and ruled as a divine king and a high priest over a network of priests who governed the people, merchandised their labor and the land's resources, and kept the gods propitiated so that they would bless and protect the kingdom. In the Egyptian system, Ra was the sun god, who ruled over a pantheon of lesser gods. Ra's son Amenhotep II[31] sat in the office of *pharaoh* and ruled as a divine king and a high priest over a network of priests who governed the people, merchandised their labor and the land's resources, and kept the gods propitiated so that they would bless and protect the kingdom.

In ancient Babylon, Shem's children would not submit to the pater as a god or a high priest. To the pater, Shem's children were insurgents who endangered the welfare of the kingdom and were thus hunted down, imprisoned, or killed. In Egypt, Abraham's children would not submit to Pharaoh as a god or a high priest. To Pharaoh, Abraham's children were insurgents who endangered the welfare of the kingdom and were thus captured and forced to serve as slaves.

Egypt Is Judged

Yahweh let the pharaohs enslave His children for four hundred years, but when the Amorites' cup of sin was full and His children were strong enough to take possession of Canaan, He anointed and appointed one of His sons to lead His children out of Egypt. In his book *Moses and the Gods of Egypt*, John J. Davis says that Moses was born in 1525 BC, and in 1445 BC, at the age of eighty, he was chosen by Yahweh to be the one who would lead His children out of Egypt.[32]

Yahweh appeared on Mount Sinai (Mount Horeb) as a burning bush and anointed Moses to be the deliverer of His people. Moses and Aaron, his brother, stood before Pharaoh and told him that Yahweh wanted him to let His people go. In essence, Pharaoh said that he did not know Yahweh and that his gods were the only gods who mattered, and since these gods had appointed him to rule Egypt, what he said went. Well, Yahweh decided to introduce Himself to Pharaoh and show him that He was far more powerful than any of the so-called gods of Egypt. The stage was now set for a showdown between Yah and the demons who were masquerading as gods in Egypt.

Pharaoh refused to listen to Moses and Aaron and to heed the signs and wonders that they performed in order to validate their testimony before his court. Yahweh sent a plague of blood to humiliate Osiris, the god of the Nile River. Pharaoh still refused to listen, so

---

[31] John J. Davis, *Moses and the Gods of Egypt*, Winona Lake, Indiana, BMH Books, 2006, p. 40.

[32] Ibid., p. 59.

Yahweh sent a frog plague to humiliate Hekt, the goddess who had a frog's head. Pharaoh still refused to listen, so Yahweh sent a lice plague to humiliate Seb, the earth god. After this, Pharaoh refused to repent, so Yahweh sent swarming creatures to humiliate Scarabus, the small beetle that the Egyptians worshiped. Pharaoh still refused to repent, so Yahweh sent a plague of dying cattle to humiliate Apis, the bull god.

After all this, Pharaoh still refused to repent, so Yah sent a plague of boils to humiliate Serapis, the god of healing. Pharaoh still refused to repent, so Yah sent a plague of hail to humiliate Shu, the god of the atmosphere, along with Isis and Seth, the two gods charged with guarding the crops. Pharaoh still refused to repent, so Yah sent a plague of locusts to humiliate Serapia, the god of the locusts. Pharaoh still refused to repent, so Yah sent a plague of darkness to humiliate Ra, the great sun god. Pharaoh still refused to repent, so Yah sent the plague of the death of the firstborn to humiliate him.

Over the course of a year, the plagues crippled the economy by destroying the crops and livestock, and sickness and confusion brought trade to a screeching halt. The people of Egypt complained to the political leaders, and the political leaders asked the priests to petition the gods for help, but help never came. In Egypt, the religious system empowered the political system, and the political system drove the economy. Therefore, the weak link in Egypt's system was the religious system, because if it failed, then the political system and the economy would fail.

Pharaoh and his priests governed the religious system, and their firstborn sons inherited their offices. In one terrifying night, Yah took the firstborn and wiped out the next generation of religious leaders and thus crippled the religious system for years to come. The total collapse of the kingdom was inevitable unless Pharaoh released the Hebrews immediately.

Yahweh gave Pharaoh every opportunity to repent, but he would not. Yahweh had to tear down his religious-political-economic system to prove that the gods who had built and sustained these systems were inferior to Him. After the religious, political, and economic systems lay in complete ruin, Pharaoh actually paid the children of Abraham to leave his kingdom.

Yah Delivers His Firstborn

The last plague, the plague of the death of the firstborn, applied to everyone in Egypt. Yahweh condemned to death all the firstborn humans and animals in Egypt. Yahweh told Moses that He would release the death angel so that he could go forth to kill the firstborn in Egypt, but if His people would kill a lamb and put its blood on their doorposts, He would not allow the death angel to kill their firstborn. Yahweh promised to *pasach* those who had the blood of a lamb on their doorposts.

When Moses heard the word *pasach*, in his mind he saw an image of a mother hen covering her chicks underneath her wings to protect them from imminent danger. Moses told the Hebrews that if they marked their doorposts with the blood of a lamb, Yahweh would accept its innocent blood in place of the condemned blood of their firstborn and would hide the door of their home underneath His wings so that the death angel would pass over them. In other words, Yahweh's presence would block the door and keep the death angel from slaying their firstborn.

Out of Egypt

Like the Babylonian mystery religion, the Egyptian religious system was complex. The Egyptian pantheon had over eighty loosely defined gods in it. The Egyptian gods tended to evolve over time. An Egyptian god took on the attributes of the other gods in the pantheon, and whenever the Egyptians encountered the gods of other nations, they would transfer the attributes of the foreign gods onto their gods. Moreover, some of the Egyptian gods were regional; that is, the gods who ruled over one part of Egypt did not necessarily rule over another part of Egypt. Therefore, it is impossible to construct a systematic theology of the religion of Egypt.

The religious institutions in Egypt were syncretistic. Therefore, it should not surprise us to learn that some of the Egyptians learned about Yahweh and gave some of their gods His attributes. Nor should it surprise us to learn that this syncretism rubbed off on the Hebrews. The Hebrews began worshiping the Egyptian gods along with worshiping the God of Abraham, Isaac, and Jacob. Yahweh let the Hebrews experience the first three plagues to remind them that He is Elohim, and there is no other.[33]

At the beginning of the fourth plague, Yahweh declared that Goshen, which means, "drawing near," would be a refuge for the Hebrews. Yahweh shielded the Hebrews who repented and separated from the Egyptians and drew near to Him in Goshen. Yahweh protected His people in order to prove to them that He would keep His covenant with Abraham, Isaac, and Jacob and to prove to the Egyptians that He was Elohim.

Yah got His point across. The Egyptians gave the Hebrews their treasures so that they could make the trip to Canaan. The Egyptians saw Yahweh's power and His faithfulness to the Hebrews, and many of them wanted to serve Him. Moses led a mixed multitude of Hebrews, Egyptians, and others out of Egypt. He led the mixed multitude straight into a canyon, however.

As the mixed multitude camped in the canyon, they realized that the Egyptians were chasing them and that the Red Sea was directly in front of them. It was a hopeless situation. Moses stretched out his rod and parted the sea, and the mixed multitude crossed over to the other side. As Moses led the mixed multitude through the waters, they passed from certain death to a new life, but when the Egyptians tried to cross over the sea, it fell on them. Yah

---

[33] *The Hebrew-Greek Key Word Study Bible*, KJV, Exodus 8:22–23; Ezekiel 20:7–9.

destroyed the power of Pharaoh and his army that day, and they were no longer a threat to the mixed multitude.

Chapter 8

The Congregation Of Moses

The Hebrews

Now we need to talk about the congregation of Moses, also known as the congregation in the wilderness. Yahweh told Moses that He had condemned the firstborn in Egypt to death. However, Yah said that the firstborn could go free if his household offered the blood of an innocent lamb in place of his blood. Moses told the people about Yah's judgment and His remedy for it. The people who believed Moses' message put the blood of a lamb on their doorposts. At midnight, Yah passed through Egypt. As Yah saw the blood of an innocent lamb on the doorposts of a home, He accepted the blood of the innocent lamb in place of the blood of the firstborn in that home. Did the firstborn do anything to merit redemption? No, the firstborn believed Yah and put their faith in the blood of the lamb. Yahweh gave the firstborn unmerited favor, or grace.

Yahweh saved the Hebrews by grace through faith. After the Hebrews' faith in the blood of the lamb had saved them, Moses led them out of the kingdom of bondage and into liberty. The Egyptians pursued the Hebrews to the edge of the Red Sea, where they were as good as dead. Moses supernaturally led the Hebrews through the waters, and they passed from death to life.

According to 1 Corinthians 10:1–4, when the Hebrews followed Moses through the waters of the sea, Yahweh baptized them into his body. The word *baptized* comes from the word *baptizo*, which means "to be identified with."[34] So the Hebrews identified with Moses, who was the head of the body (the congregation). Yeshua's Spirit was the cloud that led Moses, the manna that fed him, and the water that refreshed him. As the people

---

[34] *The Hebrew-Greek Key Word Study Bible*, KJV, p. 1,431.

who were in Moses' body followed his instructions, Yeshua's Spirit led, fed, and refreshed them too.

The Gentiles

It had been four hundred years since Yahweh had cut a covenant with Abraham. It was now time for Abraham's children to reaffirm the covenant. A Hebrew reaffirmed the covenant by believing Yahweh and proving that he believed Him by applying the blood of a lamb on the doorposts of his home and submitting to the painful process of circumcision. After a Hebrew submitted to circumcision, he could eat the covenant meal (the Passover).

Okay, but what about the Gentiles in Egypt? Were they just out of luck? No, Yahweh said that the men who were born outside the camp could eat the Passover if they submitted to circumcision. This meant that if a Gentile turned from his gods, believed Yah, put the blood of a Hebrew lamb on his doorposts, and submitted to the painful process of circumcision, he and his family could eat the covenant meal with Yahweh.[35] The Gentiles who wanted to be saved from Yah's wrath and delivered from Pharaoh put the blood on their doorposts and were circumcised with the Hebrews prior to eating the covenant meal with Yah, and they were thus redeemed and baptized into the body of Moses.[36]

Now I realize that the last paragraph does not make sense to most people. Most people assume that the Hebrew slaves circumcised their sons in Egypt on the eighth day of life, but they did not. In Egypt, circumcision was a status symbol. The pharaoh, priests, and political rulers circumcised their sons, but proletariats and slaves did not.[37] The pharaoh would not allow the Hebrew slaves to circumcise their males on the eighth day. After the plagues started and it became obvious that Yahweh was going to deliver the people who were in covenant with Him, the Hebrews met together to circumcise themselves and reaffirm the Abrahamic covenant.

The Gentiles who were in awe of Yah and wanted their firstborn to live and their family delivered from Pharaoh's kingdom submitted to circumcision, followed Moses, and claimed the promises of the Abrahamic covenant.[38] Remember, Yah promised Abraham that through him *all* the families of the earth would bless themselves. Standing on this promise, the Gentiles who wanted to escape Yah's wrath repented, believed, entered into the covenant, and circumcised themselves along with the Hebrews. The circumcised Gentiles took shelter in the homes of the Hebrews or applied the blood of a Hebrew lamb to

---

[35] Ibid., Exodus 12:48.
[36] Ibid., Joshua 5:5.
[37] *Theological Wordbook of the Old Testament*, electronic edition, Moody Press, 1999, c1980.*
[38] *The Hebrew-Greek Key Word Study Bible*, KJV, Exodus 11:8.

their own doorposts, and the death angel passed over their homes; and afterwards, they followed Moses out of Pharaoh's kingdom.

The Gentiles abandoned the traditions and gods of their ancestors and embraced the God of the Hebrews. In a sense, a Gentile died to his old life and joined himself to Abraham's camp to partake of the covenant as a newborn son. Afterwards, the Hebrews and the Gentiles shared a covenant meal with Yahweh (the Passover meal). Moses led the children of Israel (those who were natural born and those who were grafted in) through the Red Sea. The children of Israel passed from death unto life and were identified with Moses and nourished by Yeshua's Spirit.

The Passover meal was a covenant meal. A family killed a Passover lamb, and its blood served as a sin offering for their firstborn. The Passover lamb's body served as a peace offering. The fact that Yah allowed a family to sit at His table and eat with Him proved that they were at peace with Him; that is, they were in the Abrahamic covenant. Abraham's camp was a family of adopted sons; some of the sons were Hebrews, and some were Gentiles, but every son got to sit at Yah's table and eat the lamb that reconciled him to Yah. In a sense, as the people ate the lamb that reconciled them to Yah, they became one with the lamb, each other, and Yah. Unfortunately, though, the people who were not in Abraham's camp could not sit at Yah's table and eat with Him because they were citizens of a kingdom that was at war with Him; that is, they were enemies.

In sum, the congregation of Moses was a very large group of Hebrews and Gentiles. These Hebrews and Gentiles turned away from the gods of Egypt, believed Yah, and put their faith in Him. These Hebrews and Gentiles demonstrated their faith by circumcising themselves, applying the blood of a lamb to their doorposts, and eating a covenant meal with Yahweh. These Hebrews and Gentiles followed Moses through the waters of the Red Sea, passed from death unto life, and were baptized into his body. As these Hebrews and Gentiles followed Moses, they all drank of the same spiritual water that flowed from the rock (Yeshua), they all ate the same spiritual bread (Yeshua), and they were all saved, delivered, and taken care of.

I hope that it is abundantly clear that Yahweh made no distinction between a Hebrew with faith and a Gentile with faith. Most theologians say that the Hebrews were the only ones who were redeemed by believing Yah, putting their faith in Him, demonstrating their faith by circumcising themselves, applying the blood of a lamb to their doorposts, and eating a covenant meal with Yah; however, Joshua 5:5 says that a mixed multitude came out of Egypt, and they were *all* circumcised.

Mount Sinai

Moses led his congregation out of Egypt into a new life of worshiping and serving Yah, but there was just one problem: no one knew how to worship and serve Yah! The patriarchs had passed down Yah's Torah (His teachings and instructions) by word of mouth from person to person and from generation to generation, and over the years, it had been corrupted. To make matters worse, the Hebrews had just spent four hundred years in the most polytheistic nation on the face of the earth,[39] where they had fallen into idolatry and worshiped other gods. The Hebrews had also transferred the attributes of the Egyptian gods onto Yahweh and worshiped Him as the Egyptians worshiped their gods. The Hebrews did not know Yahweh or know how to walk in His ways to please Him.

Joshua 5:9 testifies of this by saying that when Joshua circumcised the congregation of Moses, Yah rolled away the reproach of Egypt. In this verse, the Hebrew word *herpa* is used, which means "to reproach," with the specific connotation of casting blame or scorn on someone, or taunting a person.[40] The Egyptians would not let the Hebrews circumcise their sons, and this played a big part in their abandoning Yahweh to worship pagan gods. After the Hebrews had forsaken Yah to worship pagan gods, evidently the Egyptians taunted them. The Egyptians asked the Hebrews why Yah had not given them Canaan. Therefore, the reproach was that they had corrupted themselves and given the pagans an opportunity to blaspheme Yah.[41] This verse makes it clear that Yah needed to cleanse the backslidden Hebrews and pagan Gentiles of the paganism that was in their hearts and minds and show them how to worship and serve Him.

Yahweh led Moses to Mount Sinai and reiterated His teachings and instructions to him. He also gave Moses some new teachings and instructions in order to implement the next phase of His plan of redeeming man, restoring the earth, and reestablishing the kingdom on it. In Egypt, the Hebrews disobeyed Yah's teachings and instructions and submitted to pagan gods. In Egypt, the Hebrews adopted symbols, rituals, and morals that came from Babylon.

In the next phase of Yah's plan, He had to give His people a mirror so they could see the dirt on their faces and wash it off before they met with Him. In other words, Yah needed to highlight His people's sins and deal with them so that they could enjoy their relationship with Him and serve Him as priests.[42] Yah's priests were to shine the light of the Torah into the darkness of the nations to attract the Gentiles. There was a problem, however. Yahweh's people liked idols, sex, drinking, and feasting, which is why He gave His people an incentive to forsake their ways and obey Him. Yah told His people He would bless them if they obeyed Him and curse them if they did not.

---

[39] John J. Davis, *Moses and the Gods of Egypt*, Winona Lake, IN, BMH Books, 2006, p. 94.

[40] *Theological Wordbook of the Old Testament*, electronic edition, Moody Press, 1999, c1980.*

[41] Matthew Henry, *Matthew Henry's Commentary on the Whole Bible*, Peabody, MA: Hendrickson, 1996, c1991.*

[42] *The Hebrew-Greek Key Word Study Bible*, KJV, Galatians 3:19.

In sum, the congregation of Moses contained Hebrews and Gentiles who had worshiped and served the gods of Egypt all their lives and did not know how to worship or serve Yahweh. Yahweh had to teach these Hebrews and Gentiles how to worship Him and walk in His ways. Yah wanted to live in the congregation of Moses with His people, lead them to Canaan, and help them to subdue its inhabitants and become a great nation. Yah wanted this great nation to bless all the other nations of the earth by bringing them into the Abrahamic covenant and teaching them His Torah. The easy part of Yah's plan was getting the people to Mount Sinai and giving the Torah. The hard part was getting the people to obey the Torah without violating their free will.

Chapter 9

Yahweh Renews His Covenant

The Congregation of Moses

Many theologians tell us that it was Yah's plan for the Old Testament saints to keep the Torah and its law to earn their salvation, but nothing could be further from the truth. Yah gave the Torah (His teachings and instructions) and the law (the legal code that He attached to His teachings and instructions at Mount Sinai) to Hebrews and Gentiles that He had already redeemed by grace through faith in the blood of the Passover lamb. Briefly stated, Yah gave the Torah and its law to Hebrews and Gentiles that He had redeemed in order to show them how to live.

The Abrahamic covenant was an unconditional, unilateral covenant of grace that was open to *anyone* who was willing to repent, believe Yahweh, trust in the blood of the lamb, and submit to circumcision. Yah took these people out of HaSatan's kingdom and put them in His kingdom, with their sin nature intact. At Mount Sinai, Yah defined sin and made a way for the saints to be forgiven and cleansed of it so that they could enjoy their relationship with Him. The Mosaic covenant defined sin and made it consequential, but more importantly, it dealt with sin until the Seed could come to take sin out of the way forever. The Mosaic covenant did not make Yah's land grant conditional; it made the enjoyment of the land conditional. Likewise, the saints did not keep the Torah to earn salvation; the saints kept the Torah to enjoy their salvation.[43]

Yahweh gave the Torah and its law to Moses. Moses offered a burnt offering and a peace offering and sprinkled some blood from the sacrifices on Yah's altar. Moses read the covenant to the people, and they accepted it, promising to live up to its terms and conditions. Moses then sprinkled the rest of the blood on twelve stones that represented

---

[43] *The Hebrew-Greek Key Word Study Bible*, KJV, Galatians 3:18; Deuteronomy 28:1–14.

Israel and ratified the covenant. The Mosaic covenant now formed the backbone of Israel's relationship with Yahweh. If Israel obeyed the Torah and complied with its law, then Yah would bless her people with peace, safety, health, prosperity, and expanding borders. If, however, Israel disobeyed the Torah and failed to comply with the law, then Yah would curse her with war, bondage, sickness, poverty, and exile.

The Mosaic Covenant

In the ancient world, there were two kinds of treaties: the *royal grant treaty* and the *suzerain-vassal treaty*.[44] In the royal grant treaty, a king swore to give a tract of land to a subject, but the subject did not have to swear an oath because there were no conditions. In the suzerain-vassal treaty, the king and his vassal swore oaths. This treaty protected the king's interests and encouraged the vassal to be loyal. The king rewarded the vassal for obedience but punished him for disobedience. Essentially, Yah cut a royal grant treaty with Abraham, but when his descendants endangered His interests, He converted the royal grant treaty into a suzerain-vassal treaty *until* the Seed could come to transform Abraham's descendants.[45]

Yah promised to give Abraham and his seed the land of Canaan. Yah promised to make a great nation out of Abraham's seed. Yah also promised to bless this great nation so that they could bless all the other nations. Abraham knew that the world had destroyed their relationship with Yah. Abraham also knew that the ultimate blessing was for that relationship to be repaired. Thus Abraham understood that Yah would use his seed to bring the nations back into a right relationship with Him. Abraham took note of the fact that Yah made the promises to His Seed, but they spilled over onto him and his seed.[46] Abraham rejoiced because Yah promised that the Seed would come through his loins and bless the nations with a right relationship with Him.[47]

Yah hoped to strengthen Abraham's seed in the oven of affliction so that they could subdue the inhabitants of Canaan and take possession of it; but HaSatan turned up the heat in the oven, and the Hebrews turned away from Yah to worship the gods of mystery Babylon.[48] The chosen ones were disloyal to Yah, and their disloyalty endangered His plans. Nevertheless, Yah had to bring Abraham's seed to Canaan and grow them into a great nation that would bring forth the Seed, because Yahweh had made the promises to the Seed,

---

[44] Tim Hegg, *The Letter Writer*, second edition, Tacoma WA, TorahResource, 2008, p. 157.
[45] *The Hebrew-Greek Key Word Study Bible*, KJV, Galatians 3:19.
[46] Ibid., Genesis 12:7; 17:7; Galatians 3:16.
[47] Ibid., John 8:56.
[48] Ibid., Joshua 24:14.

and ultimately the Seed would bring the nations into the covenant, redeem man, restore the earth, and reestablish His kingdom on it.

If Abraham's seed continued to worship the gods of Mystery Babylon, then Yah would not be able to live with them, take them to Canaan, and help them drive out the inhabitants and take possession of it. Yahweh would not be able to make a great nation out of Abraham's seed, and bring the Seed through that nation to reestablish His kingdom on the earth. Moreover, the demonic system of Mystery Babylon ruled the nations, and if Abraham's seed continued to live like the people in this system, how could they possibly draw the people of the nations to Yah's light? Well, obviously, they could not, which is why Yah had to sanctify them.

At Sinai, Yah cut a covenant of sanctification with Abraham's seed that changed the pattern of their relationship. The Mosaic covenant changed the royal grant pattern into a suzerain-vassal pattern that would last until the Seed to whom it pointed came to fulfill it.[49] Yahweh changed the terms and conditions of the covenant to motivate His subjects to be loyal to Him and to protect His interests. In other words, Yah cut the Mosaic covenant to get Mystery Babylon out of His people and to help them cut off the flesh and walk in His ways. A person still entered the Abrahamic covenant by believing Yah and trusting Him, but the enjoyment of the blessings of the Abrahamic covenant was now contingent upon their obedience to the Mosaic covenant. Circumcision was still the sign of the Abrahamic covenant, but now it reminded the people to keep their focus on the Seed while keeping the Mosaic covenant to cut off the flesh.

In those days, people made knives from stone, and Yah carved the Ten Commandments, which are the core principles behind His Torah, in stone. This means that Yahweh wanted the people who were in the Abrahamic covenant to use the sharp stone knife of the Torah to cut off their flesh so that they could serve as His priests and bring the other nations into the covenant. There was a problem, however. A sharp stone knife could permanently remove the flesh off the end of a penis, but it could not permanently remove the flesh from a heart. The written Torah could trim the flesh from a man's heart, but since his heart possessed a fallen nature, the flesh would always grow back and move the man towards Mystery Babylon and life in the flesh.

The Golden Calf Incident[50]

Yah gave Moses the terms, conditions, and protocols of the covenant of sanctification. Moses read the covenant terms, conditions, and protocols to his congregation, and they

---

[49] Ibid., Galatians 3:19.

[50] Ibid., Exodus 32.

said, "All that the LORD hath said will we do, and be obedient."[51] The congregation swore this oath, and Moses sealed the covenant of sanctification with blood. If the people obeyed the Torah, Yah would bless them with the blessings in the Mosaic covenant, but if not, He would curse them with the curses in the covenant. Moses hoped his people would keep their hearts circumcised and obey Yahweh.

Yah called Moses back up the mountain to give him some instructions. After Moses had been gone for thirty-nine days, the people assumed that he was dead. The people panicked because they thought that Yah had abandoned them. It looked like Yahweh had left His people stranded in the desert without the provisions to get to Canaan, so they asked Aaron to make them some gods. The Egyptians believed the gods rode on divine animals, and they worshiped the animal that carried a god so that it would draw near and bring the god.[52] In Egypt, the Hebrews had mixed the worship of Yah with the worship of Apis,[53] which is why Aaron made the golden calf and the people said, "These be thy gods, O Israel, which brought thee up out of the land of Egypt." [54]

The congregation worshiped the golden calf named Apis (that was associated with the fertility gods) by having sex, drinking, and feasting, hoping that he would bring Yah near![55] The people knew the Torah said not to make idols, but the mere knowledge of good and evil did not change their hearts and give them the power to obey. The people's uncircumcised hearts wanted to worship Yah as they had done in Egypt, and have sex, drink, and feast. Yahweh was not pleased.

Yahweh thought about killing the people, but Moses asked Him not to give the Egyptians a reason to glory. Moses returned to the camp, threw the stone tablets down, and broke them. This was a graphic illustration of the fact that the people had broken the covenant. Moses burned the golden calf and ground it into dust. Moses threw the dust into water and made the people drink it, which is what the Torah said to do to determine if a wife had committed adultery.[56]

The Torah was a marriage contract between Yah and Israel that Moses sealed with blood. Yahweh promised to protect and provide for Israel, and Israel promised to love and obey Him. Moses made Israel drink the water, and those who had knowingly led her into adultery were exposed. Moses told the Levites to kill the people whose bellies were swelling and whose thighs were rotting, which was the mark of adultery.

---

[51] Ibid., Exodus 24:7.

[52] James E. Smith, *The Pentateuch*, 2nd ed., Joplin, MO, College Press Publishing Company, 1993.*

[53] *The Hebrew-Greek Key Word Study Bible*, KJV, Ezekiel 20: 6–8.

[54] Ibid., Exodus 32:4.

[55] James M. Freeman and Harold J. Chadwick, *Manners & Customs of the Bible*, rev. ed., North Brunswick, NJ: Bridge-Logos Publishers, 1998.*

[56] *The Hebrew-Greek Key Word Study Bible*, KJV, Numbers 5:11–31.

Afterwards, Moses went back up Sinai to reconcile the people to Yahweh. Moses asked Yah to blot his name out of His book (the book of the living[57]) if that would reconcile Him to His wife, but this was impossible. Moses was a type of Yeshua, and his willingness to lay down his life for his wayward sheep revealed his heart; however, his blood could not atone for sin because sin had infected his blood. Yah cursed with plagues the people who remained. The golden-calf incident illustrates how man's sinful nature reacts to Yahweh's holiness.

The Sharp Two-Edged Stone Sword

Yah's Word is alive, powerful, and sharper than any two-edged sword.[58] At Sinai, this ultrasharp, two-edged spiritual sword materialized in stone. This means that Moses came down from Sinai with a sharp two-edged stone sword in his hands. Yah wanted the saints to keep their hearts circumcised with this sword so that they could do His will and live a blessed life, but sadly, the human spirit's unskilled hands nicked the heart and left it wounded and tender to the touch, which meant that it was more sensitive to the flesh. Therefore, the divine instrument that was supposed to keep the heart circumcised tended to bring out the corruption that was in it.[59]

In the Garden of Eden, man bore Yah's image until he submitted to HaSatan and took on his image. At Sinai, Yah gave man the Torah so that he could keep his heart circumcised and project His image, which is why Paul says the Torah is the standard of righteousness.[60] There was a problem, however. Fallen man misused the Torah. When Yah put the sharp two-edged sword in the hands of a fallen man, he agitated his fleshly nature with it. Instead of keeping the heart circumcised so that man could overcome sin, the Torah empowered sin to rule over him.[61] The saint who was under the custodianship of the Torah knew that it was Yah's standard and that by obeying it, he would reflect His image. The saint knew that Yahweh had redeemed him from HaSatan's kingdom, and he wanted to obey the Torah and reflect His image; but since the Spirit did not indwell him, he lacked the authority and power to subdue the soul and body. The saint's spirit often lost the war with the soul and body and did things he did not want to do and did not do the things he wanted to do unless the Spirit came on him to empower him to do otherwise.[62]

---

[57] Robert B. Hughes and Carl Laney, *Tyndale Concise Bible Commentary*, Tyndale Reference Library, Wheaton, IL: Tyndale House Publishers, 2001.*

[58] *The Hebrew-Greek Key Word Study Bible*, KJV, Hebrews 4:12.

[59] Ibid., Romans 7:5.

[60] Ibid., Romans 7:12; Psalm 19:8.

[61] Ibid., Romans 6:14, 7:5.

[62] Ibid., Romans 7:15.

What shall we say then? Did the Torah cause sin? No, it reflected the divine image. The fallen spirit's misuse of the sharp stone sword strengthened the power of sin. So if the fallen spirit was incapable of keeping itself circumcised with the Torah in order to reflect the divine image, then what hope did we have? How would we ever free ourselves from the body of death that held us captive and prevented us from living up to Yah's standards? Paradoxically, when the Torah forced a person to ask this disturbing question, it had done its job! The Torah showed man that he was incapable of keeping his heart circumcised so that he would not trust in his ability to fix himself by doing good works and trust instead in the Seed's ability to circumcise his heart perfectly.

In sum, Yah's Spirit wooed people and asked them to circumcise their hearts by believing His promises and trusting Him. Yah's Spirit gave people the ability to believe Him and put their faith in Him, and if they did, He redeemed them from the serpent's slave market and set them apart to serve Him. A saint needed to keep the Torah to keep his heart circumcised so that he could do Yahweh's will, serve as His priest, and enjoy the blessings. The saint, however, was a fallen creature who could not keep his heart circumcised. The saint was continually offering sacrifices to have his sins forgiven and his conscience cleansed. The saints longed for the Seed, who would circumcise their hearts perfectly by changing their nature. In essence, the written Torah needed to become a spiritual sword in the hands of a skilled surgeon who could circumcise man's heart perfectly. This is exactly why the Spirit who wrote the Torah took on flesh, died, resurrected, ascended, and returned to live in our hearts to circumcise them perfectly!

Part 3
The Phases of Yahweh's Plan

Chapter 10

A Deeper Look

The Fundamental Problem

It is imperative that we understand man's problem. If we understand our problem, this understanding will help us recognize Yahweh's solution and HaSatan's counterfeit of it. So please bear with me as I repeat a few things. In the beginning, Adam and Eve's spirits submitted to Yahweh's Spirit. Adam and Eve reflected Yahweh's image, and the fullness of His Spirit (His glory) clothed their bodies and crowned their heads. Adam and Eve's covering of righteousness and crown of glory gave them the authority and power to rule the earth.[63] Yahweh's teachings and instructions were simple. Yahweh told Adam to *avad* ("till") and *shamar* ("guard") the garden[64] and to eat of the fruit of any tree except the Tree of the Knowledge of Good and Evil.

HaSatan had already gotten into the garden to plant the Tree of the Knowledge of Good and Evil beside the Tree of Life. Yahweh wanted Adam to guard the garden to make sure that HaSatan did not get back into the garden to cause any more trouble.[65] Sadly, Adam failed to guard the garden, and HaSatan tricked Eve into eating the fruit of the knowledge of good and evil. HaSatan told Eve that if she ate the fruit, she would know the difference between good and evil and then could decide what was good and evil, or in other words, she could be her own god. This is man's problem: HaSatan has deceived him into believing he can be his own god.

Eve ate the forbidden fruit and gave it to Adam. Adam and Eve rose up out of submission to Yah, and as they did, their spirits disconnected from His Spirit. Adam and Eve's robe

---

[63] *The Hebrew-Greek Key Word Study Bible*, KJV, Psalm 8:5.
[64] Bill Cloud, *Enmity Between the Seeds*, Cleveland, TN, Shoreshim Resources, 2004, p. 58.
[65] Ibid., p. 64.

of righteousness evaporated, their crown of glory vanished, and their conscience sprang to life. Suddenly Adam and Eve realized that they were naked (without a covering), physically and spiritually. Since man's spirit had disconnected from Yahweh's Spirit, man's spirit could no longer project Yahweh's image into the earth, and it no longer had the authority and power to control the soul and body. This allowed HaSatan to build strongholds in the soul so that he could trigger the desires and passions of the body, rule the HSC, enslave man, and force him to build his kingdom on the earth. Man's spirit lost the ability to govern the soul, the body, and the earth.

Adam chose to be his own god and project his own image into the earth. Adam did not realize that by projecting his own image, he was actually projecting the image of a fallen angel who would enslave him and force him to build his kingdom on the earth. First, HaSatan inspired Adam to invent religion. HaSatan invented religion to keep man separated from Yah so that he could reign supreme. Religion opened a channel for HaSatan's power, and it began to flow from the spirit realm into the earth. Next, HaSatan invented a governmental system to distribute his power throughout the earth. The religious and governmental systems needed a way to control the masses, so HaSatan invented an economic system. Mystery Babylon is the name of this satanic religious-governmental-economic system that operates behind the scenes and keeps man separated from Yahweh, controlling the kings and the kingdoms of the earth.[66]

The Consequences of Sin

Yahweh wanted a creature He could fellowship with, one made in His image. Yahweh wanted this creature to project His image into the earth realm, so He created Adam. Yah's Spirit fellowshiped with Adam's spirit, and His Spirit gave Adam's spirit the authority and power to rule over his soul and body. Adam's spirit ruled his soul and body; hence Adam obeyed Yah, projecting His image into the earth realm and advancing His kingdom on the earth.

Yah loved Adam and cherished their relationship. Yah gave Adam some teachings and instructions to protect him and keep their relationship intact. As Adam obeyed Yah's Torah (His teachings and instructions), His Spirit flowed through him, which meant that Adam's spirit reflected His image and had the authority and power to keep the soul and body under control. This empowered Adam to project Yahweh's image into the earth realm and fulfill his mission.

Yahweh's Torah was a fence that separated order from disorder. As Adam's spirit submitted to Yah's Spirit, his spirit obeyed Him and had the authority and power to force the soul and body to obey Him. By obeying Yah, Adam stayed inside the fence and lived an

---

[66] *The Hebrew-Greek Key Word Study Bible*, KJV, Revelation 14:8; 17:5; Jeremiah 51:7.

orderly life where there was no lack and nothing missing or broken; that is, Adam lived the abundant life. Sadly, Adam's spirit decided to project its own image into the earth realm by doing its own will. Adam lost the power to rule over his soul and body and climbed over the fence that protected him from disorder; that is, he disobeyed the Torah. Yah called this *sin*, and sin has consequences.[67]

Adam's spirit rose up out of submission to Yah's Spirit, and when it did, it lost the power to rule over the soul and body. This was catastrophic because HaSatan had already deceived Adam's soul into obeying him (submitting to him). Since Adam's spirit no longer possessed the power to rule over the soul, and the soul had submitted itself to HaSatan, HaSatan built strongholds in it. HaSatan's strongholds in Adam cultivated strong desires to climb over the fence, and since the soul controlled the body, the body was compelled to live outside of the fence. Consequently, Adam's soul started projecting HaSatan's image into the earth realm. HaSatan enslaved Adam's spirit by shaping the desires of his rebellious soul and body to ensure that he lived outside the fence so that he could rule over him and force him to build Mystery Babylon.

Yahweh knew that this was going to happen, and He had a plan in place to deal with it. Yah's plan takes man through seven ages. In each age, Yah has taught man that the serpent lied: he cannot be his own god and build a kingdom on earth that produces the abundant life. In each age, the lesson plan has been different, but the lesson has remained the same. Yah's plan uses the different ages to demonstrate one central truth on every possible level. At the same time, Yah's plan frees man from HaSatan's kingdom, restrains Mystery Babylon, and prepares us for His earthly kingdom.

The consequences of sin are multidimensional because man is multidimensional. For example, when we sin, our conscience condemns us and our spirit's disposition shifts, which triggers the release of chemicals in our body. The chemicals circulate in the bloodstream and bind with receptors throughout the body, generating feelings of guilt, shame, and fear and igniting physiological processes that produce addiction, sickness, disease, and death. Yahweh's plan solves all the problems that we have just discussed, but since He is solving these problems concurrently by using multidimensional mechanisms implemented in progressive phases over thousands of years, it is hard to get our minds around what He is doing. This much is clear: Adam sinned, and his conscience sprang to life. The Age of Innocence ended. The Age of Conscience began, and man began his journey from the Garden of Eden to the New Jerusalem.

---

[67] Ibid., 1 John 3:4.

The Age of Conscience

In the Age of Conscience, Yahweh allowed man to use his conscience to govern himself. Yah wanted to show man that he was incapable of being his own god. Yah also wanted man to realize that the only place he would find fulfillment was in a relationship with Him. Yah created man to fellowship with him, but He did not force Himself on man; He offered man His hand in friendship.

In the Age of Conscience, Yahweh's Spirit strove with people in the hope that they would accept His invitation to relationship and find fulfillment and the abundant life in Him.[68] However, when people repeatedly rejected Yah's invitation, He had no choice but to stand by as they governed themselves and attempted to find fulfillment in fleshly and earthly pleasures that enslaved them and ultimately destroyed them. In His wisdom, Yahweh used the conscience as a testing mechanism to separate His sheep from the rebellious goats; that is, to build His ekklesia.

The Spirit's EPROM

After the human spirit separated itself from Yah's Spirit (the source of wisdom), it looked inside itself for wisdom and activated the conscience. I visualize the conscience as an *EPROM*. An EPROM is an erasable-programmable-read-only-memory. A programmer stores fixed, semipermanent information in an EPROM and can erase it and replace it with new information whenever the need arises. The EPROM is a fitting analogy for the conscience because it operates like the conscience; thus I will use the EPROM to explain the conscience.

Yahweh put an inactive EPROM in our spirit. Yah programmed the EPROM with His basic teachings and instructions. Adam's rebellion separated him from Yah's Spirit and placed a demand on the EPROM that activated it. The EPROM began judging man's actions, telling him which were good and which were evil, but there was a problem with this arrangement. The spirit could erase the information that Yah had written in its EPROM and write new information in it.

HaSatan bombarded man with new information, and periodically Yahweh updated His information. Man's spirit had to either accept the new data and write it into his EPROM or reject it. The man who submitted to Yahweh recognized His data and wrote it into his EPROM and rejected HaSatan's data. The man who did not submit to Yah (the sinner) accepted HaSatan's information and wrote it into his EPROM. The sinner embraced HaSatan's instructions, and when his soul and body engaged in behavior that violated Yah's standards, the EPROM's voice became less and less pronounced, and the behavior became

---

[68] Ibid., Genesis 6:3.

easier and easier to practice; in time, the EPROM was reprogrammed with HaSatan's standards. After this, when the spirit, soul, or body violated Yah's Torah, the conscience did not protest anymore because it was "seared".

After a man seared his conscience, Yahweh could not use it to help him make the decisions that produce the abundant life. During this age, it was obvious that man could not be his own god and that he needed the Seed to save him and empower him to live the abundant life. If people acknowledged that they could not govern themselves with their unaided conscience, responded to the wooing of Yahweh's Spirit, believed His promises, and put their trust in the Promised Seed, then Yah took them off the serpent's slave market. After these people were taken off the slave market (redeemed), they could fellowship with Yah at a bloodstained altar and submit to Him so that He could bring His will to pass through them; that is, they became saints.

Chapter 11

From The Garden To The Mountain

The Operation of the Conscience

The serpent told our parents that they could reject Yah's teachings and instructions (His Torah) and live by their knowledge of good and evil. In essence, the serpent told our parents that they could be their own gods. Our parents believed the lie, and by doing so, they forced Yahweh to take their descendants (us) on a long, arduous journey from the garden of pleasures through the desert of desire to the mountain of revelation to prove that they were not gods.

The first stop was the Age of Conscience. In the Age of Conscience, Yah allowed man to govern himself with his conscience. How does the conscience work? The conscience monitors the thoughts, intents, and actions of the spirit, soul, and body and compares them to its standard. If a person's thoughts, intents, and actions line up with the conscience's standard, then it takes no corrective action. However, if a person's thoughts, intents, or actions do not line up with the conscience's standard, then it notifies the spirit, the spirit notifies the soul, and the soul notifies the body that it needs to bring the thoughts, intents, and actions in line with its standard.

In a perfect world, the human spirit's knowledge of good and evil would enable it to choose between good and evil so that it could govern the thoughts and imaginations of the soul and keep the desires of the body under control. Man was no longer in a perfect world, however. HaSatan was running the show. HaSatan's teachings and instructions appealed to the pride of the defiant soul and the lusts of the vile body, and they embraced them. The conscience let the spirit know that these teachings and instructions were in error, the spirit notified the soul, and the soul notified the body. Man's spirit did not protest too loudly, though, because it was HaSatan's slave and did not have the authority or power to reign in the depraved duo (the soul and body). The human spirit reprogrammed the conscience with HaSatan's standards of good and evil, and HaSatan used man's defiled conscience to enslave him in sin, addiction, poverty, and sickness.

The Righteous Remnant

HaSatan enslaved man and used his dominion to rule the earth. However, Yahweh announced that the Seed would redeem man, restore the earth, and reestablish His kingdom. Yah preached the gospel of the Seed and redeemed whosoever believed it. Yah's saints could slay an animal on an altar and meet with Him to obtain the mercy and grace that empowered them to obey His teachings and instructions and bring His will to pass on the earth. The Old Testament saints believed that one day the Seed would redeem them, restore the earth, and reestablish Yah's kingdom; thus Yah credited Yeshua's sacrifice to their account, forgave their sins, and declared them righteous.[69] In each age, there was a remnant that believed the gospel of the Seed and lived out their belief by obeying Yahweh's teachings and instructions, and in the Age of Conscience, the righteous remnant included people like Abel, Enoch, and Noah.

Yahweh redeemed and justified the Old Testament saint by grace through faith. The saint looked ahead in time to the Promised Seed's sacrifice, and the blood of His sacrifice flowed backwards in time through the capillaries of faith to cleanse him of his sin. The Old Testament saint offered sacrifices that prefigured the Seed's sacrifice in order to appropriate the blood of His sacrifice into their lives. Does this mean the Old Testament saint worked for his salvation? No, Yeshua offered His life to Yahweh on behalf of man before He created the earth; hence, the only way that anyone has ever obtained grace is by faith.[70] Yahweh manifests His plan in and through history, and the Seed had not yet entered into history; thus, the Old Testament saint was living out his faith by obeying the teachings and instructions that Yeshua would fulfill.

The Two Groups

During the Age of Conscience, there were two groups of people on the earth. One group of people heard the gospel of the Promised Seed, believed it, and put their faith in it. Yahweh took these people's spirits off the serpent's slave market and brought them into His kingdom. (Yah calls the group of people that He has redeemed from HaSatan's kingdom the *ekklesia*. Yah calls people who are in the ekklesia *saints*.) A saint's spirit wanted to obey Yah, but his soul and body did not. A saint met with Yah at an altar, and Yah's Spirit helped his spirit preserve the integrity of his conscience, subdue the thoughts and imaginations of

---

[69] *The Hebrew-Greek Key Word Study Bible*, KJV, Hebrews 11:4–7.
[70] Ibid., 1 Peter 1:20; Ephesians 3:9; 2 Timothy 1:9; Titus 1:2; Revelation 13:8.

his soul, and corral the lusts of his body so that he could obey Yah, bring His will to pass, and live an abundant life.

Another group of people heard the gospel of the Promised Seed and rejected it. A person in this group was in serious trouble because he rejected the only payment that could ransom him out of the serpent's slave market. This person doomed himself to remain in HaSatan's kingdom *forever*. HaSatan built strongholds in this person's soul so that he could lord over his spirit and defile his conscience. This person could not stop obeying the rebellious soul and fulfilling the lusts of the body. In other words, this person could not stop building HaSatan's earthly kingdom.

In the Age of Conscience, Yah showed man that he could not preserve the integrity of his conscience, subdue his rebellious soul, or corral the lusts of his body. In this age, Yah showed man that the only way that he could possibly preserve the integrity of his conscience, subdue his rebellious soul, and corral the lusts of his body was by accepting His grace. In this age, a man accepted Yahweh's grace by putting his faith in the Promised Seed and meeting with Him at an altar so that His Spirit could *temporarily come upon* him in order to empower him to do His will.

In the Age of Conscience, it was a fight to preserve the conscience's integrity and to force the soul and body to adhere to its standards. So most people ignored their conscience, reprogrammed it, rejected the gospel of the Promised Seed, and perished in a global flood. A few people, like Abel, Enoch, and Noah, believed the gospel of the Promised Seed and entered Yahweh's ekklesia, where they received the grace to keep their conscience pure, subdue their rebellious soul, and corral the lusts of their body in order to do His will. In this age, if Yahweh's saints were not at an altar communing with His Spirit, or if He did not choose to come upon them and infuse their spirit with the power to overcome the flesh, the devil, and the world, then the flesh, the devil, and the world overcame them and destroyed them. In this age, man became painfully aware of the fact that the serpent had lied: man was not a god who could govern himself with his own knowledge of good and evil, build a global kingdom, and bring forth the abundant life.

The Age of Human Government

The next stop in man's journey from Eden to the New Jerusalem was the Age of Human Government. After the floodwaters receded and the ark came to rest, Noah built an altar and sacrificed to Yah. Yah met with Noah and gave him some teachings and instructions to write into his conscience, and these teachings and instructions were the foundational principles of human government. A government that adopted Yah's teachings and instructions as the basis of law could use His authority to judge and punish those who were at variance with His standards. For example, Yah said a government could take the life of anyone who took a life, which meant that the government had to set up a court system to punish the guilty and protect the innocent.

Yahweh wanted Noah's descendants to set up a government that reflected His nature so that He could rule over them and reveal His love, justice, righteousness, and mercy to the world. Yah's religious-political-economic system would witness to the world and make it easier for them to believe His promises, put their faith in the Promised Seed, and enter His ekklesia. However, Genesis 11:2 says that Noah's descendants "journeyed from the east," which means that they discounted Yah's teachings and instructions and trusted in their knowledge of good and evil. Thus HaSatan corralled Noah's descendants on the plains of Shinar and put the yoke of his religious-political-economic system on their necks to keep them away from the Promised Seed. In time, Yahweh confused their language and scattered Noah's descendants to the ends of the earth, but this scattered the old religious-political-economic system to the ends of the earth too.

Jeremiah 51:7 says that Yah used Babylon to make the nations of the earth drunk and crazy. Romans 11:32 says that Yah shut up the nations in disobedience because the people who founded them were polytheistic idol worshipers. Each group of people that built a nation had their favorite gods, dogmas, and traditions. Therefore, each nation had its own gods, dogmas, rituals, and traditions that drove its political system, which drove its economic system. Each nation was unique, but since each nation was built on the bedrock of HaSatan's religious-political-economic system, they all fit together to form his global kingdom of Mystery Babylon.

The Bible tells us about Noah's descendants:

Because that, when they knew God, they glorified Him not as God, neither were thankful; but became vain in their imaginations, and their foolish heart was darkened. Professing themselves to be wise, they became fools, and changed the glory of the incorruptible God into an image made like to corruptible man, and to birds, and four-footed beasts, and creeping things. Wherefore God also gave them up to uncleanness through the lusts of their own hearts to dishonor their own bodies between themselves: who changed the truth of God into a lie and worshiped and served the creature more than the Creator, who is blessed forever. Amen.[71]

The nations worshiped HaSatan, and he brought them into slavery to their pride and lusts. Yahweh's Spirit reached out to these people, but they turned away from Him; and after a long period of forbearance, He turned away from them. However, Yah preserved a remnant that was willing to believe Him and meet with Him at a bloody altar to receive the grace to bring His will to pass. Shem's descendants were this remnant.

---

[71] Ibid., Romans 1:21–25.

Initially, Shem's descendants kept the faith, but they grew weary and compromised with Mystery Babylon. Sadly, most of Shem's descendants embraced Mystery Babylon, and HaSatan brought them into bondage; but Yahweh poured out His grace on a remnant of Shem's line to preserve it. At the appointed time, Yahweh met with a man in Shem's line and asked him to come out of Mystery Babylon. Yahweh wanted this man to enter the remnant and expand it by bringing forth the Seed who would bring the nations into it.

The Dispensation of Promise

The next stop was the Age of Promise. It had been 375 years since Noah had prophesied that the Seed would come through Shem's line.[72] Shem's line was living on the plains of Shinar in the heart of Mystery Babylon and worshiping idols. Yahweh, however, watches over His word to perform it, so He called Abram out of Ur of the Chaldees. Yah asked Abram to leave Ur of the Chaldees (Mystery Babylon) and walk with Him. Yah made some awesome promises to Abram: He promised to bless him, and He promised to make his seed into a great nation and bless it so that it could bless the other nations. Abram's nation would bless the other nations by reconciling them with Yahweh and delivering them from Mystery Babylon so that they could live the abundant life.[73]

Yah knew that Abram's father would not forsake his idols; He also knew that Abram's nephew would not deny his flesh and focus on His interests. Yah told Abram to leave his father and nephew in order to follow Him. Sadly, Abram disobeyed Yahweh and took his father and nephew with him, so Yah let Abram live in Haran for ten years until his father (his old lifestyle) died. After this, Yah told Abram to leave Lot and follow Him, but once again, he took Lot with him. Abram's refusal to leave Lot (the flesh) behind shut up the heavens over his life and turned the Promised Land into a dry, barren place, forcing him to seek sustenance in Egypt, where he nearly lost his wife. Yah let Abram suffer with Lot (the flesh) until he was willing to part from him (crucify the flesh). Then Yah let Abram walk through the land and claim it for his children.

Yah walked with Abram for eleven years. Yah met Abram's needs and protected him. Yah proved that He was faithful. Abram was convinced that Yah would keep His promises. Abram believed that Yahweh would give him Canaan and a multitude of children to establish a line that would bring forth a nation that would bring forth the Seed, who would redeem man, restore the earth, and reestablish the kingdom. Essentially, Abram believed the gospel of the Seed, and Yah cut a covenant with him and declared him righteous. Yah redeemed Abram and justified him.

---

[72] Paul P. Enns, *The Moody Handbook of Theology*, Chicago, IL, Moody Press, 1997, c1989.*

[73] *The Hebrew-Greek Key Word Study Bible*, KJV, Genesis 12:2; Isaiah 42: 1–9.

Abram believed that Yah would keep His promises, but he got impatient and tried to help Him by siring Ishmael with Hagar. Yah waited thirteen more years for Abram and Sarai's self-sufficiency to dry up. Yahweh wanted Abram and Sarai to know that there was no possible way that they could produce a child together. Then Yah told them that Ishmael was not the son of promise. Yah changed Abram and Sarai's names and put His Spirit on them so that He could bring the promises to pass through them. Yahweh told Abraham to circumcise his males because He did not want them to forget that it was impossible for them to fulfill His promises and that they had to trust Him to fulfill the promises. After this, Yah's Spirit brought forth Isaac.

In this age, Yahweh chose to love Abraham's seed and make awesome promises to them. Yahweh wanted Abraham's seed to accept His love and believe His promises. Yahweh wanted Abraham's seed to love Him by obeying Him, but they did not. So Yahweh took Abraham's seed to Egypt to chastise them and prove that He would keep His promises.[74] Years earlier Yah had promised Abraham that his seed would be slaves in a strange land for four hundred years, but that He would judge this land and give them its wealth. So when Yah judged the strongest, wealthiest nation in Mystery Babylon and gave its wealth to His sons, this awesome event became the gold standard that they were to commemorate each Sabbath[75] and Passover to strengthen their faith.

The Dispensation of the Written Torah

The next stop was the Age of the Written Torah. Most theologians call this period the Age of Law,[76] but as we will see, the Age of the Written Torah is a more appropriate name. It was now about twenty-five hundred years since Adam had left Eden and about five hundred years since Abram had left Mystery Babylon. Abraham's children had been disobedient in Canaan and embraced the ways of Mystery Babylon, so Yah let the strongest nation in Mystery Babylon enslave them. It was now time for Yahweh to call Abraham's children out of Mystery Babylon.

Each age began with Yah's grace and the giving of new teachings and instructions, but man failed to obey the new teachings and instructions, so the age ended with Yah judging man. The Age of Promise began with Yah making promises to Abram and giving him some teachings and instructions, but ended with Yah judging Abraham's children and using Mystery Babylon to chastise them. Four hundred years after it began, Yahweh wrapped up the Age of Promise by judging the Hebrews. As Yah's judgment reached an apex, He condemned Egypt's firstborn to death, but He gave man access to His grace. As far as Yah was

---

[74] Finis Dake, *God's Plan for Man*, Lawrenceville, GA, Finis Publishing, 2004, c1949, pp. 268–271.

[75] *The Hebrew-Greek Key Word Study Bible*, KJV, Deuteronomy 5:15.

[76] Finis Dake, *God's Plan for Man*, Lawrenceville, GA, Finis Publishing, 2004, c1949, p. 301.

concerned, the firstborn were dead, but if they trusted in the blood of the lamb, He would resurrect them and give them a new life. Yah began the next age by pouring out His grace and making it available to anyone who put their faith in the blood. Thus, the next age began with grace that came through faith, not the law.

A Hebrew core and some Gentiles who attached themselves to this core followed Moses out of Egypt. Yah baptized this mixed multitude in the cloud of His presence (His Spirit) and placed a seal on their spirits, which marked them as His adopted sons.[77] Yahweh parted the waters of the Red Sea, and Moses led the mixed multitude out of their old lives into their new ones. In essence, the mixed multitude identified with the firstborn who had been counted as dead, resurrected from the dead, delivered from the kingdom of darkness by the blood of the lamb, sealed with the Spirit, given a new life, and placed in the ekklesia of Moses. Therefore, the mixed multitude was Yah's firstborn son.[78] The ancient Hebrew word for Egypt is *Mitzraim*, which means "a straight and narrow place; a birth canal"; so when the waters of the sea broke and the mixed multitude passed through them, they were reborn and given new life. This is where the concept of baptism originated[79] and where Yah's sons were reborn by blood and water.

Yahweh wanted to dwell with His people, be their king, and make them into a great nation. Yah wanted His people to believe His promises, trust Him, love Him, and obey Him. Yah wanted a nation of people who walked with Him in the cool of the evening and embraced His ways so that they could be His priests and teach the other nations His ways and bring them back to Him. There was a problem, however. Yah's sons had just come out of the strongest nation in Mystery Babylon, and they thought and acted like the people of Mystery Babylon.

Yah's sons were supposed to come out of Mystery Babylon and separate from it. Then Yah's sons were supposed to help the people of the nations come out of Mystery Babylon and separate from it. Could Yah's sons live like the people in Mystery Babylon and teach the people of the nations how to come out of it and separate from it? No, so Yah took His sons, *who had already been justified by the blood of the lamb*, to Mount Sinai to sanctify them so that they could live the abundant life and bring the nations into the Abrahamic covenant to fulfill their destiny.

---

[77] *The Hebrew-Greek Key Word Study Bible*, KJV, 1 Corinthians 10:2; Ephesians 1:13.

[78] Ibid., Exodus 4:22.

[79] John Klein and Adam Spears, *Devils and Demons and the Return of the Nephilim*, Maitland, FL Xulon Press, 2005, p. 166.

Chapter 12

The Dispensation Of The Written Torah

Exposing the Lie of the Serpent

It has taken twenty-five hundred years, but we have finally arrived at the mountain of revelation. It has been a long, hard trip, but we have learned some vital lessons along the way. Noah's flood taught us that the human spirit, which separates itself from the Holy Spirit, is incapable of governing itself by its own knowledge of good and evil. The demise of the Tower of Babel taught us that fallen man is prideful, rebellious, and lustful, and these flaws lead him into bondage and keep him separated from Yahweh. The Egyptian captivity taught us that fallen man has a heart of unbelief, and he cannot believe the promises of Yahweh, trusting Him to bring them to pass and living out that trust by loving and obeying Him. So did the Master Teacher convince man that the serpent lied to him? Did He convince man that he is not a god? Did He convince man that he is a treasonous criminal who deserves to languish in the lake of fire?

No, after all this, man still had not learned his lesson. In the next age, Yah asked man to circumcise his heart by believing Him and trusting the Seed and gave him a sharp sword so that he could keep his heart circumcised. The Torah was supposed to help man's spirit preserve the integrity of his conscience and rule the soul and body so that he could do Yah's will. Man tried to use the Torah to keep his heart circumcised, but to his horror, he discovered that he could not.

The written Torah told man what good and evil were, and it told him how to keep his self-love in check so that he could love Yah and others. However, as man tried to live up to Yahweh's standard of righteousness, he discovered that he did not have the power to choose good over evil or to keep his self-love in check so he could love Him and others. Thus the written Torah revealed Yah's standard of righteousness, but it did not give the human spirit the authority or power to subdue the rebellious soul and corral the body's lusts so that he could live up to it.

The weakness was not in the written Torah; it was in the human spirit's ability to wield the written Torah. A fallen spirit could not use the Torah to keep the heart circumcised and force the defiant soul and vile body to obey Yah. The Torah was perfect; it showed man how Yah would manifest Himself on earth. Hence Yah's Torah showed man how to project the light of His life into a dark world. The Torah projected the image of Yah, who is love. The Torah told man how to keep self-love in check so that he could love Yah and love his neighbor as himself.

Yah cut the Abrahamic covenant to provide a framework through which He could pay the redemption price that was required to take a human spirit off the serpent's slave market and bring him into His ekklesia as a son. Unfortunately, Yah's sons disregarded their inheritance and their destiny, so He cut the Mosaic covenant with them. After this, the Abrahamic covenant and the Mosaic covenant worked together to bring Yah's sons into their inheritance and destiny. The two covenants were two sides of the same coin, not two different coins that stood in opposition to each other.[80] The Abrahamic covenant *justified* Yahweh's sons, and the Mosaic covenant *sanctified* them so that He could give them their inheritance and empower them to fulfill their destiny.[81] In essence, the Mosaic covenant actualized the blessings of the former covenant.

The Written Torah Exposes the Treasonous Criminal

Yahweh designed the Age of Innocence, Age of Conscience, Age of Human Government and Age of Promise to prove that fallen man could not be some sort of god who creates the abundant life on the earth. Consequently, it should not surprise us to discover that Yah designed the Age of the Written Torah to be the *conclusive* and *irrefutable* evidence of the fact that HaSatan lied to us and that we are treasonous criminals who deserve to languish in the lake of fire with the serpent forever.

The written Torah defined good and evil; it cursed those who did evil and blessed those who did good. Now man knew the difference between good and evil and the consequences of choosing either, but this did not give him the power to choose good and shun evil so that he could live an abundant life. The written Torah exposed the criminal and showed him that he did not have the ability to overcome his father (HaSatan), which moved him to seek the one who could overcome him and give him the abundant life. Thus the written Torah

---

[80] Tim Hegg, *Fellow Heirs*, Littleton, CO, First Fruits of Zion, 2003, p. 37.

[81] Ibid., p. 37.

is the standard of righteousness that exposes sin[82] and the fallen nature while pointing man towards the Seed.[83]

The Human System Configuration under the Mosaic Covenant

It is time to look at the human system configuration in order to see how it functioned in the Age of the Written Torah. In the Age of the Written Torah, Yahweh brought the people who believed Him and put their trust in the Promised Seed into the Abrahamic covenant. Yahweh took these people out of HaSatan's kingdom and escorted them to Mount Sinai. At Sinai, Yahweh yoked His people to Himself through the Mosaic covenant. The Mosaic covenant showed man the difference between good and evil and the consequences of choosing either. The redeemed human spirit wanted to obey Yahweh, and it delighted in the written Torah;[84] but since the redeemed spirit was not a partaker of the nature of the one who wrote the Torah, it did not have the power to subdue the rebellious soul and its vile cohort and force them to obey Yah.[85]

The written Torah did not give the human spirit the authority or power to force the soul and the body to obey its statutes, but it did not leave the redeemed spirit without any recourse. The written Torah gave the spirit a small advantage. The written Torah delineated the blessings and curses that came from obedience and disobedience so that the conscience could use the written Torah as a weapon against the rebellious soul and its vile cohort. The conscience put the rebellious soul and the vile body in remembrance of the blessings that came from obedience and the curses that came from disobedience. The human spirit's new weapon got the depraved duo to cooperate from time to time, but their cooperation oozed up from the toxic well of selfishness.

The redeemed human spirit wanted to obey the written Torah, but the written Torah did not give the spirit the authority or the power to force the soul and body to obey. The redeemed human spirit goaded the soul and body towards the goal of obedience with promises and threats. The rebellious soul and its cohort played along so that they could get what they wanted, but this external motivational system built a self-dependent, self-centered, selfish, greedy, manipulative soul structure that obeyed simply because it wanted to avoid the curses and enjoy the blessings.

---

[82] *The Hebrew-Greek Key Word Study Bible*, KJV, Romans 3:20.

[83] Ibid., Galatians 3:24.

[84] Ibid., Matthew 26:41.

[85] Ibid., Matthew 26:40.

The External Motivational System Fails Under Pressure

Yah's external motivational system worked well; that is, until temptation put the soul and body under pressure. It is the nature of the rebellious soul and its depraved cohort to hunger and thirst for the pleasures of this world. Therefore, whenever HaSatan presented the depraved duo with an opportunity to gorge at a buffet of fleshly pleasures or to drink the dregs from the cup of pride, the spirit quickly lost its advantage, because as far as the seditious soul and its vile cohort were concerned, the prospect of immediate gratification outweighed the prospect of some future blessing or curse. So more often than not, the rebellious soul and its cohort ignored the spirit's weapon, cast off the restraint of the written Torah, and feasted on their favorite comfort foods.

However, after the soul and its cohort gratified themselves, the conscience weighed their conduct against the written Torah. If this conduct violated the standard of righteousness, then the conscience sent a message to the spirit and soul notifying them of the violation. After this, two things happened: (1) The spirit became conscious of the fact that it had violated the written Torah and that it could look forward to the punishment that the law prescribed, which caused the spirit's disposition to shift from a state of righteousness to a state of unrighteousness. (2) The spirit's unrighteous disposition stimulated the body's biological systems and caused them to release neurotransmitters and hormones that the soul perceived as guilt, shame, and fear.

After the saint became conscious of his sin, a stain of unrighteousness marred his spirit. The saint's conscience condemned him, and this flooded his soul with guilt, shame, and fear. The saint could not draw near to Yah to worship Him and ask for blessings. Moreover, the guilt, shame, and fear that were circulating in the saint's soul activated the strongholds in it, giving it more power to rule over the HSC.[86] Sin abounded, and the saint separated himself from Yah, violated the conditions of the Mosaic covenant, and opened himself to the covenant curses. Thankfully, though, *Yah had already released grace* and allowed the Old Testament saint to access it to restore his fellowship with Him and come back into compliance with the covenant.[87]

Yah's Grace in the Mosaic Covenant

The Torah set the standard of righteousness by telling Yah's sons how He would live in the material realm, but it also told His sons what His righteousness required when they fell short of reflecting His nature. The Torah said that if a saint sinned and separated himself from Yah, he could repent and offer a sacrifice to repair their relationship. The Hebrew

---

[86] Ibid., Romans 5:20a; 7:5; 7:8.

[87] Ibid., Romans 5:20b.

word for *sacrifice* is *korban*, which means "to bring near."[88] If a contrite saint offered a sacrifice, he could draw near to Yah and fellowship with Him. The written Torah said that Yahweh told Adam not to eat the forbidden fruit because it would kill him: The prophet Ezekiel said that if a soul sinned, it would die.[89] Yah's teachings and instructions were clear. If people sinned, then they had to forfeit their lives back to Him; but thankfully, Yah also said that the life of the flesh is in the blood, and if a person sinned, he could offer the blood of a sacrifice to atone for his soul.[90]

The Economy of the Written Torah

The written Torah pointed to a well of grace that an Old Testament saint could drink from when he sinned, defiled his conscience, stained his spirit with unrighteousness, and polluted his soul with guilt, shame, and fear. In order to drink the waters of grace, a saint had to take an animal to the temple and lay his hands on it and transfer his sin, guilt, shame, and fear to it. A priest had to kill the animal and put its blood on the altar to atone for (*kaphar*) the saint's sin. The Hebrew root word *kaphar* is often associated with an Arabic root that means "to cover," but there is very little evidence that legitimizes this association; rather, *kaphar* means "to purge."[91]

The written Torah said that the blood of bulls and goats purged sin. Yah said that if a saint believed, repented, made amends, and offered the prescribed sacrifice, He forgave that person's sin. If the saint believed Yah and offered the prescribed sacrifice, then his conscience cleansed itself, his spirit shifted its disposition back to the righteous state, and his guilt, shame, and fear vanished. After the saint offered the sacrifice, then he could draw near to Yah and fellowship with Him and receive the blessings of the covenant. Did the saint do anything to deserve this favor? No, Yah was merciful to the saint. Was this favor free, arbitrary, or cheap? No, it cost the sacrifice of a life.

Here is the bottom line: The blood of bulls and goats purged the Old Testament saint's sins to bring him back into fellowship with Yah and compliance with the Mosaic covenant so that the saint could continue to serve Yah and partake of the blessing of the Mosaic covenant. The saint deserved to die, but because of the sacrifice, Yah did not give him what he deserved. On the other side of that coin, the saint did not deserve to fellowship with Yah again or partake of the blessings of the covenant, but because of the sacrifice, Yahweh gave him what he did not deserve. Mercy is not getting what we deserve, and grace is get-

---

[88] Wood and Marshall, *New Bible Dictionary*, 3rd ed., Downers Grove, IL, InterVarsity Press, 1996.*

[89] *The Hebrew-Greek Key Word Study Bible*, KJV, Genesis 2:17; Ezekiel 18:4.

[90] Ibid., Leviticus 17:11; Hebrews 9:22.

[91] Robert Laird Harris, Gleason Leonard Archer, and Bruce K. Waltke, *Theological Wordbook of the Old Testament*, electronic ed., Chicago: Moody Press, 1999, c1980.*

ting what we do not deserve. The Mosaic covenant dispensed grace and mercy in order to fulfill the Abrahamic covenant, which is why Paul said that when the Torah was given, sin abounded, but grace abounded much more![92]

Calvary's Credit Card

The written Torah said that the blood of bulls and goats took away sins, but the writer of Hebrews said that the blood of bulls and goats did not take away sins.[93] So did Yah contradict Himself? No, the blood of bulls and goats did not expiate the saint's sin; the saint's faith in Yah's promises expiated sin as he offered the blood of bulls and goats to demonstrate his faith. If a saint repented of his sin and made amends to the people it hurt, while at the same time placing his trust in the Promised Seed, then the blood of the bulls and goats was expiatory; that is, it purged away sin.[94]

However, since the life that surrendered itself on the altar did not possess the nature of the life of the one who sinned (Adam), the blood of the sacrifice did not permanently resolve the sin issue. In other words, the blood of bulls and goats did not change man's nature and permanently resolve the sin issue between Yah and him. Thus the next time the saint sinned, his conscience condemned him, shifting his spirit's disposition to the unrighteous state, triggering the release of chemicals that corresponded to guilt, shame, and fear, separating him from Yah, opening him up to the curses.

The saint had to repent, make amends, and offer another sacrifice in order to live out his faith in the Promised Seed who would ultimately redeem man and restore the earth. Thus the writer of Hebrews was saying that the blood of bulls and goats could not take away the sin nature of a saint so that he would be perfect (his sin would never again separate him from Yah and His blessings). However, if a saint repented, made amends, and offered the prescribed sacrifice while trusting in the Promised Seed, then his sin was washed away, his conscience cleansed, his spirit's disposition returned to the righteous state, and his guilt, shame, and fear dissipated so that he could fellowship with Yahweh and enjoy the covenant blessings *until the next time he sinned*.

In the Age of the Written Torah, the saints offered the blood of bulls and goats as they looked into the future with the eyes of faith to see the Promised Seed's finished work at Calvary. The saint's faith and the works that testified of it; that is, repentance, amends, and the offering of the sacrifices, placed a demand on the Promised Seed's finished work. In essence, Yahweh gave the saints a credit card that purchased the forgiveness of sins.

---

[92] *The Hebrew-Greek Key Word Study Bible*, KJV, Romans 5:20.
[93] Ibid., Hebrews 10:4.
[94] Charles Hodge, *Systematic Theology*, Oak Harbor, WA: Logos Research Systems, Inc., 1997.*

Calvary's credit card restored the saint's fellowship with Yahweh, bringing him back into covenantal compliance and blessing him.

So if a saint obtained forgiveness on credit, did that diminish the quality or the effectiveness of the forgiveness? Well, if you go to the store and buy a loaf of bread with a credit card, do you receive the same loaf of bread that someone who pays with cash receives? Yes, of course. The saints who sinned in the Age of the Written Torah received forgiveness and cleansing through the sacrifice of the Seed, even though (from their perspective) it had not happened yet. Then, when the Seed entered the dimension of space-time and offered Himself, He paid off the credit card bill.[95] The blood of bulls and goats was a place marker that brought the sacrifice that took place in eternity into the temporal realm. Thus the forgiveness that the blood of bulls and goats secured was the forgiveness that Yah released before creating the earth.

Let me be clear. There was no intrinsic property of the blood of bulls or goats that took away sin. However, if a saint placed his trust in the Seed, confessed his sin, turned away from sin, made amends, and took the prescribed sacrifice to the temple so that a priest could present its blood to Yahweh as payment for his sin, then Yahweh forgave him. The blood of bulls and goats represented the blood of the Seed that purged the saint's sins. Or as Alfred Edersheim put it in one of his books, "Thus the Old Testament sacrifices were not only symbols, nor yet merely predictions by fact (as prophecy is a prediction by word), but they already conveyed to the believing Israelite the blessing that was to flow from the future reality to which they pointed."[96]

In sum, the Torah outlined how Yahweh's life was to be lived on the earth. Hence the Torah was the spiritual standard for Yahweh's sons. However, since Yahweh gave the Torah to redeemed, unregenerated spirits who lived in unredeemed flesh with unredeemed souls that conspired with HaSatan, they were not able to use it to keep themselves circumcised. As a saint tried to keep his heart circumcised with the Torah, he agitated his rebellious soul and its cohort. This gave the soul and its cohort more power to rule over the weak, fallen spirit. Thus Yahweh gave the written Torah to His people to prove that the serpent had lied. Man is not a god who can conform to Yah's standard in order to restore his fellowship with Him and create the abundant life on earth. In the Age of the Written Torah, when a saint acknowledged his weakness, turned to the Seed, and put his trust in Him, Yah forgave his sin. Calvary's credit card restored a saint's fellowship with Yah, brought him into covenantal compliance, and released the blessing on him.

---

[95] *The Hebrew-Greek Key Word Study Bible*, KJV, Romans 3:25.

[96] Alfred Edersheim, D.D., Ph.D., *The Temple, Its Ministry and Services as They Were at the Time of Christ*, Grand Rapids, MI, Wm. B. Eerdmans Publishing Company, 1958, p. 106.

Part 4

Israel

Chapter 13

Darkness Overtakes The Earth

Cain's Kingdom (The Kingdom of Nod)

To understand Israel, we need to understand the conditions on earth at the time Yahweh created Israel. Yahweh created man in His own image and turned the earth over to him. Yah and man enjoyed an intimate relationship. They walked and talked together and communed with each other in the Spirit. Yah's Spirit empowered man's spirit to rule his HSC, which enabled man to rule the earth. Yah wanted man to spread His kingdom to the ends of the earth, but man rebelled and separated himself from Yah. HaSatan overpowered, enslaved, and conformed man to his image. Then HaSatan allowed man to establish a kingdom on the earth. Man believed he was building his own kingdom on the earth, but actually HaSatan was working in and through man to set up his kingdom on the earth in order to keep man in spiritual slavery.

It is important to realize that the fall of man made it possible for HaSatan to build his vile kingdom on the earth. HaSatan took the first step in building this kingdom when he inspired Cain to kill Abel. After Cain killed Abel, Yah did not execute him for his crime; He tried to get Cain to repent, but he would not. Yah marked Cain to prevent his siblings from taking revenge and sent the unrepentant murderer out of His presence into the land of Nod. Yah hoped the pain of separation would drive Cain to his knees to repent and offer a sacrifice that symbolized the Seed's sacrifice so that He could forgive him, fellowship with him, and give him the abundant life.

Cain defied Yahweh by building a city. History tells us that the ancient city was a religious institution that used a political system and an economic system to control its citizens and impart power and wealth to its founder.[97] Cain was under judgment. The ground

---

[97] Fustel, De Coulanges, *The Ancient City*, Garden City, NY, Doubleday Anchor Books, 1873, p. 134.

would not produce for him. He could not support himself, but instead of believing Yahweh, repenting, and offering a sacrifice, he built a religious-political-economic system that grew into a kingdom that allowed him to remain separated from Yahweh and live what seemed to be the abundant life.[98]

The theophoric names of Cain's children indicate that they were seeking "God,"[99] but they were not seeking Yah. Yah had given man teachings and instructions that spelled out how they were to believe that He would send the Seed and how to court His presence at an altar soaked in innocent blood. Cain's followers ignored Yah's teachings and instructions (His Torah) and groped in the darkness of spiritual death with nothing more than the flickering candle of their own knowledge of good and evil, vainly searching for *a god of their own understanding*.

The kingdom of Nod corrupted the earth, so Yahweh sent a flood to destroy the earth. Noah was the only person who walked by the light of the Torah and bore Yahweh's image. Yahweh saved Noah and his family, and they began to reestablish His kingdom on the earth. Noah's children were successful; that is, until his great-grandson came into agreement with HaSatan and used the threat of death, along with the promise of peace and prosperity, to compel the people of the earth to assemble on the plains of Shinar to rebuild the vile kingdom of Nod.

Darkness Falls

Yahweh had wiped out HaSatan's earthly kingdom (the kingdom of Nod), and Noah's descendants (Shem's line) were spreading the good news that the Seed was coming to redeem man and restore the earth. Many people believed the gospel of the Seed and His kingdom and submitted to Yah at an altar covered in innocent blood. Yah was working in and through man in order to bring His promises to pass on the earth. It was obvious that HaSatan was losing control of the earth's inhabitants and needed to set up a command-and-control bunker to turn the tide.

HaSatan is not omnipresent, so he had to corral the inhabitants of earth and herd them to one central location so that he could shut down the revival. HaSatan anointed Nimrod (Noah's great-grandson) and gave him the ability to hunt down people so that he could bring them to the plains of Shinar. Nimrod assembled all the inhabitants of the earth on the plains of Shinar and rebuilt the religious-political-economic system that had been in Nod. Nimrod used the old satanic religious-political-economic system to control the people. Nimrod shut down the revival and stopped the preaching of the gospel of the Seed. Like

---

[98] Alfred Edersheim, *Bible History: Old Testament*, Oak Harbor, Logos Research Systems, Inc., 1997.*

[99] http://www.graceandknowledge.faithweb.com/cain.html [07/2010]

Cain, Nimrod used the satanic system to transform himself into a divine king and great high priest whose powers were unlimited.

Yah knew that if He allowed this intoxicating system to become entrenched, it would choke out the gospel of the Seed. If this happened, Yah and man would remain separated, and man would become so corrupt that Yah would have to destroy him again. To prevent this from happening, Yah confused man's speech and scattered him throughout the earth. At first glance, this appears to be an act of judgment, but as we look closer, we see that it was an act of mercy.

Yah brought Nimrod's kingdom to confusion and scattered it so that it could not prevent the gospel of the Seed from going forth. As people believed the gospel of the Seed and met with Yah at an altar soaked in innocent blood, He was able to work in and through them to slow the decay of society and delay the judgment and destruction that were now inevitable. Yahweh's confusion and scattering slowed the decay, postponed the judgment and destruction of man until the great tribulation, and gave him a chance to repent.

Revelation confirms that this judgment is coming, but the scattering delayed it in order to give everyone a chance to flee from HaSatan's kingdom and enter Yahweh's kingdom before judgment comes. I am glad that Yah delayed judgment, but unfortunately He delayed it by scattering the people who rebuilt the old satanic kingdom. This means that the people who rebuilt the old satanic kingdom founded the nations, which means that the nations are culturally differentiated microcosms of the old satanic kingdom.

Mystery Babylon (The New Kingdom of Nod)

After Yahweh confused and scattered Nimrod's kingdom, HaSatan had to set up a new command-and-control structure using the fallen angels and their vile offspring (the demons). HaSatan could no longer supervise and coordinate the activities of his kingdom from one central location on the earth. HaSatan now had to send commands through a hierarchy of spiritual powers and principalities positioned in the atmosphere. HaSatan's new system limited his ability to manage the situations on the ground in order to prevent the gospel of the Seed from going forth. Ever since that day, HaSatan has tried to unite the nations in order to rebuild a centralized command-and-control structure. HaSatan used Napoleon, Charlemagne, Hitler, and others to try to reunify his kingdom so that he could control the saints and prevent them from proclaiming the gospel of the Seed, but thus far his wars have failed to reunify his kingdom or stop the gospel.

HaSatan has changed tactics. Now, instead of conquering through war, he is conquering through technology and peace.[100] Technology has minimized the effects of the confusion and scattering by overcoming the barriers of distance and language, transforming the earth

---

[100] *The Hebrew-Greek Key Word Study Bible*, KJV, Daniel 8:25; 11:21, 23, 24.

into a global city. Today, as this global city comes together, it is becoming increasingly obvious to the adherents of this system that the economic inequality between nations is an impermeable barrier that must be torn down.

In a true global community, everyone should have the necessities of life and access to the resources to make their dreams come true, which ultimately benefits everyone in the global community. Currently, however, the selfish citizens of a few elite nations possess the wealth of the world while everyone else languishes in poverty. Hence there needs to be a redistribution of wealth, which necessitates the formation of a global economic system to facilitate this process.

Of course, a global socialistic economic system needs someone to oversee it. To meet this need, the superwealthy, superelite families who are leading the charge into globalism have put councils together to govern the emerging global socialistic economic system. The people in these councils are groups of self-elected technocrats who are independent from and above the nations, or in other words, these councils form a supranational governing body.[101] Or more accurately, these councils form a global government that imposes its rules and regulations on the nations of the earth to eliminate the economic, social, and political injustices on the earth.

Once the supranational governing body eliminates the economic, social, and political barriers to an egalitarian society, religion will be the only institution that divides the global city. To rectify this, the governing body will convert the currency of the global socialistic economy into bits of electronic information and store it in biometric devices in each citizen. Once the supranational governing body converts the currency, it will pass a law that brings all the religions of the earth together under a protective umbrella institution that its great high priest governs.

This great high priest (the False Prophet in the book of Revelation)[102] will intercede with "God" on behalf of the people of earth and police the great city for those who refuse to abide by the doctrines and dogmas of their universal church.[103] Everyone will have to bow to an image of "God" and submit to the False Prophet. The anti-Messiah will put a mark on everyone's right hand or forehead, which will serve as a biometric device that keeps track of their credits and debits so that they can buy and sell in the global economy. If a person refuses to take the mark, he will not be able to buy or sell. The authorities will hunt down, imprison, resocialize, or execute these religious-political-economic troublemakers for the good of society.[104]

---

[101] Dr. Robert R. Congdon, *The European Union and the Supra-Religion*, Maitland, FL Xulon Press, U.S.A., 2007, p. 129.

[102] *The Hebrew-Greek Key Word Study Bible*, KJV, Revelation 19:20, 13:11–14.

[103] Ibid., Revelation 13:12.

[104] Ibid., Revelation 13:15–17.

In sum, HaSatan is grooming another Nimrod. Soon HaSatan will anoint this man. This man will threaten the people of the earth with death while promising them peace and prosperity in order to assemble them on the plains of an electronic Shinar, where he will build a global religious-political-economic system that will make war on the saints and try to prevent Yah from reestablishing His kingdom on the earth. Until then, the people of the earth will continue to live in blindness, not realizing that Mystery Babylon is using religion, politics, and economics to set the stage for HaSatan's global city. As in the days of old, today's Mystery Babylon (the kingdom of Nod) does a marvelous job of keeping man comfortable in spiritual exile (spiritual death) from Yah in order to ensure that he remain estranged from Him and destined for the lake of fire![105]

---

[105] Ibid., John 3:18; Revelation 20:15.

Chapter 14

A Bright Light Breaks Forth

Israel Is Born

Yahweh dispersed HaSatan's kingdom and segregated it into nations. Each nation set up its own religious-political-economic system that kept its citizens separated from Yah. Darkness enveloped the earth as the nations built gods of wood and stone and shaped them like men, birds, four-footed beasts, creeping things, the sun, planets, and stars. Nevertheless, Yah had to keep His promise to Eve and Shem, so He turned on a light in order to give everyone a chance to "see the light" and reconcile with Him before He judged them and destroyed them for rebellion.

Yah called Abram out of the loosely bound confederacy of satanic microcosms (Mystery Babylon) and promised to bless him and make him into a great nation. Yah promised to bring Abraham's seed into the light by establishing a relationship with them so that they could bring the people of the nations into the light by showing them how to have a relationship with Him. Yah told His people not to marry women who served other gods because they would influence them to turn away from Him, but they disobeyed Him and intermarried with the Canaanites.[106] Yah's people started to doubt His promises and worship other gods, acting like Canaanites. Thus Yah sent the Hebrews to Egypt to discipline them and prove that He would keep His promises.

The Egyptians were separatists[107] who discouraged intermarriage. The Egyptian culture was the perfect incubator that allowed the Hebrews to prosper while holding on to Yah's Torah. The Hebrew subculture, however, prospered so much that it threatened Egypt's ruling class, and Pharaoh enslaved the Hebrews and set out to destroy their influential sub-

---

[106] *The Hebrew-Greek Key Word Study Bible*, KJV, Genesis 38:2.

[107] John Fischer, *The Olive Tree Connection*, Downers Grove, IL, InterVarsity Press, 1983, p. 24.

culture. The Hebrew subculture slowly disintegrated, and the Hebrews began worshiping the gods of Egypt.[108] Yah kept His promise to Abraham, however. At the appointed time, Yah redeemed the Hebrews and the people of the nations (the Gentiles) who put their trust in the blood of the Passover lamb. Yah brought a mixed multitude out of Egypt and baptized them into the body of Moses, which was His ekklesia, or His assembly of redeemed saints, who were free to worship and serve Him.

The Mountain of Revelation

After Yah redeemed, delivered, and baptized the mixed multitude, He took them to Sinai. At Sinai, Yah gave the mixed multitude the Torah, which showed them how He would interact with the material realm; hence it showed them how they were to interact with the material realm as His sons. Yahweh's sons were to obey the written Torah and sanctify themselves in order to project the light of His image into the darkness of the nations.[109] Yah's sons were supposed to attract the Gentiles who wanted to flee from Mystery Babylon and enter His kingdom. If Yah's sons obeyed the Torah, He blessed them, but if they disobeyed it, He cursed them.

On one hand, Yah referred to Israel as His adopted son. Yah expected His son to emulate Him by living out the written Torah. On the other hand, Yah referred to Israel as His wife. Yah expected His wife to have a passionate, purifying love for Him. The written Torah was a text that showed Yah's sons how to emulate Him, but it was also a *ketubah* (a marriage contract) between Yah and Israel that spelled out how He was to love, protect, and provide for her and how she was to love, submit, and obey Him. Thus, when the children of Israel, which is what Yah called the mixed multitude,[110] accepted the ketubah, they accepted Yah's marriage proposal.[111]

In the ancient East, an engagement was a contract that assumed a marriage had already taken place. After a woman accepted a man's ketubah, he gave her a gift as a token of his love. After this, the groom left to prepare a place for his wife and him to live. The bride did not know when the groom would return to take her to their home, or to steal her away like a thief in the night. The bride shunned other men and kept her clothes clean; she kept her body washed and perfumed as she eagerly waited for her groom's return. Yahweh expected Israel to shun the other gods and keep her clothes clean as she washed and perfumed her body while waiting on Him.[112]

---

[108] *The Hebrew-Greek Key Word Study Bible*, KJV, Ezekiel 20:5–9.

[109] Ibid., Deuteronomy 4:5–8; Isaiah 49:6.

[110] Tim Hegg, *Fellow Heirs*, Littleton, CO, First Fruits of Zion, 2003, p. 32.

[111] *The Hebrew-Greek Key Word Study Bible*, KJV, Jeremiah 2:1–3.

[112] Ibid., Isaiah 54:5–8.

The written Torah was also the constitution of Israel. The written Torah spelled out the rights and responsibilities of the citizens and the behaviors that led to blessings or curses for the citizens and the nation as a whole. Yah was the King of Israel, and He gave His Spirit and His Torah to Moses so that he could function as the head of the ekklesia. Yahweh gave the ekklesia the job of projecting His image into the nations, and Moses anointed the priests and judges so that they could teach the citizens the written Torah and judge between them in order to equip them to project Yah's image. Thus Yah governed Israel through Moses and those he anointed.

The Purpose of the Written Torah

Why did Yah give Israel the written Torah? Was it because of her ethnicity, or was it that Yah wanted to give her a set of arbitrary rules that would set her apart from the other nations? The Scriptures say that Yah gave the written Torah to the "children of Jacob" and the "children of Israel."[113] Isaac, Jacob's natural father, gave him his name, so *the children of Jacob* refers to the descendants who came through his flesh. At the brook of Jabbok, Yah, Jacob's spiritual Father, changed his name to Israel, so *the children of Israel* is an umbrella term that refers to the people who became Jacob's descendants through redemption without regard to whom their natural father was. Scripture says that Yah gave the written Torah to the whole household of faith; that is, both the Hebrews and Gentiles who turned away from the pagan gods and trusted Yah and His Seed. Clearly, Yah did not give the written Torah to any one ethnic group.

Nor was the written Torah a set of arbitrary rules that set Israel apart from the rest of the nations. No, Yahweh gave the written Torah to the children of Israel (the whole household of faith) to show them how to think and act like Him. The written Torah sanctified Israel because as she kept it, she thought and acted like Yah, while the other nations thought and acted like their gods (HaSatan and his demons). Yah created everything, so when we do things His way, we live the abundant life. As Israel diligently obeyed the written Torah, she lived the abundant life and projected Yah's image into the darkness of the nations, drawing the Gentiles to His light.

Moths to a Flame

The written Torah defined Israel's relationship with Yahweh. Israel was to be a faithful son who walked in his Father's footsteps. Israel was to be a loving wife who forsook all others, keeping her garments unspotted, her body washed and perfumed, as she waited for the day that she and her groom would live together as one. Israel was also to be a loyal

---

[113] Ibid., Exodus 19:3–6.

subject, a holy nation, and a kingdom of priests. Furthermore, Israel was to be Yahweh's body and project His image into the darkness of the nations in order to attract the people of the nations (Gentiles) to His light, like moths to a flame, while proclaiming the gospel of the Promised Seed and His kingdom.

Let me be clear. Yah did not give Israel the Torah so that she could keep it and conform herself to His image *in order to merit salvation*. Yah had already saved Israel; He gave her the Torah to show her how to live a blessed life that would attract the people of the nations. Yah wanted to show His people that they were not gods who could create an abundant life for themselves so that they would keep their eyes on the Seed and trust Him. Yah's people tried to keep the Torah as a loving son, faithful wife, and loyal subject; but whenever they failed, they offered the sacrifices that connected them to the Seed, looking to Him for forgiveness and cleansing.

The Gospel of the Seed and His Kingdom

How did Israel preach the gospel of the Promised Seed and His kingdom to the nations? Surely the children of Israel (the people of Israel) told the people of the nations (the Gentiles) that Yah had created man and man had rebelled, thus destroying their relationship, but Yah had promised to send the Seed to redeem man and restore the earth. Surely the people of Israel went on to say, "And he said unto Abram, Know of a surety that thy seed shall be a stranger in a land that is not theirs, and shall serve them; and they shall afflict them four hundred years; and also that nation, whom they shall serve, will I judge: and afterward shall they come out with great substance. And thou shalt go to thy fathers in peace; thou shalt be buried in a good old age. But in the fourth generation they shall come hither again: for the iniquity of the Amorites is not yet full."[114]

Surely the people of Israel told the people of the nations how this prophecy was fulfilled when Yah delivered them from Egypt, giving them its wealth and leading them to Mount Sinai, where He blessed them with the Torah. The Gentiles probably asked what would happen to them if they did not keep the Torah perfectly. Israel would have told the Gentiles that if they believed Yah's promise to send the Seed and trusted Him, then when they missed the mark, they could repent, make amends, and offer a sacrifice, and Yahweh would forgive them. If, however, they did not really believe Yahweh's promise to send the Seed and refused to put their trust in Him, then severe consequences such as poverty, sickness, banishment from Israel, or death would come upon them.

Surely Israel told the Gentiles how Yah had empowered them to build the tabernacle and how His presence had given them the power to drive out the inhabitants of Canaan so that they could take possession of it and establish His kingdom in it. After the Gentiles had

---

[114] Ibid., Genesis 15:13–15.

heard the gospel of the Seed and His kingdom, then they had a decision to make. The Gentiles had to choose to yield to the Holy Spirit, turn away from the gods of Mystery Babylon, place their trust in Yah and His Seed, enter the Abrahamic covenant, join Israel, and keep the Mosaic covenant in order to access the blessings of the covenants, or they could keep right on serving their gods.

Chapter 15

Who Is Israel?

The Great Evangelist

In the previous chapters, we learned that Israel was supposed to be a light to the nations. Israel was to preach the gospel of the Seed and His kingdom and walk out the written Torah. We also took a hypothetical look at how Israel would have shared the gospel with the people of the nations. Now we will look at how the people of the nations (the Gentiles) responded.

Yah called Abram out of Ur of the Chaldees. Abram and his family journeyed to Haran. After Abram's father died, Yah called Abram out of Haran. According to the Scriptures, Abram, Sarai, and Lot, his brother's son, set out for Canaan with the wealth they had amassed, and *the souls they had made*.[115] What does this mean? Well, Abram told the people in Haran how Yah had called him, promising to bless him and make him into a great nation. Since Abram was prospering and amassing wealth, the pagans believed him and wanted to worship and serve Yah too. The pagans left everything and everybody behind and attached themselves to Abram. It was as if they were reborn into a new life, or transformed into a *new soul*; hence the Scriptures refer to these people as the souls that Abram made in Haran. Thus Jewish tradition says that Abraham was a great evangelist.[116]

Laying the Foundation of the New Nation

In the beginning, Adam and Eve separated themselves from Yah, and the serpent took them captive. Yah promised that one day the Seed would step on the serpent's head and

---

[115] *The Tanach*, Stone Edition, Brooklyn, NY, Mesorah Publications, 1996, Genesis 12:5.

[116] Thomas D. Lancaster, *Grafted In*, 2nd ed., Littleton, CO, First Fruits of Zion, 2009, p. 28.

force him to release man from captivity. Adam and Eve put their hope in the Seed and passed this hope down to their children, and they passed it down to theirs. Two thousand years passed without the appearance of the Seed. Then Yah told Abram that his seed would bless the earth. Abram rejoiced because he knew Yah was finally fulfilling the ancient prophecy of the Seed.[117]

Abram told the people in Haran that Yahweh was fulfilling the ancient prophecy of the Seed. Some of the people in Haran repented and joined Abram's camp. After Abram's camp arrived in Canaan, Yah allowed him to preach the gospel of the Seed and His kingdom to the inhabitants. Yah gave the inhabitants of Canaan one last chance to repent before He judged them for rebellion. Sin had hardened their hearts, however, and they refused to repent. Finally, when their cup of iniquity was full, Yah judged them and drove them out of the land or killed them.

Undoubtedly, Abram, the great evangelist, preached the gospel of the Seed and His kingdom everywhere he went. Abram was pouring the foundation for the nation that Yah had promised him. After Abraham died, Yah reaffirmed the promise to Isaac, and he preached the gospel of the Seed in order to fortify the foundation his father had built. After Isaac died, Yah reaffirmed the promise to Jacob, and he preached the gospel of the Seed, fortifying the foundation that his fathers had built. So let us look at the foundation that the patriarchs built.

The Nation of Israel and the Israel of God

Yah founded the nation of Israel by calling Abram out of the religious-political-economic systems of the nations to love and serve Him. Israel was to trust Yahweh to bring His promises to pass as they kept the Torah. As the people of Israel kept the Torah, they projected the light of Yahweh's image into the darkness of the religious-political-economic systems of the nations, providing a way for the people who were still in HaSatan's kingdom to escape and reconcile with Yahweh before He judged and destroyed them for their rebellion. Briefly stated, Israel was Yahweh's son, who reconciled the people of the nations (Mystery Babylon) to his Father.

Abraham was the first person Yah redeemed out of the nations. Abraham and his sons formed the backbone of Israel. Abraham and his sons preached the gospel of the Seed and His kingdom to the nations, embracing those who believed, repented, and put their faith in Yahweh. Israel consisted of the redeemed children of Abraham and the redeemed people of the nations.

In response, HaSatan sowed tares among the wheat, and they grew together. Then the nation of Israel consisted of people who loved Yah and placed their faith in Him (the

---

[117] *The Hebrew-Greek Key Word Study Bible*, KJV, John 8:56; Galatians 3:8.

wheat) and people who pretended to love Him so they could partake of the national blessings (the tares). Thus Israel consisted of both a secular population and a spiritual population. We call the latter the "righteous remnant," the "congregation of the redeemed," or the "Israel of God."

Broadly speaking, the "nation of Israel" was a group of people to whom Yahweh gave a tract of land and a set of religious-political-economic axioms. More specifically, the "nation of Israel" was a group of people who loved, trusted, and obeyed Yahweh, which was a remnant of the original nation of Israel.[118] Therefore, the term *Israel* can mean "the nation of Israel," "the nation of Israel and its righteous remnant," or "the righteous remnant," depending on the context in which it is used.

The "Israel of God" has two groups. Yahweh established the covenant of redemption with a core group, redeeming them out of Mystery Babylon and bringing them into the shelter of His kingdom, forming them into a "shelter family." This shelter family was Abraham's natural seed, but the people who were born into the shelter family had to embrace Yahweh and His covenants in order to inherit the promises. If the people of the nations embraced Yahweh and His covenants, they joined the shelter family and inherited the promises; hence these people were Abraham's spiritual seed. In the final analysis, both groups were Abraham's seed *only* because Yahweh had made the promises to Abraham's Seed, and those who put their trust in the Seed became Abraham's seed.

Yah gave Abraham's seed a tract of land and a set of religious-political-economic axioms, but the people who lived on this land and kept the religious-political-economic axioms were not necessarily Israel.[119] Abraham's natural seed was not necessarily *the seed* to whom Yah had made the promises.[120] In the natural, Abraham's seed and the seed of other men composed Israel, which was a religious-political-economic society in the Middle East; but in the spiritual, Israel was a remnant of the aforementioned group who trusted Yah and His covenants. Yah's covenants pointed to the Seed, who is the King and High Priest, who built the city that Abraham looked for.[121] The temple, priesthood, and sacrifices, which all pointed to the Seed, connected the earthly Jerusalem to the heavenly Jerusalem. Hence Yahweh's kingdom flowed through Israel, which was a core group of Abraham's natural seed to which Abraham's spiritual seed attached itself.

---

[118] Ibid., Galatians 6:16.

[119] Ibid., Romans 9:6.

[120] Ibid., Romans 9:7.

[121] Ibid., Hebrews 11:10.

Isaac and Ishmael

Yah knew this would be confusing, so He gave us an object lesson. The story of Ishmael and Isaac is a real-life object lesson that shows us who is and who is not Israel. Abram and Sarai wanted to bring forth the Promised Seed and build a great nation, but she was barren. Sarai suggested that Abram have sex with her servant, and nine months later Ishmael was born. Thirteen years later, Yah told Abram that Ishmael would not inherit the promises and held to His original promise that Abram and Sarai would have a son. Yahweh also changed Abram's name to Abraham and Sarai's to Sarah. Yah told Abram to circumcise the males in his camp as a sign of the covenant, and nine months later Isaac was born. Six years later,[122] Sarah weaned Isaac, and Abraham sent Ishmael away, cutting him off from the camp. Ishmael was thirteen years old when Abraham circumcised him and twenty years old when Abraham cut him off from the camp.

What does this object lesson teach us? Yahweh preached the gospel of the Seed to Abram. Abram believed the gospel, leaving his old life (repenting) and following Yah's Spirit to Canaan. Yah declared Abram righteous (forgave his sins and redeemed him out of HaSatan's kingdom), cut a covenant with him, and made promises to him. Abram and Sarai got tired of waiting on Yah's promises, so they tried to bring His promises to pass via the works of the flesh. Since Ishmael was born of the flesh, like his parents he put his faith in the flesh.[123] Yahweh told Abram and Sarai that Ishmael would not inherit the promises, and they realized that there was no way they could bring the promises to pass; then He added the *h* to their names.

The *h* (the Holy Spirit) empowered Abraham and Sarah's redeemed spirits to rule their flesh so they could do His will and He could bring the promises to pass through them. Yahweh made circumcision the sign of the covenant because Abram and Sarai had attempted to bring the promises to pass with the flesh (Abram's penis) by using the ways of the world (Hagar). Yah asked Abraham to cut off the flesh on his penis so he would not forget that he had to cooperate with His Spirit in order to cut off the works of the flesh and allow Him to bring forth the promises. Abraham circumcised himself, Ishmael, and those who had joined him from the nations.

Now, since Isaac was born of the Spirit, like his parents he lived in the Spirit and put his trust in the Spirit to bring the promises to pass.[124] Isaac believed that Yah's Spirit would bring the promises of redemption and restoration to pass through the Seed, proving that he was the seed. However, since Ishmael was born of the flesh, he lived in the flesh and put

---

[122] Les Feldick, *Through the Bible Television Series*, lesfeldick.org.

[123] *The Hebrew-Greek Key Word Study Bible*, KJV, John 3:6a.

[124] Ibid., John 3:6b.

his trust in the works of the flesh to bring about redemption and restoration, proving that he was not the seed.

In the Abrahamic covenant, Yah said He would bring the promises to pass. So in order to be in this covenant, a person had to believe Yahweh and trust Him to bring the promises to pass. Isaac put his faith in Yah to bring the promises to pass, testifying of his position in the covenant, and those who followed him became Israel. Ishmael, however, put his faith in the flesh to bring the promises to pass, testifying that he was not in the covenant,[v] and those who followed him were not Israel.

This was nothing new. Adam rebelled and tried to save himself with fig leaves, but Yah saved him via the atonement. Cain and his sons rejected the atonement and tried to save themselves by building a city, but Yah destroyed them. Noah embraced the atonement, and Yah saved him and his family. So those who trust Yahweh to keep His promise of redemption and restoration prove that He is their God, and those who trust the flesh to bring His promise of redemption and restoration to pass prove that they are their own god (HaSatan's offspring).

Chapter 16

The Abrahamic Covenant

It's All About the Seed

Yah cut a covenant with Abram and promised to bless all the families of the earth through his seed. In general, the term *seed* referred to Abram's descendants, but more specifically, it referred to *the* Seed.[125] In essence, Yah promised that the Seed would bless the nations through Israel. Yah made the promises to the Seed and, by extension, to those who put their faith in Him. Remember, Abram's seed (Ishmael) did not inherit the promises. But Abram put his faith in the Seed, and Yah's Spirit transformed him into Abraham; and Abraham's seed (Isaac) inherited the promises. Thus, if Abram's seed wanted to become Abraham's seed, they had to put their faith in the Promised Seed, enter the covenant, and submit to circumcision,[126] which was an outward sign that pointed to an inward reality of believing and trusting Yah.[127]

The Sign of the Covenant

As Yah and Adam fellowshiped, Yah's Spirit gave Adam's spirit the power to rule its servant and slave (his soul and body). As long as Adam lived in the Spirit (his spirit stayed submitted to Yah's Spirit), his spirit was able to rule the HSC and project Yah's image in the earth. Regrettably, Adam's spirit rose up out of submission (rebelled) and lost the power to rule over the soul and body. HaSatan built strongholds in the soul, and it morphed into the self, which is HaSatan's proxy personality operating in man. Adam's self and body over-

---

[125] *The Hebrew-Greek Key Word Study Bible*, KJV, Galatians 3:16.

[126] Ibid., Romans 9:7; Galatians 4:23.

[127] Ibid., Romans 2:29.

The Abrahamic Covenant

powered his spirit and imprisoned it, forcing him to live in the flesh, projecting HaSatan's image in the earth.

Consequently, as each of us develops in our mother's womb, HaSatan begins to build his proxy personality in our soul. After we emerge from our mother's womb, HaSatan builds strongholds in our soul so that it can rule over our spirit. HaSatan uses the self and the desires of the body to enslave the spirit so that it cannot worship Yah. In short, HaSatan forces our spirit to worship his proxy personality and, by extension, him. How did this happen? Yah said that if Adam sinned, he would die. Adam sinned, so he had to die; and Yah made the serpent the administrator of the death penalty.[128] The serpent had a claim on Adam that Adam could not pay, and the wise old serpent took Adam captive and threatened to call in his debt if he did not serve him.

Here is the point: Like everyone else, Abram was a descendant of Adam. Thus Abram owed a debt to the serpent that he could not pay. Hence the serpent had a right to use him as a slave laborer.[129] This meant that Abram's spirit was on the serpent's slave market, and the serpent could use the self, the body, and the threat of death to force him to build his kingdom.[130]

Abram lived in the flesh. Yah preached the gospel of the Seed to Abram; His Spirit offered Abram's spirit the gift of repentance, and he took it. Abram put his faith in the Seed, and Yah counted the Seed's death as Abram's death. Yah paid the redemption price for Abram and took his spirit off the serpent's slave market. Is this flawed anachronistic logic? No, because Yahweh lives outside of time, and He can break into time at any point. Let me ask a question: if an eternal reality breaks into time at points A and B, is it equally valid at both points? Of course, it is. Well, the Bible says that Yeshua offered Himself before creating the earth, so that is an eternal reality. Abram's faith drew upon the eternal reality of Yeshua's atoning death, and His blood flowed through the *capillaries of faith,* breaking into the time line of history and paying the redemption price for Abram so that Yah could take his spirit off the serpent's slave market!

Yahweh redeemed Abram's spirit, but Yah's Spirit did not become one with Abram's spirit in order to empower his spirit to rule over the rebellious soul and body. In other words, Yahweh redeemed Abram, but his flesh still had power over him. Thus Abram trusted in the flesh and tried to bring the promises to pass with Hagar; but once he realized how futile this was, Yah's Spirit took an active role in empowering Abram's spirit to subdue the soul and body so that Abram could do Yah's will and Yah could bring the promises to pass through him. Yahweh's Spirit did not regenerate Abram, permanently circumcising his heart, but He did help him trim the flesh away from his heart so that he could be obedient. Yah

---

[128] Ibid., Genesis 3:14, Hebrews 2:14.

[129] Ibid., Leviticus 25:47.

[130] Ibid., Hebrews 2:15.

changed Abram's name to denote His Spirit's role in his life and told him to circumcise his penis as the outward sign of this inner reality.

Abram's Seed and Abraham's Seed

As Isaac looked at his circumcised penis, it reminded him of the fact that he had put his faith in Yahweh's Seed. Isaac knew that his faith in the Seed had caused Yahweh to set his spirit free from the serpent's slave market. Isaac knew that Yah's Spirit was helping his spirit subdue his rebellious soul and vile body so that he could keep Yah's commands and cut off the flesh (keep his heart circumcised).[131] However, as Ishmael looked at his circumcised penis, he gloried in the fact that he had shed *his blood* to enter the covenant and obeyed the commands so that Yah would accept him. Ishmael's faith was in the flesh, so his circumcision meant nothing.

Here is another way to look at this. Yah's Spirit redeemed *Abram's spirit*, but Yah's Spirit did not take an active role in empowering *Abram's spirit* to rule over his rebellious soul and body; hence Abram tried to use the flesh to produce the promises. In contrast, Yahweh redeemed *Abraham's spirit* and took an active role in empowering his spirit to rule over his rebellious soul and body so that he could do His will; that is, so he could cut off the flesh and allow the Spirit to bring the promises to pass. In sum, Abram put his faith in the Seed, and Yah's Spirit poured out His grace on him and took an active role in transforming him into Abraham, which meant that the people who followed Abraham became his seed and inherited the promises.

If this is still confusing, look at it this way. Yahweh chose to love (elected) *Abram's* seed and gave them some land along with a set of religious-political-economic instructions. If the collective group of *Abram's seed* (the nation of Israel) loved Yah, put their faith in His promises and obeyed Him, then He blessed them, but if not, He cursed them. The people within this collective group, who loved Yah, put their faith in His promises and obeyed Him, became *Abraham's seed*. Consequently, there was a subgroup within Israel (within Abram's seed), who were *Abraham's seed*. Since Abraham's seed was a part of Israel, they received temporal blessings, but more importantly, since they put their faith in Yah's promises, they received eternal redemption. Briefly, *Abram's seed* got temporal blessings, but *Abraham's seed* got temporal blessings and eternal blessings.

The Scriptures say that Abram circumcised himself after Yah changed his name. In other words, the Holy Spirit went to work to change Abram by giving him the ability to cut off the flesh and follow His lead in order to fulfill his destiny. Circumcision is the sign of the covenant because a person who is truly in the covenant of redemption cuts off the flesh and obeys Yah.[vi]

---

[131] Ibid., Deuteronomy 10:16; Jeremiah 4:4.

In conclusion, man rebelled against Yah, and HaSatan enslaved him in Mystery Babylon. Yahweh poured out His grace on Abram in order to keep His promises to Eve and Shem. Yah's Spirit chose to take an active role in Abram's life, transforming him into Abraham. Abraham performed mighty exploits while bringing Yah's will to pass. This proves three things: (1) No man comes to the Father unless the Spirit draws him: (2) The Spirit has to empower us to cut off the flesh: (3) The Spirit empowers us to do good works, thus manifesting the Father's will on the earth, and this reveals the circumcision that others cannot see, thus testifying that we know Him.[132]

Abraham's Natural Seed and Abraham's Spiritual Seed

Abraham's natural seed passed through a circumcised penis (the sign of the covenant) as theirs fathers implanted them in their mothers' wombs, and they were sanctified (set apart for Yahweh). However, this *did not* mean that Yah redeemed their spirits and they were in the covenant. Abraham's natural seed enjoyed the temporal blessings from birth, and there was a place reserved for them in the ekklesia;[133] but when they reached the age of accountability, they had to believe Yah and put their faith in the Promised Seed in order to take their rightful place.

If Abraham's natural seed believed Yah and put their faith in the Promised Seed, then Yah redeemed their spirits from the serpent's slave market and placed them in the ekklesia. After this, if Abraham's redeemed natural seed obeyed the written Torah, then Yahweh blessed them and empowered them to fulfill their calling to be a light to the nations. If, however, they disobeyed the written Torah, then Yahweh cursed them and they were powerless to fulfill their calling.

In contrast, the people of the nations did not pass through the sign of the covenant as their fathers implanted them in their mothers' wombs. As a result, they were "common" (not set apart for Yahweh). However, if the people of the nations were fortunate enough to hear the gospel of the Seed and His kingdom and receive the Holy Spirit's gift of repentance that empowered them to turn away from their gods and put their faith in Yahweh, then Yah redeemed their spirits off the serpent's slave market and placed them in the ekklesia. After this, if the redeemed Gentiles obeyed the written Torah, then Yah blessed them and empowered them to reach out to those who were still in Mystery Babylon. If, however, the redeemed Gentiles disobeyed the written Torah, then Yah cursed them and they were powerless to reach out to those who were still in Mystery Babylon.

As a Gentile placed his faith in the Seed, Yah took his spirit off the serpent's slave market and brought it into the ekklesia, and he became Abraham's seed. Abraham's spiri-

---

[132] Ibid., John 6:44; Galatians 5:16; Romans 2:25; James 2:18; Matthew 7:21.
[133] Ibid., 1 Corinthians 7:14.

tual seed, the Gentile, was now in the Abrahamic covenant, so he submitted to circumcision. Since Yah had redeemed the Gentile, he wanted to live in Israel with the rest of the redeemed and obey the written Torah like everyone else. Here is the bottom line: A Gentile did not submit to circumcision in order to *enter* the Abrahamic covenant; a Gentile submitted to circumcision because he *was in* the Abrahamic covenant. Moreover, the Gentile did not keep the written Torah in order to *get into* Israel; the Gentile kept the written Torah because he *was in* Israel.

Chapter 17

The Redeemed

The Foundation of the Israel of God

On page 407, table 1 lists some of the people who laid the foundation of the Israel of God. At the top of table 1 is Abram; to his left are his natural seed, and to his right are his spiritual seed. The first spot on the natural line belongs to Abram; the first spot on the spiritual line belongs to the souls from Haran. Spot number one depicts Abram's evangelizing of the people in Haran and their attaching of themselves to his camp.[134] The second spot on the natural line belongs to Abraham; the second spot on the spiritual line belongs to his camp. Spot number two depicts Abraham bringing his camp into the covenant.[135]

The third spot on the natural line belongs to Isaac; the third spot on the spiritual line belongs to Rebekah. This spot depicts Isaac, a descendant of Abraham, marrying a Syrian.[136] The fourth spot on the natural line belongs to Jacob; the fourth spot on the spiritual line belongs to Leah, Rachel, Zilpah and Bilhah. This spot depicts Jacob, a descendant of Abraham, marrying Syrians.[137] The fifth spot on the natural line belongs to Judah; the fifth spot on the spiritual line belongs to Shuah and Tamar. This spot depicts Judah, a descendant of Abraham, producing children with two Canaanite women.[138]

The sixth spot on the natural line belongs to Joseph; the sixth spot on the spiritual line belongs to Asenath. This depicts Joseph, a descendant of Abraham, marrying a Mitsrite.[139]

---

[134] *The Hebrew-Greek Key Word Study Bible*, KJV, Genesis 12:5.

[135] Ibid., Genesis 17:23.

[136] Ibid., Genesis 24:4.

[137] Ibid., Genesis 30:1-12.

[138] Ibid., Genesis 38:1–30.

[139] Ibid., Genesis 41:45.

The seventh spot on the natural line belongs to Moses; the seventh spot on the spiritual line belongs to Zipporah. This depicts Moses, a descendant of Abraham, marrying a Midianite (Cushite).[140] The eighth spot on the natural line belongs to the descendants of the twelve sons of Jacob; the eighth spot on the spiritual line belongs to the mixed multitude. This spot depicts Abraham's descendants bringing many different nationalities into the covenant.[141]

The ninth spot on the natural line belongs to Joshua; the ninth spot on the spiritual line belongs to Caleb. This spot depicts Joshua, a descendant of Abraham, and Caleb, a Kenizzite, taking possession of Canaan.[142] The tenth spot on the natural line belongs to the two spies; the tenth spot on the spiritual line belongs to Rahab. This spot depicts the two spies, who were descendants of Abraham, bringing a Moabite woman into the covenant.[143] The eleventh spot on the natural line belongs to King David; the eleventh spot on the spiritual line belongs to Maachah. This spot depicts David, a descendant of Abraham, marrying a Geshurite.[144]

The twelfth spot on the natural line belongs to King Solomon; the twelfth spot on the spiritual line belongs to Naamah. This spot depicts Solomon, a descendant of Abraham, marrying an Ammonite.[145] The thirteenth spot on the natural line belongs to the remnant; the thirteenth spot on the spiritual line belongs to the people of the lands. This spot depicts the descendants of Abraham who returned from the Babylonian captivity and the Gentiles who joined them and entered into the covenant.[146] The fourteenth spot on the natural line belongs to Mordecai; the fourteenth spot on the spiritual line belongs to the Persians. This spot depicts Esther and Mordecai, descendants of Abraham, bringing the Persians into the covenant.[147] The fifteenth spot on the natural line belongs to Boaz; the fifteenth spot on the spiritual line belongs to Ruth. This last spot depicts Boaz, a descendant of Abraham, marrying a Moabite.[148]

After examining table 1, three things are apparent: (1) Abraham's natural seed made up the core of the Israel of God. (2) The Gentiles could always attach themselves to this Hebrew core and partake of their covenants with Yah. (3) If a woman who lived in the nations turned away from the gods of Mystery Babylon and put her faith in Yah and the

---

[140] Ibid., Exodus 2:21; Habakkuk 3:7.

[141] Ibid., Exodus 12:38.

[142] Ibid., Joshua 14:6.

[143] Ibid., Joshua 2:18–19; Hebrews 11:31.

[144] Ibid., 1 Chronicles 3:2.

[145] Ibid., 1 Kings 14:21.

[146] Ibid., Ezra 6:21; Nehemiah 10:28.

[147] Ibid., Esther 8:17.

[148] Ibid., Ruth 4:10.

Seed, then a Hebrew man could marry her. However, these women took their place in the Israel of God like everyone else; that is, by grace through faith; and since the Israel of God was interwoven with the nation of Israel, these women had to leave their nations and take up residency in Israel.

In the Torah, Yah said that Moabites and Ammonites could not join themselves to Israel, but Ruth was a Moabite and Naamah was an Ammonite, and both became citizens of Israel. In fact, their sons became kings of Israel![149] The only way to explain this is to recognize that these two women turned away from their gods and put their faith in Yah and the Seed. In response, Yah took their spirits off the serpent's slave market and placed them in the ekklesia. Yahweh adopted Ruth and Naamah as Abraham's seed, and they were no longer a Moabite or Ammonite. Once these women *mingled their blood* with their husband's blood via intercourse, they and their offspring became Abram's seed and citizens of the nation of Israel with the right to own land.

Israel did not shun Gentiles. If famine or war displaced Gentiles from their nations, they could live in Israel as servants or slaves. Gentiles could always repent and put their faith in Yah and the Seed, and Yah would take their spirits off the serpent's slave market and place them in the ekklesia so that they could live in Israel. However, keep in mind that the Gentiles who *repented* became Abraham's seed, not Abram's seed. Since they were Abraham's seed, they could live in Israel, but since they were not Abram's seed, they could not own land in Israel. This was the only restriction on redeemed Gentiles. In every other respect, they were as the native born. In fact, Yahweh told the native born to treat the naturalized citizens (the redeemed Gentiles) as if they were native born.[150] Yah also said that there was one Torah for all covenant members, whether they were native born or naturalized.[151] So to say that the Mosaic covenant, or the Torah, applied only to the natural-born citizens (the Jews) is utterly absurd! Here is the bottom line: the Israel of God (the ekklesia) has always consisted of a Hebrew core with Gentiles attached to it.

The Native Born and the Stranger

The English translations of the Bible veil the status of Gentiles in the Old Testament. Interpreters translate the Hebrew words *neichor* and *zar* into the English words *stranger*, *foreigner*, or *alien* to describe people who were hostile to Israel and worshiped pagan gods. Interpreters translate the Hebrew word *ezrach* into *native born* or *citizen*; they also translate the Hebrew word *ger* into *foreigner*, *alien*, *stranger*, or *sojourner*. Thus, if Gentiles repented and put their faith in the Seed and married one of Abraham's seeds, they and their

---

[149] Ibid., Deuteronomy 23:3; Ruth 4:17; 1 Kings 14:21.
[150] Ibid., Exodus 12:48–49.
[151] Ibid., Numbers 15:16.

children were *ezrachs* (citizens). Moreover, if Gentiles repented and put their faith in the Seed and relocated to Israel to worship and serve Him, then they were *gers* (sojourners).

The words *stranger*, *foreigner*, or *alien* can refer to a *neichor* or a *ger*. Thus the words *stranger*, *foreigner*, or *alien* can mean "a foreigner passing through," "a foreigner who has taken up residence," or "a foreigner who has entered into the covenant and then come to live in Israel." This means that we have to look at the context of these words in order to determine their meaning. For example, Leviticus 17:15 prohibits a stranger from eating animals that died or were killed by other animals. However, Deuteronomy 14:21 permits a stranger to eat these things. An examination of the context of these verses reveals that in Leviticus, *stranger* refers to a foreigner who was in the covenant, and in Deuteronomy, *stranger* refers to a foreigner who was passing through Israel or living in Israel outside of the covenant.[152]

As we read the Old Testament, we need to be aware of the fact that the nation of Israel housed the congregation of the redeemed, which consisted of Hebrews and Gentiles living, worshiping, and serving Yah together as one. In addition, we need to remember that when the Old Testament refers to the *native born* (someone who was born in Israel), it may be referring to one of Abraham's natural seeds or to a person who was the offspring of a Gentile who had repented and put his trust in Yahweh and married a person who was Abraham's natural seed.

Furthermore, when the Old Testament talks about a stranger, alien, foreigner, or sojourner, it is talking about a Gentile. However, we have to look at the Hebrew word and its context in order to determine the Gentile's status. This is how we determine whether the Gentile was passing through; living in the land as a servant, slave, or refugee; or living as a covenant member who had repented and put his faith in Yah and the Seed and relocated to Israel to worship and serve Him. Oh, one other thing! If you are a Gentile believer, when the Old Testament talks about a stranger, foreigner, or alien who was a covenant member, take heed, because it is talking about you.

In sum, when a Gentile believed Yahweh, repented, and put his faith in the Seed, Yah brought him into the Abrahamic covenant (the covenant of redemption). Once Yahweh had redeemed the Gentile, he came under the jurisdiction of the Mosaic covenant (the covenant of sanctification). If the Gentile complied with its terms and conditions, he was in right standing with Yah, and Yah blessed him as he projected His image into the darkness of Mystery Babylon.

The Mosaic covenant established the standard of righteousness. As the redeemed Hebrews and Gentiles lived by this standard, they sanctified themselves and the blessings came upon them, but when they did not, the curses came upon them. Thankfully, the Mosaic covenant gave the redeemed access to grace via the temple, priests, and sacrifices.

---

[152] Tim Hegg, *Fellow Heirs*, Littleton, CO, First Fruits of Zion, 2003, p. 3.

If a saint fell short of the standard, he could bring a sacrifice to the temple and have a priest offer it to Yah, and He would forgive the person and cleanse him of unrighteousness. There was one drawback, however; Yah's temple was the only place where a saint could offer sacrifices, so a saint needed to live near Jerusalem.

Chapter 18

Life In The Older Covenants

The Inheritance of the Saints

In an effort to separate the New Testament from the Old Testament, and the rights, responsibilities, and inheritance of the Jews from the rights, responsibilities, and inheritance of the Gentiles, some theologians say that the concept of a Messiah originated around 100 BC. These theologians are in error. Yah's plan has always revolved around the Seed and 3,348 verses in the Tanakh prove it.[153] As early as 3999 BC, Adam and Eve named their first son Cain because they thought he was the Seed.[154] Later, Job trusted in his Redeemer (the Seed). Then, around 1977 BC, Abram put his faith in the Seed, and around 1000 BC, David followed him. From the time of Adam to the time of Isaiah, Yah's people looked for the Seed, but around 500 BC, the sages built a religion that took the focus off Him. Around 100 BC, Yah began illuminating the Tanakh, shifting the Jews' focus back to the Seed, and the rabbis started writing about Him and looking for Him again.

The Abrahamic covenant gave Hebrews an inheritance in the natural (the land of Israel), but it also offered them a spiritual inheritance (redemption). When a Hebrew reached the age of accountability, he could declare his faith in Yah and claim his spiritual inheritance. As a Hebrew claimed his spiritual inheritance, he entered into a personal relationship with Yah. The Mosaic covenant governed this relationship, and as the Hebrew obeyed the written Torah, he sanctified himself, walked in the blessings of the covenant, and was a light to the people of the nations.

---

[153] Walter C. Kaiser, *The Messiah in the Old Testament*, Grand Rapids, MI, Zondervan Publishing, 1995, p. 29.

[154] Ibid., p. 42.

Yah did not cut the Abrahamic covenant with the nations. If, however, the people of the nations heard the gospel of the Seed, turned away from the gods of Mystery Babylon, and put their faith in Yah and the Seed, then Yah brought them into the covenant. As a Gentile entered the covenant of redemption, he entered into a personal relationship with Yahweh. The Mosaic covenant governed this relationship, and as the Gentile obeyed the written Torah, he sanctified himself, walked in the blessings of the covenant, and became a light to those who were still in darkness.

The only difference between the rights, responsibilities, and inheritance of a Jew and the rights, responsibilities, and inheritance of a Gentile was a temporary one. Normally, a redeemed Gentile did not receive an inheritance of land in Israel. Yah set it up this way to keep the land in the hands of Abram's seed to fulfill His promise to Abram and to implement His plan. However, Ezekiel 47:22 tells us that in the millennial kingdom, the Gentiles will inherit land in Israel and live side by side with the Jews and rule and reign over the nations of the earth with Yeshua.

The Torah in the Older Covenants

Yah's Spirit covered Adam's body with a robe and crowned his head, but still He gave him the Torah to show him how to live. Yah told Adam not to eat the illicit fruit because he would die if he did. Thus Yah attached a legal code to the Torah, making Adam subject to it.

The serpent wanted Eve to turn her back on Yah's teaching and instruction (His Torah). The serpent encouraged Eve to disregard the Torah and follow her senses. The serpent's subtle suggestions turned Eve's spirit away from Yah's Spirit. Then the serpent planted imaginations in Eve's soul that triggered her emotions and compelled her to eat the illicit fruit. After this, Eve gave the fruit to Adam, and he made a decision to rebel against Yahweh and follow his wife.

Essentially, the serpent told Adam and Eve that they could be gods, but when they ate the illicit fruit, their consciences came to life and told them that they had broken the law and would have to die. Adam and Eve gathered fig leaves to hide their guilt and shame so that they could continue to fellowship with Yah and escape the death penalty. In other words, Adam and Eve believed that they were gods who could reconcile with Yah in order to save themselves. Yah, however, shattered this illusion when He drew near to fellowship with Adam and Eve and killed a lamb, which revealed His plan of reconciliation. Adam and Eve saw the gospel and repented by taking off the fig leaves and putting on the fur of the innocent lamb that died in their place.

Adam had to either believe Yah and trust Him to keep His promise to send the Seed to redeem him, restore the earth, and reestablish the kingdom while living by His Torah or believe the serpent and trust in his works while living by his intellect, emotions, and imaginations. In essence, this was Adam's choice: will I be God, or will I submit to Yahweh and obey Him?

Adam's children also had to choose. Abel, Enoch, Seth, Noah, and Abram chose to believe Yah, trust Him to keep His promise to send the Seed, and live by His Torah. But Abraham's children chose to live like pagans, and Yah had to chastise them by forcing them to seek provision in Mystery Babylon. Mystery Babylon enslaved Abraham's children, but this gave Yah another opportunity to demonstrate His love for His people. Yah warned man of the condemnation that was upon him and offered to save all those who put their trust in Him. Yah took a group of Jews and Gentiles to Mount Sinai, where He reiterated His Torah, attaching a legal code to it and assigning blessings for obedience and curses for disobedience. Yah asked the people that He had saved to return His love by obeying the Torah so that they and their children could live a blessed life.

The Problem with the Mosaic Covenant

At birth or before, transgression separates our spirit from Yah's Spirit, and the serpent takes us captive and puts us on his slave market. In our formative years, the serpent builds his proxy personality in our soul so that he can use it to rule over us. In the old covenant, Yah redeemed the people who put their faith in Him and the Seed; that is, in the older covenant, Yah paid the price to rescue people from the serpent's slave market so that they could worship and serve Him. There was a problem, however. Yah redeemed a person's spirit, but since this redeemed spirit came from Adam, the transgression still separated it from Yah's Spirit. Thus the redeemed spirit still lacked the authority and power to subdue the rebellious soul and body.

The saint's spirit wanted to live up to Yah's standard of righteousness, but it could not. The more a saint studied, meditated, and acted on the Torah, the more his soul came into line with the will of Yah. But the flesh, the world, and HaSatan patiently waited for an opportunity to bring the soul into disobedience, and the spirit was powerless to stop them. At Mount Sinai, Yahweh had Moses write the Torah down in order to show the saints how to live an abundant life, but more often than not, the Torah condemned the saint and produced guilt, shame, fear, curses, and death. Thankfully, however, the Mosaic covenant dispensed grace so that the saints could be forgiven and cleansed and continue to serve Yahweh and live in the blessings, being a light to the nations.

The Letter Kills

Moses wrote Yah's standard of righteousness on scrolls. As a saint fell short of Yah's standard, his conscience let his spirit know that he had sinned. After this, the disposition of the saint's spirit shifted to an unrighteous state. Once the human spirit shifted to an

Life In The Older Covenants

unrighteous state, it triggered the release of neurotransmitters and hormones into the saint's bloodstream that turned on the synaptic circuits that manifest guilt, shame, and fear. After this, the saint could no longer fellowship with Yahweh. The saint was not in right standing with Yah, and Yah stood ready to curse him; but thankfully, the Mosaic covenant gave the saint access to Yah's grace.

If a saint sinned and guilt, shame, and fear prevented him from worshiping Yahweh, the saint could take the sacrifice that the law prescribed to the temple and get a priest to offer it to Yah on his behalf. The saint's sacrifice satisfied the claim that the legal code (the law) had on him. Once the saint made amends, confessed his sins, and offered the prescribed sacrifice, his spirit shifted back to a righteous state. In this righteous state, a saint's spirit triggered the release of neurotransmitters and hormones that turned off the synaptic circuits that manifest guilt, shame, and fear so that he could enter Yah's presence to worship Him, triggering the release of neurotransmitters and hormones that turned on the synaptic circuits that manifest peace and joy.

In the older covenants, Yah freed people's spirits from slavery, but He did not change the nature of the spirit and give it the authority and power to subdue the rebellious soul and rule over the HSC. Consequently, the saints often failed to live up to the standard of righteousness and had to take sacrifices to the temple and give them to a priest while confessing his sins and asking for forgiveness, which was good because the temple, priests, and sacrifices pointed to the Seed. The Torah's legal code was a schoolmaster that kept pointing the saints to the Seed so they would not get proud and self-righteous.[155] The older covenants were all about the Promised Seed. As a person believed Yah and put his faith in the Promised Seed, Yah redeemed him. The temple, priests, and sacrifices pointed the saints back to the Promised Seed whenever they sinned so that they never forgot that it was the Promised Seed who redeemed them and kept them in right standing with Yahweh.

In the older covenants, the people who turned away from the works of the flesh and the gods of Mystery Babylon, putting their faith in Yahweh's Seed, entered into the Abrahamic covenant. A saint was declared righteous by faith through grace, but after his positional righteousness had been established, then he had to keep the written Torah to experience its benefits (be blessed). A saint's positional righteousness was secure, but his experiential righteousness was contingent upon keeping the written Torah. When he missed the mark, he had to partake of the Seed's finished work via the temple, priests, and sacrifices in order to be in right standing with Yah.

Moses wrote the Torah on scrolls, and it killed.[156] It killed because it established the goal of righteousness, along with the penalties for falling short of this goal, without giving

---

[155] *The Hebrew-Greek Key Word Study Bible*, KJV, Galatians 3:24.

[156] Ibid., 2 Corinthians 3:6–7.

the spirit the power it needed to reach the goal.[157] Thus the letter of the Torah produced guilt, shame, fear, separation, curses, and death. Nevertheless, the Torah was not at fault; it was perfect.[158] Adam's spirit was at fault because it chose to be its own god and separated itself from the power it needed to rule over the HSC; that is, the fallen spirit that Adam passed to each of us was the problem. Thus the Torah's role was to reveal the standard of righteousness and the fallen spirit's inability to reach the standard of righteousness so that fallen men and women would reach out for the Seed.

---

[157] Ibid., Romans 7:5, 11, 18.

[158] Ibid., Romans 7:12; Psalm 1:1–3; 19:7–8; 1 Timothy 1:8.

Part 5

From Religion to Relationship

Chapter 19

Religion Takes Over

Yahweh proved that He was faithful when He freed Abraham's descendants from Pharaoh's chains so that they could worship and serve Him. After this, Yah took His people to the mountain of revelation and commanded them to love Him with all their heart, with all their soul, and with all their might so that they would live long, prosperous lives and be a witness to all the nations.[159] This was the greatest commandment,[160] and the next greatest was to love thy neighbor as thyself.[161] Every other commandment explained exactly how Yahweh's people were to express their love for Him and their neighbors, which kept their self-love in check.[162]

In the older covenants, love was the driving force. Yah freed the saint's spirit from the serpent's slave market, so he loved Him and His Torah and wanted to obey.[163] The soul still ruled the HSC, however, and it had a tendency to side with the flesh, the world, and HaSatan. Thus the saint did the things he did not want to do and did not do the things he wanted to do.[164] The saint was painfully aware of the fact that the Torah was good,[165] but he did not have the power to obey it. A saint could repent, confess, make amends, and offer sacrifices so that Yah would forgive him, cleanse him of unrighteousness, and restore

---

[159] *The Hebrew-Greek Key Word Study Bible*, KJV, Deuteronomy 6:1–5.
[160] Ibid., Matthew 22:36–38.
[161] Ibid., Leviticus 19:18; Matthew 22:39.
[162] Ibid., Matthew 22:40.
[163] Ibid., Romans 7:22.
[164] Ibid., Romans 7:15.
[165] Ibid., Romans 7:16.

him to fellowship, but this did not correct the root problem.[166] The saint lived on a spiritual-emotional roller coaster: one day he was righteous, but not the next; one day he was clean, but not the next; one day his spirit could fellowship with Yah, but not the next. Paul described this frustrating condition by saying the body of death held captive the redeemed spirit, which was unable to subdue the soul and body.[167]

The Mosaic covenant showed man that even after Yah liberated his spirit from the serpent's slave market, he still could not choose between good and evil or rule his HSC in order to bring forth the abundant life. After the saints who were under the custodianship of the Mosaic covenant came to terms with this unpleasant reality and cried out to Yahweh for help, He announced that He would cut a new covenant with Israel. In the Mosaic covenant, Yah had dealt with the symptoms of man's spiritual disease, but in the new covenant, He would cure man's disease.

In the new covenant, Yah would cure man's spiritual disease by putting his spirit to death, resurrecting it, giving it His nature, and writing the Torah on his heart.[168] Yah's Spirit would satisfy the Mosaic covenant's legal demands and free the saint from its custodianship. A saint's righteousness would not be contingent on his keeping the Torah, and his spirit would possess the authority and power to rule the HSC and bring forth the abundant life. This was the good news the saints had hoped for, for thousands of years, but when Yah sowed this word in Judah's heart, the serpent slithered into the ekklesia, hoping to uproot it and abort its harvest.

The Serpent Slithers into the Ekklesia

Yahweh spoke through Jeremiah and announced that He would cut a new covenant with Israel. In the new covenant, Yah's Spirit would *indwell every saint*. Yah's promise terrified the serpent. Over the centuries, he had watched helplessly as Yah's Spirit empowered kings, priests, prophets, and others to do mighty exploits establishing His kingdom in Israel. The serpent knew that if Yah's Spirit indwelt the saints, His Spirit would empower them to fulfill their mission to bring the nations into the covenant. The serpent devised a plan to erect a wall between Israel and the nations that would separate them and prevent them from embracing the new covenant.

In 1953 BC, Yah commanded Abraham to circumcise all his male descendants on the eighth day after birth. Hence the Hebrews circumcised their infants, but the recipients of the ritual had no remembrance of this traumatic event. The Gentiles, however, did not circumcise their infants. Still, Yah said that they had to submit to circumcision when they

---

[166] Ibid., Hebrews 10:1.

[167] Ibid., Romans 7:24.

[168] Ibid., Ezekiel 11: 19–20; 36:26–27; Jeremiah 31:33–34; 2 Corinthians 3:3; Hebrews 8:10; 10:16.

accepted the covenant, and this dissuaded many adult Gentiles from doing so. In 722 BC, Yah chastised Israel and scattered her to the ends of the earth, and this gave Gentiles another reason not to embrace the covenant. The net result was that by 586 BC, there was very little Gentile blood flowing into Judah, and she was becoming very Hebraic.

In 586 BC, the Babylonians destroyed the temple and took Judah captive. This event threatened to destroy the identity of the people of Judah and wipe Israel off the map. Yah told Judah that He was chastising her and that her captivity would last only seventy years, but the serpent whispered in her ears and planted fear in her heart. The serpent took advantage of Judah's fear and built a stronghold of pride on it that resulted in her people attempting to protect their identity and their nation by defining how a person from Judah (a Jew) was to live. The crafty old serpent used Jewish pride to *redefine* their identity and *change* their nation. The Jewish people began to take their focus off trusting in Yahweh's promise to send the Seed and put it on their own works.

In 331 BC, Alexander the Great began conquering the East, forcing it to worship his gods, speak his language, and adopt his culture, but the Jews' brush with assimilation in Babylon had prepared them for this threat. Israel's sages began to regulate every aspect of life in order to define Jewishness in an effort to preserve their identity and protect their culture. In 323 BC, Alexander died, and his generals began fighting with each other, trapping Israel in the middle.

In 165 BC, Antiochus took control of Israel and offered a pig on Yahweh's altar. The Gentile king set up an idol in the Holy of Holies, burned the Torah, and outlawed circumcision. The Gentile king outlawed the keeping of the Torah and forced Jews to offer sacrifices to his gods. The Gentile king tortured or killed Jews who refused to go along with his plan and assimilate into the Greek world. Many Jews abandoned the Torah and the sages' code of conduct, thus having their circumcision reversed so that the Greeks would not persecute them.[169]

Antiochus defiled Yah's temple for three years until a revolt broke out.[170] The Maccabees, a family of devout Jews, refused to offer sacrifices to the gods and recruited an army that took back the temple. The army forced the men in the land to prove they were Jews. A man proved he was a Jew by showing his circumcision and reaffirming his commitment to the Torah and the sages' code of conduct. The Jewish army allowed a man and his family to remain in Israel if he proved he was a Jew or became a Jew by submitting to circumcision and swearing to keep the Torah and live by the sages' code of conduct, but they expelled or killed those who resisted.[171] After this, the sages took steps to make sure that their identity as a people would never be lost.

---

[169] Flavius Josephus, *The Works of Josephus*, Peabody, MA, Hendrickson Publishers Inc., 1987, p. 323.

[170] Finis Dake, *God's Plan for Man*, Lawrenceville, GA, Dake Publishing Inc., 1949, p. 312.

[171] Flavius Josephus, *The Works of Josephus*, Peabody, MA, Hendrickson Publishers Inc., 1987, p. 325.

The sages put Yah's mission to bring the nations into the covenant on the back burner. The sages saw Gentiles as a threat to their identity and began making rules, regulations, and laws to govern every aspect of Jewishness, creating a sharp dividing line between Jews and Gentiles that grew into an invisible dividing wall that eventually manifested in the temple as an actual dividing wall. The sages began teaching that Yah had cut the covenant with Jews, and the only way a Gentile could get into the covenant was to become a Jew via the proselyte ritual that they invented.

The sages believed that Yah gave them the wisdom to interpret the written Torah and revelations to add to it.[172] The sages called these new revelations the "oral Torah," and they *superseded* the written Torah! The sages ruled on how the people were to live out the written Torah and oral Torah, and their rulings became a code of conduct that defined Jewish life. The sages taught that everyone with legal status as a Jew had a place in the Abrahamic covenant and the world to come. If a Jew kept the written Torah, oral Torah, and legal rulings, he got to keep his legal status, his place in the Abrahamic covenant, and his place in the world to come; but if not, he lost his legal status as a Jew, his place in the Abrahamic covenant, and his place in the world to come. The Jews became fanatical about protecting and guarding their legal status.

The sages said that if a Gentile was circumcised, baptized, offered a sacrifice, and kept the written Torah, oral Torah, and legal rulings (*halachah*), then, in a legal sense, he had died and been reborn as a Jew. Since this proselyte was now considered a Jew, he was in the Abrahamic covenant, but of course this Jew had to keep the written Torah, oral Torah, and halachah in order to keep his legal status. Clearly, the sages taught that salvation came by *ethnicity*, and *works* determined ethnicity. Regrettably, the sages took the next logical step and began to teach that Gentiles were unclean. The sages forbade Jews from fellowshiping with Gentiles, entering their homes, eating with them, or using their water pots or utensils to prepare food, because they were contaminated.

The Enmity Between Jews and Gentiles

The sages said Gentiles were unclean, and a Jew could become unclean by interacting with Gentiles. The sages said Gentiles would be accepted if they would be circumcised; baptized; offer a sacrifice; keep the written Torah, oral Torah, and legal halachah; and leave their families, nations, and traditions and move to Israel. However, the proselyte Jew would then have to keep the written Torah, oral Torah and legal halachah, or the sages would revoke their status as a Jew and Yah would expel them from the covenant. Thus the sages'

---

[172] Fritz A. Rothschild, *Between God and Man*, New York, NY, Simon and Schuster Inc., 1959, p. 160.

rules, regulations, and laws created a lot of enmity between Jews and Gentiles, making it impossible for Israel to evangelize the nations.

In sum, the sages said that salvation was an ethnic issue, and works defined ethnicity. They said that Jews were born into salvation, but they had to maintain their ethnic status and hence their salvation by keeping the written Torah, oral Torah, and halachah. They said Gentiles had to be reborn as Jews via the proselyte ritual and then keep the written Torah, oral Torah, and halachah in order to keep their new ethnic status and hence their salvation. The sages forsook the gospel of the Seed and preached works, and those who placed their trust in their system died in their sins and perished. The serpent's plan was working. The Jews had taken their eyes off the Seed and put them on their works, and they became self-righteous and excluded the Gentiles from their exclusive club. Jews were reluctant to reach out to Gentiles, and Gentiles resented Jews for treating them as if they had a disease; consequently, most Gentiles did not want anything to do with Jews or their God.

Chapter 20

The Spiritual Exodus

Looking Back at the Physical Exodus

Yahweh spoke to Abraham hundreds of years before He sent his seed into the strongest nation in Mystery Babylon so that Pharaoh, Mystery Babylon's high priest, could chastise them for their unbelief. Yahweh told Abraham that a strange nation would enslave his seed and oppress them for four hundred years, but then He would deliver them, along with the wealth of that strange land. At the appointed time, Yahweh kept His promise by releasing His power through Moses so that Abraham's seed would believe that He had sent Moses to fulfill His promise to Abraham.

A remnant of Abraham's descendants believed Yahweh would keep His promise to deliver them. This remnant embraced Moses. The rest of Abraham's descendants gave up on Yah keeping His promise. These Hebrews forsook Yah, adopted the ways of the pagans, and bowed down to their gods. They did not believe Moses was the deliverer until they saw him release the plagues.

Moses released the power of Yahweh's kingdom and preached repentance and the blood. The Hebrews shared this message with the Gentiles, and Yahweh freed everyone who repented and put their trust in the blood, giving them a new life as they passed through the Red Sea. Yah's Spirit led the mixed multitude to Sinai and showed them how to establish His kingdom on the earth. In sum, Moses preached repentance, the blood, and the kingdom.

Setting the Stage for the Spiritual Exodus

The mixed multitude did not believe Yah, so He kept them in the wilderness until they died. Yahweh let the mixed multitude's descendants enter Canaan, but after 1,100 years,

His people were still unwilling to trust Him wholeheartedly, so He chastised them.[173] In the past, Yah had taken His people to the strongest nation in Mystery Babylon so that pagans could rule over them and give them a desire to repent, but this time He let the strongest nation in Mystery Babylon march into Israel to oppress them and entice them to worship their gods. Regrettably, instead of repenting and trusting Yah, the sages followed Cain's example and built a religion.

The sages' religion looked biblical because it used biblical terms, but actually it was the religion of Mystery Babylon clothed in biblical garb. HaSatan's children believe that they are gods and that they can use religion to restore their relationship with Yah, which means that the sages were operating as priests of Mystery Babylon, which means that Yah's people were in bondage to Mystery Babylon again. Nevertheless, Yahweh preserved a remnant that met each Sabbath to recall how He had kept His promise to deliver their ancestors from Mystery Babylon, which strengthened their faith to believe that He would send a prophet like Moses[174] to deliver them from Mystery Babylon again. The sages oppressed the remnant from one side, and the Romans oppressed the remnant from the other, but still the remnant waited for the deliverer (the Seed).

A Prophet Like Moses

Yah told Israel He was going to send the Seed, and He would be like Moses. Yah cut the Mosaic covenant to keep the people that He had redeemed focused on the Seed so He could bless them and to expose the people that He had not yet redeemed and point them to the Seed so that He could redeem them. Regrettably, the sages misused the Mosaic covenant. They used the law unlawfully by using it to establish their own righteousness, so when the Seed came, they rejected Him. Let us look at Moses and Yeshua to see if the sages should have recognized the Seed.

In the book *Israel, The Church and the Jews*, James Jacob Prasch points out that both Moses and Yeshua were born under oppressive foreign rule. A wicked king threatened both Moses and Yeshua. The faith of a mother and father saved both Moses and Yeshua. Egypt sheltered both Moses and Yeshua. Moses' wisdom was unsurpassed, and so was Yeshua's.

The Hebrews rejected both Moses and Yeshua. The Gentiles accepted both Moses and Yeshua. Moses was willing to bear the sins of his people, and so was Yeshua. Moses fasted forty days, and so did Yeshua. Moses spoke face-to-face with Yah, and so did Yeshua. Moses' face shone, and so did Yeshua's. Moses fed people supernaturally, and so did Yeshua. Moses performed signs and wonders, and so did Yeshua. Moses cut a covenant,

---

[173] *The Hebrew-Greek Key Word Study Bible*, KJV, Jeremiah 14:10–11; Isaiah 5:5–7; Ezekiel 24:21–23; Daniel 9:24.

[174] Ibid., Deuteronomy 18:15–19; Isaiah 9:6–7; 53:1–12; Daniel 2:44.

and so did Yeshua.[175] Clearly, Moses and Yeshua were theological twins, so the apostate sages were without excuse.

At Mount Sinai, Yah's people could not touch the mountain while He was giving the Torah and its legal code to Moses, but fifteen hundred years later, Yah's people sat with Him (Yeshua, who is Yah in human flesh) on a mountain as He taught them the Torah's intent.[176] Yeshua wanted the people in the sages' religion (the lost sheep of the house of Israel) to know that they could do the works of the Torah without fulfilling its intent and think they were in right standing with Yah when in reality they were not. As Yeshua taught the people the intent of the Torah, they realized that religious works did not change their hearts so that they could fulfill the intent of the Torah.

In order to illustrate to the lost sheep just how futile it was for them to perform religious works with the wrong motives (seeking to establish their own righteousness), Yeshua told them that unless their righteousness exceeded the righteousness of the sages and Pharisees (who dedicated their whole lives to doing religious works), they would not enter the kingdom![177] On the other hand, however, if they craved the righteousness that the Messiah would reveal when He established His kingdom, then Yah accepted their works because their hearts were right. The intent of the Torah was for people to love Yah with their whole hearts and to love their neighbors as themselves, but sadly, their fallen spirits prevented them from reaching this goal.

Yeshua, the embodiment of the written Torah, rebuked the religious rulers because they had marred His image by twisting His teachings and instructions around to defraud the sheep and lead them into hell. Yeshua told these "vipers" that they worshiped Yahweh in vain[178] and that they, their sheep, and the proselytes they made were children of hell![179] Yeshua preached the gospel of the kingdom and released the power of the kingdom in order to prove that He was the Seed,[180] and a needy remnant accepted Him, but the proud, self-righteous masses rejected Him.

The Spiritual Exodus

Around 430 BC, Yah spoke to the prophet Malachi and told him that the Lord (the Seed), who was the messenger of the covenant (the prophet like Moses), would come soon. After this, the native priests of Mystery Babylon (the sages) enslaved Abraham's seed and

---

[175] James Prasch, *Israel, the Church and the Jews*, Springfield, MO, 21st Century Press, 2008, pp. 99–114.

[176] *The Hebrew-Greek Key Word Study Bible*, KJV, Matthew 5:1–7:29.

[177] Ibid., Matthew 5:20.

[178] Ibid., Mark 7:7–13.

[179] Ibid., Matthew 23:13–15.

[180] Ibid., Matthew 22:41–46; Mark 12:36–37; Luke 5:20–21; 20:41–44; John 8:24, 58; 14:20; 17:5; 20:28–29.

oppressed them for four hundred years, but then Yah sent the deliverer. Yah released His power through Yeshua so that the people of Israel would believe that He had sent Yeshua to fulfill His word to Malachi. A remnant recognized Yeshua and followed Him. The lost sheep saw Him release the power of the kingdom and some believed, but most of the religious rulers refused to see or hear.

Essentially, Yeshua preached repentance,[181] the blood,[182] and the kingdom[183] to the people who were in the false religion (the lost sheep), and this did not go over well with the religious rulers. The religious rulers were furious. The religious rulers charged Yeshua with blasphemy, but their court (the Sanhedrin) could not execute Him because under Roman law the Romans were the only ones who could put a convicted criminal to death. The Jews (the apostate religious rulers) told the Romans that Yeshua was starting a rebellion by telling the people that He was their king. So the Romans crucified Yeshua on the preparation day as the people were slaying their lambs for Passover, which revealed His identity as the Passover Lamb.

Yeshua's disciples buried Him, and on the third day, the Holy Spirit resurrected Him. The glorified Yeshua taught His disciples for forty days and then returned to heaven. Ten days later, on the day of Pentecost, Yeshua's Spirit began His ministry of implementing the new covenant. As people repented and put their faith in Yeshua, His Spirit sealed them, applying the blood of the Passover Lamb on the doorposts of their hearts so that HaSatan could not kill them or take them to hell. Yeshua's people followed Him through the waters, passing from death to life so that HaSatan could not force them to serve him anymore. Yeshua's Spirit took the saints to Mount Zion, where He wrote the Torah on their hearts, establishing His kingdom in them.

In sum, in the physical exodus, Yah set people free from Pharaoh's slave market as they repented from worshiping idols and put their faith in the blood of a Passover lamb. Yah's people followed Moses in baptism, leaving their old life behind to begin a new one. Yah's Spirit took His people to Mount Sinai, where He wrote the Torah on stone tablets to show them how to live in the kingdom. In the spiritual exodus, Yah sets people free from the serpent's slave market as they repent from worshiping idols (primarily the idol of self) and put their faith in the blood of the Passover Lamb. Yah's people follow Yeshua in baptism and leave the old life behind to begin a new one. Yeshua's Spirit comes to live in His people to connect them to Mount Zion (the New Jerusalem), write the Torah on their hearts, set up the kingdom, and release its blessings.

In the era of the Mosaic covenant, a person repented and put his faith in the blood of a Passover lamb to enter the Abrahamic covenant. Then Yah's Spirit wrote the Torah on

---

[181] Ibid., Matthew 4:17.

[182] Ibid., Matthew 20:28; Luke 18:31–33, 22:20.

[183] Ibid., Matthew 6:33.

stone tablets, and as the saint obeyed the Torah, Yah sanctified him so that he could walk in the blessings and project His image into the darkness to draw the lost to Him. In the era of the renewed covenant, a person repents and puts his faith in Yeshua's blood to enter the Abrahamic covenant. Then Yah's Spirit writes the Torah *on his heart* and sanctifies him and releases the blessings. Yah's Spirit gives him a desire to overcome the flesh, world, and HaSatan to project His image into the darkness to draw the lost to Him. The objectives of the two covenants of sanctification are *identical*, but the mechanisms that bring about these objectives are *different*.

Chapter 21

A Change In The Ekklesia's Government

The Ekklesia

The ekklesia was born in the Garden of Eden, but it grew from infancy into adolescence as the mixed multitude of Hebrews and Gentiles passed through the sea with Moses. Yah gave Moses the Torah and the Holy Spirit so that he could build a community that functioned as His body on the earth. As Yah's body followed His Spirit and obeyed the Torah, He sanctified and blessed it so that it could project His image into the darkness of the nations and draw the Gentiles into the covenant. Yahweh made Moses the head (the instruction giver) of His body and placed the people who passed through the sea with him (followed him in baptism) into His body. As Moses' ekklesia obeyed Yah, they accomplished His will, blessing the nations of the earth.[184]

About 750 years after Moses died, the sages stole his mantle. The sages morphed from interpreters of the Torah into Torah givers. The sages invented the oral Torah, the halachah, the legal ethnic status, and the ethnic gospel and used these manmade devises to divert power from the kings, priests, and prophets so that they could be the arbiters of salvation and exalt and enrich themselves. By 100 BC, the Great Sanhedrin was the head of the ekklesia, and its instructions flowed down through the lesser Sanhedrins and town councils, oppressing the saints of Yah.[185]

---

[184] *The Hebrew-Greek Key Word Study Bible*, KJV, Acts 7:38.
[185] Merrill Unger, *The New Unger's Bible Dictionary*, Chicago, IL, Moody Press, 1966, pp. 998; 1,126.*

Mystery Babylon Rules Over the Ekklesia of Moses

The sages, elders, and priests were religious rulers and Rome's puppet officials. These religious rulers governed the ekklesia of Moses through the Great Sanhedrin, lesser Sanhedrins, and town councils. The Great Sanhedrin consisted of seventy-one of the most prominent religious rulers in Israel. The regional councils (lesser Sanhedrins) consisted of twenty-three religious rulers, and the town councils (houses of judgment) consisted of three religious rulers.

The religious rulers used this three-tiered legal system to pass thousands of laws. The local authorities accused people of violating a law, and the religious rulers judged these people, imposing harsh penalties on the guilty. Normally, the Sanhedrin judged officials and passed laws, the regional councils judged capital cases, and the town councils judged noncapital cases.[186]

After Israel gained her independence from the Greeks, the religious rulers split into two sects: (1) the Sadducees (the rich upper class), who controlled the courts, priesthood, and government; and (2) the Pharisees (a poorer class of very pious men), who controlled the masses. In 135 BC, the two sects began fighting for control of Israel, and this led to a bloody civil war. In 63 BC, the Pharisees asked the Romans to help them stabilize Israel, and they marched in and conquered it. The Romans installed provincial governors, who appointed kings, priests, and judges to rule in order to keep the peace. At this time in history, Rome was the strongest nation in Mystery Babylon, and she ruled over the ekklesia of Moses and oppressed the saints.

The Gates of Hell Prevail Over the Ekklesia of Moses

There were two groups who thought they were in the ekklesia: the wheat and the tares. The tares believed that the people who were born Jewish inherited a Jewish legal status that entitled them to a place in the age to come. The tares also believed that the people who were not born Jewish had to go through the proselyte ritual in order to obtain Jewish legal status and a place in the age to come. Moreover, the tares believed that those who had Jewish legal status had to keep the written Torah, oral Torah, and legal halachah in order to keep their status. In short, the tares put their faith in the flesh (in their ethnic status) and the works of the law to get them into the ekklesia. Thus the tares were HaSatan's children, whose inheritance was the fiery lake.[187]

---

[186] Herbert Danby, *Tractate Sanhedrin*, 1919, pp. 24–42, http://www.sacred-texts.com. [10/2010]

[187] *The Hebrew-Greek Key Word Study Bible*, KJV, Matthew 13:30.

The wheat believed that Yahweh would keep His promise to send the Seed to reestablish His kingdom and circumcise their hearts in order to make them whole.[188] The wheat obeyed the written Torah because they loved Yah, but their hope was not in perfectly keeping the law—it was in the Seed. Yah counted the wheat's faith as righteousness.[189] Sadly, the gates of hell (the powers of hell) worked through the sages, shutting up the kingdom of Yahweh so that the wheat (those who were in Moses' ekklesia) could not enjoy its fruits and its many blessings.[190]

Yeshua's Ekklesia

Yeshua came for the lost sheep; that is, He came for those who were in the sages' religion. Yeshua exposed these wolves in sheep's clothing, along with their teachings and traditions that circumvented or nullified the written Torah. Yeshua said that He was going to build *His* ekklesia and that the gates of hell would not prevail over it.[191] Yeshua told His disciples that He would give them the keys of the kingdom so that whatever they bound on earth, He would bind in heaven, and whatever they loosed on earth, He would loose in heaven.[192] In essence, Yeshua said that He would return to heaven to sit on His throne, where He would rule on what to permit or prohibit, and His Spirit would relay His rulings to them so that they could build His ekklesia.

The sages were fallen men, and they governed the ekklesia. This means that in the ekklesia of Moses, fallen men decided what to loose (permit) or bind (prohibit), which is exactly why the gates of hell prevailed over it. The ekklesia of Moses did not fulfill its mission to bring the nations into the covenant, because fallen men governed it. These fallen men were emissaries of Mystery Babylon, who oppressed the saints and exploited them for financial gain. Yeshua told His disciples that He would make the halachah for His ekklesia and deal with each saint directly so that hell could not control the ekklesia and she would fulfill her mission. In Yeshua's ekklesia, He is the head who tells the members of His body how to live out the Torah. Yeshua took the keys of the kingdom away from the sages and *gave them to the people who were in Israel's righteous remnant*. Do not feel sorry for the sages, because Yeshua told them that He was going to take the kingdom from them and give it to a people who would bring forth fruit.[193]

---

[188] Ibid., Deuteronomy 30:6; Jeremiah 32:37–42; Ezekiel 11:17–20.

[189] Ibid., Acts 2:29–37; Job 1:1; 1 Kings 9:4; Matthew 1:19; Luke 1:6; 2:25, 37.

[190] Ibid., Matthew 23:13.

[191] Ibid., Matthew 16:18.

[192] William Morford, *The Power New Testament*, Lexington, SC, Shalom Ministries, 2003, Matthew 16:19.

[193] *The Hebrew-Greek Key Word Study Bible*, KJV, Ezekiel 34:2–15; Matthew 21:33–46.

Restructuring the Ekklesia

Yeshua told His disciples to go into the nations and preach repentance and the remission of sins in His name, but before they got started, He told them to go to Jerusalem to wait for the promise of the Father (the Holy Spirit). See, Bezaleel was filled with Yah's Spirit and given the wisdom and the ability to build His old dwelling place (the tabernacle),[194] and now Yah needed to fill the apostles with His Spirit so that they would have the wisdom and the ability to build His new dwelling place (Yeshua's ekklesia).[195] The apostles and 108 of their disciples waited for the Spirit to come upon them and establish the kingdom in their hearts so that He could give them the wisdom and the ability to build Yeshua's ekklesia on the earth.

On the day of Pentecost, the Holy Spirit filled the righteous remnant of the nation of Israel. After this, the people who were in the righteous remnant went about preaching repentance and the remission of sins in Yeshua's name. Many of the lost sheep of Israel renounced their faith in the sages' religion, put their faith in Yeshua, and entered the righteous remnant, but most of the religious rulers did not. The apostles told their disciples to abide by the sages' halachah that did not conflict with the written Torah so that they could worship Yahweh and study the written Torah in the synagogues. Yeshua wanted His disciples to remain in the synagogues so that the apostate religious rulers and their sheep could hear the truth and repent.

Yahweh Grafts the Gentiles into the Righteous Remnant

When a Jew believed that Yeshua was the Messiah, he did not convert to a new religion called Christianity. The righteous remnant of Israel had always known that faith in the Seed was what brought them into the Abrahamic covenant and that once they were in the covenant, they were to keep the written Torah to demonstrate their faith by their works and live the abundant life. At Sinai, Yah reiterated the Torah to Moses and attached a legal code to it to form the core of the Mosaic covenant. It was easy for the righteous remnant to keep the Torah and comply with its law because their focus was on the Promised Seed and His righteousness. The righteous remnant had always had saving faith and the corresponding works, and when a Jew came to believe that Yeshua was the Messiah, he became part of the righteous remnant.

At this point, the righteous remnant was a sect of Judaism. The messianics and nonmessianics had different beliefs, but so did the Sadducees and Pharisees. The fact that the messianics believed that the Messiah had come and the nonmessianics were still waiting

---

[194] Ibid., Exodus 35:30–31.

[195] Ibid., Ephesians 2:19–22; 1 Peter 2:3–5; 1 Corinthians 3:9, 16.

for Him to come did not preclude the sects from worshiping or studying the Torah together. Now, of course, there were some heated debates and lively discussions, but in the end the sects simply agreed to disagree in order to keep the peace in the community, because, after all, everyone was still a Jew.

Then the apostles started preaching Yeshua's sacrificial death to the Gentiles, and suddenly things were a bit more complicated. Things were a bit more complicated because when a Gentile believed, Yahweh's Spirit grafted him into the righteous remnant, but the sages were still teaching that Gentiles were unclean and that Jews could not fellowship with them. How could Jews and non-Jews worship and study the Torah together? Did the Gentiles have to become Jews via the proselyte ritual, or was there another solution to the Gentile problem?

Chapter 22

Rebuilding The Tabernacle Of David

The Tabernacle of David

Yahweh promised Abraham that his seed would bless all the families of the earth.[196] Yahweh also promised Abraham that kings would come out of his loins.[197] In 1000 BC, Yahweh partially fulfilled these promises and opened a channel that would bring about their complete fulfillment. The great King, Yahweh, anointed David with His Spirit so that he could rule on earth as His vice regent. David was a man after Yahweh's heart, keeping the written Torah as an expression of his love for Him, longing to see the Seed and His kingdom come to the earth.

Yah redeemed David, declared him righteous, and anointed him with His Spirit. Yah's Spirit gave David the wisdom and power to govern his kingdom and expand its borders. David conquered the nations around Israel, annexing them into his kingdom and making their people (the Gentiles) his subjects.[198] Yah promised David that his seed would sit on the throne forever.[199]

The Davidic kings worshiped idols, and their dynasty fell into disrepair. In 933 BC, the kingdom of Israel split into a northern half and a southern half. Around 750 BC, the prophet Amos said that in the latter days, Yahweh would rebuild the tabernacle of David. The people of Israel longed to see the son of David (the Seed). When the son of David appeared, He would take His place on His father's throne, overthrow Israel's Gentile oppressors,

---

[196] *The Hebrew-Greek Key Word Study Bible*, KJV, Genesis 12:3.
[197] Ibid., Genesis 17:6.
[198] Ibid., 2 Samuel 8:1–14.
[199] Ibid., 2 Samuel 7:12–17.

conquer the nations, force the Gentiles to serve Him, reestablish the kingdom, and rebuild the dynasty of David.

In 722 BC, the Assyrians took the northern kingdom captive and scattered its inhabitants to the ends of the earth. In 605 BC, the Babylonians took the southern kingdom captive and enslaved its people in Babylon. In 535 BC, the Babylonian captivity ended. Yahweh's people returned to Judah, but, unfortunately, the *times of the Gentiles* had begun. The times of the Gentiles was a period of time in which Gentiles would rule over Israel. During the times of the Gentiles, there was no sovereign kingdom. Thus there was no king, and there was no seed of David on the throne. Over the course of the next 670 years, the Gentile powers of Persia, Greece, and Rome ruled Israel. During this time, the Jews looked back at the golden age of David and longed to see his son reestablish it. The Jews longed for the son of David who would overthrow Israel's oppressors, conquer the nations, force the Gentiles to serve Him, and restore the kingdom.

The terms *tabernacle of David*, *house of David*, and *dynasty of David* are synonyms. In the phrase *tabernacle of David*, the word *tabernacle* hints at the Feast of Tabernacles (the Feast of Ingathering). The Feast of Tabernacles points to a time when Yah will gather the fruit of His labor; that is, it points to a time when Yah will gather His saints from every nation. In other words, the Feast of Tabernacles points to the millennial age. In the millennial age, Yeshua will return to the city of Jerusalem (not the city of Rome) to take His place on David's throne (not Saint Peter's throne) and restore the kingdom of Israel, reestablishing His Father's kingdom on the earth, and He and His saints will rule the nations for a thousand years.

The Jerusalem Council

In the first century, four groups met in the synagogues to worship and study the Torah: (1) nonmessianic Jews, (2) messianic Jews, (3) proselytes, and (4) God-fearers. The nonmessianics did not believe that Yeshua was Messiah. The messianic Jews did believe that Yeshua was Messiah. The proselytes were Gentiles who had been "reborn" as Jews; some believed in Yeshua, and some did not. The God-fearers were Gentiles who had repented from idolatry and were on their way to becoming proselytes; some believed that Yeshua was Messiah, and some did not.[200]

After Yeshua returned to heaven, the apostles shared the gospel with the Gentiles. They began repenting and putting their trust in Him, and Yah grafted them into the righteous remnant. Many Gentiles began coming to the synagogues to worship Yahweh and study the Torah. The Pharisees wanted these Gentiles to submit to circumcision and keep the Torah of Moses.

---

[200] Tim Hegg, *The Letter Writer*, 2nd edition, Tacoma, WA, TorahResources, 2008, p. 102.

To understand what the Pharisees meant, we need to consider two issues. First, did the Tanakh teach that a person entered the covenant by submitting to circumcision or keeping the law? No, the Tanakh never taught that circumcision or keeping the law brought anyone into the covenant. It taught that Yah brought people into the covenant as they believed Him and put their trust in His promises. The Tanakh taught that after Yah had grafted a person into the covenant, that person submitted to circumcision, kept the Torah, and complied with its legal code in order to walk out his faith, which proved that it was real. In light of what the Tanakh taught, the Pharisees' demand seemed reasonable. It looked as if they wanted the Gentiles to prove that their faith in Yahweh was real by submitting to circumcision and keeping the Torah of Moses.

This brings us to the second issue: Pharisees did not follow what the Tanakh said about bringing Gentiles into the covenant; they followed the sages. What did the Pharisees' phrase *keep the Torah of Moses* mean? In the first century, the sages referred to the written Torah, oral Torah, and halachah by the generic phrase *the Torah of Moses*.[201] The Pharisees were saying that Gentiles had to confess Messiah and become Jews via the proselyte ritual of submitting to circumcision, baptism, sacrificing, and keeping the written Torah, oral Torah, and halachah, but the apostle Paul disagreed. In AD 49, the Council of Jerusalem met to solve the Gentile problem.

The Resolution

The Gentiles who repented and put their faith in Yeshua started showing up at the synagogues, but the historical, cultural, sociological, and religious cards were stacked against them. The Jews viewed the Gentiles with suspicion, separated from them, or kicked them out. Ritual purity was the issue. A person who participated in idolatry was considered impure (unclean). If the sages allowed an impure person into the synagogue, he would defile everyone else, and Yahweh would reject their prayers. The council had to address the sages' concerns before they would allow Yeshua's Gentile followers to attend the Sabbath services to worship Yah and study the Torah.

Peter was the first to speak. Peter told everyone about the vision he had experienced. Peter had fallen into a trance and seen a sheet that was full of unclean animals and heard a voice tell him to kill and eat. Peter said that he had objected to the directive because he had never eaten anything that the written Torah said was unclean, but the voice told him not to call anything unclean that God had cleansed.

Peter told the council that this vision had confused him. It confused Peter because he knew that Yeshua had never changed one jot or tittle of the written Torah's dietary instructions. Peter went on to tell the council that the Lord had clarified the vision by sending

---

[201] Ibid., p. 237.

three Gentiles to the place where he was staying. Peter accompanied the men to Cornelius's home and preached the gospel of Yeshua to the Gentiles. Yah filled the Gentiles with His Spirit, and they spoke in tongues as His Spirit gave them utterance. Yahweh made it very clear that He had redeemed the Gentiles, declared them righteous, and brought them into the kingdom to dwell with them. Peter told the council that he came to realize that Yah was telling him not to call the Gentiles who had repented and put their trust in Him unclean, because He had accepted them, cleansed them, and indwelt them.

Paul and Barnabas told the council that they had preached the gospel of Yeshua to the Gentiles, and the Holy Spirit had performed signs and wonders confirming their message. James reminded the council that Amos had spoken of a day when Yah would rebuild the tabernacle of David. James probably reminded everyone that Yah had promised David that his son would sit on the throne and rule the kingdom forever and that this son of David (the Promised Seed) would rebuild the dynasty of David (tabernacle of David) by gathering the Gentiles into the kingdom.

Once the discussions were over, it was clear to everyone on the council that Yahweh treated the Gentiles just as He treated the Jews. It did not matter whether a person was a Jew or Gentile. When people repented and put their faith in Yeshua, Yahweh gave them the Holy Spirit, and the Holy Spirit sanctified them (cleansed them and set them apart for Yahweh). The council ruled that since Yahweh had cleansed the Gentiles, they should be welcomed into the synagogues without having to go through the sages' proselyte ritual in order to become a Jew.

The messianic council members were passionate about keeping the Torah, and their rulings carried a lot of weight with unbelieving Jews. In fact, the Pharisees called Yeshua's half-brother "James the Just" because of his meticulous observance of the law.[202] The unbelieving Jews also accepted the ruling of the council because they knew that if they were to split Israel into two warring factions, it would give Rome a reason to take away their religious freedoms.

The sages agreed to let the messianic Gentiles worship Yah and study the Torah in the synagogues as long as they submitted to the halachah that protected everyone from idolatry. The sages already allowed the Gentile God-fearers, who lived by the halachah on idolatry, to worship Yah and study the Torah inside the synagogues; and if the messianic Gentiles lived by the same rules, then they could too. The sages' halachah did not always line up with Yeshua's halachah. In this case, however, the sages' halachah complemented the Holy Spirit's work of separating people from their old lives and giving them a desire to please Yahweh by keeping His Torah, accomplishing Yeshua's will while maintaining ritual purity. The council's ruling satisfied the sages and permitted the messianic Gentiles to worship Yahweh and study the written Torah.

---

[202] Paul Maier, *Eusebius: The Church History*, Grand Rapids, MI, Kregel Publications, 1999, p. 71.

In sum, the Council of Jerusalem demonstrated how the keys of the kingdom were to be used in order to build Yeshua's ekklesia so that the gates of hell could not prevail over it. This is how it worked: Yeshua was in heaven, but He ruled on the issue before the apostles, and His Spirit, who was in the apostles, relayed His ruling to their spirits. Their spirits relayed His ruling to their souls, and their souls relayed His ruling to the council. The sages did not want to lose their positions. Their halachah already permitted the God-fearers to worship and study in the synagogue after they turned from idolatry and abstained from meat offered to idols, blood, strangled things, and temple prostitutes,[vii] so they accepted the messianic Gentiles who did the same.[203]

---

[203] Ibid., pp. 247–258.

Part 6

The Apostle Paul

Chapter 23

The Apostle Paul

A Jew, a Pharisee, and a Roman Citizen

In the Roman Empire, Jewish men had Roman names. Saul's Roman name was Paul. Paul was a Jew, a Pharisee, and a Roman citizen. Yah sent Paul to the Gentiles to share Yeshua with them and show them how to follow Him. Paul's target audience was in the synagogues and pagan temples. However, if he had entered a pagan temple before going to a synagogue, the synagogue rulers would not have allowed him to enter to proclaim the gospel, so he went to the synagogue to share the gospel with his Jewish brothers and then shared it with the Gentiles.[204]

Paul was not an enemy of the synagogue. The synagogue was the only institution that worshiped Yahweh.[205] Paul, however, had to walk a tightrope. In the synagogues, Paul had to proclaim Yeshua and teach the people who accepted Him how to walk in His footsteps, without dishonoring the leaders of the synagogues, who proclaimed the ethnic gospel and its doctrines.

A few synagogues embraced Yeshua, but most rejected Him. Some of the synagogue leaders punished Paul by beating him with rods, giving him thirty-nine lashes with a whip, imprisoning him, or stoning him. Paul was a Roman citizen and a citizen of the New Jerusalem. So Paul did not have to submit to the punishment of the synagogues, whose authority came from the earthly Jerusalem; but since he loved his Jewish brothers and did not want the Romans to get involved, he submitted to their authority, took their punishment, and moved on to the next town.

---

[204] *The Hebrew-Greek Key Word Study Bible*, KJV, Romans 1:16.

[205] Tim Hegg, *The Letter Writer*, 2nd edition Tacoma, WA, TorahResources, 2008, p. 69.

Paul's Bible

In Paul's day, Scripture consisted of the Torah (Ta), the Nevi'im (Na), and the Ketuvim (Kh), or the books of Moses, the Prophets, and the Writings. Scribes combined the abbreviations of the three sections of Scripture and came up with the acronym *Tanakh*.[206] Yahweh had not yet written the gospels or the epistles,[207] so when Paul referred to *the Scriptures*, he was referring to the Tanakh. Sadly, theologians have minimized the Tanakh by calling it the "Old" Testament.

Before his conversion, Paul had memorized every word of the Tanakh, but his faith was in his legal status and his ability to keep the law. Paul believed that the goal of the law was for a man to keep it perfectly in order to establish his own righteousness and maintain his place in the covenant. This means that Paul, at that time, was not in the covenant; he was a highly educated slave in the serpent's slave market. At the appointed time, Yeshua filled Paul with His Spirit and led him into the desert to meditate on the Tanakh. In the desert, Yah's Spirit showed Paul that the goal that the Torah's law pointed to was the Seed. Paul realized that the works in the Torah's law pointed to Yeshua and His righteousness, so the people who believe in Him and trust in His righteousness reach the goal of righteousness.[208]

The Torah (the first five books of the Bible) is the foundational revelation of Yah and His plan for man. Yahweh told His people to reject any prophet whose words did not line up with the Torah.[209] This means that the section of Scripture known as the Prophets lines up with the Torah, and so does the section known as the Writings (Psalms, Proverbs, Chronicles, etc.). If Yeshua had come to destroy the Torah, the Prophets, or the Writings, then He would have been a false prophet.[210]

Yeshua came to fulfill the Torah, the Prophets, and the Writings; that is, to bring their words to pass and reveal their true meaning. If Paul taught something that did not show how Yeshua had lived out the words of the written Torah in order to reveal their true meaning, then he was a false prophet. Moreover, if Paul taught something that did not show how Yeshua's Spirit in us would cause us to walk in His ways and fulfill the intent of the written Torah, then he was a false prophet.[211]

Think about it. If Paul taught that Yahweh had replaced the written Torah, he was teaching that Yah had replaced his Bible, and he then had no foundation on which to stand. If Paul nonetheless shared his insights with the sages or their sheep, how could he possibly

---

[206] Arthur Green, *These Are the Words*, Woodstock, VT, Jewish Lights Publishing, 1999, p. 65.

[207] Tim Hegg, *The Letter Writer*, 2nd edition, Tacoma, WA, TorahResources, 2008, p. 146.

[208] *The Hebrew-Greek Key Word Study Bible*, KJV, Romans 10:4.

[209] Ibid., Deuteronomy 13:5.

[210] Ibid., Matthew 5:17.

[211] Ibid., Deuteronomy 13:5.

convince them that his insights were accurate and that theirs were not? If Paul could not stand on the Tanakh, then all he could stand on were the "revelations" that some spirit had given him in the wilderness.

The pagans might have accepted a revelation that did not line up with the Tanakh, but not the people in the synagogues. The people in the synagogues knew that if a revelation did not line up with the Torah, it was not from Yah. Paul preached Yeshua's death, burial, and resurrection and expounded on how He had fulfilled the Torah, the Prophets, and the Writings; and the Spirit bore witness with him and gave eternal life to those who accepted the testimony of these three witnesses.

The Holy Spirit illuminated the Tanakh for Paul in order to explain Yeshua and what He had accomplished, which is why Paul validated his teaching by quoting it. In Berea, Paul went to the synagogue and shared the gospel with the assembly; and they searched the Scriptures—that is, the Torah, the Prophets, and the Writings—to see if what he was saying was true. Since it lined up with the Torah, the Prophets, and the Writings, they accepted his and the Spirit's testimonies and believed.[212]

Paul's Letters

Paul wrote thirteen letters to Yeshua's ekklesia. Yahweh gave Paul the keys of the kingdom, along with an assignment of unlocking its gates for the Gentiles so that people from every nation could attach themselves to Israel's righteous remnant and worship Him. As Jews and Gentiles worshiped Yah together, their unity testified to the fact that Yeshua was the Seed.[213]

Paul described what the renewed covenant (the new covenant) accomplished in the lives of the saints. More specifically, Paul described how the Holy Spirit changes people's desires, giving them the ability to love Yahweh with all their heart, soul, and strength and love their neighbors as they *already* love themselves.

Paul's letters are a *divine commentary on the Tanakh* that gives us a tangible guideline to follow as we walk out our salvation. Yeshua expects His ekklesia to live by the halachah that He has revealed in Paul's letters. As we study Yeshua's halachah in Paul's letters, His Spirit writes it on our heart. This empowers us to walk out the intent of the written Torah; that is, to do Yahweh's will and reflect His image into the darkness.

Let me be clear. The letters that the apostles wrote are the halachah for Yeshua's ekklesia, but Paul's letters form the pinnacle of these writings, and so it is imperative that we understand his letters. To understand Paul, we must adopt the presuppositions he adopted, while envisioning the religious backdrop and cultural settings of his day. If we

---

[212] Ibid., Acts 17:10–12.
[213] Ibid., John 10:16; 17:20–21; Galatians 3:28; Ephesians 2:14–15.

interpret Paul's letters with a Greco-Roman mind-set, against an anachronistic backdrop that is divorced from the social dynamics of his culture, then invariably we will draw erroneous conclusions and fail to walk in the fullness of Yeshua's finished work and enjoy all of its blessings, privileges, and freedoms.

Paul's Message

Paul's message: Yeshua took the sins of the world onto Himself. He allowed the high priest to present Him to the Romans for execution. Yeshua's death paid the penalty for the sins of the world. Yeshua became a curse, taking the curses that Israel deserved for breaking the Mosaic covenant, so that Israel could receive the blessings that He deserved for keeping it. The Spirit resurrected Yeshua and restored Him to eternal life, and those who accept Him and identify with Him are put to death, buried, resurrected, restored to eternal life, and grafted into Israel.

Paul wrote his first letter around AD 48 to the congregation in Galatia. The letter to the Galatians gives us the historical-religious-cultural-sociological context we need to interpret the rest of his letters. If we divorce Paul's letters from this context, we will misinterpret his message. The church disconnected from its Hebrew roots and concluded that Yeshua did away with the Torah, but nothing could be further from the truth! Yeshua did not destroy the Torah; He made a way for His Spirit to write it on our hearts so that we could fulfill its intent. Paul's letters tell us how to cooperate with the Spirit so that we can fulfill the intent of the Torah.

The Situation in Galatia

Paul shared the gospel with Gentiles. Many Gentiles repented from worshiping the gods of Rome, placed their faith in Yahweh, bowed their knee to Yeshua, and entered the synagogues. Yahweh put His Spirit in these Gentiles and removed the veil from the Tanakh. The Gentiles were studying the Tanakh and breaking free from the religious men who were controlling them.

The sages in Jerusalem sent agents to Galatia to tell the Gentiles that it was nice they believed in a Jewish Messiah, but they also needed to submit to circumcision and to keep the written Torah, oral Torah, and halachah. In other words, the sages' agents told the Gentiles that they had to go through the proselyte ritual and obtain Jewish legal status to get into the covenant and obtain a place in the world to come, and then they had to keep the Torah and its law (their way) to stay in it.

The sages were losing control, and they could not stand it. The rapid growth of the Yeshua sect shocked the sages, and they realized that they could not stop it. The sages sent their emissaries into the synagogues in Galatia in an attempt to preserve their religious-political power. If the sages could convince the Gentiles that they had to live out the written Torah within the legal framework that they had established (the oral Torah and legal halachah) in order to share in the wealth of Israel's covenants, then they could control them and rule over them. In short, the sages were attempting to integrate the people who believed that Yeshua was the Messiah into their system so that they could remain in power. Paul realized that the gates of hell were trying to prevail against Yeshua's ekklesia, so he wrote a letter to expose the lies of the usurpers.

Chapter 24

The Book Of Galatians

A Historical Perspective

All residents within the Roman Empire had to participate in the Imperial Cult and worship its gods in order to demonstrate their loyalty to Rome. Yahweh gave the Jews favor with the Roman government, however. The Romans passed a law that said that the people who worshiped in the synagogues did not have to participate in the Imperial Cult or worship its gods. Therefore, the Roman government did not require the Gentiles who believed Yahweh, put their faith in Yeshua, and assembled in the synagogue on the Sabbath to study the written Torah to participate in the Imperial Cult or worship its gods, but this put these Gentiles in a very precarious position.

If a Gentile believer stayed in good with the synagogue authorities, he did not have to worship the emperor, the emperor's family, or the other gods, but if he fell out of favor with the synagogue authorities, it could cost him his life. See, if a synagogue authority kicked a believing Gentile out of the synagogue, the Romans would either force him back into idolatry or execute him!

The sages in Jerusalem set the guidelines for the synagogues. Thus the rulers of the synagogues in Galatia listened to the troublemakers from Jerusalem. The synagogue rulers told the Gentiles that they had to submit to circumcision and keep the written Torah by keeping the oral Torah and halachah in order to obtain a place in the covenant and keep it. If the Gentiles obeyed the synagogue rulers, they would in effect be proclaiming that what Yeshua had done on the execution stake was not enough to save them and that they had to save themselves by keeping the law. However, if the Gentiles refused to obey the synagogue rulers, the synagogue rulers could kick them out of the synagogue; and the Romans would either force them to worship their gods and keep their religious calendar with its days, months, seasons, and years that they set aside to appease their gods, or kill them! Either way, the Gentiles would be exchanging their freedom in Messiah for the bondage of religion. So some Gentiles played it safe and mixed the three conflicting systems together.[214]

Paul's Letter to the Galatians

Paul wrote the book of Galatians in an effort to strengthen the Galatian congregation so that it could withstand the sages' emissaries who were trying to bring them into bondage by yoking them to the false religious system by making them obtain Jewish legal status. Since the troublemakers from Jerusalem were trying to convert the Gentile believers into Jews, we call them *Judaizers*. Hence the letter of Galatians is a theological defense against the Judaizers.

The Judaizers said that Abraham's children were those who were born in his bloodline, circumcised on the eighth day, and lived out the Torah within the fences the sages erected to protect the covenant community. The Judaizers said the Gentiles could repent, submit to circumcision, be baptized, offer a sacrifice, and put themselves under the custodianship of the written Torah, oral Torah and halachah, in order to be reborn into Abraham's bloodline and enter the covenant.

Paul agreed that Abraham's seed were the men who were born in his bloodline, circumcised on the eighth day, and lived within the fences the sages erected to protect the covenant community, but he pointed out that their mother was Hagar (the earthly Jerusalem). According to Paul, whatever a Hebrew put his faith in revealed who had given birth to him. Those who put their faith in the sages' religion revealed that their mother was Hagar the Egyptian (Mystery Babylon); but Yah had not promised to give her a son, so like Ishmael, these men would not inherit the promises.

Yahweh had promised that He would give Sarah a son, and He sent His Spirit from the New Jerusalem to empower her to conceive and bring forth this son, who would inherit the promises. A Hebrew who believed Yahweh and put his faith in Yeshua revealed that his mother was Sarah (the Holy Spirit from the New Jerusalem), and like Isaac, they would inherit the promises.[215] Paul also said that the people who were not born in Abraham's bloodline (the Gentiles) could repent, believe Yahweh, put their faith in Yeshua, and receive His Spirit; and since Yeshua was Abraham's Seed to whom Yahweh made the promises, the Gentiles then became his seed and inherited the promises.[216]

The conflict between the apostle Paul and the Judaizers was a conflict between the New Jerusalem and the earthly Jerusalem, Yahweh's kingdom and HaSatan's kingdom, Yeshua's

---

[214] *The Hebrew-Greek Key Word Study Bible*, KJV, Galatians 4:7–11.

[215] Ibid., Genesis 21:8–14; Galatians 3:6–9; 4:21–31.

[216] Ibid., Genesis 12:3; 17:4–6; Galatians 3:29.

ekklesia and Mystery Babylon. The gates of hell were coming against Yeshua's ekklesia, so Paul opened the Torah and recorded the Holy Spirit's insights, taking the keys of the kingdom and opening its gates so that everyone with faith could enter and take refuge from religion.

Paul validated the Spirit's insights by examining the lives of Abraham, Sarah, Hagar, Isaac, and Ishmael. Paul said that the covenant Yah made at Mount Sinai represented Hagar and that the covenant He made with Abraham represented Sarah. Paul went on to equate Hagar with the earthly Jerusalem and Sarah with the heavenly Jerusalem. Paul said that Hagar, or the religious rulers in the earthly Jerusalem, who had built fences around the written Torah that became more important than the written Torah, gave birth to slaves, who had to strive to keep the written Torah, oral Torah, and legal halachah in order to obtain a place in the world to come.[viii]

Paul said that the children of Abraham and Hagar were slaves who would not inherit the promises. Paul said that the Holy Spirit worked through Sarah (the Abrahamic covenant, or the heavenly Jerusalem), giving birth to sons who would inherit the promises. Yah's sons were free to worship Him in Spirit and truth, and He freely gave them a place in the world to come. The apostle reminded his readers that the son of the flesh (Ishmael) persecuted the son of the Spirit (Isaac), and the Spirit (Sarah) prompted the father (Abraham) to cast him out of the camp.

Paul's message was clear. Those who believed Yah, put their faith in Yeshua, and bowed their knee to Him as Lord entered the Abrahamic covenant and the age to come. Those who believed the sages and put their faith in the flesh (Jewish legal status) via circumcision and obeying the written Torah, oral Torah, and halachah did not enter the Abrahamic covenant or the age to come. For Paul, redemption, sanctification, and eternal life came by faith in Yah's grace, and Yeshua was the full manifestation of Yah's grace; so it was pointless to submit to the sages.

The sages did not put their faith in the Seed and receive redemption and justification (as Abraham did). Nor did the sages embrace the Mosaic covenant as a way to show their love for the one who had redeemed and justified them (as Moses did). They discounted the Abrahamic covenant (the covenant of redemption) and put their faith in the Mosaic covenant (the covenant of sanctification) for redemption and justification. In Galatians 3:17, Paul lets us know that the apostate sages believed that the Mosaic covenant disannulled the Abrahamic covenant, so they tried to obtain Abraham's inheritance by keeping the law and made the promise to no effect.

A Fork in the Road

The Gentiles had two options: (1) The Gentiles could contend for the faith that Paul had shared with them by standing up to the Judaizers, which could anger the synagogue president, causing him to banish them from the synagogue. This would be bad because the Romans would then force the Gentiles to worship their gods, or else they would execute them. (2) The Gentiles could give in to the Judaizers and put their faith in circumcision and the written Torah, oral Torah, and halachah.

Two roads claimed to lead to covenant inclusion and right standing with Yahweh. The sages in Jerusalem built one of these roads by setting the parameters that Jews were to live by. As long as they lived by these parameters, they were the seed of Abraham, and as the seed of Abraham, they had a place in the covenant. Yahweh built the other road by pouring out His grace and inviting everyone to put their faith in Abraham's Seed so that His Spirit could become one with their spirit, transforming them into Abraham's seed and bringing them into the covenant. The Gentiles were at an important intersection, and they had to take either the road the Tanakh pointed to or the road the sages in Jerusalem pointed to. The Gentile believers had to choose between following God or man, Spirit or flesh, faith or works, grace or legalism, relationship or religion.

The rulers of Mystery Babylon were trying to incorporate Yeshua's life, death, and resurrection into their religion so that they could enslave the people who believed in Him. The rulers wanted to prevent people from trusting in Yeshua alone for redemption, sanctification, and eternal life because they wanted to control them and use them for financial gain. Paul told the Gentiles that Yeshua had redeemed them and that His Spirit was sanctifying them, giving them the ability to walk out the intent of the written Torah without the sages' rules and regulations.

If the sages and their emissaries could trick the people who believed that Yeshua was the Messiah into putting their faith in circumcision and keeping the written Torah by keeping the oral Torah and legal halachah, these people would fall from grace. In other words, Yeshua's finished work would count for nothing! Clearly, this was an attempt by the gates of hell to prevail over Yeshua's ekklesia. Thankfully, Yeshua promised that the gates of hell would not prevail over His ekklesia and spoke through Paul, giving the Galatians the truth that would keep them free.

Paul contrasted faith in Yeshua with faith in circumcision and keeping the whole Torah of Moses for redemption and sanctification, and shed light on the sociological, historical, cultural, and religious conditions of his day. Paul attacked the men who were teaching that circumcision and keeping the whole Torah of Moses could transform a Gentile into a Jew and bring him into the covenant. Paul's letter upset the sages, so they told their sheep that he was not to be trusted because he destroyed the Torah; that is, he taught against the Torah. The sages injected their toxic venom into unsuspecting victims, and as these poor souls read Paul's letter, they concluded that he was bashing the patriarchs and the Torah, and rejected the gospel, thus reserving their spot in hell.[217]

---

[217] Ibid., 2 Peter 3:16.

Centuries later, for political reasons, the Gentiles in Yeshua's ekklesia broke away from the mooring of their Hebrew roots and rebuilt the dividing wall between Jews and Gentiles. The pride of the Gentile theologians blinded them to the fact that Yah had established a relationship with the patriarchs through grace by faith and that centuries later the sages had perverted this relationship into a religion. The church concluded that the Torah was a curse that Yeshua freed them from, but Yeshua and Paul were not against the Torah; they were against the people who perverted the Torah in order to enslave people in a religion that separated Jews and Gentiles.

Chapter 25

Divine Bookends

The Early Letters[218]

In AD 48, Paul wrote the letter of Galatians. In AD 50, Paul wrote a letter to the congregation in Thessalonica, addressing behavioral issues and the end times. The Jews (the apostate religious rulers) and Romans persecuted the saints in Thessalonica. The persecution got so severe that the congregation feared that they had missed the rapture and were going through the tribulation. Paul wrote 1 Thessalonians to reassure the congregation and clarify some of his earlier teachings, but after they read his letter, some of the people in the congregation stopped working because they thought that the rapture was imminent. In AD 51, Paul wrote 2 Thessalonians to get the saints back to work and to educate them about the timing of the rapture.

In AD 52, Paul wrote a letter to the congregation in Corinth. In 1 Corinthians, Paul addressed some behavioral, housekeeping, and discipline issues. Paul explained how the gifts of the Spirit operate, how to partake of the Lord's Supper, and the doctrine of the resurrection. Most of the people in the Corinthian congregation took Paul's correction, but some of the congregants refused his correction because he was not one of Yeshua's twelve disciples. In AD 54, Paul wrote a second letter to the congregation in Corinth. In 2 Corinthians, the apostle Paul defended his apostleship, encouraged the congregation, and explained the proper motives for giving.

---

[218] Theologians disagree on the exact dates that Paul wrote his letters.

A Bookend Epistle

Israel's rulers were supposed to guide the ekklesia of Moses by the light of the Torah so that she would prosper until the prophet who was like Moses came to circumcise her heart and lead her into the world to come.[219] It was obvious that Yeshua was the prophet whom Israel had been waiting on for 1,500 years, because the miracles He performed were reminiscent of the ones Moses had performed. Peter, James, and John stood with Yeshua on a mountain and saw Moses and Elijah (the Law and the Prophets) talk with Him about His death, burial, and resurrection, and they heard Yahweh call Him His Son; that is, the Promised Seed. Moreover, like Moses' face, Yeshua's face shone with Yah's glory, proving beyond any doubt that He was the prophet like Moses.[220]

Moses was disobedient, so he did not get to lead his ekklesia into the Promised Land; but Yeshua was obedient unto death, and Yah gave Him the honor of leading His ekklesia into the New Jerusalem, the millennial kingdom, and the renewed earth. Here is my point: Yahweh gave the sages the pure milk of the Torah so that they could nurture the ekklesia with it, and they poisoned it and tried to kill her with it. The prideful sages misinterpreted the passage that commanded them not to boil a kid in its mother's milk, which is exactly what they were doing! Yeshua transformed Moses' ekklesia into His ekklesia and wrote Galatians to protect her from the attacks that came from within the camp; therefore, Galatians serves as a *bookend epistle*.

The Other Bookend Epistle

Normally, a collection of books will stand in an upright position only when two equal but opposite forces overcome the force that seeks to topple them (gravity). The book of Galatians serves as the right bookend that keeps the collection of books known as the apostolic writings from falling too far to the right. In keeping with the bookend analogy, there has to be a left bookend to prevent the books in the apostolic writings from falling too far to the left. So which epistle serves as the left bookend? Well, if the right bookend repels the attacks that come from inside the camp, then the left one must repel the attacks that come from outside the camp.

The Attacks That Come from Outside the Camp

High atop the Tower of Babel, Nimrod and his wife built a religion around a counterfeit Messiah and enslaved the people of the earth, but Yah scattered the people in this religion

---

[219] *The Hebrew-Greek Key Word Study Bible*, KJV, Deuteronomy 18:15–19.

[220] Ibid., Matthew 17:1–13.

to the ends of the earth, forming the nations. Each nation had its own people, dynamics, and geography, which meant that each nation had a unique set of political and economic problems. The leaders of each nation built a religion around some aspect of the tower religion so that they could solve their political and economic problems. Remember, the ancient city was a religious institution that utilized a political system and an economic system in order to keep its citizens in line, promote the common good, and enrich its founders; and a nation is merely a collection of cities.

In essence, HaSatan planted a tree in Babylon, and man flocked to this tree to wear its leaves and eat its fruit. In an act of mercy, Yah scattered man to the ends of the earth, forming the nations. Much as Johnny Appleseed did, man carried the seeds of HaSatan's tree with him and planted them in each nation. As men died and returned to dust, their dust covered the root systems of these trees, covering them in tradition. The leaves on the trees were different colors, textures, and shapes, but all the trees produced the same fruit (eternal death). In other words, the pagan religions sprang from the tower religion, but tradition has obscured their true origin.

Technically, the terms *HaSatan's kingdom, Mystery Babylon*, and *the world system* refer to the religious-political-economic system that controls the earth. The goal of HaSatan's kingdom, Mystery Babylon, the world system, is to deceive, enslave, and keep people comfortably separated from Yahweh so that they end up in the lake of fire with HaSatan. In a general sense, the term *paganism* refers to the religious component of Mystery Babylon.

The attacks that come from outside the camp are from paganism. Fortunately, however, Yah put a witness in us that lets us know we are accountable to Him. Yah also wrote the gospel in the stars and designed nature so that it testifies of Him. Moreover, Yah sent His Word and His Spirit to testify. Since these witnesses testify of the existence of Yahweh, there are no atheists; however, there are fools, who are educated above their intellect, who refuse to seek their Creator.

Since most people respond to the testimony of the witnesses and seek Yahweh, Mystery Babylon puts most of its energy into ensnaring people in one of its many religions. Yeshua told the righteous remnant of Israel to proclaim the gospel to all the nations. The gospel opens the mind and works in concert with the Holy Spirit to convict the heart of sin, giving people an opportunity to repent and put their faith in Yeshua to save them from sin, poverty, sickness, disease, death, hell, and the lake of fire. Yeshua's bride is a threat to HaSatan's kingdom, so its religious arm (paganism) tries to infiltrate her and contaminate her halachah in order to wrinkle and stain her garments and diminish her glory so that she cannot accomplish her mission.

Infiltrating Yeshua's Ekklesia

By the time Yeshua arrived, Rome was the most powerful empire on earth. Its military was invincible. Its political system was effective. Its economy prospered above all others. Its religious system was all-inclusive. The Romans were brilliant strategists. As the Romans conquered a city, they captured its gods and put them in their pantheon.[221] After that, if the defeated people wanted to worship their gods, they had to submit to Rome. So essentially, Rome kidnapped and exploited the gods of a city in order to force its citizens to be loyal to her.

The Romans also took a portion of the conquered people to Rome as slaves. Rome was a melting pot that contained every god and religion on earth.[222] In essence, Rome regathered the religions that sprang forth from the tower and reconstituted them; that is, Rome became a modern-day Babylon.[223] If paganism was to mix its teachings with Yeshua's, Rome was the place to do it.

Mystery Babylon needed to separate Yeshua's ekklesia from its Hebrew roots so that it could integrate pagan philosophies, ideologies, and traditions into it. The Torah stood in the way, however. The Torah told about the covenants that Yahweh had cut with Israel, how people could enter those covenants, and how covenant members were to walk out their relationship with Him. The Torah left no room for paganism, so HaSatan had to separate Yeshua's ekklesia from it.

The ekklesia in Rome was strong, but trouble was brewing. The Romans thought that Yah was finished with Israel and the Jews and that they had replaced them. The Romans became proud and boasted against the Jews. The Spirit, foreseeing the future, inspired Paul to write a letter to get them back on track before they unhooked from their roots and opened the door for paganism.

Moving the Bookends

Paul's letter to the Romans was the barrier that repelled attacks from outside the camp. If we wish to keep the apostolic writings in place, we need to keep our interpretations of these writings between the bookends of Galatians and Romans. In other words, we must filter our interpretations of the apostolic writings through the sociological, historical, cultural, and religious context of Galatians to screen out the ideologies of the Jews' false

---

[221] George Smith, *The Gentile Nations*, New York, NY, Carlton and Porter, 1854, p. 490.

[222] Philip Schaff, *History of the Christian Church, Volume 1: Apostolic Christianity*, Logos systems, 1997, Sect 36.*

[223] *The Hebrew-Greek Key Word Study Bible*, KJV, 1 Peter 5:13; Revelation 17:5; (Rome is spiritual Babylon).

religion, and then filter them through the sociological, historical, cultural, and religious context of Romans to screen out the ideologies of the Gentiles' false religions. The former steals our liberty, but the latter inspires liberties that glorify HaSatan and diminish the glory and power of Yeshua's ekklesia.

Over the centuries, Mystery Babylon has tried to topple the Galatian bookend so that the corrosive ideologies of the Jews' false religion could eat away at the execution stake and bring it down, but it has failed. Mystery Babylon has also tried to topple the Romans bookend so that it could flood the ekklesia with paganism and destroy her, but this too has failed. However, Mystery Babylon has managed to move the bookends to spot and wrinkle the ekklesia's garments. Hence Yeshua's bride has not operated at *full power*, but this is changing. Today Yeshua is giving His bride a desire to return to her roots. The ekklesia is embracing her Hebrew roots and moving the Galatian bookend back to its original position. This will shift the Romans bookend back to its right position, flush paganism out of the ekklesia, and return her to her former glory.

Part 7

Establishing the Context of Romans

Chapter 26

Rome

A City Is Born

Near the west coast of Italy on the plain of Latium, there is a river called the Tiber. One thousand years before Yeshua arrived in Israel, the clans in this area began to cooperate with one another, and small settlements began to spring up in the hills that surround the Tiber River. The settlements grew into small villages and towns. In 600 BC, these villages and towns came together to build a meeting place called the Forum, giving birth to the city of Rome.[224] Rome grew rapidly, taking control of the land and resources of the Latium plain and the rest of Italy.

Just to the east of Rome, there was another prominent power: the Greek city-states. The Greek city-states were jockeying for position, fighting with each other, and paying tribute to the Persians and plotting their revenge on them; thus they were not a threat to Rome. The Persians had conquered the Greek city-states and were extracting high tributes from them. The Greeks spent their days trying to figure out how to escape from the Persian yoke.[225] Still, Rome kept a watchful eye on the Greeks.

In 338 BC, Philip of Macedon forced the Greek city-states into a confederation, and in 334 BC, his son, Alexander, marched east to take revenge on the Persians. Alexander the Great defeated the Persians, took control of their territories, and drank himself to death. Alexander's four generals divided his vast kingdom and began fighting with each other.

---

[224] Martin Goodman, *Rome and Jerusalem: The Clash of Ancient Civilizations*, New York, NY, Random House, 2007, p. 34.

[225] Everett Ferguson, *Backgrounds of Early Christianity*, Grand Rapids, MI, Eerdmans Publishing, 2003, p. 7.

In 264 BC, Rome's lust for power and control brought her into conflict with Carthage on the northern coast of Africa. After a long, bitter war with Carthage, Rome prevailed, and her navy controlled the sea lanes of the Mediterranean. Rome prospered and built up her military. Rome was strong and stable, so some of the weaker Greek city-states asked her to protect them from the stronger Greek city-states. The Romans stepped in to "help" these Greeks and in 149 BC annexed Macedon into their republic. In 146 BC, Rome sacked the city of Corinth and annexed Greece into its republic. In 133 BC, Pergamum's dying king realized that the Romans were gunning for his kingdom and bequeathed it to them in order to avoid war.[226]

The Evolution of Rome

As we have seen, Rome began as a conglomeration of clans that evolved into a network of towns that merged to form a city. Legend claims that Romulus and Remus spearheaded this effort in 753 BC. Legend also claims that Romulus was the first king of Rome and that six other men ruled the kingdom after him for a total of 250 years. However, as I noted above, history indicates that villagers founded Rome in 600 BC. Whatever the case may be, legend and history agree on a point that is far more germane to the subject matter of this book: Rome evolved into a vast kingdom, and a king ruled the monarchy of Rome until 509 BC.[227]

In 510 BC, a man named Brutus killed the king of Rome (Lucius Tarquinius Superbus). A representative government (republic) replaced the monarchy.[228] The Roman Republic was an oligarchy led by two consuls and a senate that governed through a complex constitution that revolved around the principle of separation of powers and a system of checks and balances.[229] The Romans had a profound reverence for the traditions of their ancestors, so they added new checks and balances to the ancient laws, but the checks and balances soon got out of hand. The checks and balances hindered their ability to govern and led to confusion, disorder, and violence.

Two Classes

During the republican era, there were two classes: *patricians* and *plebeians*. The patricians were families that traced their roots back to the founding of Rome and who had grown rich and influential during the monarchy; the plebeians (*plebs*) were newcomers,

---

[226] Ibid., p. 23.

[227] Merrill F. Unger, *The New Unger's Bible Dictionary*, Chicago, IL, Moody Press, 1988, p. 1,089.*

[228] http://www.roman-empire.net/kings/kings-index.html [02/2011]

[229] http://www.theancientworld.net/civ/roman_republic.html [02/2011]

who were poorer and less influential. Class warfare between the patricians and plebs is what fueled Rome's evolution.

In the early republic, the patricians controlled the government and grew richer and richer as Rome subdued the surrounding territories and took their possessions. As the patricians got richer, they bought up all the real estate around Rome, and this created a need for a large pool of cheap laborers to work their estates. The patricians asked their generals to capture people from the conquered territories and bring them back to Rome as slaves. Sadly, the massive influx of slaves into Rome took employment away from the plebeians, and they grew poorer and poorer.

Teetering on the Brink of Destruction

The patricians' large estates used slave labor to grow grain and other commodities. The patricians' government-subsidized estates sold commodities at a discount and drove the peasants' farms out of business. Most of the displaced peasants came to Rome to find jobs, but more often than not, they ended up taking handouts from the state. Once the peasants were on the state's payroll, the patricians bought their farms for pennies on the dollar and grew richer.

The patricians also used the military to grow richer. Patricians were officers in the military, and plebs, who owned small farms, were soldiers. The people in the military had to buy their own weapons and supplies; thus inner-city peasants were not compelled to serve. Rome began fighting long, protracted wars, and as the plebs returned home, they found their farms in disrepair. Reprehensibly, the patricians offered them pennies on the dollar for their dilapidated farms and purchased them with the spoils of war that the soldiers had spilled their blood to obtain.

Patricians and aristocrats organized to pass laws favoring the rich; plebeians and peasants organized into urban mobs trading political support for government food and housing. Two political parties emerged: the *Optimates* drew their support from the Senate and other nobles, and the *Populares*, relied on the Tribal Assembly and the urban mob for support.[230] The situation in the provinces was just as dire: unscrupulous men who exploited the people under their care for personal gain governed. The republic teetered on the brink of destruction.

The Tipping Point

The plebeians fought to gain a political voice, and slowly but surely, they obtained it. Eventually the plebeians gained political equality with the patricians. The plebeian Popu-

---

[230] http://www.flowofhistory.com/units/birth/4/FC30 [02/2011]

lares set up social programs to help the poor, but got rich and lost touch with the plight of the poor. After a while, the only thing that distinguished the plebeian Populares from the patrician Optimates was their label. In fact, there was little difference between the two political parties. However, it was politically expedient for the patricians to look out for the aristocrats and for the plebs to keep handing out aid to the poor. The politicians had to protect their power base while walking a tightrope to appease both the aristocrats and the poor in order to hold the republic together.

The politicians looked to the military to expand the tax base and deposit spoils into the treasury, but they did not support the military. Remember, the soldiers had to buy their own weapons and supplies. This changed when Marius, a politician and general, passed a law that allowed poor city dwellers to serve in the military. Rome began to purchase weapons and supplies for soldiers, and if they obtained a favorable discharge report from their generals, the state gave them a plot of land.[231] The soldiers became fiercely loyal to their generals, but the generals started building personal armies to compete with each other for glory and control of Rome. One general would back the patricians, and another would back the plebs. Finally, the class warfare, the superfluous checks and balances, the attempts to redistribute the wealth, the inept provincial governors, and the competition between generals led to a series of civil wars.

A Death Spiral

Rome was now five hundred years old. Rome had absorbed Italy and the surrounding territories and taken their wealth. Rome had used this wealth to build a very powerful military machine and to provide goods and services for her citizens, but now she was in a death spiral. The patricians, plebs, Optimates, and Populares were constantly struggling with each other, and often this culminated in political violence. The wealthy aristocrats and their associates gobbled up the state revenues and war spoils, leaving the scraps for the commoners, peasants, and slaves. The disappearance of the middle class led to mobs, riots, crime, and violence between the classes.

The politicians tried to keep the peace by offering "carrots" to the two classes, but it became increasingly difficult to squeeze carrots through the intricate maze of checks and balances that was supposed to level the playing field between the classes. Ultimately the politicians had to rely on their ability to dispatch the military to keep the peace. Rome was skillful at dangling carrots, but she was even more skillful at wielding the proverbial big stick. However, the political aims of the generals made it hard for the politicians to wield the big stick.

---

[231] Cormac O'Brien, *The Fall of Empires*, New York, NY, Fall River Press, 2009, pp. 256–257.

The republican system of government began to break down as its generals became political superstars. The Roman generals controlled the strongest military on the face of the earth and were responsible for the prosperity, so they began to take on mythical qualities. Eventually the citizens of Rome glorified and worshiped the generals as gods, and Rome's soldiers idolized the generals and became more loyal to them than to the state. The Roman generals began to command the politicians and set policy, competing with each other for control of the government, and this divided the military, the political parties, and the classes even more.

Chapter 27

The Rise Of The Roman Empire

The Republic Becomes a Military State

The generals were the most powerful and influential people in the Roman Republic. The Senate "gave" three generals consulship over Rome. Pompey, Crassus, and Caesar formed the First Triumvirate (the board of three). Gaius Julius Caesar was born on July 13, 100 BC. Caesar was a patrician, and his family, the Julia family, had roots that stretched back to the founding of Rome. Caesar had climbed the political ladder to become very powerful, but this upset the aristocrats because he fought for reforms that benefited the proletariats and the middle class.

Caesar's popularity with the people of Rome concerned the rich patricians and plebs in the Senate, so they got rid of him by giving him a governorship over the province of Gaul. In Gaul, Caesar put down a rebellion, killed over a million people, and annexed over 350,000 square miles of territory into the Roman Republic. Caesar also sent vast sums of wealth and thousands of slaves back to Rome to fuel the economy, but the Senate accused him of going to war without their approval and decided to arrest him and force him into an early retirement.

The Dynamics of Change

Once the Senate decided to take a certain course of action, the only ones who could stop it were the tribunes. Most of the men in the Senate were aristocrats, so by law tribunes had to be plebs who held that office to balance out the power of the aristocrats. The tribunes could overrule any vote of the Senate. The Senate ruled that Caesar had to surrender his command, become a private citizen, and face trial for his crimes, but the tribunes vetoed their ruling. The Senate, however, ignored the checks and balances set forth in the constitution and planned to enforce its ruling. Unfortunately, mobs now ruled Rome: the proletariat mobs ignored the law and ruled the streets, taking what they wanted by force; and the Roman Senate, an aristocratic mob, ignored the constitution and ruled the capital, taking what they wanted by force.[232]

The triumvirate held Rome together, but General Crassus died in a battle with the Parthians. After this, General Pompey sided with the Senate, and the people of Rome sided with Caesar. In 49 BC., Caesar marched his legions to the Rubicon, crossed it, and started a civil war. Caesar's legions, with the support of the Roman people, drove Pompey and the Senate out of Rome. Caesar appointed a Senate that was friendly to him. The new Senate made Caesar the dictator of Rome. Caesar's legions chased Pompey's legions and defeated them. Pompey fled to Egypt, but the king of Egypt did not want any trouble with a man who had killed over a million people, so he cut off his head and gave it to Caesar when he came looking for him. Ptolemy's gift did not impress Caesar, but his sister did. Cleopatra captivated the mighty Caesar, and he helped her fight a bloody civil war against her brother for the control of Egypt.

The combined forces of Caesar and Cleopatra defeated Ptolemy's forces. Cleopatra then married her youngest brother and began to rule Egypt. Later Caesar returned to Rome with Cleopatra, and the Senate and the people of Rome vied with each other to confer dignities on him. Caesar accepted all the principal offices and titles that the Roman constitution specified— consul, dictator, censor, tribune, etc.—and garnered the support of almost all the rest.[233] Caesar began a large number of very extensive public works projects, changed the tax code, and quickly transformed Rome from a city of violence and anarchy into a peaceful city of law and order.

Caesar took the title of *imperator* (head of state). Caesar also took the office of *pontifex maximus* (high priest of the state religion). Caesar made ivory statues of himself. Caesar had these statues carried in all the official religious processions and placed one in the temple of Quirinus with the inscription "To the Invincible God." To the Romans, Quirinus was the deified likeness of Romulus, the city's founder and first king. This clearly identified Caesar with the gods who had laid the foundations of Rome and the kings they appointed to rule it.[234]

Caesar implied that he was a god by minting coins with his image on them. It looked as if Caesar was transforming himself into a divine king so that he could reestablish the monarchy. A group of senators who saw the value of a republican form of government

---

[232] http://historion.net/american-encyclopedia-history-i/triumvirate-caesars-gallic-wars-war-between-caesar-and-pompey [02/2011]

[233] http://historion.net/american-encyclopedia-history-i/dictatorship-and-death-caesar-second-triumvirate-civil-wars-mark-ant [02/2011]

[234] http://www.unrv.com/fall-republic/caesar-the-god.php [03/2011]

came up with a plan to stop Caesar. The senators' plan was pregnant with irony. In 44 BC, Brutus and twenty-two republican senators stabbed Caesar to death to prevent him from becoming a divine king and reestablishing a monarchy, but by killing him, they empowered him to achieve his goal.

The Sons of God Fight over Rome

Caesar's heir, Octavianus, and his two trusted generals, Marc Antony and Lepidus, formed a triumvirate and defeated the republican legions. This triumvirate split Rome's territory into western, eastern, and southern regions. Antony governed the eastern region, Octavianus governed the western region, and Lepidus governed the southern region.

Octavianus and Lepidus got into a dispute. Lepidus surrendered his command to Octavianus, and the western region merged with the southern region. Octavianus ruled the western territories from Rome, and Antony ruled the eastern territories from Alexandria.

In 42 BC., the Senate recognized Caesar as a god, which meant that Octavianus was the son of a god. Antony got involved with Cleopatra and followed in Caesar's footsteps (in more than one way). Antony declared that he was the incarnation of the Greek god Dionysus (the Roman Bacchus, the Egyptian Osiris) and that Cleopatra was the Greek goddess Aphrodite (the Roman Venus, the Egyptian Isis), giving them divine authority in Greece, Rome, and Egypt. Marc Antony also declared Cleopatra the Queen of Kings, and Caesarion, her son with Caesar, was declared the son of a god and the King of Kings, challenging Octavianus's claim as Caesar's heir and casting doubt on his authority to rule.[235] In 31 BC, Octavianus's navy defeated Antony and Cleopatra's navy, and they committed suicide. After this, Octavianus took the title of *pharaoh*, and Egypt became his personal possession. Rome treated Egypt as if it were a province, but the personal rule of Egypt and title of pharaoh belonged to every emperor.[236]

The Buck Never Stopped

Rome's republican experiment was a disaster. It produced four hundred years of class warfare, political unrest, and civil strife that culminated in a century of civil war. The people of Rome grew tired of fighting with each other for control and squandering their precious resources on endeavors that did not advance their standard of living. The Romans found out the hard way that when everyone is in charge, no one is in charge. The

---

[235] http://www.unrv.com/fall-republic/death-antony-cleopatra.php [03/2011]

[236] http://www.unrv.com/fall-republic/death-antony-cleopatra.php [03/2011]

Roman government had too many checks and balances and offsetting political offices. The buck never stopped with anyone.

In the Roman Republic, power, wealth, and privilege clashed with hopelessness, poverty, and servitude, prompting its founders to put checks and balances and offsetting offices into place to bring these two opposing forces, both of which would destroy the republic, into equilibrium. The power that this equilibrium generated was supposed to advance the interests of everyone, but it did not work. The complex mixture of checks and balances and offsetting offices needed to be simplified, and someone needed to be in charge. Clearly, the buck needed to stop with someone.

The Buck Stops Here

The proverbial passing of the buck led to a civil war that paved the way for a supreme ruler. By 30 BC., Octavianus, the son of a god by adoption, had executed Caesarion, the biological son of the god, and secured for himself the divine authority to be the supreme ruler of the Roman territories. Octavianus brought the eastern territories back into submission and killed those who resisted; he added Egypt to the list of provinces and deposited its wealth into the Roman treasury.

In 29 BC, Octavianus returned to Rome to a hero's welcome. The people of Rome practically begged him to be their supreme ruler and he "reluctantly" complied with their requests. Octavianus was brilliant. In a series of backroom deals, Octavianus positioned the right people in the right places at the right times in order to ensure that the people of Rome transferred their power to him and consolidated it in his person. In public, however, Octavianus played it cool and let the people think that it was their idea to invest all their power in him.

The Roman Senate gave Octavianus the title of imperator (emperor), and he became the permanent commander of the military. Next, Octavianus secured the position of censor, which was in charge of the Senate's role. As censor, Octavianus reduced the number of senators and set new qualifications for them. Octavianus made sure that the people who were loyal to him and his cause populated the Senate. Next, Octavianus secured the position of princeps (prince), a title that implied that he was the first citizen and the head of the Senate. Octavianus secured the position of tribune so that he could veto the Senate's votes when they did not suit him.

Octavianus also secured the title of *augustus* (exalted one) and the office of proconsul, which allowed him to govern Rome's provinces. As proconsul, Octavianus immediately appointed governors, who reported directly to him. Octavianus made it an act of treason to extort money or otherwise mismanage a province, bringing good government to the provinces. Next, Octavianus obtained the office of consul. As consul, Octavianus had twelve lictors and a seat between the regular consuls, who became figureheads with little choice but to side with him. With the help of his father, who was a god, Octavianus now had absolute control over Rome's military, government, and economy. The buck stopped with Octavianus now.

Chapter 28

The Empire Of Augustus

From Bricks to Marble

Augustus was now the supreme ruler of Rome, and he had to make some changes. Augustus did not want the changes to be too abrupt because he did not want to clash with the Senate. Augustus wanted to avoid another civil war, so he allowed the old checks and balances and offsetting political offices to remain in place. However, the checks and balances and offsetting offices were part of a carefully crafted facade that produced an illusion of a functioning republic. It looked like the republican system of government was finally working, but behind the scenes, Augustus continued expanding his power by making allies and restructuring the government.

Augustus had absolute control over the most powerful military on earth. Augustus was also considered the son of a god, so he supposedly had a direct line to the gods. This meant that Augustus's power was unlimited because the gods in heaven and the military on earth were at his beck and call.

Augustus took some of the money that he had confiscated from Egypt and purchased plots of land for about forty thousand military veterans. Augustus restructured the military and got the soldiers to swear an oath to him. Augustus had the soldiers look to him for compensation and made it illegal for the generals to glorify themselves. Rome's generals had to give Augustus the glory for their victories. Augustus put together nine cohorts of highly skilled legionnaires to protect him (the Praetorian Guard), stationing them on the outskirts of Rome and giving them double pay. Augustus sent the rest of the military to the provinces to maintain order and repel attacks from barbarians, which prevented the generals from joining forces against him. Augustus treated the military extremely well because they actualized his will and his power on the earth.

Augustus built or rebuilt eighty-two temples in Rome, along with a new capitol complex.[237] Historians say that Augustus found Rome in bricks and left it in marble; they also say that he kept the poor happy with bread and circuses. Augustus gave food and entertainment to the poor, while building bathhouses, gyms, schools, and parks for those in the middle and upper classes. He established Roman cities in the provinces and built bathhouses, gyms, schools, and parks in them to reacculturate the citizens. Augustus built roads, aqueducts, and sewers to improve the quality of life, and he promoted trade and economic growth by keeping the roads and sea lanes safe.

The Carrot and the Stick

The Roman Republic stretched from Spain to Egypt and from Britain to North Africa. The Roman Republic spanned 750,000 square miles and incorporated more than a hundred million people. In the Roman Republic's infancy, patrician rule brought peace and stability to the capital, projecting an image of a strong republic to the rest of the world. However, the patricians got greedy and started making decisions that increased the proletariat population in the capital. Rome's proletariats united, organized, and forced the patricians to give them a place in government.

Divisive political brawls between patricians and plebs led to violence that destabilized Rome's capital, projecting an image of weakness to the whole world. Rome's perceived weakness emboldened the rebels in her provinces, and they did their best to ignite a civil war. The counsel of history was clear. For Rome to continue to be a superpower, she would need a strong leader who could unite her people, end political violence, and stabilize the capital. The capital had to project an image of strength and stability to its provinces and the outside world.

Well, as providence would have it, Caesar Augustus was the perfect man for the job. Augustus was an expert at dangling carrots while holding a big stick. Augustus dangled the carrots of peace, prosperity, culture, entertainment, and a better quality of life before the eyes of those he wanted to befriend, while holding the big stick of the Roman military in his other hand. If people did not take the carrots, then they got the big stick! Rome tried to entice people into her franchise, but if that failed, then she beat them with her big stick until they got on board.[238]

One of Caesar's best carrots; that is, one of his most effective enticements, was the promise of Roman citizenship. If people cooperated and freely integrated into the system, Rome gave them full citizenship in the emerging empire. However, if they resisted and Rome had to force them into the system, they often came in as noncitizens or perhaps even

---

[237] http://www.unrv.com/early-empire/augustus-empire.php [03/2011]

[238] http://www.roman-empire.net/diverse/faq.html#romerise [03/2011]

slaves. The smartest thing to do was to take Caesar's carrot, because citizenship had its privileges. A citizen could vote, hold political office, was exempt from certain taxes, and could own property or a business. A citizen could obtain an education and enjoy the gyms and the parks. The Roman government could not jail Roman citizens without cause or punish them unless it had given them a fair trial. The rights and privileges of the noncitizens were limited, and slaves had no rights or privileges.

Augustus's primary concern was for Rome to project an image of stability and strength. Pride counseled him to initiate a clandestine program to consolidate political power in one man through psychological manipulation and deceit. Logic counseled him to restructure the military and modernize the capital. Wisdom counseled him to build an educational system that promoted literacy, rhetoric, and the writing of Roman propaganda. Common sense counseled him to build the infrastructure to facilitate trade, stimulate economic development, and start programs to help the poor. The gods counseled Augustus to spend millions of dollars on building eighty-two temples. The prince of the gods, HaSatan, counseled him to go the way of Cain and Nimrod.

The Way of Cain

After Yahweh kicked Adam and Eve out of the garden, they told their sons about their interactions with Him and the two supernatural trees. Adam and Eve told Cain and Abel how Yah had killed a lamb and clothed them with its wool so they could continue to fellowship with Him. They showed their sons how to build an altar and offer the blood of a lamb to Yah in order to draw near to Him. Cain and Abel had no excuse for not drawing near to worship Yah.

One Sabbath Abel offered a sacrifice of innocent blood to Yah. Yah sent fire down to consume it and fellowshiped with Abel. HaSatan whispered in Cain's ear and told him to offer as a sacrifice to Yah some of the crops that he had produced from the cursed ground. Cain rejected Yah's teachings and instructions that said that he had to approach Him through the blood of an innocent lamb, which, of course, was an expression of faith in the Seed, and instead offered Him the works of his own hands. In essence, Cain believed that his works could bring him near to Yah.

Yahweh rejected Cain's sacrifice, and he got angry and killed Abel. Yah told Cain that his brother's blood cried out from the ground. Yah gave Cain an opportunity to confess and repent, but he would not. Since Cain would not repent, Yah sent him into the land of Nod so he would experience the pain of separation and the barrenness of a life lived without fellowship with Him. Yah wanted Cain to repent and do things His way, but Cain and his sons built the first city, which evolved into a religious institution that used a political system and economic system to control the people who joined themselves to it, in order to enrich and glorify themselves.

Cain and his sons knew Yahweh, but they did not glorify Him or give Him thanks. Cain and his sons shunned the light; therefore, they lived in darkness. Cain and his sons invented a religion that venerated trees, fire, hearths, and ancestors. In Cain's religion, the father of a family was its high priest. The father became a god when he died, and his son became the high priest.

Cain's religion spread, and Seth's line fell away from the faith. Fallen angels mixed their DNA with man's DNA, filling the earth with violence. Yahweh sent the flood to destroy man. After the flood, Noah's son (Ham) told his sons about Cain's religion. Later Noah's great- grandson (Nimrod) gathered everyone on the plains of Shinar and reformed Cain's religion. Yahweh scattered the people in this religion, forming the nations. Italy was one of the nations.

The Religion of the Hearth and Its Sacred Fire

The flood occurred in the year 1,656 FC (From Creation) or 2,348 BC. The confusion of tongues and the scattering occurred in the year 1,757 FC (2,247 BC) The descendants of Japheth's fourth son, Javan, founded Greece in the year 3,004 FC (1,000 BC). Romulus and Remus founded the city of Rome in the year 3,251 FC (753 BC).[239] Rome came into existence 1,595 years after the flood and 1,494 years after the confusion and scattering. The religion that Nimrod invented on the Tower of Jupiter Belus (Tower of Babel) evolved over the course of 1,494 years, but its principles lined up with the foundational principles of the religion that Cain invented in the land of Nod.

Romulus and Remus were familiar with Cain's religion and embraced the concept of a divine king who was the father of the city and its high priest, and who joined the hierarchy of the gods when he died. In the hierarchy of gods, the oldest and most powerful gods were those of nature and fertility; the *strong gods* were below them, and *the ancestral gods* were below them. The ancestral gods were said to be the spirits of the "mighty men" who ruled the earth and gained favor with the strong gods; after these men died, their spirits went to heaven to rule with the gods. Cain's religion showed the living how to worship the gods at hearths that housed the sacred fire.

In this religion, the king of a city, who was also its high priest, offered sacrifices to his father, an ancestral god (a man who became a god after his death), and asked for his blessings. In response, the ancestral god petitioned the strong gods to pour out their blessings on his relatives on the earth. After the son of an ancestral god died, he joined his father and became a god; his son now became the king and the high priest and offered sacrifices and prayers to his deceased father, who used his influence to secure blessings. The city built a

---

[239] James Ussher, *The Timechart of Biblical History*, Chippenham, England,Third Millennium Press Ltd., 2002.

hearth for the sacred fire, and the high priest offered sacrifices to the gods, supplicated them for blessings, and honored them with symbols, rituals, and feasts. I present this background information on Cain's religion and the religion that Nimrod put together at the Tower of Babel, along with my assumptions about Romulus's religious convictions, to offer insight into why Augustus built eighty-two temples in Rome.

Chapter 29

The Religion Of Romulus And Remus

The Pontifex Maximus

Augustus was the supreme commander of the Roman army. In times of war, Rome's provinces had to supply her with men whom she could equip and train in order to replenish her legions. Hence Augustus commanded the largest, most powerful military on earth. Moreover, Augustus had tribunician and proconsular powers; thus he had the power to direct all the affairs of domestic and foreign administration.[240] This meant that Augustus was in complete control of the government, economy, and military; however, Augustus did not have absolute power. The people of Rome knew that there was a spirit realm that interacted with the material realm and that the gods empowered the rulers ("mighty men") who courted them with sacrifices and worship. Augustus needed the endorsement of the heavenly gods in order to have absolute power on earth.

Well, as providence would have it, Augustus had a direct line to the gods. Julius Caesar was a descendant of the goddess Venus.[241] Caesar was also closely related to Romulus,[242] who was the son of the god Mars and the father of the city; he was the first king-high priest, who died and became the god Quirinus. Right before Caesar died, he bequeathed his office to Augustus, which meant that he adopted him as a son. After Caesar died, the Senate recognized him as a god and added his image to the pantheon of strong celestial gods who ruled all the other gods.

In 44 BC, Julius Caesar passed the office of emperor to Augustus, and in 13 BC, the man who occupied the office of high priest (Lepidus) died, so now Augustus could take his

---

[240] http://www.roman-emperors.org/auggie.htm, p. 12. [03/2011]

[241] http://www.unrv.com/fall-republic/gaius-julius-caesar.php. [03/2011]

[242] http://www.britannica.com/EBchecked/topic/88114/Julius-Caesar. [03/2011]

rightful position as the high priest, or pontifex maximus (the chief bridge-builder between god and man). The transition to absolute power was now complete. Like Cain, Nimrod, and Romulus before him, Augustus was now a king (emperor) and a high priest, and he controlled the political system, the economic system, and the religious system and was predestined to become a god! In 2 BC, the Roman Senate gave Augustus the title of *Pater Patriae*, "Father of the Country."

Projecting the Right Image

Rome was the seat of the emperor's power, and Alexandria was his personal possession. Both cities were reflections of the emperor and his power; that is, his ability to rule the empire. Essentially, Rome was his western capital, and Alexandria was his eastern capital. If both cities were peaceful, stable, and prosperous, then the provinces knew that they were safe and secure, and the outside world knew not to mess with the empire. Rome and Alexandria had to remain peaceful, stable, and prosperous in order to keep the provinces in line and project an image that repelled foreign enemies and discouraged internal ones. In short, the emperor secured peace by projecting an image of overwhelming strength. So naturally, the emperor used every available resource to keep the cities of Rome and Alexandria peaceful, stable, and prosperous.

Cultivating Loyalty, Unity, and Strength

The Roman army stood behind the emperor, but it was an oppressive, destructive force. The Roman military machine was extremely effective at setting geographical, sociological, cultural, and behavioral boundaries for people through the threat of violence, destruction, and death, but it was unable to change their hearts and minds and cultivate a sense of loyalty in them.

The emperor's changes brought peace and prosperity to the Roman Empire, but a citizen's emotional response to peace and prosperity cultivated a loyalty that was superficial and transitory. This loyalty was not bedrock that the emperor could build on. This loyalty was contingent on a citizen's subjective perceptions of peace and prosperity, which were transitory.

The emperor needed to tap into something deeper than the emotions that a citizen's soul generated when the emperor threatened it with violence, destruction, or death, or promised it peace and prosperity. The emperor needed to tap into something deeper that would deposit a layer of bedrock loyalty in the hearts of the people of his empire and bring them into unity, because unity maximizes strength. Remember, the emperor's primary goal was to protect his empire by making sure that his capitals projected an image of stability and strength that would discourage his domestic enemies and repel his foreign ones. So what is deeper than soulish emotions?

The emperor knew that man had three components: body, soul, and spirit. He also knew that his body and soul were simply temporal agents of his eternal spirit. Moreover, the emperor knew that if he could control the spirits of the people in his empire, he could control their hearts and minds and deposit a bedrock loyalty that would bring unity and strength to his empire.

An Umbrella Institution

The emperor needed to bring the people in his empire into spiritual unity. There was a problem, however. The beliefs and practices of the people in his empire were extremely diverse. In those days, every city had its own gods and religious practices, and there were thousands of cities in the empire. The emperor's task was somewhat simplified by the fact that many of the gods came from Mount Olympus, which narrowed the field to about two hundred gods. Still, how could the emperor possibly bring the congregants of two hundred religions into spiritual unity?

Well, the first step was to place a renewed emphasis on spiritual matters and pious living, which is exactly why Augustus built or rebuilt eighty-two temples in the city of Rome. The next step was to bring the diverse religions together underneath an *umbrella institution* that allowed them to keep their gods, dogmas, rituals, and feasts as long as they submitted to the leadership of the powerful quasi-governmental umbrella institution and its gods, dogmas, rituals, and feasts.

Once the religions were in the Roman institution, they lost control of their gods. The Roman institution integrated the gods into its pantheon. Jupiter ruled the pantheon, so the other gods became subservient to him and his high priest (the emperor). The objective of the Roman umbrella institution was not to replace or eliminate religions, but to bring their people together "on the plains of Shinar" and unify them with a mixture of "iron" (military power) and "clay" (religion) to achieve the emperor's goal. Since the emperor was the son of one of the strong gods (Julius Caesar) and the pontifex maximus (the high priest), he had a direct line to heaven and hence absolute power on the earth. In sum, the *Imperial Cult* enabled the emperor to exercise absolute control over his empire. If people wanted to get to the gods, then they had to go through the emperor; thus he was in command of religion, government, and the economy.

The Imperial Cult

The emperor erected statues of himself and his ancestors in the temples in order to identify himself with all the different gods and religions. On special occasions, the emperor would offer sacrifices to his ancestors and the other gods so they would bless the empire with a military victory or peace and prosperity. The emperor appointed priests to conduct regular services in the temples. These regular priests offered animal sacrifices, poured out libations, served ritual cakes, burned incense, conducted elaborate ceremonies, and officiated at feasts.

In Rome and the western provinces, the priests usually offered sacrifices to the gods *on behalf of the emperor*, but occasionally they offered sacrifices *to the emperor*, which indicated that he was a god or at least that he would become one when he died. The deity of the emperor was a touchy subject in Rome and the western provinces. The emperors did not want to be associated with the divine kings because the people had overthrown them, or with the god-man Julius Caesar because the people had assassinated him. Understandably, the emperors did not want to share in the fate of either the divine kings or Julius Caesar, so they came up with a somewhat ambiguous compromise: the emperor's will (*numen*), or his essence (*genius*), was divine.[243]

The eastern provinces had been Greek city-states that began as independent entities that formulated their own civic cult, but when the Macedonians defeated them and forced them into the league, they adopted their gods. The Greeks believed that the Macedonians overpowered them because their gods overpowered the Greek gods. The Greeks also believed that the men who defeated them were agents of the strong gods or related to them, so they worshiped the gods by worshiping the men. The emperor's deity was not a stumbling block for these people.

In 336 BC, Alexander of Macedon took control of the League of Corinth and conquered all the territories in Asia Minor that later became the eastern provinces of the Roman Empire. Alexander conquered these territories and "encouraged" them to adopt the Greek gods, religion, and worldview. Consequently, the people in the eastern provinces of the Roman Empire certainly saw nothing wrong with offering sacrifices to the gods on behalf of the emperor, or even offering sacrifices to the living emperor, his family, his deceased ancestors, the city of Rome, or the Roman gods and the Greek gods; nor did the emperor object to these practices.[244]

In sum, Julius Caesar derived his authority from his unique relation to both the gods and man. Julius Caesar inherited his body of flesh from Romulus, who was Rome's founder, first king, and high priest. Julius Caesar inherited his spirit from the gods Venus and Mars, which proved that he was a god-man with the unique right to rule the empire. Nevertheless, his own received him not and put him to death. Julius Caesar bequeathed his spirit to

---

[243] http://www.roman-emperors.org/auggie.htm; p. 20, [03/2011], Garrett G. Fagan, Pennsylvania State University.

[244] S. R. F. Price, *Rituals and Power*, Cambridge, UK, Cambridge University Press, 1984, pp. 25–30.

his adopted son, giving him the power to rise to an exalted position, and gave him a name above all others; that is, Augustus.

If a person believed that Augustus was the son of a god (Julius Caesar) and confessed him as lord, then that person entered a body of believers (the Imperial Cult) who worshiped and served him as he established his kingdom that would subdue the nations and bless them with peace and prosperity. This is exactly what happened when Jupiter (Marduk) and Venus (Semiramis) begot Tammuz, and he set up his kingdom in Babylon. Evidently Tammuz's spirit (the spirit of anti-Messiah) anointed Romulus, and he anointed Julius Caesar, and he anointed Augustus so that he could rebuild the Tower of Babel and reestablish Cain's religion with its political and economic systems that kept people comfortably separated from Yahweh so that they would not repent.

Pax Romana

The Imperial Cult was integral in the development of the Roman Empire because it accomplished what the military, political system, and economic system could not accomplish. Namely, it brought hundreds of different groups with different spiritual beliefs and religious practices into a spiritual unity that caused them to be loyal to the emperor and his empire.[245]

The Imperial Cult integrated the emperor and his ancestors into the various religions; thus the congregants of a religion had to honor the emperor, his family, his ancestors, and the city of Rome before they could honor their gods with sacrifice, ritual, food, drink, and athletic competition. This common thread (the worship of the emperor, his family, his ancestors, and the city of Rome) wove the colorful, irregular patches of society (the different groups and their religions) into a beautiful quilt that kept the people of the Roman Empire safe and warm.[246]

The Imperial Cult brought unity out of diversity while preserving diversity. It linked the emperor, his family, his ancestors, and Rome to the peace, prosperity, and strength of the empire and transformed the emperor into a messiah. The citizens of the Roman Empire called this anti-Messiah the living god, lord, son of god, great high priest, and savior of the world![247]

---

[245] Martin Goodman, *Rome and Jerusalem: The Clash of Ancient Civilizations*, New York, NY, Random House, 2007, p. 66.

[246] http://www.philipharland.com/publications/articleAHB.html, p. 103. [04/2011]

[247] Tom Thatcher, *Greater Than Caesar*, Minneapolis, MN, Fortress Press, 2009, p. 136.

The Imperial Cult brought a hundred million people with differing beliefs into spiritual unity and laid down a bedrock loyalty that was unshakable.[248] The people in the Imperial Cult were fiercely loyal to the emperor, his family, his ancestors, the capital city, and the empire. The Imperial Cult charged the atmosphere with a strong flux field of patriotism that greatly potentiated the dangers of public dissent, and the people who dared to disrupt this strong flux field by opposing the emperor's policies paid a horrible price for their disloyalty and rebellion. Thus the Imperial Cult restrained public dissent and kept the empire's internal enemies in check.

In Rome, the Imperial Cult generated an especially intense flux field of patriotism that radiated outwardly into all the provinces. In response, the provinces established cities that were miniature versions of Rome and tried to imitate her. Moreover, a massive military machine with a voracious appetite for blood and booty patrolled the borders of the empire. Thus the outside world saw a strong, unified people who had favor with the strong gods and an army that stood ready with great anticipation to bring vengeance upon anyone who dared to violate her borders.

Remember, an ancient city was a religious institution that put together its own political system and economic system to bring the favor of the gods to the earth for its citizens. This means that when the ancients saw an empire with a strong capital, a network of provincial cities that reflected its image, and a powerful military, they saw a people who had favor with the gods. The ancients knew that if they attacked this empire, they would be attacking the strong gods, and this proved to be a powerful deterrent that kept the empire's foreign enemies in check.

To the Romans, there was one city (Rome), and they set out to build a religion with a political system and an economic system that would slowly spread across the whole earth and bring all the nations into this city.[ix] The emperor's Imperial Cult led Rome into an age of unprecedented peace and prosperity that historians call the age of *Pax Romana*, which is Latin for the "Age of Roman Peace." The Pax Romana spanned a period of about two hundred years. It began sometime around 27 BC and ended sometime around AD 180.

---

[248] William Halliday, *History of Roman Religion*, Liverpool, UK, University Press of Liverpool, 1922, p. 175.

Chapter 30

The Context Of Romans

A Key to Ecclesiology, Eschatology, and Recovery

The social dynamics and culture of the Roman Empire acted as a corrosive agent that dissolved the barriers between different philosophies and religions so that they could be absorbed into one system. The Imperial Cult played a pivotal role in bringing people into this all-inclusive system. The Imperial Cult allowed everyone to worship the gods that appealed to them, just as long as they worshiped the emperor, his family, his ancestors, and Rome. The Imperial Cult curried favor from the strong gods so that they would bless the empire and protect it from its enemies. The Imperial Cult helped the emperor maintain peace and stability in Rome and Alexandria and thus project an image of strength to the provinces and the outside world.

If we will read the book of Romans in context, while considering the information that is in the book of Galatians, then we will accurately interpret it. This is important because the book of Romans represents the apex of the apostolic writings and contains the key to understanding what the ekklesia is (ecclesiology) and how Yah will glorify it to bring about the end of the age (eschatology). The book of Romans also contains the keys that will enable us to recover from the Adamic nature with its compulsions, obsessions, and addictions and live the abundant life.

The Earthly Jerusalem Submits to Rome

In 63 BC, Pompey captured Jerusalem. Normally, when a Roman general conquered a city, he offered sacrifices to the gods of the city and invited them to switch sides. The Roman general invited the weaker gods to join the stronger gods and receive better wor-

The Context Of Romans

ship in Rome.[249] Without fail, the Roman generals returned to Rome with a statue of a new god. The Romans added the new god to the roster of state gods and built a temple for it. Historians often say that in Rome there were more gods than there were men. Jerusalem was another story, however.

The Romans knew that they would have to kill everyone in Jerusalem in order to offer a sacrifice to Yah in the temple. The Romans also knew that Yah accepted sacrifices only from Levitical priests and that there was no statue of Him. The Romans forced the Jews to offer daily sacrifices to Yah on the emperor's behalf as a sign that they submitted to Rome. Really, the Romans were courting Yah in the hope that He would abandon the Jews and move to Rome.

General Pompey returned to Rome with a large number of Jewish prisoners to sell to the patricians as slaves. However, the Romans soon discovered that it was extremely hard to keep a Jewish slave. The Jewish slaves insisted on keeping the traditions of their fathers. Among other things, they refused to eat the typical diet or work on the Sabbath (the seventh day). The Romans quickly manumitted large numbers of Jewish slaves. After the Romans had freed their Jewish slaves, the former slaves formed their own community on the far side of the Tiber River.[250]

The Sovereignty of God Intersects with the Will of Man

The Jewish community in Rome prospered and became an indispensable part of the economy. Since Jews were a vital part of the economy and had supported Caesar during the civil war, the emperor allowed them to worship Yahweh and keep the traditions of their fathers. The emperor exempted Jews from military service, certain taxes, Sabbath labor, and Caesar worship. The emperor gave the Jews jurisdiction over their community.[251] The Jews took advantage of their privileges and insulated themselves from the corrosive forces that could dissolve their identity and culture. The Jews built a state within a state, and the people of Rome resented it.

Jews refused to fellowship with Romans, eat the meat in the markets, or celebrate the holy days (holidays) that honored the gods, the emperor, his family, his ancestors, and Rome. In essence, the Jews stepped into the flux field of patriotism and induced powerful eddy currents of anger that caused the Romans to hate them and view them with suspicion. The Romans kept an eye on the Jews and tried to catch them violating a law so the gov-

---

[249] Martin Goodman, *Rome and Jerusalem: The Clash of Ancient Civilizations*, New York, NY, Random House, 2007, p. 431.

[250] George Edmundson, *The Church in Rome in the First Century*, London, Longmans, Green and Co., 1913, p. 3.

[251] Ibid., pp. 3–4.

ernment could punish, expel, or execute them. Since Jews would not eat with Romans or worship their gods, the Romans called them "haters of man" and "atheists." However, the Jewish lifestyle appealed to a few Romans, and they repented and became God-fearers or proselytes and worshiped Yah in the synagogues.

The emperor could have infused more resources into the economy, refused to honor the Jews' loyalty to his father, and kicked them out of the empire. Why did the emperor give the Jews so many privileges and let them build a city within a city that divided the people and endangered the welfare of the empire? This is where the sovereignty of God intersects with the will of man. Yah, foreseeing the birth of Yeshua's ekklesia, arranged things to ensure that the empire would give the synagogue an exemption from the state religion. Yah wanted the people in Yeshua's ekklesia to gather in the synagogues so that they could hear the Torah and share their faith with the Jews, God-fearers, and proselytes until the ekklesia could stand on its own two feet.

Expelled for the Sake of the Empire

Normally, the Romans could tolerate the Jews and their city within the city and be civil towards them, but occasionally the Romans lashed out at the Jews. In AD 19, a rich Roman woman became a proselyte. A Jewish scoundrel persuaded her to send an offering of purple and gold to the temple, but he and his associates spent her offering.[252] This angered the people of Rome, and they took advantage of the situation. The people of Rome used the theft as an excuse to release their pent-up anger on the Jewish community, and things got out of hand.

Since the emperor's primary objective was to keep Rome peaceful and stable in order to project an image of strength to the provinces and the outside world, he took drastic measures to restabilize it. Tiberius forced four thousand Jews to join the army and sent them to Sardinia to die. Tiberius told the Jewish community that they had to renounce their traditions or leave Rome.[253] Well, of course, most of the Jews refused to renounce their traditions, so Tiberius kicked them out of Rome; however, by the late twenties, the Jews were back and things had returned to normal.[254]

---

[252] William Whiston, *The Works of Josephus*, Peabody, MA, Hendrickson Publishers, Inc., 1987, Book 18:81–84.

[253] Michael Grant, *Tacitus: Annals*, London, Penguin Books, 1956, Book II:85.

[254] Martin Goodman, *Rome and Jerusalem: The Clash of Ancient Civilizations*, New York, NY, Random House, 2007, p. 369.

The First Ghetto

In Alexandria, the situation was much the same. The Jews occupied two of the five boroughs and built a temple where they worshiped according to their traditions.[255] The sages' rules, regulations, and laws separated the Jews from the Greeks and built a Jewish subculture in the city or, more accurately, built a wall that separated the Jews from the Greeks and created enmity between the two groups.[256] The enmity between the Jews and the Greeks resulted in frequent arguments that were very intense and periodic outbreaks of violence. In AD 37, Tiberius died, and Caligula took his place. Caligula tried to force everyone to worship him as a living god. The Greeks complied, but the Jews refused, increasing the tension between the two groups.[257]

In AD 38, Agrippa visited Alexandria. The pomp and circumstance of the Jewish king appalled the Greeks. The Greeks insulted Agrippa and demanded that the Jews erect statues of Caligula in the synagogues. Well, of course, this put the governor between a rock and a hard place. If the Roman governor complied with the Greeks' request, then the Jews would start a rebellion; but if he refused the Greeks' request, then he would have to explain to the emperor Caligula, who was insane, why he did not want to put up statues of him in the synagogues.

The Roman governor ordered the Jews to erect the statues of Caligula in the synagogues, and riots broke out. The Roman government rounded up the Jews and confined them in a small section of Alexandria (a ghetto), while the Greeks looted, ransacked, and destroyed their homes and stores.[258] The Roman rulers stood by and allowed the looting and destruction to go on as a way of dissipating the pent-up anger of the Greeks. The Jews sent ambassadors to the emperor Caligula to petition him for relief, and their humbleness persuaded him to grant their request.[259]

The Second Expulsion

In AD 49, Claudius expelled the Jews from Rome for a second time. The Roman historian Suetonius wrote, "Since Jews constantly made disturbances at the instigation of Chrestus, he [Claudius] expelled them from Rome."[260] The Scriptures also indicate that the

---

[255] Tom Thatcher, *Greater Than Caesar*, Minneapolis, MN, Fortress Press, 2009, p. 24.

[256] *The Hebrew-Greek Key Word Study Bible*, KJV, Ephesians 2:15–16.

[257] Tom Thatcher, *Greater Than Caesar*, Minneapolis, MN, Fortress Press, 2009, p. 24.

[258] http://www.livius.org/am-ao/antisemitism/antisemitism01.html#agrippa. [04/2011]

[259] Tom Thatcher, *Greater Than Caesar*, Minneapolis, MN, Fortress Press, 2009, p. 24.

[260] Martin Goodman, *Rome and Jerusalem: The Clash of Ancient Civilizations*, New York, NY, Random House, 2007, p. 370.

emperor expelled the Jews from Rome around this time.²⁶¹ Thus it is clear that the emperor Claudius expelled the Jews from Rome around AD 49, but it is not clear why he expelled them.

Some scholars think "Chrestus" was a reference to Christ and that the Jews who rejected Him were fighting with the Jews who accepted Him and thus destabilizing Rome. I do not agree with this reasoning, because at this point Yeshua's ekklesia was still a sect within Judaism that met in the synagogues. The people in Yeshua's ekklesia needed the synagogue because if they left it, the Romans would force them into the Imperial Cult. The leaders of the synagogues did not agree with the people in Yeshua's ekklesia and attempted to control them with threats and intimidation that sometimes escalated to violence, but surely both parties had enough sense to handle their disputes before they escalated into riots that the Romans would have to quash.

The Chrestus Question

It had been only twenty years since the emperor had kicked the Jews out of Rome over a religious issue. Moreover, it had been only ten years since the governor of Alexandria had thrown the Jews into a ghetto and stood by as they lost their homes and businesses over a religious issue. Surely the Jewish religious leaders would have handled their internal conflicts with the people who put their faith in the man who claimed to be the Messiah wisely and thus discreetly.

The social dynamics of Rome and Alexandria were not like the dynamics in the rest of the empire. The Jews were under a magnifying glass in these two cities. In AD 41, when Claudius became emperor, he wrote that the Jews were free to practice their religion, but he warned them not to interfere with the rights of other people to practice their religion.²⁶² Claudius prohibited Jews from meeting outside of the synagogues and closed down all the clubs and unruly taverns. The Jews were welcome to practice their religion as long as they did it orderly and discreetly.²⁶³

Chrestus was a common name. Therefore, it seems more probable that Chrestus was a Jew who got his people worked up until they lashed out at the Romans, and the Romans lashed back. If the emperor had expelled the Jews because of an internal dispute between a sect that believed that Yeshua was the Messiah and the sects that did not, surely the religious rulers would have studied the messianic sect and been able to explain why it was a heresy. However, ten years later, when the Roman authorities brought Paul to Rome,

---

[261] *The Hebrew-Greek Key Word Study Bible*, KJV, Acts 18:2.

[262] Martin Goodman, *Rome and Jerusalem: The Clash of Ancient civilizations*, New York, NY, Random House, 2007, p. 370.

[263] Ibid., p. 370.

The Context Of Romans

the Jewish religious leaders said they had heard of this sect but did not know much about it.[264] I believe it is more probable that the people who were in the two sects (the people who rejected Yeshua and the people who accepted Him) met in different sections of the synagogues, met at different times, or met in altogether different synagogues. This would be the wisest course of action in order to prevent the Roman government from taking the synagogue's exemption and rounding up the Jews to throw them into a ghetto, destroy their homes and businesses, or kick them out of the city again.

Another thing to consider is that Caligula was insane. Surely an insane emperor made some decisions that destabilized Rome. This would mean that when Claudius came to power, he had to clean up Caligula's mess in order to restabilize Rome. History tells us that Claudius got the people of Rome refocused on the gods and reinstituted many of the old practices.[265] I believe that Claudius was trying to propitiate the gods and gain their favor in an effort to restabilize Rome. I also believe that the trouble that Chrestus was causing gave Claudius an opportunity to rid Rome of the "atheists" who refused to worship the gods so that the gods would help him.

In sum, I believe that Chrestus was a Jew who took advantage of the issues between his people and the Romans to promote his own agenda for status or finances, and it got out of hand. Nevertheless, in Rome there were historical, cultural, sociological, and religious forces at work to separate the Jews who rejected Yeshua from the Jews who accepted Him. Once the Jews formed two sects in the synagogues, the Gentiles were free to join either sect. Some Gentiles joined the messianic sect, and some joined the other sect.

In AD 49, when Claudius kicked the Jews out of Rome, the Jews who believed in Yeshua left at the same time as the Jews who did not believe in Him. Thus Claudius's decree separated *the Jews* who believed that Yeshua was the Seed from *the Gentiles* who believed in Him. Yeshua had just torn down the dividing wall that had separated Jews and Gentiles, and this was the first brick that HaSatan laid to rebuild it!

---

[264] *The Hebrew-Greek Key Word Study Bible*, KJV, Acts 28:22.

[265] Martin Goodman, *Rome and Jerusalem: The Clash of Ancient Civilizations*, New York, NY, Random House, 2007, p. 370.

Part 8
Repositioning the Bookends

Chapter 31

Repositioning The Bookend Of Galatians

The Ekklesia and the Gates of Hell

In these last days, Yeshua's Spirit is giving His bride a desire to wash in the water of the Word. Yahweh's Word is washing away the paganism that has spotted His bride's garments. The Holy Spirit is beckoning us to return the bookend of Romans to its original position, but before we can do this, we have to reposition Galatians. So let us begin.

Paul wrote Galatians to keep the sages' teachings and traditions out of the ekklesia. The Galatian Gentiles believed that Yeshua was the Messiah, but the Judaizers were trying to convince them that they had to submit to circumcision and keep the written Torah, oral Torah, and legal halachah. If a person believed Yeshua was the Messiah, but trusted in the flesh (circumcision) and keeping the written Torah, oral Torah, and halachah, his belief in Yeshua did not save him. Moreover, if a *saint* believed that he had to submit to circumcision and keep the written Torah by keeping the oral Torah and halachah to be in right standing with Yah, His grace did not benefit him (he fell from grace).

The sages wanted to keep people out of the kingdom and to enslave the people who were in it. Paul wrote Galatians to keep the kingdom's gates open, the saints free, and the ekklesia strong. The fourth-century church theologians had Greco-Roman worldviews. These Gentiles despised Jews and wanted to rid the ekklesia of them and their Torah. These Gentiles were not familiar with the Jewish culture or with how a first-century Jew expressed theological concepts, so they interpreted the Scriptures with an anti-Semitic slant and wrote commentaries that generated strong emotions against legalism without accurately defining legalism. They confused keeping the Torah with the sages' legalism and turned Galatians into an argument against the Torah.

The Gentiles said that the Mosaic covenant was an instrument of bondage and cursing because Yahweh had told the Jews they had to keep the *whole Torah* or He would curse them. The Gentiles said Yeshua fulfilled the Torah, so we do not have to try to obey it and curse ourselves. They said the Mosaic covenant was the polar opposite of the new covenant. Sadly, the Gentile church dismissed the Torah, misinterpreted Romans, and opened the door for paganism.

Right before Yeshua went to the execution stake to tear down the dividing wall that His people had built to separate themselves from the Gentiles, He prayed that the Jews and Gentiles would be one so that His glory would flow through them in order to glorify the ekklesia and prove to the nations that He was the Seed.[266] However, by the fourth century, HaSatan had tricked the Gentiles into rebuilding a dividing wall between Jews and Gentiles so that he could separate the ekklesia from the written Torah and get her to adopt pagan ideologies, philosophies, and traditions.

This is ironic, but it was in Yah's plan. In Genesis, Joseph looked like an Egyptian, and his brothers did not recognize him; but at the right time, he took off his Gentile garb, revealing himself to his brothers. In Esther, Mordecai told Esther not to reveal her Hebrew roots so that she could position herself to fulfill her destiny; but at the right time, she embraced her Hebrew roots, and the king saved her people. Today Yeshua is taking off his Egyptian garb, revealing Himself to His brothers (the Jews), and Esther (the ekklesia) is embracing her Hebrew roots so that the King can save her people (the Jews) and glorify her so that Yeshua can return for her.

The Gentile Disguise

Today Yeshua is taking off His Gentile disguise and showing Himself to a remnant of Jews. Messianic Jews are providing valuable insights into the proper interpretation of the Scriptures. If we listen to messianics like Tim Hegg, Robert Gorelik, Curt Landry, and Sid Roth, we will gain insight into the Scriptures that will expose the paganism that we have embraced. The Torah is a preserving agent that has preserved the Jewish people over thousands of years as they dwelt in the nations, worshiping Yah in their homes on the Sabbath and keeping His feasts.

The Torah kept the Jewish culture alive so that when the time came, they could return to Israel, reestablish their culture in their own land, and set the stage for the return of the Messiah. Moreover, the Torah preserved the Jewish culture so that when the Jews returned to the ekklesia, they could teach the Gentiles about the Torah so that the bride could purify herself,[267] embrace her Hebrew roots, and fulfill her destiny. Like Esther, the ekklesia is embracing her roots and purifying herself so that the King will save the Jews, glorify the

---

[266] *The Hebrew-Greek Key Word Study Bible*, KJV, John 17:20–22; Romans 11:13–15; Ephesians 5:27.

[267] Ibid., Ephesians 5:26.

ekklesia, and the Messiah can return. Let us look at some of the insights that the messianic Jewish remnant has given the Gentiles.

The Religion of the Apostate Jews

The written Torah reveals Yahweh's nature. It reveals how Yah interacts with the material realm; thus the written Torah reveals how Yahweh's people are to interact with the material realm. Hence the written Torah is the standard of righteousness, and when we measure ourselves against it, we fall short. In other words, the written Torah identifies and reveals sin and lets us know that we are sinners. The written Torah is a schoolmaster that points us to the Messiah. The written Torah has always pointed to the Messiah, but the sages perverted the Torah's message to feed their pride and satisfy their lust for position, power, and monetary gain.

The sages invented a religion that was radically different from the patriarchs' way of life. The sages twisted the standard of righteousness that revealed sin and pointed to Messiah, turning it into rules, regulations, and laws that people had to obey before Yahweh would save them. The sages said that if individuals submitted to circumcision and then walked out the Torah by obeying their rules, regulations, and laws, then they were part of Israel; hence they were in the covenant and had a place in the world to come. However, if they did not submit to circumcision and then walk out the Torah by obeying the sages' rules, regulations, and laws, then they were not part of Israel; hence they were not in the covenant and would not enter the world to come.

The sages turned the Torah into a list of rules, regulations, and laws that defined who was and who was not a Jew. The sages defined a Jew as a person who had submitted to circumcision and walked out the written Torah by obeying *their* rules, regulations, and laws. Moreover, a Gentile was a person who had not submitted to circumcision and did not walk out the written Torah by obeying *their* rules, regulations, and laws. A person's ethnicity was the central issue. The sages said that all Jews were righteous and had a place in the world to come. The sages proclaimed an ethnic gospel that said Yahweh saved anyone who would submit to circumcision, keep the *whole Torah*, and become a Jew. This was convenient for the sages because the "whole Torah" was the written Torah and their interpretation and application of it. The sages had complete control over their captives, and they kept them bound in the chains of legalism.

Circumcision and the Torah

The sages taught that circumcision was the sign that a person had promised to obey the written Torah, oral Torah, and legal halachah. In Galatians 5:2–4, Paul said, "Behold, I Paul say unto you, that if ye be circumcised, Christ shall profit nothing. For I testify again to every man that is circumcised, that he is a debtor to do the whole law. Christ is become of no effect unto you, whosoever of you are justified by the law; ye are fallen from grace."[268] Paul was saying that if a reborn Gentile believed the Judaizers and submitted to circumcision as a sign that he promised to obey the written Torah, oral Torah, and halachah in order to become a Jew and be grafted into Israel and her covenants, then his actions proclaimed that Yeshua's sacrifice on the execution stake was pointless. Yeshua's grace would not benefit this person because the sages would enslave him. Sadly, Gentile theologians said that these verses prove that we should not try to obey the Torah, because if we obey one of its commandments, we will have to obey all of them; and since this is impossible to do, we will open ourselves to the curses for not obeying the whole Torah.

Under the Law and the Works of the Law

It is essential to realize that "linguistically, meaning is not an intrinsic possession of a word; rather, it is a set of relations for which a verbal symbol is a sign."[269] In other words, we do not determine the meaning of a word through etymology; we determine the meaning of a word through etymology and context. Simply put, if we know a word's origin and development, along with its historical, cultural, sociological, and theological use, then we know its meaning.

For example, translators translate the Hebrew word *Torah* into Greek as *nomos* and *nomos* into English as *law*. But *Torah* means "teaching" or "instruction," and *law* means a "statute." So depending on the context, *law* can mean a statute, or it can mean teaching and instruction and refer to Yah's teachings and instructions, or it can mean the law that Yah attached to His teachings and instructions at Sinai, or it can mean the sages' teaching and instructions in the oral Torah and halachah.[270]

The phrase *under the law* can indicate that a person is subject to the penalties of the law or that a person is trusting in circumcision, the written Torah, oral Torah, and halachah for covenant inclusion. In Galatians 3, Paul said that Abraham was justified by faith, and if the Gentiles followed his example, they too would be justified by faith. In verse 10, Paul anticipated the sages' objection and said, "For as many as are of the works of the law are under the curse: for it is written, Cursed is every one that continueth not in all things which are written in the book of the law to do them." Paul was saying that if the Gentiles followed the sages and put their trust in circumcision and keeping the written Torah, oral Torah, and halachah, they were under the curse.

---

[268] Ibid., Galatians 5:2–4.

[269] D. A. Carson, *Exegetical Fallacies*, Grand Rapids, MI, Baker Book House, 1993, p. 31.

[270] Tim Hegg, *Paul's Epistle to the Galatians*, 1st ed., Tacoma, WA, TorahResource, 2010, pp. 98–99.

Yah did not cut the Mosaic covenant so that people could obey the Torah and comply with its law in order to enter the Abrahamic covenant; He cut the Mosaic covenant with the people who were already in the Abrahamic covenant to show them how to live a blessed life. The sages refused to believe that people entered the covenant of redemption by faith and that the covenant of sanctification merely described the works that were necessary to walk out that faith; thus *they did not continue in all that Yahweh had written in the book of the law (the Torah) and were under the curse.*

The sages' desire for power and wealth blinded them to the parts of the Torah that proved that Yahweh justified Abraham by faith, and all they saw were the parts of the Torah that appealed to their fallen nature and allowed it to establish its own righteousness. In essence, the sages taught that the works of the flesh (circumcision) and the works of the law (doing the things that the law prescribed) brought people into the Abrahamic covenant (redemption) and kept them in it. The sages were trampling on Yeshua's blood, counting it as a worthless thing. Paul warned the Gentiles not to follow the sages and encouraged them to continue in all the Torah.

In essence, Paul told the Gentiles not to divide the Torah and pick what they liked. The Torah testified to the fact that Yahweh had condemned all those in HaSatan's kingdom and doomed them to eternal death, but if they would apply the blood of the Lamb to the doorposts of their heart, He would redeem them from HaSatan's kingdom and lift them out of eternal death. However, those who trampled on Yeshua's blood by putting their trust in circumcision and obeying the written Torah, oral torah, and halachah remained under the curse of eternal death.

Another problematic phrase is *the works of the law*. This phrase can refer to the works that Yah described in the five books of Moses, the works that Yahweh required to fulfill the legal code that He attached to the Torah at Sinai, or the works that the sages required to fulfill the written Torah, oral Torah, and legal halachah. In Galatians 3:2–3, Paul said, "This only would I learn of you, Received ye the Spirit by the works of the law, or by the hearing of faith? Are ye so foolish? having begun in the Spirit, are ye now made perfect by the flesh?" Paul was asking the Gentiles if they had received the Holy Spirit by being circumcised and keeping the written Torah, oral Torah, and legal halachah, or by putting their faith in Yeshua as Messiah.

Paul let the Gentiles know that it was foolish for them to think that they could gain anything by cutting the skin off the end of their penis and submitting to the sages' ideas about how people were supposed to walk out the Torah, because Yah had already brought them into His kingdom by indwelling them. Yah's Spirit had sanctified the Gentiles and was leading them to walk out the Torah's intent. So what could the Gentiles gain by submitting to circumcision and striving to walk out the Torah the sages' way? Paul was not saying that when Yah gives His Spirit to people, they no longer need to obey the Torah. To the contrary,

Yah's Spirit empowers them to go beyond the letter of the Torah and fulfill its intent so that they live an abundant life.

In sum, Galatians is a polemic against the Judaizers and their perversion of the Torah. It is not a polemic against the Torah. Paul never said that those who obey Yah and His Torah are in bondage to legalism. Paul said that those who accept man's rules, regulations, and laws and strive to live by them in order to secure a place in Israel and partake of her covenants are in bondage. In other words, those who yoke themselves to man's religions by blindly accepting their interpretation and application of the Scriptures, obeying their rules, regulations, and laws so that Yah will accept them and bless them, are in bondage to legalism. A person who puts his faith in Yeshua is free. Yeshua's blood redeems us from HaSatan's kingdom and pays the penalty for our violation of the Torah, and His Spirit gives us eternal life, sanctifying us and giving us the ability to *live out the intent of the written Torah* so that we can live the abundant life.[x]

In the new covenant, the Spirit writes the Torah on our hearts and gives us the ability to live out its intent. What does this mean? Yahweh's Torah tells us how to love Him with all our heart, soul, and strength and how to love our neighbors as ourselves. Thus, if we follow Yah's Spirit, we will love Him with all our heart, soul, and strength and love our neighbors as ourselves. So if the Spirit is empowering us to walk out the intent of the Torah, is it wrong to let the Torah teach us how to love Yahweh and our neighbors? Is it wrong for a disciple of Yeshua to do the things that He taught in the Torah? No, Yahweh expects us to seek guidance from His Torah.

Chapter 32

Repositioning The Bookend Of Romans

Expelled from Rome

The book of Romans is the magnum opus of the apostolic writings. It gives us the key to ecclesiology (the study of the ekklesia), eschatology (the study of the end times), and recovery (recovering from the Adamic nature with its obsessions, compulsions, and addictions).

In AD 49, the emperor Claudius set out to restore the worship of Rome's older gods and reinvigorate the worship of her newer ones. No one knows why Claudius thought that this was necessary, but for some reason, he wanted to be sure he did not withhold worship and sacrifice from any of the gods that watched over Rome. Evidently Claudius perceived a grave danger and needed to be sure that he had propitiated all the gods so that they would bless the Roman Empire.

If a person refused to worship the gods, then the gods could get angry and punish Rome. Hence it was against the law not to worship the gods. Julius Caesar gave the Jews an exemption from this law. Claudius, however, was serious about making sure that no one in Rome offended the gods and caused them to withhold their blessings from his empire. Claudius needed to find some way to get rid of the Jews, until he got things right with the gods, without dishonoring his spiritual father (Julius Caesar) by revoking their privileges. When Claudius heard that a Jew named Chrestus was causing trouble, he used him as an excuse to expel the Jews from Rome.

The Parting of the Ways

As I stated above, it was illegal not to worship the gods, but Julius Caesar had given the synagogues an exemption, so the Jews and their converts did not have to worship the gods. It was also illegal to start a new religion in Rome. These two political realities forced Yeshua's ekklesia to meet in the synagogues with nonbelievers. In one of the Roman synagogues, there was a Jewish couple named Aquila and Priscilla. Aquila and Priscilla accepted Yeshua and became close friends with the other Jews and Gentiles who had accepted Him. When Claudius issued his decree to expel the Jews, Aquila and Priscilla had to pack their bags and leave Rome. Aquila and Priscilla knew that when they left, the Romans would close the synagogues, and their Gentile brothers would have no place to meet. Aquila and Priscilla loved Yeshua, so they gave their home to their Gentile brothers so that they would have a place to worship Him.

Now remember, in that culture, if a person kept the written Torah by keeping the oral Torah and halachah, then, by definition, he was Jewish. After the Jews left Rome, the Gentiles discarded the written Torah along with the oral Torah and the halachah so that the government would not label them as Jews and expel them. *The Gentile believers parted ways with the traditions of the Jews and started meeting in private homes.*[271] The Gentiles had to be very cautious because if the Roman government found out that they were not worshiping their gods and were worshiping instead the God of the Jews, they would imprison, expel, or execute them.

Paganism Takes Root

The Romans believed that the age of a religion validated it. Since the Yeshua sect worshiped a Jewish man and was relatively new, it was especially distasteful to the Romans.[272] To the Romans, the ekklesia was an illegal cult that worshiped a Jewish man and refused to bow to the emperor. Yeshua's ekklesia declared that He was Lord and Savior. Yeshua's ekklesia believed that He would establish His kingdom on earth and bring peace and prosperity to it. The ekklesia in Rome kept a low profile, and it was almost as if they were *ashamed of the gospel*.

The ekklesia in Rome grew slowly. The only Scripture the ekklesia in Rome possessed was the Tanakh, and since the Jews were no longer there to teach them how to interpret it, they had to rely on their intellect and the Spirit. The saints in Rome had spent their whole lives worshiping the gods and building their worldviews on the shifting sands of paganism with its ideologies, philosophies, and traditions. The saints in Rome filtered the Tanakh and the Spirit's promptings through their pagan worldviews and planted the seeds of paganism in the ekklesia.

---

[271] Robert Wilken, *The Christians as the Romans Saw Them*, London, Yale University Press, 1984, pp. 112–13.

[272] Ibid., p. 122.

After a few years, the Jews started trickling back into Rome. In AD 54, Nero reversed Claudius's expulsion decree.[273] As the Jews returned to Rome, those who believed sought out the homes where the Gentile believers met, and those who did not believe returned to the synagogues. The Jewish believers discovered that the Gentile believers no longer kept the Torah and had their own interpretations of the Tanakh. The Gentiles believed that Yah had rejected the Jews and accepted them in their place.[274] Jews had a hard time reintegrating into the ekklesia.

As long as the ekklesia did not cause any trouble, the government overlooked it. The synagogues were careful not to cause any trouble because they did not want the government to put them in a ghetto or expel them again. The ekklesia kept to itself, and the synagogue kept to itself. If a synagogue member decided to become a believer, he migrated from the synagogue to the ekklesia, and the religious rulers did not protest or cause trouble. In Rome, the synagogue and the ekklesia separated and began to develop into two distinct entities. Yahweh needed to correct some doctrinal issues in the Roman ekklesia and bring the Gentiles down a few pegs, while nipping in the bud the ethnic pride of the Jews, in order to bring the two groups together. In AD 55, Paul wrote a letter to reground the Romans and give them instructions on how to build the *one new man*; that is, a congregation of Jews and Gentiles that was one in Yeshua.[275]

So why did Paul write Romans? The Roman ekklesia was full of Gentiles who had just come out of the Imperial Cult and the worship of celestial bodies, nature, and fertility gods. Now, most of these Gentile believers had assembled in the synagogues with the Jews, and the Jews had introduced the Gentiles to the written Torah. However, after the expulsion of the Jews, it was dangerous to appear Jewish, so the Gentiles distanced themselves from the Jews and stopped keeping the written Torah. The Gentiles formulated doctrines that were similar to the doctrines of the Imperial Cult and superimposed paganism onto the worship of Yeshua. The Gentiles became proud and came to believe that they had replaced Israel.[276]

After the Jews returned to the Roman ekklesia, they had to defend their heritage and the written Torah. Some of the Jews went too far and began to boast of their superiority as a Jew. Paul had to correct the doctrinal issues and put everyone on a level playing field to ensure that no one rebuilt the dividing wall and destroyed the one new man.

---

[273] Neil Elliott, *The Arrogance of Nations*, Minneapolis, MN, Fortress Press, 2008, p. 91.
[274] Ibid., pp. 108–109.
[275] *The Hebrew-Greek Key Word Study Bible*, KJV, Ephesians 2:15–16.
[276] Neil Elliott, *The Arrogance of Nations*, Minneapolis, MN, Fortress Press, 2008, pp. 109–111.

Distorting Romans

The letter to the Galatians protected the ekklesia from the influences of the Judaizers. The Judaizers wanted to get the people in the ekklesia to keep the written Torah by obeying the rules, regulations, and laws in the oral Torah and the legal halachah. If the Judaizers could get the people in the ekklesia to believe that they had to keep the written Torah by keeping the oral Torah and the legal halachah in order to be a member of the covenant community and partake of the covenants, then they could keep their positions and control the ekklesia.

The sacrifice of Yeshua flew in the face of the Judaizers. Yeshua's blood sanctified believers. Yeshua's Spirit indwelled believers and proved that they had entered the covenant. Yeshua's Spirit showed believers how they were to walk out the written Torah. Believers were to follow Yeshua, not the sages!

Fourth-century church theologians failed to realize that Galatians was a polemic against people having to submit to circumcision and keep the written Torah by obeying the rules, regulations, and laws in the oral Torah and halachah to obtain Jewish legal status so Yah would bring them into the covenant and the age to come. The Gentiles thought Galatians was a polemic against keeping the Torah and superimposed this misunderstanding onto Romans, distorting it.

A Different Situation

In Rome, Yeshua's ekklesia separated from the synagogue. The ekklesia and the synagogue were two separate entities.[277] The Judaizers were familiar with the situation, but they knew better than to stir up trouble in Rome. The synagogues did everything they could do to not give the government a reason to put them in a ghetto or expel them again. The sages knew where Yeshua's ekklesia met, but they did not "rat them out" because of the large number of Jews in their meetings. The sages knew that if the Romans caught a large number of Jews in these illegal assemblies, it would be disastrous. The people in the illegal assemblies refused to worship the emperor, but worshiped a Jewish man and bowed to Him as Lord and Savior while promoting His kingdom. If the Romans raided the illegal assemblies, they would probably put the Jews in a ghetto or expel them again. Hence the Judaizers were not a problem in Rome.

Paul wrote Romans to correct a Gentile ekklesia that rejected their Hebrew roots and formulated doctrines by filtering Yeshua through their pagan worldviews.[278] Galatians pro-

---

[277] Ben Witherington, *Paul's Letter to the Romans*, Grand Rapids, MI, Eerdmans Publishing Co., 2004, p. 14.

[278] Neil Elliott, *The Arrogance of Nations*, Minneapolis, MN, Fortress Press, 2008, p. 20.

tected the ekklesia from the religion the Jews invented, and Romans protected it from the religions the Gentiles invented. All the other books in the apostolic writings must fit between these two bookends.

Gentile interpreters treat chapters 1–8 of Romans as the main point, chapters 9–11 as a theological afterthought, and chapters 12–15 as a potpourri of unrelated ethical exhortations, but this is a major mistake.[279] Chapters 1–11 tell what humans have done in their fallenness and how Yah has responded in Messiah. Chapters 12–15 tell what the believers in Rome ought to do because of what Yah has done.[280] Chapters 9–11 are the climax of the letter that defends Yahweh, Israel, and His Word and refutes the idea that He has rejected Israel and the Jews.[281]

---

[279] Ben Witherington, *Paul's Letter to the Romans*, Grand Rapids, MI, Eerdmans Publishing Co., 2004, p. 48.
[280] Ibid., p. 50.
[281] Ibid., p. 237.

Part 9

A Survey of Romans: We All Have Fallen

Chapter 33

Romans 1:1–3:20

Verses 1:1–17

Paul begins his letter by introducing himself and establishing his credentials. In verses 16 and 17, he gives his thesis statement: "For I am not ashamed of the gospel of Christ: for it is the power of God unto salvation to every one that believeth; to the Jew first, and also to the Greek. For therein is the righteousness of God revealed from faith to faith: as it is written, The just shall live by faith." In other words, as Jews or Gentiles believe the gospel of Yeshua, Yah declares them righteous, and that righteousness manifests in their lives, as they live by faith, in order to uphold and reveal His righteousness. In the body of his letter, Paul unpacks this thesis statement and explains how Yah makes a sinner righteous and inspires him to live by faith so that the righteousness that He imputes to him manifests in his life in order to uphold His righteousness. Paul closes his letter by explaining what righteousness looks like in real life.

The phrase *the just shall live by faith* is from Habakkuk. Yah told Habakkuk He was going to allow the Chaldeans to punish Judah for her sins, and Habakkuk questioned His righteousness. Yah told him that the punishment of the unrighteous and the salvation of the righteous would not happen instantly, but it would happen. Yah said that those who lifted up their souls and refused to believe His report would perish, but those who were just would believe His report and live by faith.[282] Paul is saying that those who believe the gospel will escape Yah's wrath and live by faith to reveal His righteousness, but those who do not believe the gospel will perish. In the next eleven chapters, Paul discusses the nature of faith

---

[282] Tim Hegg, *Paul's Epistle to the Romans*, Tacoma, WA, TorahResource, 2005, p. 24.

and faithfulness: Yah's faithfulness in Messiah to the Jews, Yah's impartiality towards Jews and Gentiles, and human faith and faithfulness.[283]

Verses 1:18–32

In these verses, Paul brings the Gentiles down a few pegs by giving them a history lesson. Paul tells how Yahweh's wrath came on the Gentiles because they once knew Him but turned away from Him to worship idols. This section has many parallels to texts in which the Jews criticized the Gentiles for their sins.[284] Interpreters think this section alludes to the fall of man, the apostasy that caused the flood, or perhaps what happened at the Tower of Babel. Regardless of what Paul was alluding to, his message was that the Gentiles have no reason to glory because they and their ancestors were idolaters who worshiped the celestial bodies, nature, and fertility gods.

The Gentiles could not deny Paul's indictment. The temples of their ancestors littered the landscape of Rome. Every day they had to pass by these temples and try to avoid the prostitutes and homosexuals who ministered in them, trying to lure them in to worship their gods. Paul destroyed any illusion the Gentiles had about being more worthy than the Jews. Paul painted a picture that made it abundantly clear that the Gentiles deserved to experience Yah's wrath.

Verses 2:1–16

In this section, Paul uses a teaching method called a *diatribe* (a dialogue with an imaginary disputant). By using the diatribe technique, Paul can discriminate undesirable attitudes or sentiments through a fictive device without directly confronting (and possibly alienating) his real audience, but if we do not realize that he is using this technique, we will misinterpret this section.[285] This is why scholars do not agree on whether Paul addressed this section to Jews or to Gentiles. Some think Paul was dealing with the pagans who lived moral lives and did not commit the sins named in the previous section.[286] Others think he was addressing Jews. Both opinions are viable, but I believe he was addressing the moral pagans. Paul was telling the moral pagans that they deserved Yah's wrath and had no right to judge the Jews.

---

[283] Ben Witherington, *Paul's Letter to the Romans*, Grand Rapids, MI, Eerdmans Publishing Co., 2004, p. 47.

[284] D. A. Carson, *New Bible Commentary*, 4th ed., Downers Grove, IL, InterVarsity Press, 1994.*

[285] Ben Witherington, *Paul's Letter to the Romans*, Grand Rapids, MI, Eerdmans Publishing Co., 2004, pp. 75–76.

[286] Warren W. Wiersbe, *The Bible Exposition Commentary*, Wheaton, IL, Victor Books, 1996, Romans 2:1.*

Verses 2:17–29

In this section, Paul turns his attention to the *religious* Jew. In our review of Galatians, we saw that Paul was not against the Torah; he was against the misuse of the Torah. It is not the pursuit of the Torah or even relying on it as revealing the truth about Yah's heart that Paul casts in a negative light, but rather pursuing the Torah apart from faith.[287] The sages read the Torah and invented the oral Torah and halachah to prevent their sheep from breaking any of its commands. However, they ended up inventing a *religion* that said that if people kept the written Torah by obeying the oral Torah and halachah, they were Abraham's seed and heirs to the covenant.

The sages' interpretations of the Torah became more important than the Torah itself. The sages' rulings often contradicted the Torah by allowing things it forbade and forbidding things it allowed. The sages made up rules, regulations, and laws that turned the Torah into a heavy burden that crushed people. Paul says that the sages taught what the Torah said about stealing, but their rulings allowed them to steal by loaning money and collecting interest. The sages also taught that adultery was wrong, but their rulings allowed them to send their wives away without giving them a bill of divorce, which caused others to commit adultery by marrying them. The sages taught about forsaking idolatry and everything that idols polluted, but their rulings created loopholes that allowed them to accept donations stolen from pagan temples.[288]

The apostate sages said that people were Jews (righteous) if they submitted to circumcision and kept the written Torah by obeying the oral Torah and legal halachah. However, the apostle Paul said that Hebrews were Jews (righteous) if they circumcised their hearts; that is, if they responded to Yahweh's love, put their faith in His promises, and obeyed the written Torah. Paul said that if an uncircumcised Gentile circumcised his heart; that is, if he responded to Yahweh's love, put his faith in His promises and obeyed the written Torah, Yahweh counted his uncircumcision as circumcision (counted him as righteous). Moreover, if circumcised Hebrews failed to circumcise their hearts, Yahweh counted their circumcision as uncircumcision (counted them as unrighteous).

By the time we arrive at the end of this section, there is no room for Gentile or Jewish boasting about ethnic or moral superiority because all stand in need of grace, and Paul has laid the groundwork to present salvation by grace through faith in Yeshua.[289]

---

[287] Tim Hegg, *Paul's Epistle to the Romans*, Tacoma, WA, TorahResource, 2005, p. 50.

[288] Ibid., pp. 51–53.

[289] Ben Witherington, *Paul's Letter to the Romans*, Grand Rapids, MI, Eerdmans Publishing Co., 2004, p. 89.

Verses 3:1–8

After Paul rebukes his Jewish brothers for their hypocrisy, he anticipates the questions that his readers would ask: If the pious Gentile and the pious Jew both stand in need of Yeshua's mercy and grace, then what was Yah's purpose for the nation of Israel and the Jews? Did Jews have any advantage over Gentiles? Paul answers by saying that Jews had an advantage over Gentiles because Yahweh gave them His oracles that showed them how to live. Paul was referring to Yah redeeming His people from slavery and coming down to give them the Torah at Mount Sinai. The Torah was the foundational revelation of Yahweh and His instructions, and all other revelations had to line up with it. Rather than seeing the written Torah as a burden that Israel had to bear, Paul saw Yahweh's self-revelation in the written Torah as Israel's greatest treasure.[290]

Paul said that some of the people in Israel did not believe Yah, circumcise their hearts, put their faith in the Seed, and obey the Torah. Instead, these people circumcised their penises and then tried to walk out the written Torah by obeying the oral Torah and legal halachah. Here was Paul's question: if some of Abraham's offspring did not believe Yah and trust Him and instead invented a false religion, did this mean that He would not keep the covenant that He cut with Abraham?

Paul said that even if everyone in Israel yielded to the fallen nature and became a liar by teaching the Abrahamic covenant but not keeping it, Yahweh would still keep His covenant. So, if Israel's unrighteousness highlighted Yahweh's faithfulness and accentuated His righteousness, was it right for Him to punish her? I mean, human logic says that if disobedience glorifies Yahweh, then disobey more and give Him more glory! This is exactly what the sages accused Paul of doing when he taught that the Gentiles did not have to submit to circumcision or keep the written Torah by obeying the rules, regulations, and laws in the oral Torah and legal halachah. The sages accused Paul of promoting lawlessness as a way of glorifying Yahweh. This is not as outlandish as it may seem. Have you ever heard some people say that they do not have to obey Yahweh's commands because they are not under the law, but under grace? The people who say this are trying to glorify Yahweh by disobeying Him, and Paul says that these people do not know Him.

Verses 3:9–20

In verse 9, Paul says, "What then? are we better than they?" This is what Paul is getting at. Yah cut a covenant with Abraham, and He will move heaven and earth to keep it. However, just because a person is a child of Abraham (a Jew), does that mean that he possesses a righteousness that sets him above the Gentiles and ensures that Yah will find him

---

[290] Tim Hegg, *Paul's Epistle to the Romans*, Tacoma, WA, TorahResource, 2005, p. 60.

not guilty? No, Paul says that he has already proven that both Jews and Gentiles are fallen creatures who live in sin. On judgment day, Jews and Gentiles will stand before Yahweh, and He will find them both guilty.

Paul gives some scriptures to prove his point. Paul says that the written Torah and its law was given to Israel to point out her sin and her inability to rise above it so that she would acknowledge her guilt and seek the Promised Seed and His righteousness. Moreover, when Israel acknowledged her guilt, the whole world would realize they were guilty too. In sum, Yahweh gave the Torah and its law to reveal man's sin and his inability to rise above it so that he would humble himself and seek the Promised Seed and His righteousness. He did not give the Torah and its law to justify the people who kept it; thus no one will be justified by keeping it.

Chapter 34

Romans 3:21–31

Verses 3:21–22

During the Age of the Written Torah, a person had to believe Yah's promises about the Seed, put his faith in Him, and demonstrate his faith by keeping the written Torah and complying with its legal code in order to be in right standing with Him. When a saint disobeyed Yahweh or transgressed the written Torah, he had to comply with the law and offer the blood of an innocent substitute so that Yahweh would forgive him, cleanse his conscience, and cancel the curses. Yahweh had redeemed this person from the serpent's slave market and declared him righteous, but this person had to maintain his righteousness by offering the sacrifices that Yahweh called for in the law.

The sacrifices that the Mosaic covenant's legal code called for served as temporal place markers that allowed the saints to benefit from Yeshua's eternal sacrifice before He entered the dimension of space-time to manifest it. In Romans 3, verses 21 and 22, Paul says now that Yeshua has brought His eternal sacrifice into the dimension of space-time, the righteousness of Yahweh is manifested without our having to offer the sacrifices that the Mosaic covenant's law called for. Paul says that this grace is not contrary to the Law or the Prophets; the Law and the Prophets testify of this grace, and it is available to all who believe (Jews and Gentiles).

Verses 3:23–26

Paul says that everyone who puts his faith in Yeshua will be in right standing with Yah because (as he has already proven) there is no difference between Jews and Gentiles, for all have sinned and come short of the glory of Yah. Remember, in the Garden of Eden, Adam and Eve rebelled and disconnected from Yah's glory. Adam and Eve's spirits lost dominion over their souls, and their souls started deciding what was good and evil. Since both Jews and Gentiles are children of Adam and Eve, we all are born spiritually separated from Yahweh and in bondage to our souls. HaSatan takes advantage of this and builds strongholds in our souls so that he can control us and hold us in bondage. There is one problem that causes both Jews and Gentiles to fall short of Yah's glory: the rebellion and fall of Adam; and there is one solution to this problem: faith in Yeshua. Paul shoots down dual covenant theology by saying that Yah saves *everyone* the same way.

Yahweh told Adam and Eve that if they sinned, they would surely die, and He meant it. The reason that Yahweh did not kill Adam and Eve and send them straight to hell was because Yeshua had already offered Himself for their rebellion. However, it was not time for Yeshua to enter the dimension of space-time to manifest His sacrifice, so Yah killed a lamb. The blood of the lamb served as a temporal place marker for Yeshua's eternal sacrifice that made it possible for Yahweh to forbear, clothe, and continue to fellowship with Adam and Eve. From HaSatan's perspective, Yahweh was unjust because He had made Adam and Eve in His image and likeness but allowed a substitute that He had not made in His image and likeness to die in their place. From man's perspective, Yahweh's righteousness was imperfect because He had said that if they disobeyed Him, they would surely die; but they disobeyed and did not die and go straight to hell.

This is what HaSatan and man did not understand: the blood of an innocent animal was merely a place marker in the dimension of space-time that represented Yeshua's eternal sacrifice that permitted people to benefit from His sacrifice prior to His entering the dimension of space-time. So it was not the animal blood that took away sin; it was the blood of Yeshua, which is why the Scriptures say that it was impossible for the blood of bulls and goats to take away sin. When Yeshua finally manifested His sacrifice in space-time, He redeemed all of the place markers with His blood, paid all of Yah's outstanding debts, and vindicated His righteousness.

Paul says that Yah is just in justifying those who trust in Yeshua and His righteousness. Yeshua lived up to the standard of righteousness, which means that He was righteous, and the corruption that Adam and Eve loosed on the earth could not touch Him. Death had no claim on Yeshua, but He chose to die and go to hell to pay the penalty that Adam and Eve and their descendants (Jews and Gentiles) deserved in order to vindicate Yah's name and manifest His righteousness. Thus Yah is just in justifying those who place their faith in Yeshua's blood.

Verses 3:27–31

In these verses, Paul says no one can brag about being in right standing with Yah. What prevents a person from bragging? Is it the law of works? No, Paul says it is the law of faith that prevents people from bragging. In the Age of the Written Torah, Yahweh declared a person righteous as he believed His promises, put his faith in Him, and walked out his faith by keeping the Torah. If a saint failed to obey the Torah, the law convicted him of sin and opened him to a curse. Yah's Spirit pricked the saint's conscience, and he went to the temple and offered the sacrifice the law required so that Yah would forgive him and release him from the curse and return him to right standing, which reinforced his faith in the Seed. *This was the law of faith*. The sages, however, said that if a man submitted to circumcision and kept the written Torah by keeping the oral Torah and halachah, he was in right standing with Yahweh. *This was the law of works*.

Paul taught that Yeshua fulfilled the law, and if a person received Him, then he was justified and made righteous apart from the works of the law. Did this mean that the written Torah and its law were void? No, the only way that people could come to that conclusion was if they thought that Yahweh had given the Torah and its law to the Old Testament saints so that they could obtain right standing by keeping it. However, the Old Testament does not teach *the law of works*. It teaches that a person obtains right standing by faith; that is, it teaches *the law of faith*.

In sum, the sages invented a religion that used the works of the Torah to define who was and was not a Jew. The sages said that Yahweh cut the covenant with the Jews, and if you were a Jew, then you were in the covenant and in right standing with Him, and He would bring you into the world to come. The sages said a person became a Jew by submitting to circumcision and obeying the written Torah by obeying the oral Torah and legal halachah. Essentially, the apostate sages were trying to use the Mosaic covenant to obtain redemption, but Yahweh did not design the Mosaic covenant to produce redemption; He designed it to produce sanctification.

Yah brought people into the Abrahamic covenant (redeemed people) as they put their faith in the Promised Seed, and then they kept the Mosaic covenant so that He could sanctify them. The sages took the emphasis off faith and put it on works; thus they took the emphasis off the Seed and His righteousness and put it on man's ability to establish his own righteousness. In verse 31, Paul says that faith in Yeshua does not do away with the law, faith in Yeshua establishes the law. Paul demolishes the sages' *law of works* and proclaims *the law of faith* that the Tanakh taught.

Part 10

A Survey of Romans: Inheriting Yeshua's Nature

Chapter 35

Romans 4:1–25

An Overview

In this section, Paul proves that the Tanakh teaches the law of faith. Paul proves to his Jewish brothers that justification by faith is *the central theme* of the Torah and that the belief that Yahweh makes people righteous in response to their righteous works is a heretical doctrine. Now what this tells us is that since being justified by faith is the central theme of the Torah, being justified by faith is not a New Testament theme that is incompatible with the Torah. The Torah bears witness to the fact that Yahweh preached the gospel of the Seed to Abraham, and he believed it. Yahweh redeemed Abraham, and *then* he circumcised himself and obeyed the Torah. Abraham and his camp walked out their faith by obeying the Torah, but sadly, HaSatan used the Torah to divide the Roman ekklesia: the Jews kept it woodenly, and the Gentiles shunned it. Paul put the Torah and its law in its place so the one new man could arise and fulfill its mission.

Verses 4:1–4

In these verses, Paul asks whether Abraham was justified by faith or by works. The sages said that Abraham was justified when he tied Isaac to the altar. James seems to promote this dogma in his letter when he says, "Was not Abraham our father justified by works, when he had offered Isaac his son upon the altar?"[291] However, we must remember that James was writing to people who tended to forget that saving faith expresses itself in

---

[291] *The Hebrew-Greek Key Word Study Bible*, KJV, James 2:21.

action.[292] James is saying that when Yahweh redeems a person from the power of sin, that person's works will testify of this reality.

The sages forgot that Abraham submitted to circumcision twenty-nine years after he *believed* Yah would give him a son and make a nation out of him.[293] They also forgot that Abraham had so much *faith* that he believed Yah would keep His promise even if He had to re-form Isaac's body from smoke and bring him back to life! Abraham's faith empowered him to do righteous works; his righteous works did not make him righteous. The sages said that as Abraham tied Isaac to the altar, he fulfilled the law before it was written, thus securing Yah's favor for him and his seed.[294]

The sages also said that Abraham's descendants were justified by submitting to circumcision and keeping the whole Torah. However, in Genesis 15:6, the Torah says that Abraham believed Yahweh, and He declared him righteous. Paul says that Abraham believed that the Seed would come through his loins in order to crush the head of the serpent and bless all the nations. Yahweh justified Abraham as he put his trust in the Seed, and He justifies all those who follow his example.[295] However, those who follow the sages and do works of righteousness in order to place Yahweh in their debt so that He will repay them by justifying them will perish.

Verses 4:5–25

In these verses, Paul drives his point home by saying that if the ungodly will humble themselves and believe Yahweh's promises and trust Him to bring them to pass, then He will count their faith as righteousness (justify them). Paul uses David as an example. David believed Yahweh's promises about the Seed and trusted Him; in response, Yah declared him righteous.[296] Afterwards, David committed adultery and murder.[297] The law said David had to die, but since his faith was in the Seed who *had already* offered Himself for him, Yahweh did not require David to forfeit his life.[298] The Holy Spirit (via Nathan) humbled David; he confessed his sins with a broken, contrite heart, and Yah forgave him and cleansed him without the works of the law.[299]

---

[292] R. H. Mounce, *The New American Commentary*, Nashville, TN, Broadman & Holman Pub., 2001, vol. 27; p. 122.*

[293] Tim Hegg, *Paul's Epistle to the Romans*, Tacoma, WA, TorahResource, 2005, p. 88.

[294] Ibid., p. 82.

[295] *The Hebrew-Greek Key Word Study Bible*, KJV, Galatians 3:6–8.

[296] Ibid., 1 Samuel 16:13; 2 Samuel 7:12–17; Psalm 89:26; 110.

[297] Ibid., 2 Samuel 12:9.

[298] Ibid., Exodus 20:14; Deuteronomy 5:18; Leviticus 20:10; 2 Samuel 12:13.

[299] Ibid., Psalm 32:5; 51:3.

Yahweh redeemed David and declared him righteous. Thus Yahweh responded to David's sin with mercy, not imputing it to him. In other words, Yahweh did not allow David's sin to change His declaration that David was righteous. Yahweh did not set the law aside for David; He fulfilled it by dying in his place so that He could forgive him. Yah's grace does not set the law aside to dispense mercy; Yah's grace fulfills the law to release the full measure of mercy.

Here is the point: The Torah teaches that Yah justifies the ungodly based on their faith without the works prescribed in the law. The Torah has always taught justification by faith, but the sages built a religion around a few verses that seemed to say that justification came by doing righteous works. By the time Yeshua appeared, the concept of being justified by faith seemed like a heresy. Paul had to prove that Yah had always redeemed and justified people by faith.

The sages said that Abraham was righteous because he submitted to circumcision and kept the whole Torah (via the binding of Isaac). However, Paul said that Yah declared Abraham righteous because he believed His promises and trusted Him to bring them to pass. Paul pointed out that Yah declared Abraham righteous *before* He asked him to submit to circumcision. Thus, if Gentiles (who are also uncircumcised) believe His promises and trust Him to bring them to pass, then He will declare them righteous. Submitting to circumcision was what Yah demanded of covenant members, but submitting to circumcision did not *make* one a covenant member.[xi]

Yahweh promised Abraham that his Seed would bless all the families of the earth (by redeeming them from HaSatan's kingdom and taking them off his slave market). Essentially, Abraham and his Seed would inherit the whole earth! Abraham staggered not at the promise of Yah, but was strong in faith. However, the sages refused to believe that Abraham's Seed would redeem them. The sages tried to earn their right standing with Yah and hence redemption by keeping the law. If Yahweh allowed the sages to earn their redemption, then His promise was pointless, because there would be no need for the Seed to suffer and die for all the families of the earth.

Paul says that it is impossible for a man to be justified by the law because Yahweh commissioned the law to point out sin and punish it (to stir up His wrath) so that man would realize he needed a Savior. Once Yah had saved a person, the law forced him to keep his eyes on the Savior. Hence the law was not a way to bring the promise to pass; the law was a way to humble man so he would take hold of the promise by faith. Abraham and David believed Yah's promises and put their trust in Him. Yah redeemed Abraham and David and counted their faith as righteousness (justified them). Yah did not impute Abraham's and David's ungodly actions to them, and if we follow them, He will not impute our ungodly actions to us!

Excursus (Supplemental Information)

The Dual Role of the Law

Yahweh chose Israel to be His representative. Yahweh cut the covenants with Israel and made promises to her. Yah desired to have a special relationship with Israel. Yah gave Israel the Torah with its sacrifices and feasts to cleanse her so that she could enjoy her relationship with Him. In the Feast of the Passover, Israel remembered how Yahweh redeemed her from slavery. In the Feast of Unleavened Bread, Israel remembered how Yahweh delivered her from Pharaoh's power. In the Feast of Firstfruits, Israel remembered how Yahweh brought her through the sea from death to life. In the Feast of Pentecost, Israel remembered that Yahweh gave her the Torah. Yahweh's feasts were shadows that drew upon Yeshua's sacrifice that took place before He created the earth.

Yahweh's feasts sanctified Israel, but they did not necessarily sanctify the individuals in Israel. In order for Yah to redeem, justify, and sanctify individuals, they had to believe Him and obey His teachings and instructions. Israel was redeemed and holy unto Yah, but there were two groups of people in Israel.

The first group was composed of people who circumcised their hearts by putting their faith in Yah's promise to send the Seed and obeyed His teaching and instructions to maintain their relationship with Him and enjoy the blessings of the covenants. For these people, the Torah and its law served as a guide that showed them how to live and appropriate the forgiveness that Yah had given them so that they could put away guilt and shame when they failed to obey Him or keep the Torah. Yah's Spirit pricked their conscience and let them know that they needed to repent, and they took a sacrifice to the temple and got the priests to offer it to Him. For these people, the sacrifices pointed to the Promised Seed and His righteousness, and these sacrifices made them yearn for Him more. *This was the righteous remnant.*

Those who did not circumcise their hearts by humbling themselves and putting their faith in Yah's promise formed another group. These people kept the written Torah by keeping the rules, regulations, and laws in the oral Torah and halachah in order to be in the covenant. For these people, the Torah and its law were a list of rules, regulations, and laws they had to obey in order to establish their own righteousness so that they could be righteous, sanctified, and blessed. Since these people failed to believe Yahweh's promises about the Seed and did not put their faith in Him, He did not declare them righteous. When these people sinned, their pride drove them to the temple with a sacrifice to repair their own righteousness. For these people, the sacrifices did not point to the Promised Seed, so Yahweh could not forgive their sins and take away their guilt and shame. *This group had to hide their uncircumcised hearts behind the fig leaves of religion.*

In sum, the righteous remnant saw the Torah and its law as a light and a lamp unto their feet that showed them how to walk humbly before Yah. The Torah and its law was a blessing to these people because it showed them how to avoid the curses of poverty, sickness, bondage, and death, and they meditated on it day and night. The apostate sages and their sheep saw the Torah and its law as a list of things they had to do to be righteous so that Yah would redeem them. The Torah and its law brought guilt, shame, condemnation, and fear on these people to lead them to repentance, but they hid behind the fig leaves of religion and remained in HaSatan's kingdom.

End of Excursus

Chapter 36

Romans 5:1–21

Overview

Paul begins Romans by cutting away at the pride of man in general. Next, Paul narrows his focus and cuts away at the pride of the pious pagan. Paul then performs a surgical procedure on his Jewish brothers, who took pride in the fact that they were Abraham's seed. Finally, Paul shears the sages and their sheep, who gloried in their own works. At this point, Paul's readers should realize that no one has a reason to boast about his spiritual heritage. Everyone is born with a nature that separates him from Yahweh, and everyone needs to bow to Messiah. Paul has made it clear that all have sinned and come short of Yah's glory. Hence the Jews who were not in the righteous remnant were under Yah's condemnation and impending wrath. Equally, the Gentiles who were not in the righteous remnant were also under Yah's condemnation and wrath. Paul proves that a person's ethnic status has no bearing on whether he is righteous.

Verses 1–11

In these verses, Paul says that since those in the Roman ekklesia had put their faith in the Lord Yeshua Messiah, Yahweh justified them, and thus they now had peace with Him. Paul says that through faith in Yeshua, they could draw near to Yahweh and take hold of grace whenever they needed it, looking forward to Him one day returning the crown of glory that Adam lost. Paul says that saints should rejoice when trouble befalls them because when they, through the power of the Holy Spirit and the love that He has poured into their hearts, patiently endure, He strengthens their faith and they more intently look forward to receiving the promises. Thus tribulation tempers faith and makes us more resolute in our expectation that Yahweh will keep His promises. Yah assures us that He will keep His promises by sending His Spirit to live in our hearts in order to remind us that He loved us when we were His enemies and took the punishment that we deserved to reconcile us. Since we have been justified by Yeshua's death, we can be confident that His life; that is, His continual intercession for us, will complete the work (save us).

Verse 12

In verse 12, Paul says that Adam brought death into the world by sinning, and death passed to everyone. Now, we have already discussed how this happened, but it will not hurt to discuss it once more. Adam was in perfect fellowship with Yahweh. Adam's spirit submitted to Yah's Spirit, and Yah's Spirit empowered Adam's spirit to rule over his HSC and keep his soul and body in line so that he could do Yah's will on the earth. However, as Adam turned away from Yah to obey his wife, his spirit disconnected from its source of authority. Adam's spirit lost the power to rule the HSC and keep the soul and body in line. Adam's soul took control of his HSC and took on what appeared to be a life of its own, and the body sided with it.

The serpent built strongholds in Adam's soul so that he could use it to control him. This is how the serpent stole Adam's dominion and forced him to build HaSatan's kingdom on the earth. Adam's rebellion stained his spirit with sin, and thus he could no longer draw near to Yah. Yah's Spirit could not infuse Adam's spirit with the power it needed to break free of HaSatan's control. Adam's spirit was in bondage to his soul, and his soul was in bondage to HaSatan.

The consequences were severe. The crown of glory vanished, and Adam lost dominion over the earth. The robe of glory vanished, and Adam was naked (without a spiritual covering). Adam's body began drawing energy from the earth, and Yahweh cursed the ground. Adam's blood began to assimilate the curse, and his body began to die. Clearly, Adam's spiritual death led to his physical death.

As Adam's children, we are all born spiritually dead and subject to physical death. HaSatan uses our fallen spirit, soul, and body to rule over us. We have all inherited Adam's nature, and it separates us from Yah and allows HaSatan to rule over us. Consequently, there is no way that any of us can manifest Yah's glory. In other words, we all fall short of Yah's glory, and we all die, which means that we were all born with fallen natures.

In sum, Adam separated himself and his seed from Yahweh's Spirit. Therefore, Adam separated every Jew and every Gentile from Yah's Spirit. This means that every Jew and every Gentile falls short of Yah's glory. It means that every Jew and every Gentile will die. It also means that if a Jew or Gentile dies while separated from Yah's Spirit, he will remain separated from Him forever. In short, both Jew and Gentile inherited spiritual, physical, and eternal death.

Verses 13–14

In these verses, Paul anticipates a question. The Gentiles thought that disobeying the Torah and not complying with its law was what made men sinners. So naturally, Gentiles would ask how Yah could call them sinners and condemn them to die without giving them a chance to obey the Torah and its law. Paul says that Adam's children inherit his nature, and it separates them from Yah so that HaSatan can rule over them. Since HaSatan rules over Adam's children, they sin. So sin has been in the world since Adam, but Yah did not impute sin to man's account and systematically punish it until He gave the law. Yet everyone from Adam to Moses died. Hence Yah labeled men as sinners and condemned them to die long before He gave the law.

In the Garden of Eden, Yah gave Adam an instruction with a legal provision attached to it. Adam disobeyed Yah's instruction and fell under the penalty prescribed in the legal provision (he died). Later Yah gave Adam's children instructions without legal provisions, but they still died. Then, at Sinai, Yah reiterated His instructions and attached legal provisions to them, but Adam's children still died. Death is the punishment for Adam's sin. Yahweh's agent carries out the punishment of death regardless of whether or not Yah had given man instructions with legal provisions attached to them. So the Gentiles, who did not receive the Mosaic law, were sinners subject to death, just as the Jews, who did receive the Mosaic law, were sinners subject to death, because the Mosaic law did not create sin, the Mosaic law highlighted sin. Simply stated, Adam's rebellion—not the Mosaic law—turned man into a sinner. The Mosaic law showed man that he was a sinner in order to prepare his heart to receive the Messiah.[300] Therefore, a valid use of the Mosaic law is to use it to show a man that he is a sinner who needs to submit to the Seed and receive His righteousness.[301]

Verses 15–21

In this section, Paul contrasts the works of Adam with the works of Yeshua in order to emphasize that righteousness is a gift that Yah gives to those who believe Him and put their trust in Yeshua. Yah put Adam in a garden and gave him an opportunity to eat of the Tree of Life and all the other luscious trees, which represented all His blessings. However, there was one tree that Yah told Adam not to eat from because it would kill him. This tree, the Tree of the Knowledge of Good and Evil, represented the curses. It is sad that Yahweh set life, death, blessings, and curses before Adam and that he chose the curses and death for him and his descendants. This is why we are all born separated from Yahweh's Spirit and in bondage to the flesh, the world, and the devil.

---

[300] *The Hebrew-Greek Key Word Study Bible*, KJV, Galatians 3:24.
[301] Ibid., 1 Timothy 1:9–11.

Yah put Yeshua in the same garden and gave Him 613 commandments with blessings and curses attached to them. If Yeshua obeyed all the commandments, then the blessings would come upon Him, but if He disobeyed one, then the curses would come upon Him. Yeshua obeyed the 613 commandments and earned the blessings of the Mosaic covenant. Afterwards, Yeshua offered His sinless life as a ransom for Adam's children. If Adam's children will trust Him and bow their knee to His lordship, then He will give them His righteousness as a gift. As a mother's water breaks, she forces her child down a bloody birth canal, and the baby emerges with Adam's nature. Adam's nature identifies us with him and the curse, but we can accept Yeshua's blood and follow Him through the baptismal waters to be reborn and identify with Him, and His blessings will swallow up the curse!

Through Adam's disobedience, sin, addiction, sickness, disease, poverty, and death rule; but through the obedience of Yeshua, righteousness, freedom, health, sufficiency, and eternal life rule through the gift of righteousness and the indwelling Holy Spirit. The gift of justification and righteousness clears the way for the Holy Spirit to join Himself to the human spirit and infuse it with the authority and power it needs to rule the human system configuration. The Holy Spirit gives the human spirit the authority and the power it needs to rule over the rebellious soul and vile body so that we can do the will of our heavenly Father on the earth. The Holy Spirit empowers us to reign in life by overcoming sin, addiction, sickness, disease, poverty, spiritual death, eternal death, and ultimately physical death, which proves that the gift is more powerful than the curse.

In verse 15, Paul emphasizes Yeshua's humanity in order to combat some of the *Gnostic philosophies* that were taking root in the Roman ekklesia.[302] In verse 20, Paul returns to the subject of the law that Yahweh attached to the Torah. Paul wanted to be sure that the Roman ekklesia understood that the Mosaic law did not make man a sinner; it showed man that he was a sinner, and its penalties drove him to the sacrifices that drew upon the Seed's grace and pointed to Him so that man would long for Him to arrive with healing in His wings.

Yah gave Israel the Torah to instruct her in righteousness so that she could instruct the other nations in righteousness. Yah attached the law to the Torah to point out man's failures and make them grievous. The law gave sin a platform to stand on so that it could expose what was in man's heart, and so sin abounded. Nevertheless, Yahweh poured out His grace on a remnant so that His promise to Abraham would not fail. Yahweh's grace enabled the remnant to believe Him and put their trust in the Seed so that He could redeem them and declare them righteous. Yah's grace empowered these saints to live out their faith by obeying the written Torah. Yah's grace cleansed these saints when they failed to obey Yah or the Torah. Hence Yah's law caused sin to abound, but grace superabounded in order to keep the saints in right standing with Him.

---

[302] Tim Hegg, *Paul's Epistle to the Romans*, Tacoma, WA, TorahResource, 2005, p. 123.

Chapter 37

Romans 6:1–13

Verses 1–3

In these verses, Paul says, "What shall we say then? Shall we continue in sin, that grace may abound?" Paul knew that some people would think he was promoting lawlessness as a way of glorifying Yahweh; that is, saying that since Yah's grace swallows up sin and its penalties, sinners can continue to sin in order to glorify Him. For example, an addict might say that Yah saved him and allowed him to keep doing dope to bring Him glory. This is the logic: the law has convicted me of being an addict, so I will accept Yeshua so He can pay for my sins, and I can keep violating the law in order to show everyone how merciful He is. This logic reflects an error that Paul begins to correct by saying, "God forbid. How shall we, that are dead to sin, live any longer therein?"

For Paul, it was inconceivable to think that Yahweh would justify a person and permit him or her to continue living in sin. In verse 3, Paul begins to explain why. Paul says that when the people in the Roman ekklesia believed the gospel and bowed their knees to Yeshua, Yah's Spirit baptized their spirits into Yeshua. Thus Yah's Spirit baptized their spirits into Yeshua's death, and they died with Him. According to Joseph Shulam, the primary meaning of the Greek verb *baptidzo* is "to dye," in the sense of immersing something in liquid.[303] As Yahweh justifies a person, His Spirit immerses the person's spirit (who was a slave to sin) into Yeshua to absorb His death.

---

[303] Joseph Shulam, *A Commentary on the Jewish Roots of Romans*, Baltimore, MD, Lederer Books, 1997, p. 213.

Verses 4–13

In verse 4, Paul finishes explaining why a saint cannot live in sin. Yeshua lived a sinless life, so death could not touch Him. But He loved the human beings that He created, so He took our sins and got on the execution stake in order to pay for them by shedding His blood, suffering through the pain of separation from His Father, and leaving His body to go to hell. In Psalm 16:10, Yahweh promised that He would not leave Yeshua's soul in hell, so His Spirit came on Him in hell, and He emerged from hell cleansed of sin and back in perfect fellowship with Yahweh. Yeshua's Spirit and soul returned to His body, resurrecting and glorifying it. Later Yeshua ascended, and Yah gave Him all authority and power, which are what our spirits absorb.

In verses 5–13, Paul unpacks his explanation. Adam's nature separates us from Yahweh, and this gives HaSatan the ability to rule over us. HaSatan compels us to sin and torments us with lack, addiction, sickness, disease, and fear. As we bow our knee to Yeshua, Yahweh's Spirit puts us to death on the execution stake with Him. Next, Yah's Spirit comes on us to cleanse us, resurrect us, and take up residence in us; hence we are alive to Him forevermore. Paul says that Yah has destroyed "the body of sin" and freed us so that we can live for Him. Paul says that we are to think of ourselves as being dead to sin and alive to Yah through Yeshua. In other words, we need to believe that Yah has set us free from HaSatan and that he can no longer control us unless we let him. This raises two questions: what is the body of sin, and how does Yahweh destroy it?

Excursus

The Body of Sin

In the Garden of Eden, Adam rebelled. Adam stained his spirit with iniquity. Adam's iniquity separated his spirit from Yahweh's Spirit. After this, Adam's spirit no longer had the authority or power to rule the human system configuration. HaSatan took advantage of this schism between Yah and Adam and built strongholds in Adam's soul. HaSatan's strongholds gave Adam's soul a life of its own called "the self." However, the self was HaSatan's proxy personality manifesting itself on earth through man. Adam's body began assimilating the curse, and it corrupted its passions and desires. The corrupted body sided with the defiant soul, and the depraved tag team ganged up to rule over man's spirit and the human system configuration.

The rebellious soul (the self) shuns Yahweh's will, exalts itself, and does its own will. The self believes that it is an autonomous entity, but this is illusion. HaSatan uses the self to build his kingdom on the earth. However, since the soul has separated itself from Yahweh's Spirit, it is in darkness. Hence the self is not able to see that it is actually a slave that is being forced to build a kingdom that is not its own. By doing its own will, the self does HaSatan's will on the earth and builds his kingdom. HaSatan is the self's lord, and he uses sin to control it.

So what is the body of sin? It is what Adam formed when his spirit separated itself from Yah's Spirit and lost the authority and power to rule over the soul and the body, which allowed HaSatan to build strongholds in the soul in order to project his image through it and corrupt the desires and passions of the body. The body of sin is the instrument HaSatan plays in order to get us to follow him, just as the Pied Piper played his instrument to get the children of Hamelin to follow him to their deaths. If we follow our pied piper, we will live with him forever in a fiery lake! Figure 2, on page 409, depicts the body of sin (body of death), or *corrupted HSC*, that gives HaSatan the ability to rule us and force us to build his kingdom on the earth.

Destroying the Body of Sin

How does Yah destroy the body of sin? The Holy Spirit offers the human spirit the gift of repentance. If the human spirit accepts the gift, then it is empowered to repent. In other words, the Holy Spirit empowers the human spirit to break free of the control of the soul and body so that it can bow its knee to Yeshua. Next, the Holy Spirit comes on the human spirit that has stained itself with iniquity and separated itself from Yahweh. The Holy Spirit baptizes this defiled spirit into Yeshua and puts it to death on the execution stake with Him. Next, the Holy Spirit resurrects this spirit, cleanses it of sin, and releases it from condemnation and wrath. Then, the Holy Spirit takes up residence in this person's heart and joins Himself to this new spirit.

The human spirit is now in perfect fellowship with the Father, Son, and Holy Spirit. Consequently, the human spirit has the authority and power to subdue the soul and restrain the body. Essentially, Yah returns the HSC to its original state in order to destroy the body of sin. As Yeshua destroys the body of sin, He establishes His kingdom in us. As we accept this as a reality and cooperate with the King's Word and the promptings of His Spirit, we learn how to operate the re-created HSC in order to break free from compulsions, obsessions, and addictions.

Change

When a person believes Yah and bows his knee to Yeshua, Yah's Spirit puts the old defiled spirit to death, resurrects it, and joins Himself to it. Now this person's spirit wants to obey the King, and the person has a desire to bring every area of his life into conformity with His will. Hence a saint will study the King's Word, meditate on it, renew his mind with it, and allow the Spirit to write it on his heart. If an area of a saint's life does not line up with the King's will, his heart will generate a desire that propels him towards the goal of bringing it in line. In other words, a saint will have a sincere desire to change. Some areas of a saint's life will change as the saint repents and Yah's Spirit puts the old spirit to death, but other areas will change as the person's new spirit cooperates with Yah's Spirit in order to tear down the strongholds in the soul.

As Yahweh regenerates a person, He returns the HSC to its original state, destroying the body of sin, freeing the person to change. So why do some areas of a believer's life change instantly and some change slowly? As Yah regenerates individuals, He establishes His kingdom in them, and they have access to everything in it. As a saint's spirit submits to the King, the King's authority and power flow through the spirit in order to force the rebellious soul and the vile body to obey the person's will, which is to obey the King. However, a saint's spirit has to learn to submit to the King and comply with His Word while following His Spirit's promptings so that together they can tear down the strongholds in the soul and bring it into compliance with the King's will. It takes time to learn how to operate the new HSC, and so some strongholds come down as we repent, but most come down over time. Hence recovery is most often a process, not an event.

A saint must focus on conforming to Yah's Word and following His Spirit's promptings so that together they can tear down strongholds and force stubborn areas of the soul into submission. As Yah justifies a person, He destroys the body of sin (figure 2, p. 409), reordering the HSC and returning it to its original state (figure 1, p. 408). But it takes a while for a saint to learn how to operate the new HSC, so some areas of his life change instantly, but others change in time.[xii]

End of Excursus

In verse 11, Paul says that a saint must believe that Yahweh has put his old spirit to death with Yeshua and resurrected him as a new creature who is dead to sin and alive to Yahweh. Paul says that if a saint does this, he will have the power to prevent sin from ruling him and forcing him to fulfill the lusts of the body. A saint must believe that Yahweh has destroyed the corrupted HSC and restored it to its original state, while submitting to His Word and Spirit, so that together they can tear down the strongholds of unrighteousness in his soul and replace those strongholds with strongholds of righteousness, which changes his character. If a saint fails to do these things, he will wander in the desert of addiction until he goes to heaven.

The Spirit resurrects those who have died with Yeshua and gives them desires that propel them towards righteousness. As saints obey Yah, peace fills their hearts. When saints sin, they forfeit peace until they confess and repent. Hence saints cannot *comfortably* live in sin. If saints choose to live in sin, they will have to fight the Spirit. Consequently, they will have no peace or joy, and Yah will allow the consequences of their behavior to bring them to a place where they will cooperate with Him. If you have been justified, you will change, one way or the other. Make it easy on yourself: reckon yourself dead to sin and alive to Yah, and tear down the strongholds so that you do not yield your members to sin and suffer the consequences.

Chapter 38

Romans 6:14

Misinterpreting Paul

In this verse, Paul says, "For sin shall not have dominion over you: for ye are not under the law, but under grace." Most people read this verse and think Paul is saying that when we bow our knee to Yeshua and receive grace, the Torah no longer applies to us. However, Yeshua said that He did not come to destroy the Torah. Yeshua kept the Torah. Paul kept the Torah. In 1 Corinthians 11:1, Paul tells us to follow him as he follows Yeshua, so what is he saying in this verse? Paul is simply telling believers how the Torah and its legal code fit into the paradigm of Yahweh's Spirit putting a person's old defiled spirit to death on the execution stake with Yeshua and resurrecting it as a new spirit empowered to obey Him. To understand what Paul is saying, we have to understand why Yahweh cut the Mosaic covenant with Israel and how it operated.

Excursus

The Mosaic Covenant and Its Operation

Abraham believed Yahweh. Yahweh declared Abraham righteous. Abraham's works manifested his righteousness. Abraham's seed was supposed to believe Yahweh so that He could declare them righteous and empower them to manifest their righteousness by their works. However, Abraham's seed was disobedient, so Yah placed them in a controlled environment so they could multiply without destroying themselves. After Abraham's seed was in Egypt, they began worshiping Egyptian gods and thinking and acting like Egyptians. At the set time, Yah reaffirmed the Abrahamic covenant with Abraham's seed and delivered them. After that, Yah gave Abraham's seed the Torah and attached a legal code to it. The Torah identified sin, and its law punished it in order to discourage it. If saints disobeyed Yah, the law dealt with their guilt, shame, and condemnation so that they could continue to enjoy their relationship with Him.

In the Age of the Written Torah, Yahweh expected the people who put their faith in the Seed to demonstrate their faith by obeying the Torah and complying with its law. If the saints obeyed the Torah and complied with its law, the blessings came on them; but if they did not, the curses came on them. Hence the Mosaic covenant was not a covenant of works. The Mosaic covenant was a covenant of faith that spelled out how saints were to walk out their faith.[304]

Yahweh cut the Mosaic covenant so that He could sanctify His people until Yeshua could manifest His finished work in space-time. So how did the HSC function in the Age of the Written Torah? In Eden, man's spirit turned away from Yah and lost the power to force the soul to carry out its will. HaSatan took advantage of this schism and built strongholds in man's soul so that he could lord over his spirit. Man's spirit takes on the image of whomever it submits to; thus, when HaSatan forced man's spirit to submit to him, man's spirit took on HaSatan's image.

Yahweh's Spirit strove with man's spirit and tried to draw him to repentance. Yahweh redeemed the people who repented, put their faith in the Promised Seed, and met with Him at an altar soaked in innocent blood. At times, the Holy Spirit came upon these people in order to strengthen their spirit so that it could subdue the rebellious soul and vile body to do Yah's will. As these people meditated on the Torah and its law, they were acutely aware of Yah's will, His rewards for obedience, and His punishment for disobedience, which helped their spirits restrain their hands from doing evil, their feet from drawing near to mischief, and their mouths from speaking guile.

However, Yah's Spirit had not yet begun His ministry of regeneration (changing the nature of the human spirit). Thus Yah had redeemed these people, but their hearts remained bent towards sin and self. In the Age of the Written Torah, Yahweh wrote the Torah and its law on scrolls, and it did not change a person's heart and empower him to obey Him. Hence the law constantly reminded the people that they were sinners and pointed them to the Messiah.

Yahweh cut the Mosaic covenant with Israel so that He could deal with His people's sin until Yeshua came to put sin away. When guilt, shame, condemnation, and fear overwhelmed saints, they offered a sacrifice, confessed their sin, and turned away from it so that Yahweh could forgive them and cleanse their conscience. However, since they were fallen creatures, they had to repeat this process regularly and meet with Yah three times a year in

---

[304] *The Hebrew-Greek Key Word Study Bible*, KJV, Deuteronomy 10:12–13; Romans 9:31–32.

order to renew the covenant, repent, and allow Him to cleanse them. The law constantly reminded saints that they were fallen creatures who needed the Seed to heal them; thus it produced a sin consciousness.

The Mosaic covenant's sacrifices were merely temporal place markers that made it possible for Yah's saints to reach out by faith and connect with the eternal sacrifice of Yeshua. The sacrifices did not please Yahweh; the sacrifices were conduits of faith that connected the saints to what did please Him. The sacrifices made people aware of the cost of sin, discouraged them from sinning, and kept them focused on the Promised Seed and connected to His sacrifice. This allowed Yahweh to dispense mercy to His saints without compromising His righteousness. Thus the attitude of the person giving the sacrifice was more valuable than the sacrifice itself.

David's life illustrates this truth. David was a humble man. The Holy Spirit abode with David, teaching him His ways, and they enjoyed an intimate relationship.[305] When King David committed adultery with Bathsheba and killed her husband, his behavior was so putrid to him that he hid his sin from himself. David opened the door for the curses of the Mosaic law. A curse of sickness came on him, and his bones began to waste away. David hid his sin for a year, but then the Spirit sent Nathan to confront him so that He could heal him. David confessed his sins with a broken, contrite heart, and Yahweh forgave David without the works of the law and healed him. After Yah had forgiven him, David offered sacrifices to fulfill the Mosaic law.[306]

Daniel's life also illustrates this truth. Daniel lived in Babylon. It was impossible for Daniel to offer sacrifices when he sinned. Nevertheless, Yah said that he was an example of righteousness.[307] Why was Yahweh so fond of Daniel? Daniel had an intimate relationship with the Spirit, and it broke his heart when he sinned; thus he repented with a broken, contrite heart. This was what Yah was trying to instill in His people, which is why it was such an affront to Him when they offered sacrifices with the wrong heart and turned the law into a religion.[308]

The lives of David and Daniel prove that the people in Israel's righteous remnant were partakers of Yeshua's sacrifice and that the Holy Spirit helped them obey Yahweh. However, when their fallen natures got the better of them and they sinned, the law opened an avenue for the curses. A saint's transgressions did not affect his justification; it affected the quality of his life, his witness, and his reward. After a saint sinned, he felt guilty and ashamed. The saint feared that Yahweh would release the curses of the Mosaic covenant

---

[305] Ibid., 1 Samuel 16:13; Acts 13:22.

[306] Ibid., Psalm 32:3, 4; 2 Samuel 12:1–20; Psalm 51:16-19.

[307] Ibid., Ezekiel 14:14.

[308] Ibid., Psalm 51:16–17; Isaiah 1:11–17, 66:2–3; Jeremiah 6:19–20; Amos 5:21–27; Micah 6:6–8; Hebrews 10:6, 8.

on him, so he lost his peace. The saint's conscience (or the Holy Spirit) drove him to the temple with sacrifices that he offered with a broken, contrite heart while longing for the Seed to heal him. Yahweh forgave the saint, cleansed his conscience, and released him from the curses.

Israel's righteous remnant did not live under the condemnation of the law or the dominion of sin. However, the sages and their sheep refused to believe Yah and trusted in their ability to please Him by complying with every jot and tittle of the Torah and its law. When they sinned, the law imputed transgression to their accounts, and they took a sacrifice to the temple. But since they offered the sacrifice seeking to repair their own righteousness, Yah did not forgive them, cleanse them, or release them from condemnation. Thus the sages and their sheep lived under the law; that is, under the law's condemnation. Yahweh's law condemned the sages and their sheep because they were HaSatan's children. Consequently, sin had dominion over them.

In sum, prior to creating the earth, Yeshua offered Himself to pay for man's sin. Yeshua offered Himself so His Father could bestow His grace on man and be merciful to man without setting His righteousness aside. After the fall, Yahweh poured out His grace on a remnant. The remnant believed Yah's promises, and He declared them righteous. After Sinai, the remnant walked out their faith by obeying the Torah and complying with its law. When saints sinned, they offered a sacrifice that connected them to Yeshua's sacrifice so that Yah could erase the sin from their record and release them from the curses. The remnant included people like Zacharias, Elizabeth, and Simeon, who knew they were sinners and waited eagerly for the Seed who would heal them of their "leprosy." The righteous remnant embraced Yeshua when He came to earth.

Yeshua said that the people who believed had access to the kingdom. The people in the righteous remnant believed Yeshua, and He established the kingdom in them. The people in the righteous remnant told the sages, their sheep, and the nations that if they would believe in their heart that Yahweh's Spirit had raised Yeshua from the dead and bow their knee to Him, then His Spirit would establish the kingdom in them and bring them into Israel's righteous remnant.

In the Mosaic covenant, a saint's weak, fallen spirit fought with the soul and body in an effort to overcome sin and offered sacrifices to connect with Yeshua's sacrifice when he failed. However, Yeshua brought His sacrifice into space-time, revealing the fullness of Yah's grace. So, in the new covenant, we do not have to offer sacrifices, and Yah's Spirit puts our fallen spirit to death, resurrects it, and infuses it with power so that it can overcome the soul, body, and sin.

End of Excursus

In verse 14, Paul is saying that the fallen human spirit is under the custodianship of the Mosaic law, and it is subject to its condemnation; but Yah's Spirit puts this fallen spirit to death, resurrects it, and joins Himself to it. This reborn human spirit is not under the custodianship of the Mosaic law or subject to its condemnation; this reborn spirit is under the custodianship of Yah's Spirit, and His grace gives this reborn spirit the power to overcome sin.

Chapter 39

Romans 6:15–23

Verse 15

In this verse, Paul anticipates a question his readers would have as they realized that they were not under the custodianship of the law and not subject to its condemnation: "What then? shall we sin, because we are not under the law, but under grace?" That is, since Yeshua has taken the penalty for our sins, Yahweh has poured out His grace upon us, the Holy Spirit has taken custodianship of us and released us from the custodianship of the law, and the law cannot condemn us when we violate the written Torah, is it now okay for us to violate the written Torah? Paul answers by saying, "God forbid."

Excursus

The Torah and Its Legal Code

The Torah is the first five books of the Bible. The Torah is Yahweh's teachings and instructions. The Torah spells out how Yahweh wants His people to live. The Torah is the foundational revelation of Yahweh and His will for man. In the Torah, Yah says that if a prophet tries to turn His people away from obeying the Torah, the people are to put the prophet to death, for he is a false prophet. All that is why Yeshua said that He did not come to destroy the Torah.[309]

---

[309] *The Hebrew-Greek Key Word Study Bible*, KJV, Deuteronomy 13:5; Matthew 5:17.

As we have seen, Yahweh's people spent four hundred years with the Egyptians, and they started worshiping their gods and thinking and acting like the Egyptians.[310] Yahweh redeemed and baptized His people and took them to Mount Sinai, where He reiterated His teachings and instructions for them. Thus the Torah was given to people who were already in relationship with Yah through their faith in the blood of a lamb and the baptismal waters of the Red Sea to show them how to live a blessed life; it was not given to strangers to show them how to work their way into a relationship with Him.

Yahweh took His people off Pharaoh's slave market by the blood of a lamb. Yah brought His people through the waters of the sea into the body of Moses so they could worship and serve Him and establish His kingdom in Canaan. Yah redeemed the mixed multitude of Hebrews and Gentiles, but His Spirit had not regenerated them, so they still had fallen natures.

The fallen nature is rebellious, prideful, and selfish, so Yah attached the law to the Torah to deal with it and the sin it produced so He could sanctify and cleanse His people and hold the Abrahamic covenant in place until Yeshua came to put the fallen nature and sin away. Yah cut the Mosaic covenant with His people, and they entered into a relationship that revolved around the law. The Mosaic covenant made *the enjoyment* of the blessings of the Abrahamic covenant contingent upon obedience. If Yah's people obeyed the Torah and complied with its law, He blessed them. If they disobeyed the Torah and failed to comply with its law, He cursed them.

The Mosaic covenant set forth the standard of righteousness (the Torah). The blessings and curses in the Torah's legal code gave the fallen spirit an incentive to obey Yah's teachings and instructions; thus the legal code provided some restraint against the fallen spirit sinning. The restraint was not very effective, though, so the legal code provided a way for Yah to forgive and cleanse His people when they did not obey Him or His Torah. Nevertheless, the Mosaic covenant restrained sin and dealt with its effects until Yeshua could come to the earth.

The Abrahamic covenant is the covenant of redemption, and the Mosaic covenant is the covenant of sanctification. If Yahweh justified people without sanctifying them, He would be unrighteous. Thus when there is justification, there is *always* sanctification.[311] Justification and sanctification are two sides of the same coin. Hence when Yah justifies a person, He will also sanctify that person. For instance, Abram believed Yah, and He justified him. Yahweh changed Abram's name to Abraham to denote that His Spirit came upon him and abode with him in order to give his spirit the power to rule his soul and body in order to bring about his sanctification.

---

[310] Ibid., Ezekiel 20:5–11.

[311] Ibid., James 2:18, 24, 26.

Later, in the Mosaic covenant, the Holy Spirit would temporarily empower the people who were justified so that they could do Yah's will, but He did not regenerate them and change their nature.[312] Why did Yah not change their nature? In the Garden of Eden, the serpent told Eve that we could be our own god and create the abundant life for ourselves. Yah put fallen man under the custodianship of the law to make sure that he understood that the serpent had lied. Yah put redeemed, unregenerated people under the custodianship of the law, and His Spirit worked through its provisions in order to sanctify and cleanse them until Yeshua could come.[313]

Yahweh's people were under the custodianship of the law for about 1,500 years. At the appointed time, Mary gave birth to Yeshua. Yeshua was not born of Adam's spirit; He was born of Yah's Spirit. Thus Yeshua was justified and sanctified from birth. Yeshua obeyed the Holy Spirit and the written Torah perfectly. Death had no claim on Yeshua, but He chose to die for His sheep in order to set them free from HaSatan and his religions. Yeshua surrendered His life for His sheep on the execution stake, and Yah's Spirit resurrected Him. Yeshua ascended to sit at the right hand of the Father, where He intercedes for those who bow their knee to Him and put their trust in Him. Yeshua and His Father commissioned their Spirit to begin His ministry of regeneration, and He began indwelling all believers in order to sanctify them and bless them.

Yeshua embodied and thus transformed the institutions that administered the Mosaic covenant. Yeshua's Spirit is in us performing the operations that sanctified the people in the Mosaic covenant. Hence Yeshua transformed the Mosaic covenant into the new covenant. In the new covenant, Yahweh's Spirit works through our regenerated spirits in order to sanctify us. Remember, the backbone of the Mosaic covenant was the law that Yah attached to the Torah to sanctify His people. As Yah's Spirit regenerates saints and indwells them, He sanctifies them; hence He releases them from the Torah's law, but He does not release them from the Torah, because it is the foundational revelation of who He is and how He wants His people to live.

Some of the Torah's instructions relate to the implementation of the Mosaic covenant and the maintenance of its institutions; that is, the temple, priests, sacrifices, and the rituals that emphasized Yah's holiness and distinguished His system from pagan religions. Today there is no temple; therefore, there is no priesthood and thus no way to offer sacrifices. Thus it is impossible for us to obey these instructions. All we can do is renew our minds with these instructions so that the Spirit can show us how to walk out the intent of the written Torah.[xiii]

---

[312] Ibid., Exodus 28:3; 35:31; Numbers 11:17; Deuteronomy 34:9; Judges 6:34; 15:14; 1 Samuel 16:13; 1 Peter 1:11.

[313] Ibid., Exodus 31:13; Nehemiah 9:14–20; Ezekiel 20:12; Galatians 3:19.

The written Torah is still the standard of righteousness, so we should obey it whenever possible. The Torah is a fence that protects us so that we can live the abundant life. The Torah was the hedge of protection that Yahweh placed around Job and his family. If we obey Yahweh's teachings and instructions, they will protect us and produce the abundant life. If, however, we deliberately step over the fence; that is, disobey the Torah, we will step on HaSatan's territory and submit to him and open ourselves to the curses that Yeshua delivered us from.

Picture this: Life is a highway that winds through mountains. A governor has set the speed limits for the highway and an engineer has put signs beside the highway to protect us and ensure that we enjoy a safe, prosperous trip. The signs are the Torah. If we obey the signs, we will make it home. If we ignore the signs, we will get a ticket or crash and burn and never make it home.

Now let us say that a new governor takes office. This new governor decides not to give any more tickets or arrest anyone for recklessness. Are we now free to drive as fast as we want? Yes, but if we do, we will tear our car up and suffer unnecessary expense and delay, or we will crash and burn and never make it home. To help us, the engineer who designed the roads and put up the signs comes to ride in our car with us. If we pay attention to the signs and listen closely to the engineer's guidance, we will have a safe, prosperous trip and arrive on time and on budget.

End of Excursus

This is Paul's question: if we will not be ticketed and penalized for ignoring the traffic signs, shall we ignore the traffic signs because the engineer who put them up is riding with us? Paul responds, no, do not even think like that! The engineer uses the signs to guide us to ensure that we have a safe, prosperous trip and arrive alive. So just because we have been set free from the legal consequences for speeding does not mean that we should disregard the signs and speed.

In verse 16, Paul explains why we should not violate the Torah's commandments: "Know ye not, that to whom ye yield yourselves servants to obey, his servants ye are to whom ye obey; whether of sin unto death, or of obedience unto righteousness?" In other words, if you step over the fence of the written Torah, you will be on HaSatan's territory, and he will kill, steal, and destroy; but if you stay within the fence of the Torah, you will enjoy the fruits of righteousness, which are unbroken fellowship with Yah, peace, freedom, and prosperity.

Here is the bottom line: If we listen to the engineer who designed the roads and pay attention to the signs that he put up, then we will arrive on time, on budget, and enjoy our trip. However, if we listen to the voice on the radio that tells us to go as fast as we want because the signs were put up for Old Testament drivers, and ignore the engineer in our front seat who is trying to get us to obey the signs, we will tear up our car, crash, or never reach our destination.

In verses 22 and 23, the apostle Paul uses the analogy of slavery to drive his point home. Every man has to serve a master, and ultimately there are only two masters: Yahweh and HaSatan. Paul says that we came into the world as a servant of HaSatan, and he paid us the wages of sickness, disease, addiction, poverty, death, and eternal death.

As HaSatan's slaves, we were in bondage to sin; but Yah offered us the gift of repentance, and we bowed our knee to Yeshua, confessing Him as Lord. Yah's Spirit put our spirit to death and resurrected it. Yah's Spirit purified our spirit so that we could fellowship with Him. Yah's Spirit prompts our spirit to follow Him and gives our spirit the authority and the power to force our rebellious soul and vile body to obey. As we cooperate with Yah's Spirit, He produces the fruit of holiness in our life. Paul encourages us to serve our new master and shun the old one.

Part 11

A Survey of Romans: Putting the Law in Its Place

Chapter 40

The Debate Over Romans 7

Two Issues

Theologians have debated Romans 7 for hundreds of years. The debate revolves around two issues: (1) Does the "I" in Romans 7 represent Paul, a hypothetical man, or life in Adam? (2) Is this person describing his life under the law that Yahweh gave in the Garden of Eden, his life under the law Yahweh gave at Mount Sinai, or his life after he died to the law that Yahweh gave in the garden and unpacked at Mount Sinai, and was resurrected and joined to Yahweh's Spirit? The only way that we can settle this debate and determine who and what Paul wrote about in Romans 7 is by filtering what he wrote through what we know about the human system configuration. So let us get started.

In the beginning, Yah's Spirit and the human spirit were in perfect fellowship together. Yah's Spirit infused the human spirit with the authority and the power it needed to keep the soul and the body in submission so that they would carry out the spirit's will, which was Yah's will. So originally, the HSC brought Yah's will from the spirit realm into the physical realm with no interference from the soul and the body, which were both bent towards the material realm.

In the fall, the human spirit turned away from Yahweh, forfeiting the authority and power it needed to keep the soul and body in submission, and HaSatan built strongholds inside the soul. HaSatan took over the HSC and began bringing his will to pass on earth through it. Man's spirit takes on the image of whomever it submits to, and it does not matter whether it submits willingly or a more powerful being forces it to submit. Hence man's spirit took on HaSatan's image. Man's spirit now leaned toward rebellion, strove to be self-sufficient, and sought to please the flesh.

After the fall, Yahweh's Spirit reached out to the fallen human spirits. If a fallen human spirit believed His promise about the Seed and submitted to Him, He redeemed and justified that person. Yahweh expected these people to circumcise their hearts and love Him by obeying Him. This means that Yahweh's Spirit helped people circumcise their hearts, because He would not ask them to do something that could not be done and then punish them for not doing it.[314]

After a human spirit had *chosen* to yield to Yah's Spirit and believe His promises about the Seed, Yah credited the Seed's sacrifice to the person's account. The Seed's blood paid the ransom price so that Yah could release the fallen spirit from the serpent's slave market. Yah's Spirit placed these human spirits in His kingdom, but He did not unite Himself with them and indwell them. In other words, Yahweh redeemed the human spirit, but He did not regenerate it. Hence the redeemed human spirit did not have the power to rule over the rebellious soul and vile body.

The redeemed human spirit appreciated being free from the serpent's slave market. The redeemed human spirit wanted to worship, serve, and obey Yah, but he wanted to do it in a way that exalted him and allowed him to satisfy the desires of the soul and body. The saint was in a precarious position, but the more he looked to the Promised Seed, meditated on the Torah, and sought Yah, the more the Spirit helped him keep his fallen nature in line and his soul and body under control. Nevertheless, when the fallen nature got the better of him, he could offer the prescribed sacrifices, drawing upon the finished work of the Seed, and be forgiven and cleansed.

If a human spirit chose not to yield to Yah's Spirit, believe His promises about the Seed, and put his faith in Him, then Yah could not redeem that person and help him keep his heart circumcised as he *walked out his faith* by keeping the written Torah and complying with its law. Hence this person's fallen nature deceived him into believing that he could overpower his evil inclination by keeping the Torah and complying with its law so that he could be righteous. In other words, some people in Yahweh's earthly kingdom (Israel) did not put their trust in His promises about the Seed. Yah could not place these people in His spiritual kingdom and declare them righteous. These people (the apostate sages and their sheep) tried to keep every jot and tittle of the Torah and meticulously comply with its law *to establish their own righteousness*.

The apostate sages and their sheep delighted in the Torah and its law for the wrong reasons. The sages and their sheep looked at the law as a tool that they could use to overcome their evil inclination (fallen nature) so they could enter the age to come (save themselves). On the outside, these people did everything that the law required, but on the inside, they were at enmity with the law and full of fear, unbelief, criticism, guilt, lust, hatred, and violence. As these people went to the temple to offer sacrifices, they shed innocent blood; but since their faith was not in the Seed and His righteousness, Yahweh did not forgive these

---

[314] *The Hebrew-Greek Key Word Study Bible*, KJV, Deuteronomy 10:12, 16.

people and cleanse them. Hence these people had to sew together fig leaves to hide their nakedness, pain, fear, and shame.

Thankfully, Yah preserved a remnant in order to fulfill His promise to Abraham. If Yah's Spirit had not entered into,[315] overpowered,[316] clothed,[317] filled,[318] come upon,[319] fallen upon,[320] and rested upon[321] His people to preserve a remnant, everyone would have joined the sages' religion, and there would not have been a righteous line to bring the Seed through. Yah preserved a remnant so that Yeshua could come through it and graft the rest of the nation into it, because it is written: "And the LORD thy God will circumcise thine heart, and the heart of thy seed, to love the LORD thy God with all thine heart, and with all thy soul, that thou mayest live."[322]

The remnant was waiting on the Seed, so they accepted Him when He appeared, but the apostate religious rulers and their sheep rejected Him and persecuted Him. After the Romans crucified Yeshua, His Spirit began implementing His plan by indwelling His disciples in order to bring His will to pass through them. In response, the apostate religious rulers began to persecute and kill Yeshua's disciples.

Paul had been one of these religious rulers. He had thought he could keep the Torah and comply with its law to merit salvation; thus Yahweh's condemnation was on him. On the Damascus road, Yeshua showed Paul how his religious education had blinded him. Paul repented, believed, and bowed his knee to Yeshua, and He gave him His Spirit and his sight.

In Romans 7, Paul looks back to when he was spiritually blind and under the condemnation of the law, trying to keep every jot and tittle of it. Outwardly Paul kept the Torah's commandments, but on the inside, there was a conflict raging. Paul's spirit delighted in the Torah (because his spirit wanted to use it to fix itself up), but it was powerless to rule over his soul and body. Consequently, he knew what was right, but could not do it, and he knew what was wrong, but did it. Paul's spirit was not ruling his HSC; his soul and body were ruling it.

---

[315] Ibid., Ezekiel 2:2; 3:24.

[316] Ibid., Judges 14:6, 19; 15:14; 1 Samuel 10:10; 11:6.

[317] Ibid., Judges 6:34; 1 Chronicles 12:18; 2 Chronicles 24:20.

[318] Ibid., Exodus 31:3; 35:31.

[319] Ibid., 1 Samuel 16:13.

[320] Ibid., Ezekiel 11:5.

[321] Ibid., Numbers 11:25.

[322] Ibid., Deuteronomy 30:6; Romans 11:26.

Paul's Experiences Under the Law

Early in Romans 7, Paul says that as we die with Yeshua, we die to the law. Paul does not contradict himself by later describing a regenerated person's battle with the law. Many theologians think that Romans 7 discusses how the regenerated spirit, which Yah has become one with, struggles to bring the soul and body under control. This is unlikely, however. Paul does not mention "Spirit" in this chapter and mentions "spirit" only once. Hence I believe that in Romans 7, Paul looked back to when he was in the apostate religion and described the frustration he felt as he tried to overcome his sin nature by keeping the Torah. This means that Yahweh had not yet redeemed, justified, or regenerated Paul and that HaSatan ruled his HSC, thus influencing his soul and body. Augustine,[323] Chrysostom,[324] John Stott,[325] Douglas Moo,[326] Ben Witherington III,[327] Franklin Paschall, and Herschel Hobbs [328] concur.

Paul was a Jew. Paul addressed this chapter to his brothers who knew the law. Thus, to understand this chapter, we have to filter it through a Jewish worldview. I have enlisted the help of three men with Jewish worldviews to accomplish this task: Abraham Heschel, Tim Hegg, and Joseph Shulam. Tim Hegg is a messianic Jew. Mr. Hegg says the sages' religion evolved into modern Judaism, which defines sin as a failure to do the commandments. So, in Judaism, a person is supposedly able to overcome his sinful nature by keeping the commandments.[329]

Abraham Heschel, a nonmessianic Jew and an expert on Judaism, writes, "We believe that there is a law, the essence of which is derived from prophetic events, and the interpretation of which is in the hands of the sages"; and "in Judaism allegiance to God involves a commitment to Jewish law, to a discipline, to specific obligations."[330] "Halakhah is the rationalization and schematization of living; it defines, specifies, sets measure and limit,

---

[323] Ben Witherington, *Paul's Letter to the Romans*, Grand Rapids, MI, Eerdmans Publishing Co., 2004, p. 180.

[324] Ibid., p. 194.

[325] John Stott, *Romans*, Downers Grove, IL, InterVarsity Press, 1994, pp. 50–51.

[326] Douglas Moo, *The Epistle to the Romans*, Grand Rapids, MI, Eerdmans Publishing Co., 1996, pp. 445–451.

[327] Ben Witherington, *Paul's Letter to the Romans*, Grand Rapids, MI, Eerdmans Publishing Co., 2004, p. 195.

[328] F. Paschall and H. Hobbs, *The Teacher's Bible Commentary,* Nashville, TN, Broadman & Holman, 1972, pp. 713–15.*

[329] Tim Hegg, *Paul's Epistle to the Romans*, Tacoma, WA, TorahResource, 2005, pp. 191–95.

[330] Fritz A. Rothschild, *Between God and Man*, New York, NY, Harper & Row, 1959, p. 158.

placing life into an exact system. Agadah deals with man's ineffable relations to God, to other men, and to the world."[331]

According to Heschel, Judaism stresses *kavvanah* (purpose, motive, and intention), and the study of *agadah* (the Scriptures that do not deal with the law) builds faith and cultivates the right *kavvanah*, ensuring that a person keeps the law with the right motive. Heschel shows how the serpent has tricked man into believing that he can fix himself by keeping the Torah and establishing his own righteousness so that he does not have to admit that he is a treasonous criminal, humble himself, and receive righteousness as a gift. Heschel also writes, "It is agadah that keeps on reminding that the purpose of performance is to transform the performer, that the purpose of observance is to train us in achieving spiritual ends... It is well known that the purpose of all mitzvot is to purify the heart, for the heart is the essence."[332] "Indeed, the purpose of all mitzvot is to refine man."[333] "Yet there is power in the deed that purifies desires."[334] Hence Judaism teaches that when a person performs Yahweh's commands, he takes on His image.

Heschel writes, "Good deeds alone will not redeem history; it is the obedience to God that will make us worthy of being redeemed by God."[335] In other words, if we perform the commandments, we will become worthy enough for Yah to save us. This means that ultimately redemption rests on our shoulders because we have to merit salvation before Yah will save us. Thus, in Judaism, salvation is not by grace through faith; it is by the works of the law. Very clearly, Judaism leaves plenty of room for boasting. Heschel affirms this by writing, "The world is in need of redemption, but the redemption must not be expected to happen as an act of sheer grace. Man's task is to make the world worthy of redemption. His faith and his works are preparations for ultimate redemption."[336] Apparently, the Jews' "ultimate redemption" will come through a messiah who will cut a new covenant when they deserve it; but until then, they will redeem themselves by keeping the law. Heschel affirms this by writing, "Yet we [Jews] are never lost. We are the sons of Abraham.[337]

Joseph Shulam is a messianic Jew. Mr. Shulam wrote *A Commentary on the Jewish Roots of Romans*. In his informative book, Mr. Shulam says that in chapters 5 and 6 of

---

[331] Ibid., p. 175.

[332] Ibid., p. 175.

[333] Ibid., p. 185.

[334] Ibid., p. 190.

[335] Ibid., p. 197.

[336] Ibid., p. 197.

[337] Ibid., p. 197.

Romans, Paul deals with the issue of Yahweh's justification of the Gentiles through faithfulness, and in chapter 7, he addresses some of the concerns of his Jewish brothers.[338]

Paul was often misunderstood. There was a rumor that Paul taught against the Torah and its law, promoting lawlessness in order to glorify Yahweh.[339] Hence Paul needed to clarify his position and let the Jewish believers know where they stood in relation to the Torah and its law. Mr. Shulam says that some of the Jews of that day (like those in Judaism today) thought that they could overcome the fallen nature (the evil inclination) by keeping the Torah's commands.[340] To combat this heresy, Paul explained how the Torah's law affected an unredeemed, unregenerated person by writing about his struggles with the law before Yahweh's Spirit put him to death on the execution stake with Yeshua and resurrected him to live in Him.

Paul was putting the Torah and its law in its place within the messianic paradigm for his Jewish brothers to show them how futile it was for them to try to keep the Torah and its law in an effort to overcome their fallen nature. Yeshua suffered and died so that His Spirit could put our fallen spirit to death and resurrect it in Him to empower it to overcome the fallen nature's residual effects. Paul did not say that we should ignore the Torah and continue to sin as a way of magnifying Yahweh's grace, nor did he say that we could overcome and change our fallen nature by keeping the Torah.

Hegg, Heschel, and Shulam give us valuable insight into what Paul would have been thinking before he was redeemed and regenerated, and their thoughts validate our analysis of the HSC. As we consider the mechanics of the human system configuration, the religion of the sages, and the tenets of modern Judaism, and remember that a Jew wrote this section of Scripture to Jews about the Torah's law, we understand that Paul was describing *his struggle with the law before Yah regenerated him*. I know some people object to this reasoning because Paul said that when he was a Pharisee in the apostate religion, he was blameless in respect to the law. This objection is not valid because an unredeemed, unregenerated person could fail to do good and do evil and then perform every ritual that the law called for without being right with Yahweh.[341]

---

[338] Joseph Shulam, *A Commentary on the Jewish Roots of Romans*, Baltimore, MD, Lederer Books, 1997, p. 235.

[339] *The Hebrew-Greek Key Word Study Bible*, KJV, Acts 21:21; Romans 6:1.

[340] Joseph Shulam, *A Commentary on the Jewish Roots of Romans*, Baltimore, MD, Lederer Books, 1997, p. 236.

[341] *The Hebrew-Greek Key Word Study Bible*, KJV, Matthew 23:28.

Chapter 41

Romans 7:1–14

Verses 1–4

Paul addressed this section to his brothers who knew *the law*. Some interpreters say that Paul addressed this section to the people who knew *Roman law*; that is, he addressed it to Gentiles. This does not make sense. Everyone in Rome would have been familiar with Roman law. Why would Paul address a section on Roman law to one group? No, Paul addressed this section to his Jewish brothers who knew the *Mosaic law*. Paul did not want his brothers to misconstrue his teachings and think that he was validating the sages' teachings that said they could keep the Torah in order to overcome their evil inclination. Moreover, the sages had accused Paul of teaching against the Torah, and he wanted his Jewish brothers to know that this was not true.[342]

Paul says that the legal code that Yahweh attached to the Torah has jurisdiction over a man as long as he lives. Paul uses the marriage relationship to illustrate his point. In this case, the sages' halachah was in line with Yahweh's heart, so Paul used their halachah to prove his point to those who were familiar with Jewish law. Hegg[343] and Shulam[344] cite references that prove that the sages taught that if a woman's husband died, she died to him, and she was, therefore, free to remarry another man. The apostle Paul picks up this theme and runs with it.

---

[342] Joseph Shulam, *A Commentary on the Jewish Roots of Romans*, Baltimore, MD, Lederer Books, 1997, p. 236.

[343] Tim Hegg, *Paul's Epistle to the Romans*, Tacoma, WA, TorahResource, 2005, p. 164–65.

[344] Joseph Shulam, *A Commentary on the Jewish Roots of Romans*, Baltimore, MD, Lederer Books, 1997, p. 237.

The Torah said that if a man sent his wife away without a bill of divorce and she married another man, she was an adulterer. If, however, she received a bill of divorce prior to her husband sending her away, she was free to marry. The sages' halachah said if a woman's husband died, she died to her husband; thus she was free to marry, and the law could not condemn her. Paul's point: At Mount Sinai, fallen human spirits entered into a relationship with Yahweh through the law, but when these spirits die in Yeshua, they are released from the law's custodianship. Thus the Torah's law cannot condemn them anymore. Yah's Spirit resurrects their spirit and becomes one with it. Hence Yah's Spirit is now the custodian of their relationship with Him.

Verse 5

In this verse, Paul explains the effect that the law has on the fallen nature when grace is absent; that is, the effect the law had on those outside of the remnant. A fallen spirit believes the serpent's lie and strives to prove that he is a god; hence he will not admit that he is a criminal, humble himself, and circumcise his heart. Instead, a fallen man tries to keep the commandments in order to prove that he is righteous enough to have a relationship with Yahweh. Daniel Fuller expressed this well when he wrote the following: "When one is convinced that the Mosaic law, as well as the other commandments in the Bible, comes from God, then all these commands provide the ego with the greatest opportunity (aphormen!) for satisfying its cravings."[345]

The people outside of the remnant refused to humble themselves and circumcise their hearts. These people tried to keep the commandments as a way to become righteous so that Yah would save them, which proved that their fallen nature was ruling over them. The law provoked their fallen nature to sin (by misusing the commandments), so when they sacrificed animals, they did not receive forgiveness or cleansing from the Spirit. Thus these people remained under the condemnation of the law (under the law), and this caused them to be more zealous for the law because they needed more and more fig leaves to cover their guilt, shame, and condemnation!

At Mount Sinai, Yahweh joined Himself to redeemed fallen men through the Torah and its law. The Torah and its law showed the redeemed how to walk out their faith so that Yahweh could bless them and bring His plan to pass. Not long after this, HaSatan deceived the Israelites into reversing Yahweh's plan by trying to use the written Torah and its law to establish their own righteousness so that Yah would redeem them. This is silly. The Torah is Yah's standard of righteousness, and the fallen nature opposes the nature of the Torah. Thus there is no way a fallen man can reach the goal of righteousness. This was what Yah was

---

[345] Daniel P. Fuller, *Gospel & Law: Contrast or Continuum?*, Pasadena, CA, Fuller Seminary Press, 1982, pp. 94–95.

showing fallen man, but he rose up in pride and tried to prove that he could reach the goal. Of course, he could not reach the goal, and this frustrated him, releasing diseased emotions in his soul and body that caused him to sin more.

Verses 6–13

In verse 6, Paul tells his brothers that Yah has released them from the custodianship of the Torah's law. Yah's Spirit has put their spirits, which were under the custodianship of the law, to death with Yeshua. Yah's Spirit has resurrected their spirits and become one with them. So they are no longer under the custodianship of the Torah that was written on stone; they are under the custodianship of the Spirit, and He writes the Torah on their hearts and empowers them to obey it.

In verse 7, Paul asks, "What shall we say then? Is the law sin?" Paul answers this rhetorical question by saying, "God forbid." The law revealed sin. Sin, however, took advantage of the platform that the law gave it and triggered diseased desires in the soul and body that produced more sin that produced death. Paul explains this further by using his own life as an example. Paul essentially says, "I was alive once, but the commandment came and sin revived, and I died. The commandment that I thought would lead me to life became death unto me because sin capitalized on the opportunity that the commandment gave it and deceived me and slew me."

Paul parallels his experience with what happened in the Garden of Eden. Eve was grown and accountable for her behavior. Yahweh gave the commandment to Adam. Adam gave it to Eve. The serpent took advantage of the platform that the commandment gave him, deceived Eve, and slew her. Paul, however, was not accountable to the commandments until his bar mitzvah, which is why he says that there was a time when he was alive apart from the law.[346]

When Paul was thirteen, his dad turned him over to Yah's commandments. Paul was then accountable to the commandments, and via his fallen spirit, the serpent took advantage of the commandments, deceived him, and slew him. In other words, the serpent tricked Paul into misusing the Torah and its law, proving that he was spiritually dead. However, Paul says that the Torah and its law are holy, just, and good. In verse 13, Paul asks if Yah gave the Torah and its law to kill us. He answers by saying that Yah put His people under the custodianship of the law to expose their sin and make it grievous so that they would realize they had a sin nature.

---

[346] Joseph Shulam, *A Commentary on the Jewish Roots of Romans*, Baltimore, MD, Lederer Books, 1997, p. 245.

Chapter 42

Romans 7:14–25

Background

Regenerated interpreters identify with the struggles that Paul described in this section of Romans, and their emotional involvement with the text causes them to presuppose that Paul was writing about their struggles. But this presupposition skews their perception and affects their hermeneutical and exegetical skills, and they interpret the text to support their presupposition.

Ben Witherington III, who is an expert in rhetoric, describes the situation in more technical terms, saying, "So then, there is the passing of the baton. Failure to recognize this rhetorical way of introducing the next argument before concluding the previous one has helped lead to the incorrect conclusion that Paul is speaking about Christians in 7:14–25, a mistake various early Greek Fathers, who knew rhetoric did not make."[347] In other words, Paul is still writing about the fallen man's struggle with the law, describing how it provokes him to sin.

At Sinai, Yah entered into a relationship with fallen man that revolved around the law. Yah condensed the Torah into the Ten Commandments and wrote them on stone tablets. Then Yah gave Moses the Torah in its expanded form and attached a legal code to it. Moses wrote the Torah and its law on scrolls, and fallen man struggled with it. Fallen man struggled with the Torah and its law because it was holy, but he was not. The Torah that Yahweh wrote on stone tablets established the standard of righteousness, but it did not change man's heart so he could live up to it.

---

[347] Ben Witherington, *Paul's Letter to the Romans*, Grand Rapids, MI, Eerdmans Publishing Co., 2004, p. 196.

Romans 7:14–25

However, once a fallen man chooses to circumcise his heart by repenting from his sin, believing Yahweh's promises, and bowing his knee to the lordship of Yeshua, he dies on the execution stake with Yeshua. The fallen human spirit that had a relationship with Yahweh through the Torah and its law is dead, so the Torah's law cannot condemn it anymore.

It does not end there. The Holy Spirit resurrects the human spirit and becomes one with it. Now obviously, this makes the human spirit righteous, holy, above blame, and beyond reproach. As regenerated individuals study the written Torah, Yahweh's Spirit writes it on their hearts, changing their desires, giving them the power to walk it out. The reborn human spirit is holy, so the holiness of the Torah does not frustrate the reborn man. This diffuses the power of sin. The reborn human spirit is free to serve Yah. A regenerated person has no quarrel with the Torah or its law; therefore this section is not describing a regenerated person's struggle to obey the Torah.

However, if a regenerated person thinks that this section of Romans is describing his struggle, he will not enjoy the victory that Yeshua gave him. If we think that we have to struggle with the Torah or its law, then, on some level, we think that we are still at odds with Yahweh. Yah defines sin as not obeying the Torah, and the law makes sin a crime that He has to punish. If we think that we are still under the custodianship of the law, then, when we sin, we will think that there is an unresolved legal issue between Yah and us and that He is going to punish us for our sin. Thus we will live with guilt, condemnation, and fear and give HaSatan a platform to stand on so he can deceive us, torment us, manipulate us, rule over us, and bring death into our lives. It is imperative for us to understand that we have died to the law and that it can no longer condemn us, because if we do not, HaSatan will convince us that we can lose our salvation.

Yeshua gave us the victory, but to walk in it, we must realize that our old rebellious, spirit has died, and we have died to the law. Accordingly, Yah has no basis on which to punish us in hell or to act as if there is an unresolved legal issue between Him and us and condemn us or curse us for our sins in this life. So does this mean that we can sin without consequences? No, when we sin, there is an unresolved legal issue between HaSatan and us! We have stepped over the protective fence of the Torah and onto his land, and he has a legal right to attack us. If, however, we jump back over the fence (repent), confess, and sprinkle the blood of the Lamb on our conscience, then HaSatan has no legal claim against us and no basis on which to attack us.

Misinterpreting this section of Romans also promotes a mentality of defeat because we get the mistaken idea that we cannot overcome sin or the flesh. This is a lie. Our old fallen spirit that had a relationship with Yah through the law died on the execution stake in Yeshua, and we died to the law. Consequently, Yah no longer imputes our sins to us. Yah's Spirit resurrected our spirit and became one with it. We are now holy, so the holy Torah does not provoke us to sin. Yeshua has removed the platform that gave sin the ability to rule over us through the flesh.

Yahweh's Spirit resurrected our spirit as a *new creature* and became one with it. As a result, our spirit is in agreement with the Torah, clothed in Messiah's righteousness, and sitting at the right hand of the Father. Consequently, when a regenerated person sins, it is because he *chooses* to let his defiant soul and vile body feed on their favorite comfort foods. In other words, sin does not overpower a regenerated person; sin entices him to surrender to it. There is a big difference between someone surrendering to sin and sin overpowering someone. This section of Romans describes sin overpowering a person, not a person who surrenders to it. Thus this section is not describing a regenerated person's struggle with sin and the flesh; this section is describing how the law gives sin and the flesh an opportunity to rule over a fallen man.

Verses 14–15

Paul begins this section by stating the obvious: Yah gave Israel the Torah and its law. Hence the Torah and its law came from the spirit realm; that is, the Torah and its law are spiritual. Paul says, "But I am fleshly, sold under sin." Paul is referring to the fact that Adam rebelled against Yah and separated himself from Him. HaSatan captured Adam and built strongholds in his soul so that he could control him and manifest his will on earth through him. Adam's spirit took on HaSatan's image. Then Adam had sex with Eve, and she gave birth to children who possessed his spirit. Adam's iniquity separated his children from Yahweh and made it possible for HaSatan to rule over them. Thus Adam sold Paul and everyone else into slavery to sin.

Paul contrasts the fallen man, who is a slave to sin, with the Torah and its law, which is good, righteous, and holy. Paul is pointing to the fact that the Torah and its law serve as the pure white canvas that accentuates the black ink of our sin in order to paint a portrait of our fallen nature. In verse 15, Paul tells us how he struggled with the law when he was hiding behind the fig leaves of religion. Incredibly, even though Paul was beating, imprisoning, and killing his Jewish brothers and sisters who were in Yeshua's ekklesia, he said that he was blameless in respect to the law! This shows us how deceptive sin is and how powerless religion is to stop it. Paul says that since he was in the flesh (carnal), he did the things he hated; and the things that he wanted to do, he could not do, while the things that he did not want to do, he did. In essence, Paul is telling us that his rebellious soul and vile body were ruling his HSC; hence they prevented his spirit (him) from doing what he wanted to do, and they forced him to do what he did not want to do.

Verses 16–20

In verses 16 and 17, Paul says that his fallen spirit knew that the written Torah was the standard of righteousness, and he wanted to improve himself to meet that standard. However, since he consistently failed to do the things that he wanted to do, it became obvious that sin was ruling over him and preventing him from living up to the standard of righteousness. In verse 18, Paul says that he was aware that his spirit was not in charge of his HSC and that his flesh was, and that HaSatan was pulling the strings of the flesh. Paul (his spirit) wanted to obey Yah and do good (in order to fix himself), but he could not force his rebellious soul and vile body to carry out his will. In verses 19 and 20, Paul says that he was powerless to do the good he wanted to do, and he did the evil he did not want to do, and this brought him to the realization that he was controlled by the sin that dwelt in him. In other words, Paul was powerless to do good and shun evil, so he knows that HaSatan was using his corrupted HSC to control him.

Verses 21–25

In verse 21, Paul says that just as he is unable to overcome the law of gravity, he was also unable to overcome the law of evil that was in him in order to do good. In verses 22 and 23, Paul says that his inner man delighted in the law of Yah (because he wanted to use it to fix himself up and establish his own righteousness). However, even though his mind embraced Yah's law (for its own purpose) and wanted to obey it (to build itself up), it was obvious that there was a law at work in his body that prevented him from reaching his goal. In verse 24, Paul cries out, "O wretched man that I am! Who shall deliver me from the body of death?"

Paul reached the breaking point; he realized that it was impossible for him to fix his fallen spirit and establish his own righteousness by keeping the law. Hence Paul did what any pious Jew would have done: he recited a prayer that thanked Yahweh for sending Yeshua to deliver him from the body of death![348] With this, Paul tells his readers what the solution is, but before he discusses the solution in detail, he sums up what it is like being a fallen man under the law by saying that with his mind, he served the law of Yah, but with his flesh, he served the law of sin.

In sum, in Romans 7, Paul is describing his struggle with the Torah's law. Paul is describing how the Torah's law gave his prideful soul and his vile body an opportunity to rule over him (his fallen spirit). In Romans 7, Paul paints a dark, depressing, hopeless backdrop that highlights Yeshua's victory and the light, joy, and hope it brings.

In Romans 8, Paul paints a vivid picture of the victory we have in Yeshua. Yeshua delivers us from the torment that Paul described in Romans 7 by redeeming us from the *custodianship* and *condemnation* of the law, which diminishes the power of the rebellious soul and the vile body. Moreover, Yeshua's Spirit comes to live in our hearts, which changes

---

[348] Joseph Shulam, *A Commentary on the Jewish Roots of Romans*, Baltimore, MD, Lederer Books, 1997, p. 261.

our natures and writes the Torah on our hearts (as we study it), giving us the power to obey. Yeshua restores our human system configuration to its original state, but we have to learn how to operate it. Until we learn how to operate the restored HSC (mature in Christ), we will experience some of the symptoms that Paul described in Romans 7 and live beneath our potential, which is why we must cooperate with the Holy Spirit and mature in Him.

Part 12

A Survey of Romans: Life in the Spirit

Chapter 43

Romans 8:1–2

Verse 1

In Romans 7, Paul used "I" thirty-three times, which tells us who was on the throne running his temple and thus his life. In Romans 8, Paul uses "I" three times and "Spirit" twenty times, which tells us that he got off the throne so that Yeshua could run his temple. Essentially, this is what it means to repent. In Romans 8, Paul describes what happens to us after we step down from the throne and turn it over to Yeshua. Yeshua's Spirit comes to live in our temple with us in order to deliver us from the body of death.

In verse 1, Paul says, "There is therefore now no condemnation to them which are in Christ Jesus." In the King James Version, this declaration is modified by the phrase "who walk not after the flesh, but after the Spirit." Translators tell us that this phrase is not in the earliest manuscripts. A scribe who was copying an early manuscript probably added the phrase because he was afraid that basing salvation on Yeshua plus nothing else promoted sin. The scribe added the phrase to make the verdict of no condemnation conditional. In other words, according to the scribe, a believer has to walk by the Spirit and not the flesh in order to escape condemnation. The scribe's motives for altering Yahweh's Word were probably noble, but he demonstrated that he did not understand why there is no condemnation in Messiah Yeshua. Unfortunately, the scribe's addition to Yahweh's Word also breeds confusion, error, and fear.

Tim Hegg points out that the assertion that there is no condemnation to those who are in Yeshua is "the core of the Gospel and the central pillar of our salvation."[349] How do we escape condemnation? Paul says, "For by grace are ye saved through faith; and that not

---

[349] Tim Hegg, *Paul's Epistle to the Romans*, Tacoma, WA, TorahResource, 2005, p. 196.

of yourselves: it is the gift of God: Not of works, lest any man should boast."[350] Yahweh's Spirit gives us the *grace* to repent, and if we *choose* to repent, then we step down from the throne and ask Yeshua to be our Lord (King) so that He can establish His kingdom in us and empower us to be His ambassadors so that we can introduce others to Him.[351] Yah declares us not guilty and frees us from condemnation and wrath because He condemned Yeshua for our sin and poured out His wrath on Him instead of pouring it out on us.

How did Yahweh pour out His wrath on Yeshua? Yahweh allowed the Romans to afflict Yeshua's body with a cat-o'-nine-tails. Yahweh allowed Yeshua to suffer the pain of separation, sickness, disease, and death. Yahweh allowed the demons to take Yeshua's human spirit to hell. At the appointed time, Yahweh's Spirit came upon Yeshua's spirit, delivered Him from hell, reunited Him with His body, and He arose with the keys to the grave, death, and hell!

According to 1 Corinthians 12:13, as we put our trust in Yeshua and bow our knee to Him, Yah's Spirit baptizes our fallen spirit into His spiritual body. This baptism puts our fallen spirit, which deserves the punishment that Yeshua received, to death. After this, Yah's Spirit resurrects our spirit. Our new spirit is blameless, so the Holy Spirit unites Himself with our spirit, infusing us with His life and nature. Yahweh credits Yeshua's punishment to our account and hence releases us from condemnation, wrath, and punishment.

The old spirit man, who was under the custodianship of the law and wanted to use it to establish his own righteousness, died on the execution stake, and Yahweh resurrected him as a humble spirit who wants to obey Him and His Torah. The scribe did not understand that man's new spirit is one with Yah's Spirit; thus Yah's life and nature are his life and nature. Man's new nature propels him towards righteousness, and since the Torah is the standard of righteousness, he wants to walk out its intent. Man's new nature mirrors the nature of the Torah, so he is not under the custodianship of the law; hence Yahweh no longer imputes his sins to him. The new man is under the custodianship of the Holy Spirit, who doggedly restrains him from sin, propels him towards righteousness, and makes it *impossible* for him to live *comfortably* in sin.

---

[350] *The Hebrew-Greek Key Word Study Bible*, KJV, Ephesians 2:8–9.
[351] Ibid., Romans 10:9.

Excursus

The Ministry of the Holy Spirit

In the beginning, the Spirit moved upon the face of the waters. Yeshua spoke, and the Spirit brought His words into being. Yeshua created Adam and Eve, and they were in perfect fellowship with Yahweh. However, Yahweh needed to test Adam and Eve to see if they would follow Lucifer and lift themselves up in pride to rebel, or if they would remain humble, trusting and obeying Him.

Yahweh tested Adam and Eve by giving them a commandment with a legal provision attached to it. After this, the serpent tempted Eve. Eve turned away from Yah's Spirit, and the serpent used the law to slay her. Adam followed Eve, and their consciences came to life and began to judge between good and evil. The first couple died spiritually; that is, their spirits were no longer in fellowship with Yah's Spirit and infused with His authority and power. Hence the first couple forfeited their dominion over the HSC. After this, the serpent built strongholds in their souls so that he could control their HSCs and force them to build his kingdom on the earth.

After this, Yahweh's Spirit worked in concert with man's conscience to restrain him from sin. Yah's Spirit strove with man and tried to get him to believe His promise to send the Seed and to show that he believed by coming to an altar with a sacrifice. A few people (like Enoch and Noah) believed that Yahweh would send the Seed to restore things to the original condition and fellowshiped with Him through the blood of an innocent sacrifice. Most people ignored Yah's Spirit and their own consciences and lifted themselves up in pride to satisfy the lusts of the flesh.

Yah raptured Enoch shortly before He poured out His wrath on the earth, and Noah and his family passed through His wrath in an ark that was sealed with pitch (atonement) and steered (led) by the Holy Spirit. After the flood, Yah gave man some basic principles of government that He could work through to restrain sin, but fallen men ignored His Spirit, their consciences, and His principles of government and built a religion that birthed their own governmental and economic systems. So Yah confused their language and scattered them to the ends of the earth.

After this, Yah called Abram out of Babylon and promised to make a great nation out of him. Yah placed Abraham's descendants in an incubator called Egypt until they were strong enough to take possession of the Promised Land. In Egypt, Yah's people learned the ways of the Egyptians, so He took them to Mount Sinai. At Sinai, Yah gave His people 613 commands that His Spirit could work through in order to identify sin, restrain sin, and forgive them when they did sin. Yahweh used the Mosaic covenant to hold the Abrahamic covenant in place until the Seed could come and cut a new covenant that would put away sin and enable Him to fulfill the Abrahamic covenant. At Mount Sinai, Yahweh also betrothed Himself to the nation of Israel.

Over time, Israel got prideful, and she would not respond to the Holy Spirit. Yahweh, however, made sure that there was a remnant that would respond to His Spirit. The people in the remnant responded to the Holy Spirit, humbled themselves, and put their trust in the Promised Seed. Yahweh redeemed and justified the people in the remnant, and they waited expectantly for the Seed; but the Holy Spirit had not yet begun regenerating man (permanently circumcising his heart), so the flesh that the saints trimmed from their hearts grew back, causing them to sin again.

Yah's Spirit forgave the sins of His saints, cleansed their consciences, and helped them retrim the flesh from their hearts as they offered sacrifices. However, Israel's religious rulers lost sight of Yahweh's promise and the true meaning of the Abrahamic covenant. Israel's religious rulers refused to respond to the Holy Spirit and tried to exalt themselves by misusing the law. These men would not trim the flesh from their hearts by humbling themselves and putting their trust in the Seed. Consequently, the serpent took advantage of the law and used it to slay them.

In sum, the Holy Spirit has always tried to get man to humble himself, believe Yah's promises, and put his trust in Him. The Spirit tried to keep Adam humble, but he wanted to follow his wife and judge between good and evil, so he turned his back on Him. After man's conscience came to life, the Spirit tried to use it to restrain his fallen nature, but man would not listen to his conscience. The Spirit also tried to restrain the fallen nature through the principles of government, the promises to the patriarchs, and the law of Moses, but fallen man disregarded the principles of government, disbelieved the promises, and used the Mosaic law to exalt himself. So at the appointed time, Yeshua made it possible for Yah to put a fallen spirit to death, resurrect it, and regenerate it as a spirit that submits to Him, loves Him, and desires to obey Him. The Spirit has no trouble restraining a regenerated spirit because they are of like nature. Hence the scribe did not have to add a modifying phrase to Yahweh's Word, because in the new covenant, the Spirit regenerates man and ensures that he walks humbly before Him in love.

End of Excursus

Verse 2

In this verse, Paul says, "For the law of the Spirit of life in Messiah Yeshua hath made me free from the law of sin and death." In essence, Paul says that he used to misuse the Torah and its law. In other words, Paul used to try to keep the Torah and comply with its law in order to establish his own righteousness in order to keep his position in the covenant. Hence Paul was provoking his fallen nature to sin, and Yah could not forgive and cleanse him when he offered sacrifices. Therefore, HaSatan used the Torah to slay him; that is, HaSatan used the Torah to bring sin and death into his life. This is the law of sin and death.

What is the law of the Spirit of life? In the Mosaic covenant, the Spirit wrote the Torah on stone tablets, which did nothing to change man's heart. The heart of a fallen man is deceitful and desperately wicked, so he used the Torah and its law to exalt himself. As fallen men tried to live up to Yah's standard of righteousness without His grace, then guilt, shame, condemnation, and fear overtook them, prompting them to hide behind the fig leaves of religion. In the new covenant, the Spirit writes the Torah on man's heart and changes it. The Spirit nudges a believer towards the goal of living out the intent of the Torah. The *Spirit* is now the *law* that restrains us from sin and moves us to seek Yahweh's kingdom so the blessings come upon us and we live the abundant life. This is the law of the Spirit of life in Messiah Yeshua that has made us free from the law of sin and death.

Chapter 44

Romans 8:3–17

Verses 3–6

In verse 3, Paul tells his readers that when Yahweh wrote the Torah on stone tablets, it did not change man's heart and empower him to obey it. In other words, Yah did not give us the Torah so that we could keep it and repair our fallen natures, making ourselves acceptable to Him. If the Torah could have transformed man into a new creature, then life would have come through the law, and there would have been no need for Yeshua to suffer and die on the execution stake. The Torah reveals our fallen nature and points to Yeshua as the only remedy for it. Yeshua took the sins of man into Himself so that Yah could judge, condemn, and punish them in His flesh.[352]

In verse 4, Paul tells us that Yahweh condemned and punished Yeshua for our sins so that the Holy Spirit could regenerate our spirits and become one with us in order to empower us to walk out the intent of the written Torah (fulfill the righteousness of the written Torah). Paul says that the Holy Spirit fulfills the righteousness of the Torah in us; hence He prompts us to turn away from the flesh and turn to Yahweh so that we can walk out the intent of the Torah.

In verse 5, Paul says there are two kinds of people. There are those who are born of the flesh, who set their minds on the things the flesh desires, and there are those who are born of the Spirit, who set their minds on the things the Spirit desires. In verse 6, Paul describes the fruit that people reap. A person who is born of the flesh will seek to please the flesh and will reap death in this age and in the age to come. However, a person who is born of the Spirit will seek to please the Spirit and will reap life and peace in this age and in the age to come.

---

[352] Paul probably wrote this to combat docetism, which was the belief that Messiah did not come in the flesh.

Verses 7–8

In these verses, Paul says that when a person's mind is controlled by the flesh (the old nature), it will not submit to the Torah (as a law of faith that shows him how to be faithful), but it will try to use the Torah or anything else that it can find to fix itself. He says that those who are in the flesh (controlled by the old nature) cannot please Yah because they are at war with Him.

David Stern says it this way:

The primary psychological fact of life—deeper than any analysis of id, ego and superego; or of genetic, physiological, behavioral, environmental or educational conditioning; or birth traumas, complexes, sexual experiences, interpersonal communication, family background or games people play—is that the sinful "old nature" (the "flesh") is utterly irredeemable. This is why no self-help measures, psychotherapeutic methods, educational programs, environmental changes or resolutions to improve can enable us to **please God**; all of them are based on **having the mind controlled by the old nature**, which **is death**, rather than by the Holy Spirit, which is life and *shalom*—not only "peace" but "tranquility, safety, well-being, welfare, health, contentment, success, comfort, wholeness and integrity," in short, everything secular and popular psychology promise but cannot deliver.

Stern continues:

This is why Yeshua said, "You must be born again from above" (Jn 3:7), and Sha'ul wrote, "If anyone is united with the Messiah, he is a new creation—the old has passed; look, what has come is fresh and new!" (2C5:17). If there were no new nature, Sha'ul's (Paul's) psychology would offer the most pessimistic picture of the human condition—as he himself admits (1C15:16–19). But since there is a new nature, only Sha'ul's solution of letting one's mind be controlled by it, through the Holy Spirit, offers any real hope to mankind; all other psychologies offer palliatives and ultimate failure.[353]

Amen!

Verses 9–13

In verse 9, Paul says that if Yahweh's Spirit dwells in a person, he is not in the flesh, but in the Spirit. However, if a person does not have Yeshua's Spirit (Yah's Spirit) dwelling

---

[353] David Stern, *Jewish New Testament Commentary*, Clarksville, MD, Jewish New Testament Publications, 1992, p. 382.

inside, that person does not belong to Him; that is, He has not regenerated the person and become one with him. Paul says that if Yeshua's Spirit is in a person, Yahweh has redeemed the spirit of that individual and released it from condemnation and death by regenerating it. Though Yah has become one with the spirit, He has not redeemed the body and released it from condemnation and death. Thus the outer man (flesh) is perishing, but Yah's Spirit is renewing the inner man (spirit) day by day.

In verses 11, 12, and 13, Paul tells us not to get upset over the fact that our bodies will die, because if the Spirit that raised Yeshua's body dwells in us, He will raise our bodies at the end of this age when He resurrects the righteous. This means that the flesh is not the source of our lives, so we do not owe it anything. Paul tells us that we should not seek to please the flesh, because if we seek to please the flesh, we will die; but if we walk in the Spirit, putting to death the desires of the flesh, we will live.

Paul is not saying that a person has to put the deeds of the body to death so that Yah will save him or allow him to keep his salvation. Paul is describing the fruit that Yahweh's Spirit will bring forth in those He has regenerated. Paul is saying that a regenerated person will seek to follow the Spirit and put the flesh to death, so if a person does not seek to follow the Spirit and put the flesh to death, Yah has not regenerated him.

If we set our mind on the Holy Spirit, submit to Him, and follow Him, we are putting our flesh to death. Never forget, however, that our regenerated spirit lives in our unredeemed body and operates through our soul that Yah is in the process of redeeming. This means that every day we will be tempted to give in to the desires of the partially redeemed soul and indulge our unredeemed flesh, and sometimes we will. When we choose to give in to the desires of the soul or the body, *our regenerated heart* will convict and condemn us and drive us to our knees to confess and repent so that the Spirit can cleanse our conscience and restore our peace and joy.

The moment a person bows his knee to the King of the Jews, the Spirit of the King comes to live in that temple and sit on its throne, establishing His kingdom in him. The person then has to cooperate with the King's written and verbal instructions and do His will so that together they can tear down the strongholds and bring the soul into submission, establishing the kingdom throughout it. As a person cooperates with the King, he matures and learns how to live in the kingdom and begins to eat the fruit of the kingdom, which is righteousness, peace, and joy. This becomes the most important thing in his life, so he will till and guard his garden in order to keep the serpent out. Justification is instant, but sanctification is a lengthy process.

In Galatians 5:25, Paul says, "If we live in the Spirit, *let us* also walk in the Spirit" (emphasis added). Here Paul tells us that we play a role in the process of sanctification. To experience the fullness of salvation in this life and maximum rewards in the next, we have to yield to the Spirit and follow Him, putting the desires of our flesh to death. If Yahweh has justified a person, He will also sanctify him, but the exact process is a little different in each individual. Each person has cooperated with HaSatan and configured his flesh in a unique way, so the Holy Spirit sanctifies each person in a unique way.

For example, if HaSatan has built a soul structure in a person who has an appetite for gossip, the path that this person has to follow in order to get free is a little different from the path that a person whose flesh has an appetite for drugs has to follow. If HaSatan has configured a person to indulge in gossip, he may not feel a sense of urgency to follow the Holy Spirit as He asks him not to speak evil about others. A gossiper may not see the damage that he is doing to himself or others, so he may ignore the Holy Spirit's counsel or act as if he does not hear it and thus cheat himself out of temporal and eternal blessings.

If, however, HaSatan has configured a person to have an appetite for drugs, this is another story. Those who have fed their bodies drugs and conditioned their souls to depend on them have to pursue drugs. HaSatan uses drugs and the pursuit of drugs to destroy addicts. At some point, addicts realize that HaSatan is destroying them, and they feel an urgency to cooperate with the Spirit and yield to the sanctification process so that they do not end up in prison, a mental ward, or a grave.

The comfort food that my flesh craved was drugs. Drugs brought me to the end of myself and forced me to cooperate with Yahweh. Today I am at peace with Yah, myself, and everyone else. Am I perfect? No, I still have a few strongholds that I struggle with, but I know that if I continue to follow the Holy Spirit and renew my mind in the Word, the walls of these strongholds will fall, and I will be free in those areas of my life. Until then, I will be content to be in Yahweh's washing machine. Yahweh sets His washing machine on the repentance cycle and agitates us in His holiness, washing us in the water of His Word, using the detergent of His blood and the softener of His Spirit. As long as our regenerated spirit lives in an unredeemed body and expresses itself through a partially redeemed soul, we will fail; but if we stay in Yahweh's washing machine, renewing our mind and following His Spirit, we will fail less often.

Verses 14–17

In verse 14, Paul says that Yahweh's Spirit leads those who are His sons. Paul goes on to say that before Yahweh regenerated our spirits, we were HaSatan's slaves, and he used the fear of death to control us. You see, deep down on a subconscious level, we feared death because of the judgment, condemnation, and punishment that awaited us, so we sought to please our master because he held the power of death over us. Yeshua, however, took the keys of death and hell away from HaSatan. When we bowed our knee to Yeshua, Yah executed our old fallen spirit and resurrected it as a new spirit. Then Yahweh's Spirit became one with our spirit to transform us into His son. Yahweh's Spirit assures us that we belong to Him and leads us in order to mold us into the image of His eldest Son, Yeshua, so our spirit cries out to Him and says, "Abba Father."

In verse 17, Paul says that the Spirit of Messiah lives in us, giving us the desire to follow Him and suffer as He suffered. In other words, Yeshua's Spirit gives us the desire to surrender our will, just as He surrendered His will in the garden of Gethsemane, and to put our flesh to death on the execution stake, just as He put His flesh to death on the execution stake. Paul goes on to say that if we suffer with Yeshua, Yahweh will glorify us with Him as joint-heirs!

Chapter 45

Romans 8:18–39

Verses 18–39

*I*n this section, Paul writes about hope. Paul writes about living with an expectation of receiving everything that Yahweh has promised. Yahweh has promised that He will give us our full inheritance after He resurrects us or raptures us into heaven. In heaven, we will enjoy intimate fellowship with Yeshua for a short time and return to earth with Him to set up His kingdom. After a thousand years, Yeshua will re-create the earth, transforming it into a paradise. We will then live with Yeshua in paradise forever. Paul says that if we focus on these things, then the things of this world, the desires of the soul, and the lusts of the body will lose their appeal, and we will be able to submit to the prompting of the Holy Spirit and live the abundant life.

In verse 20, Paul says that Adam's sin brought disorder into the universe. Paul says that the universe is frustrated and anxiously awaiting its redemption. Paul goes on to say that the whole universe is waiting for the full manifestation of Yahweh's sons because when His sons are fully manifested, this will mean that it is about to be redeemed and reborn. Hence the whole universe is groaning and travailing in pain, waiting for the full manifestation of Yahweh's sons.

In verse 23, Paul says that the universe does not groan alone. Yahweh has regenerated the saints by becoming one with their spirits, and He brings forth fruit in their lives through their spirits, but their souls and bodies fight against this process and frustrate them. Yah's people are aware that the measure of the Spirit that they have now is just a small down payment of the glory that awaits them. Thus their spirits groan and yearn for the full measure of the Holy Spirit that will glorify their bodies and transform them into the image of Messiah Yeshua.

In verse 26, Paul says that the universe and man are not groaning alone. As the Holy Spirit labors in us to bring forth our sanctification, He makes intercession for us with groanings that we cannot put into words. Since we do not know what to ask Yahweh for so that He can help us overcome our weaknesses, His Spirit prays His perfect will for us, making all things work together for our good. The Holy Spirit's prayers build us up so that we can fulfill our destiny, not our selfish desires. I agree with Kasemann. This is a reference to praying in tongues, because 1 Corinthians 14:4 says that we build up our spirits by praying in tongues.[354]

Here is the point: Yahweh is on the throne in heaven. Yeshua sits at Yah's right hand, making intercession for us. The Holy Spirit in us is speaking forth that intercession through us. Hence the Godhead is vested in and active in bringing about our salvation, because those whom Yah foreknew, He predestinated to be conformed to the image of His Son; and those whom He predestinated, the Holy Spirit called; and those whom He called, He justified; and those whom He justified, He also glorified.

Brothers and sisters, please take note of the fact that Yahweh describes the actions and activities of the Godhead in the past tense in order to let us know that nothing will prevent Him from glorifying the people that He foreknew, predestinated, called, and justified. When individuals come to the realization that the Godhead's involvement in their salvation spans from eternity past to eternity future, they are either overwhelmed with joy or overwhelmed by fear because they suddenly realize that the bridge of sanctification connects eternity past to eternity future.

On one hand, when saints perceive the Holy Spirit in them prompting them to follow Him and put their flesh to death, they are overwhelmed with joy because they realize that they are on the bridge of sanctification and that nothing can prevent Yah from escorting them across this bridge into glory and eternal life. On the other hand, when individuals do not perceive the Holy Spirit in them prompting them to follow Him and put their flesh to death, they are overwhelmed with fear. These people suddenly realize that they are not sharing in Yeshua's sufferings and hence are not on the bridge of sanctification crossing over into glory and eternal life. Salvation and sanctification are two sides of the same coin. No one can have one without the other. When Yah declares people righteous, His righteousness demands that they actually become righteous, and His Spirit goes to work to bring this about through the processes of sanctification and glorification. Reader, be honest. Are you on the bridge of sanctification?

Before we move on, let me say a word about the concepts of foreknowledge and election. In Romans 11:2, Paul says that Yahweh foreknew Israel. In Romans 9:6, Paul says that a person who is born in Israel is not automatically a part of Israel. In Romans 10:9–13, Paul says that a person must believe what Yahweh has said about Yeshua and confess Him

---

[354] Ernst Kasemann, *Commentary on Romans*, Grand Rapids, MI, Eerdmans Publishing, 1980, pp. 239–41.

as Lord (bow his knee to Him) in order to be baptized into His death and resurrection and be grafted onto the olive tree (the righteous remnant of Israel).

There is a dynamic tension between Yahweh's sovereignty and man's free will. Yah inhabits the timeless realm of eternity and sees things from a dimension where time can be whatever He wants it to be.[355] However, time lords over us and forces us to see things in reference to it. Thus it is impossible to reconcile foreknowledge with free will without coming up with some creative doctrines that divide people. The best thing to do is to acknowledge that Yah is bigger and wiser than we are and accept that He is sovereign and has a sovereign plan for man, but in some way at some time, man chooses whether he will cooperate with Him. Remember, the goal is love, but love is not love if Yah has to coerce it or predestinate it. Yahweh is love, and we *choose* to love Him or to reject Him. Election is not favoritism, and it does not negate free will. Election is the instrument that makes salvation available to us all.

In verse 31, Paul asks, who can be against Yahweh's sons? Yah's Spirit gives His sons the power to renew their minds and put their flesh to death as the Godhead escorts them over the bridge of sanctification, moving them from eternity past to glorification and eternity future. So who can prevail over Yah's sons? In verse 34, Paul says that Yahweh has declared His sons righteous and sent His Spirit to live in them in order to make them righteous, and any failure that they have is attributable to the residual effects of the fallen nature. Yahweh, however, clothed Himself in human flesh and surrendered to death in order to pay for the crimes of the fallen nature. Thus Yahweh has paid for the sins that His sons committed in the past, the sins they commit today, and the sins they will commit tomorrow![356] So who can condemn Yah's sons?

Yeshua is in heaven talking with the Father about us and communicating His will to the Holy Spirit. The Holy Spirit is releasing the power of the Godhead in us in order to conform us to Yeshua's image. Yahweh has declared us not guilty and released us from the law; hence He no longer counts our sins against us because where there is no law, there is no transgression. Is anyone able to reverse Yahweh's not guilty decree? No! If Yeshua died to pay for our sins, will He now condemn us? No! So what is able to separate us from Yeshua's love? Nothing is!

The Crown Jewel

Most commentators do not know what to do with chapters 9, 10, and 11. Some commentators say that these chapters form a codicil or an afterthought that Paul *inserted* in his

---

[355] David H. Stern, *Complete Jewish Bible*, Clarksville, MD, Jewish New Testament Publications Inc., 1998, p. 882.

[356] *The Hebrew-Greek Key Word Study Bible*, KJV, Hebrews 9:12.

letter, but this is a serious error. These three chapters are the precious stones that transform Romans into the crown jewel of Paul's letters! The whole purpose of writing Romans was to convey the information in these chapters. Everything that Paul wrote up to this point laid a theological foundation that supports what he writes in chapters 9, 10, and 11.

Ben Witherington III puts it this way: "It is a very serious error indeed to treat these chapters as an afterthought, unrelated discussion, or mere appendix to chs. 1-8. It is nearer to the mark to call it the climax of the theological portion of the letter. It is an argument for the defense of both God and of Israel and as such is meant to refute certain assumptions Gentiles in Rome seem to be making about God and Israel, and about Israel's failure."[357]

If we do not filter Romans through the political and social atmosphere that existed in Rome at the time it was written, we will fail to recognize that chapters 1–8 form the bedrock on which the conclusions in chapters 9–11 rest. We will turn Paul's main point into an afterthought, and it will lose its impact. The book of Romans is the crown jewel of the apostolic writings, and chapters 9, 10, and 11 are the precious jewels that make it thus. Romans 9, 10, and 11 come together to form the keystone of the faith that was once delivered to the saints and is not simply an afterthought to be dismissed!

Rome's political and social dynamics prompted the government to expel the Jews from the city, which caused the Gentiles to recoil from everything Jewish so that the government would not expel them. The Roman ekklesia thought that they had replaced Israel and the Jews. The Roman ekklesia pulled away from their Hebrew roots and broke away from the theological mooring of the Torah. The Romans filtered Yeshua and His finished work through their Gentile minds and came up with doctrines, philosophies, and traditions that were inconsistent with Yah.

The Jews returned to the ekklesia to find that the Gentiles had marginalized them and devalued the Torah. Yahweh had told Israel to teach the Torah to the nations, so the Jews remained loyal to the Torah. The Jews' loyalty to the Torah and the Gentiles' rejection of it split the ekklesia, dividing it along ethnic lines, crippling the one new man. Paul wrote Romans to correct the misconceptions of Yah, His nature, and His plan for Israel and the nations, as well as to set straight the relationship between Jews and the Gentiles and their relationship to the Torah and the law.

In chapters 1–8, Paul describes the ancestries of Gentiles and Jews. Paul proves that the pious and nonpious in each group possess a fallen nature that has to be put to death on the execution stake in Messiah and resurrected in Him, and tells how the Spirit sanctifies people and how the Torah and its law fit into the scheme of things. In chapters 9–11, Paul gets to the heart of the matter and corrects the errors about Yah, Israel, Jews, and Gentiles.

---

[357] Ben Witherington, *Paul's Letter to the Romans*, Grand Rapids, MI, Eerdmans Publishing Co., 2004, p. 237.

Chapters 1–8 contain the keys to recovering from the Adamic nature with its compulsions, obsessions, and addictions. Chapters 9–11 contain the keys to ecclesiology and eschatology. *Recovery in Christ* is about addiction and recovery, so we will forego a detailed analysis of chapters 9, 10, and 11. However, since paganism is pressing in on the ekklesia today and Romans is a defense against that, and since it helps us keep the other books in the apostolic writings in place, we will briefly summarize chapters 9, 10, and 11.

Part 13

A Survey of Romans: The Crown Jewel

Chapter 46

Romans 9 And 10

Romans 9:1–33

In chapter 9, Paul expands on the concepts that he introduced in Romans 8:28–30 and defends Yahweh's character and sovereignty. Paul says that it saddens him when he thinks about how his Jewish brothers and sisters are refusing to follow Abraham by putting their faith in the Promised Seed and are instead blindly following the teachings and traditions of man, seeking to establish their own righteousness. Paul does not understand why Yahweh has hardened his people; nevertheless, he knows that He is just in having mercy upon whomever He chooses to have mercy and in hardening whomever He chooses to harden.

Paul says that it was Yahweh's prerogative to elect Israel and call, justify, glorify, and use her to bring the nations back to Him. However, Paul says that the people who are born in Israel are not automatically the elect whom Yahweh has called, justified, and glorified. Paul reminds us that Isaiah said that the people of Israel were as numerous as the sand of the sea, but Yahweh would save only a remnant of them. Paul says that Yah gives mercy to whomever He chooses to give mercy and hardens whomever He chooses to harden so that those He calls may rejoice in His mercy. Paul says that by works, not faith, his people pursued the righteousness that the Torah pointed to and stumbled at the stumbling stone (Yeshua), never attaining righteousness.

Romans 10:1–4

Yahweh revealed Himself to Israel and gave her the Torah. This gave Israel a unique opportunity to reveal the full extent of the fallen nature. The Jews accepted the assignment and built a religion to fix their fallen nature (overcome their evil inclination) by keeping the law. The Jews refused to admit that they were treasonous criminals who deserved to die for their crimes, believe Yahweh, bow their knee to the Seed, and receive His righteousness as a gift.[358] So in verse 2, Paul says that his Jewish brothers and sisters were relentless in their pursuit of Yahweh, but they did not pursue Him according to knowledge; that is, according to the Torah. In verse 3, Paul says that the Jews refused to believe what the Torah said about Yahweh's gift of righteousness and tried to establish their own righteousness by keeping the Torah and its law.

In verse 4, Paul says Yeshua is the *telos* (the goal) of the law for righteousness to everyone who believes. In other words, Yeshua is the righteousness that the law pointed to, and those who believe in Him and bow their knee to Him so He can establish His kingdom in them will receive His righteousness as a gift. The Torah pointed to the Seed. The Mosaic covenant's institutions, protocols, ceremonies, and sacrifices pointed to the Seed's finished work and drew upon it so that Yahweh could forgive redeemed, fallen people and cleanse them. In sum, the Mosaic law allowed redeemed, fallen people to enjoy their relationship with Yahweh until the Promised Seed could come to embody the Mosaic law and then indwell them to fulfill the Mosaic law in them and regenerate them.

Romans 10:5–8

These four verses are very important because they prove that Yahweh's plan is one progressively revealed, fully consistent, continuous, contiguous plan. Tragically, a couple of very influential Gentile theologians misinterpreted these very important verses and used them to validate their doctrines that perverted the grace of Yahweh and turned into lawlessness.

Remember, Paul wrote Galatians to protect the ekklesia from the people who promoted the sages' apostate religion and tried to impose it on her to control her. Centuries later John Calvin (1509–1564) and John Darby (1800–1882) interpreted Galatians through the old Roman mind-set that recoiled from everything Jewish. Calvin and Darby tried to protect the ekklesia from Jewish legalism without understanding what Jewish legalism was. Since the Roman church had expelled the Jews, these Gentile theologians lifted Galatians out of its Jewish context and failed to distinguish between the written Torah and the sages' perversion of the written Torah.

Remember, the sages said that a person had to submit to circumcision, offer a sacrifice, go through baptism, and keep the whole law (keep the written Torah by keeping the oral Torah and legal halachah) to be saved. However, Paul said that a person did not have to submit to circumcision, offer a sacrifice, submit to baptism, and keep the whole law (keep the written Torah by keeping the oral torah and legal halachah) to be saved. Paul said that

---

[358] *The Hebrew-Greek Key Word Study Bible*, KJV, Genesis 3:15; 12:3; John 8:56; Acts 3:25; Galatians 3:8.

Yahweh saved a person as he believed in Yeshua and confessed Him as Lord; then His Spirit indwelt him to circumcise his heart by writing the Torah on it and prompting him to walk out its intent.

Calvin left the Roman Church, but unfortunately, he hung on to parts of his old Roman mind-set and misinterpreted Galatians and superimposed his errors onto Romans to validate his interpretation of Galatians. Atheists use this same kind of circular logic to confirm the theory of evolution by assigning an age to a fossil based on which layer of the geologic column they unearthed it in and assigning ages to the layers of the geologic column based on which fossils they unearthed in it. Neither atheists nor theologians can make circular logic work, however.

After filtering Romans 10:5–8 through a worldview that he had built on the old Roman mind-set and a misinterpretation of Galatians, "Calvin thought that Paul clearly made an antithesis between grace and faith on the one hand, and law and works on the other. [So] These passages are the root cause of all the law-grace difficulties in Lutheranism, Calvinism, covenant theology, and the dispensationalism of yesterday and today."[359]

Calvin believed that these verses taught that there was righteousness in the old covenant that came from keeping the Torah and its law, but in the new covenant, righteousness came by faith. In other words, Calvin taught that there was a pathway to righteousness for the people in the old covenant that was separate and distinct from the pathway to righteousness for the people in the new covenant. After Calvin, people began to view the old covenant as being the antithesis of the new covenant. Those who taught that the commands in the Torah applied to the ekklesia were accused and convicted of mixing the old covenant, which Yahweh cut with the Jews, they said, with the new covenant, which Yah cut with the ekklesia, they claimed. These teachers were condemned for stealing the saints' liberty and shackling them in the chains of legalism.

Did Paul share Calvin's adversarial relationship with the Torah? No, Paul quoted the Torah to substantiate his teachings on the new covenant. What is Paul saying in these verses? Paul is explaining why his brothers' zeal for Yah is misguided and proving that there has always been one pathway to righteousness. Let us look at the *Jewish New Testament* translation of these verses: "For Moshe writes about the righteousness grounded in the *Torah* **that the person who does these things will attain life through them.** *Moreover*, the righteousness grounded in trusting says: **'Do not say in your heart, "Who will ascend to heaven?"'** ' —that is, to bring the Messiah down—or, **"Who will** descend to

---

[359] Daniel P. Fuller, *Gospel & Law: Contrast or Continuum?*, Pasadena, CA, Fuller Seminary Press, 1982, p. 63.

Sh'ol' '—that is, to bring the Messiah up from the dead. What, then does it say? **'The Word is near you, in your mouth and in your heart.'** " [360]

This translation shows that Paul equated the righteousness that Yahweh built the Torah and its law on with the righteousness that came by faith, because they were one in the same![361] This takes us right back to Romans 9:30–32. Through faith in Messiah, the Gentiles attained the righteousness that the Torah spoke of without seeking it by keeping the law, but the Jews kept the law without attaining it because they sought it by works and not by faith. This tells us that if the Jews would have followed in Abraham's footsteps, believed Yahweh, put their trust in His promises about the Seed, and lived out their faith by keeping the Torah and its law, they would have obtained the righteousness they were seeking.

Now let us look at John Darby. John Darby took Calvin's teachings to the next level. Darby taught that Yahweh gave the Torah to Israel and that Yeshua's ekklesia has nothing to do with Israel or her righteous remnant. Therefore, the Torah does not apply to Yeshua's ekklesia.

In Ezekiel 36:24–30, Yah said He would cut a new covenant with Israel so that His Spirit could live in His people's hearts to transform them from stone to flesh so that they would obey His Torah. Since the goal of the new covenant is to empower people to keep the Torah, Darby said that the new covenant was for Israel, not the ekklesia. Darby's misinterpretation of Galatians forces the radical dispensationalist to insist that the ekklesia is not in the new covenant! This is absurd.

Ultradispensationalists say that Yeshua's ekklesia is not in the new covenant, that she is "under grace." Where does this grace come from if it does not come from the older covenants or the new covenant? No, Yeshua shed His blood to establish the new covenant with Israel's righteous remnant. It should be completely obvious that Darby's logic is a product of the old Roman mind-set that Paul was dispelling in his letter to the Romans. After Calvin and Darby, Yeshua's ekklesia began to shun the Torah and to believe that obeying it was a form of Judaizing.

So are the old covenant and the new covenant polar opposites? No, the fundamental difference between the two covenants is where Yahweh placed the Torah.[362] The old covenant was dealing with people with fallen natures, so Yahweh wrote the Torah and its law outside of them on stone tablets in order to reveal their fallen nature to them. Unfortunately, the stone tablets did not change their hearts so that they could live up to Yah's standard

---

[360] David Stern, *Complete Jewish Bible*, Clarksville, MD, Jewish New Testament Publications Inc., 1998, p. 1,413.

[361] David Stern, *Jewish New Testament Commentary*, Clarksville, MD, Jewish New Testament Publications, 1992, p. 398.

[362] Daniel P. Fuller, *Gospel & Law: Contrast or Continuum?* Pasadena, CA, Fuller Seminary Press, 1982, p. ix.

of righteousness. In the new covenant, however, Yahweh's Spirit executes man's fallen spirit, resurrects him, indwells him, and becomes one with him, imparting His nature to him. Yah's Spirit writes the Torah on man's heart and moves him towards obedience by prompting him to walk out its intent.

So is Yeshua's ekklesia in the new covenant? In 1 Corinthians 11:25, Paul quotes Yeshua as saying, "This cup is the new testament in my blood." In 2 Corinthians 3:6, he says that Yah has made us able ministers of the new testament. If you look up the Greek word *diatheke* (Strong's 1242), you will find that it means "covenant" or "testament," and the translators of the literal versions usually render it as "covenant."[363] So according to Paul, Yeshua's ekklesia is definitely in the new covenant. This brings us to the next question. Is Yeshua's ekklesia separate and distinct from Israel? Paul will answer this important question in chapter 11.

Romans 10:9–21

In these verses, Paul says if a person confesses with his mouth that Yeshua is Lord and believes in his heart that Yahweh's Spirit raised Him from the dead, He will save him. Essentially, Paul says we have to bow our knee to Yeshua, making Him our Lord, and believe that He is the Seed that the Tanakh spoke of before Yah will save us. Paul emphasizes that Yah will save *whosoever* calls upon Yeshua. In other words, it does not matter whether a person is a Jew or a Gentile; anyone can call upon Yeshua, bow his knee to Him, confess Him as Lord, and believe that He is the Promised Seed that the Tanakh spoke of, and Yahweh will save him.

Paul says that a person cannot call upon Yeshua unless he hears the good news about Him. Paul says that faith comes by hearing and hearing by the Word of Yahweh. In other words, as a sinner hears Yah's Word about Yeshua and His finished work, His Spirit knocks on the door of his heart and offers the gift of repentance. Yah's Spirit gives the sinner's spirit the faith it needs to receive the gift of repentance, and hence faith comes by hearing Yah's Word.

If the sinner pulls the trigger by *choosing* to believe and confess Him as Lord, Yah's Spirit baptizes his fallen spirit into Yeshua. As Yah's Spirit baptizes a sinner's fallen spirit into Yeshua, the sinner dies on the execution stake. Yah's Spirit resurrects the spirit as a brand-new creature (a new spirit). Yeshua's Spirit becomes one with this spirit, and this person is now *in Messiah (Christ)*. As this saint studies the Torah, the Holy Spirit writes it on his heart and gives him the desire to walk out its intent so that he can obey Yah and live the abundant life.

---

[363] *Young's Literal Translation, Concordant Literal Translation, Jewish New Testament and the Power NT.*

Fallen men and women are powerless because they are HaSatan's slaves. HaSatan holds his slaves in the chains of sin and forces them to build his kingdom on the earth. Fallen men and women want to live free and enjoy an abundant life, so HaSatan goes out of his way to make them believe that they are free and living an abundant life as he prompts them to build up his kingdom on the earth. Fallen men and women may think that they are free or that they live an abundant life, but actually they are slaves in HaSatan's kingdom. Does this mean that HaSatan will not allow a person in his kingdom to be moral or help others? No, HaSatan will permit his slaves to do good things and live moral lives if it will deceive them and others into believing that they do not need the "opiate of religion" to drug them into doing these things.

Do not let HaSatan deceive you in Alcoholics Anonymous. It is impossible to rise above temptation, overcome sin, and live the abundant life without Yahweh, and the only way to get to Yahweh is through His Messiah. A person has to be in Messiah (Christ), obey His Word, and follow His Spirit to live the abundant life. There is no other way to recover from the Adamic nature and its addictions, compulsions, and obsessions, which is why I wrote *Recovery in Christ*.

Romans 10:19–21

In verses 19, 20, and 21, Paul tells how Moses and Isaiah warned Israel that if they did not believe Yahweh, put their faith in His promises, and obey His teaching and instructions, He would turn to the nations. Yahweh said that He would turn to the nations and offer them the gift of justification by faith and the abundant life that comes to those who obey His teachings and instructions. Paul expresses sadness over the fact that these prophecies were materializing right before his eyes, but still his people refused to hear with their ears and see with their eyes so that Yahweh could heal them of the spiritual leprosy that was destroying them.

Chapter 47

Romans 11

Verses 1–10

In verse 1, Paul begins to transition to the main point of his letter by asking a rhetorical question. Paul says, "I say then, Hath God cast away His people?" Paul answers this question by saying, "God forbid!" In effect, he is saying, "Look at me. I am an Israelite of the seed of Abraham of the tribe of Benjamin. Clearly, Yahweh has not cast away His people whom He *foreknew*." Paul is pointing back to Romans 8:29–30 and saying, "Reader, do you not remember that Yahweh said whomever He foreknows, He also predestinates, calls, justifies, and glorifies?"

In verse 2, Paul begins a discussion on the remnant to show how Yahweh preserves a remnant in order to preserve the elect as a whole. Paul points to Elijah, who tried to get Yahweh to enter into judgment against Israel for breaking the covenant. Elijah thought that Israel had forfeited the right to be Yahweh's elect. Elijah thought that he was the only one who was still serving Yahweh. Yahweh corrected Elijah by revealing that seven thousand men were still serving Him. Yahweh let Elijah know that He had poured out His grace on a remnant and preserved it, and he was just a small part of this remnant. Paul says that just as Yah preserved a remnant during Elijah's day, He had preserved a remnant in his day, and he was a small part of it.

In verse 5, Paul says that Yah gave the remnant the grace to circumcise their hearts, believe His promises, and put their faith in Him so that He could justify them and sanctify them as they kept the written Torah and complied with its law. The rest of Israel, however, was blind because as Isaiah said, they honored Yah with their mouths, but their hearts were far from Him. Most of Israel followed the teachings, instructions, and traditions of man instead of Yah's Word, and since they rejected the truth, He blinded them so that they could not see or hear the truth.[364]

In verses 8, 9, and 10, Paul reminds his readers of what Moses told the people who roamed the wilderness for forty years and watched their parents die. Moses said that since these people witnessed signs and wonders that proved Yahweh was faithful and still refused to circumcise their hearts by believing His promises, He gave them hearts that did not perceive, ears that did not hear, and eyes that did not see. However, this time in the wilderness prepared these people to repent, believe, and obey so that they could prosper.[365] Paul provides a second witness to validate this principle by quoting Isaiah 29:10 and drives his point home by reminding his readers of what David prophesied. David foretold that Yah would darken the eyes of those who would come against Messiah and His ministry so that they would not be able to see.[366]

Paul, Moses, Isaiah, and David tell us that when people knowingly reject the truth, Yahweh blinds them so that the pain and calamity that blindness brings will humble them. Yahweh humbles us so that we will believe His promises and trust Him. Yahweh gave Israel the Torah. The Torah told Israel about Yahweh's promise to send the Seed, and it told her how Abraham trusted Him and received the gift of righteousness. However, Israel chose to trust the sages' teachings and attempted to establish her own righteousness, so Yahweh blinded her.

Verses 11–16

In verse 11, Paul asks if Israel is still the elect who will bring the rest of the world into the covenant or whether her refusal to believe has caused Yah to take back His promise. Paul says, "God forbid!" It is impossible for Yahweh to go back on a promise. Israel was still the elect that would draw the Gentiles into the covenant. Yah wanted Israel to cooperate with Him so that He could bring the nations into the covenant, but since she would not cooperate with Him, He blinded her and used her disobedience and blindness to draw the nations into the covenant. There is a reason behind everything. I believe that if Yahweh had not blinded the Jews, then they would have received Yeshua and tried to get the Gentiles on board, but the Gentiles would have thought the Jews were exalting themselves so they could rule the world and would not have received Him.

Israel's religious rulers believed Messiah would come as a king. According to the sages, the Anointed One would conquer the nations and bring the Gentiles into the covenant to rule over them. Yahweh had other plans, however. Yeshua assumed the role of Messiah

---

[364] *The Hebrew-Greek Key Word Study Bible*, KJV, Isaiah 29:9–24.

[365] Ibid., Deuteronomy 29:1–10.

[366] Ibid., Psalm 69:21–28.

ben Joseph, a suffering servant, who humbled Israel in order to draw the nations into the covenant. In turn, Yah commissioned the Gentiles to provoke the Jews to jealousy to bring them into the covenant. In verse 12, Paul says Israel's rejection of Yeshua brought riches to the nations. So how much more will Israel bless the nations when Yah lets her recognize Yeshua? In other words, if Yah cast Israel aside so He could bring the nations into Yeshua's ekklesia, then what will happen when He brings Israel into Yeshua's ekklesia? Paul says that it will bring it to life!

Some assume Paul was talking about the resurrection. However, Robertson wrote, "Many think that Paul means that the general resurrection and the end will come when the Jews are converted. Possibly so, but it is by no means certain. His language may be merely figurative."[367] I believe that if Paul wanted us to infer that he was referring to the resurrection, then he would have used the Greek word *anastasis*. Nonetheless, Paul was talking about the impact Jews have on Gentiles and the channel through which that impact flows; that is, Yeshua's ekklesia.

I do not believe that Paul is referring to the eschatological event that will signal that the tribulation has started (the rapture and resurrection of the righteous remnant of Israel). Nor do I believe that he is referring to the eschatological event that will occur at the end of the tribulation as Yahweh pours out the spirit of grace on the nation of Israel so that they can see whom they have pierced and mourn for Him as one mourns for his only son and then repent and accept Him.[368] I believe that Paul is using a little wordplay in order to let us know that the ekklesia will spring to life, and this will signal that the rapture/resurrection of the righteous remnant of the nation of Israel is imminent, and hence the time of Jacob's trouble (the tribulation) is imminent as well.

I also believe that Paul is telling us that the return of the Jews will bring the one new man to maturity. The one new man is the rebuilt tabernacle of David, where there is no veil separating man from the presence of Yah and no middle wall of separation between Jews and Gentiles.[369] Amos said that when Yahweh rebuilds David's tabernacle, the plowman will overtake the reaper.[370] So when the Jews return to the ekklesia, we will proclaim the Word and plant seed for souls, deliverance, healing, and prosperity, and the harvest will be so abundant that we will not be able to gather it in before it's time to plant again! Surely this is life from the dead. This is Yah's glorious bride, and He will rapture her before He pours out His wrath on the earth.

---

[367] A. Robertson, *Word Pictures in the New Testament*, Oak Harbor, WA, Logos Research System, 1997, Romans 11:15.*

[368] *The Hebrew-Greek Key Word Study Bible*, KJV, Zechariah 12:10.

[369] Sid Roth, *The Incomplete Church*, Shippensburg, PA, Destiny Image Publishers Inc., 2007, pp. 132–133.

[370] *The Hebrew-Greek Key Word Study Bible*, KJV, Amos 9:11–15.

Verses 17–22

In verse 17, Paul begins a discussion that is a key to understanding ecclesiology. Paul shifts from the example of the consecration of a part of the dough that made the whole lump of dough holy unto Yah[371] to a discussion of an olive tree. In the Scriptures, sometimes Yah depicts Israel as an olive tree, [372] so when Paul writes about the root of the olive tree, he is referring to the patriarchs and the covenants that Yahweh cut with them.

Yahweh promised Abraham that his seed would multiply and grow into a great nation that would bless all the other nations of the earth, and He sealed this promise with a blood covenant. Yah set Abraham and his seed apart and built a great nation out of them so that He could use them to bring the people of the other nations into the covenant. So since Abraham, Isaac, and Jacob were holy, so is Israel.

Yahweh made the promises to Abraham and his seed. Abraham's seed became Israel, but those who were born in Israel were not the seed who would inherit the promises unless they shared Abraham's faith in the Seed and manifested that faith by obeying the Torah. The people who were born in Israel and kept the Torah apart from faith in the Seed did not become the seed that would inherit the promises, and hence they severed themselves from the tree. Yahweh turned to the people of the nations (Gentiles) so that they could put their faith in the Seed and He could transform them into the seed that would inherit the promises and graft them onto the tree. Yah grafted Gentiles into the covenant He made with Abraham, transforming them into the seed that would inherit the promises, and He expected them to walk as Abraham walked by obeying the Torah.

In verse 18, Paul warned the Gentiles not to become proud and boast against the branches that grew up on Yah's tree and were broken off because of unbelief so that He could graft the wild branches onto His tree. In other words, Paul warned the Gentiles not to think that Yah had rejected Israel as the elect and broken His covenants with her so that they could become the elect; that is, he warned the Gentiles against thinking that Yeshua's ekklesia had replaced Israel. The apostle to the Gentiles wanted the Gentiles to understand that the ekklesia was an outgrowth and an extension of Israel's righteous remnant. Israel's roots (the covenants that Yahweh cut with the patriarchs of the righteous remnant) supported the ekklesia, not the other way around!

Paul warned the Gentiles not to think that Yah had rejected Israel and the Jews and replaced them with a church that was independent and separate from Israel and her covenants. Yahweh grafted the Roman ekklesia into Israel's righteous remnant and her covenants. Paul tells the Gentiles in the Roman ekklesia that they needed to be careful about impugning Yahweh's character by boasting against Israel and the covenants, because if

---

[371] Ibid., Numbers 15:17–21.

[372] Ibid., Jeremiah 11:16–17.

their conduct proved that their confession of faith was not genuine, He would cut them off from the tree because of their unbelief.

Believers get upset over verses 21 and 22 without cause. Paul was merely expounding on Yeshua's teaching. Yeshua said that the wheat (believers) and tares (unbelievers) grow in the same field. As fruit appears on the wheat stalks, it is obvious that they are wheat plants and that the other plants are tares, but He lets the two plants grow together until harvest time because if He pulls up the tares, He will damage the wheat. At harvest time, His workers will pull up the tares to burn them and will put the wheat into His barn.[373] Paul is not saying we can lose our salvation. Paul is saying that there are branches on the tree that appear to be connected to the root, but they are not because they produce no fruit, and these branches will be broken off and burned in the fiery lake.

Ultradispensationalists tread on dangerous ground because they believe that Yahweh cut the covenants with Israel and that they do not apply to Yeshua's ekklesia because He has regenerated its members. Ultradispensationalists believe they are regenerated sons who partake of Yahweh's life and nature through His Spirit and thus do not need a covenant. Ultradispensationalists think that they have a deal with Yahweh that is apart from Israel and her covenants.[374] Paul, however, warned Gentiles not to think like this, because Yah has planted only one Tree of Life.

The Abrahamic covenant is the covenant of redemption. Yah cut the Mosaic covenant to hold the Abrahamic covenant in place until Yeshua implemented the new covenant. Yeshua implemented the new covenant by shedding His blood on the execution stake, resurrecting, and ascending to sit at the right hand of the Father, where He released the Holy Spirit to begin His ministry of regenerating and sanctifying the Jews first and then the people of the nations in order to fulfill the Abrahamic covenant. A messianic Jew named Daniel Gruber puts it this way: "Gentiles who recognize the sovereignty of Messiah, the King of the Jews, are brought into the commonwealth of Israel alongside the faithful Jewish remnant. The King of the Jews reigns over them, too. So then, you [Gentiles] are no longer strangers and foreigners, but you are fellow-citizens [sumpolitai] with those set apart [Jewish believers], and are built upon the apostles' and prophets' foundation; Yeshua Messiah being the cornerstone (Eph. 2:19-20)."[375]

---

[373] Ibid., Matthew 13:24–30.

[374] Paul P. Enns, *The Moody Handbook of Theology*, Chicago, IL, Moody Press, 1997, p. 522.*

[375] Daniel Gruber, *The Separation of Church & Faith, Volume. 1: Copernicus and the Jews*, Hanover, NH, Elijah Publishing, 2005, p. 244.

Verses 23–36

In verses 23 and 24, Paul tells the Gentiles in the Roman congregation that they grew up on a wild tree, but when they responded to Yahweh's Spirit and *chose* to put their trust in Yeshua, He grafted them onto His tree. Paul says that some of the natural branches that grew on Yahweh's tree refused to believe His promises and to put their trust in Him. Yahweh cut these natural branches off His tree, but the Gentiles should not think that He could not graft them back onto His tree if they should repent, believe, and trust Yeshua. Paul says that it is easy for Yahweh to graft the natural branches back onto the tree that they grew up on (His tree).

In verse 25, Paul tells the Gentiles that he is going to let them in on a secret so that they do not act like fools. Paul says that Yahweh has blinded the Jews until the full number of Gentiles comes into the new covenant in order to partake of the Abrahamic covenant and join with Israel's righteous remnant to form a global commonwealth. After the fullness of Gentiles comes into the righteous remnant, Yah will remove the scales from the eyes of the Jews. The Jews will bow to Yeshua, and He will bring them into the righteous remnant to partake of the fullness of the Abrahamic covenant. Thus the first shall be last, and the last shall be first.

In verse 28, Paul says Israel is an enemy of the gospel for the Gentiles' sake, but they are still the elect for the Father's sake because He will not change His mind and take back His gifts and callings. Paul sums it up by alluding to the fact that man rebelled against Yah and formed the nations in unbelief. Yahweh, however, called a man named Abram. Yah made the nation of Israel out of Abraham. Israel fell into unbelief, and their unbelief helped Yah bring the nations into the covenant. Now the nations offer Yah's mercy to Israel, who is in unbelief, so that she might believe. Yah's plan was to save Israel and the nations while they were in unbelief so that all would know that salvation is by grace through faith and that no one has a reason to boast.

Part 14

A Survey of Romans: Walking It Out

Chapter 48

Applied Theology

Background

In the previous chapters, the apostle Paul discussed Israel, the righteous remnant, the Gentiles' position, the covenants, the Torah, and the law. In the remaining chapters, Paul gives the ekklesia some instructions on how to walk out their faith; that is, he gives the ekklesia its halachah. Paul's halachah tells us how to walk out the Torah, but these instructions also lay a foundation that helps us recognize the Spirit's promptings, which are His specific instructions on how we are to handle the situations in our lives, walk out the Torah's intent, and live the abundant life.

Yahweh expects His people to follow His Spirit (walk in the Spirit) so that they do not fulfill the lust of the flesh. How do we walk in the Spirit? If there is no standard that defines what it means to walk in the Spirit, then walking in the Spirit is a subjective experience. If walking in the Spirit is a subjective experience, then everyone will do what is right in his own eyes, divide the ekklesia, and hinder it from accomplishing its mission. Hence there has to be an immutable standard that sets the parameters and establishes boundaries for walking in the Spirit so that we can differentiate between the Spirit's voice, the flesh's voice, and the devil's voice.

Well, of course, Scripture is the immutable standard that defines what it means to walk in the Spirit. The Ten Commandments set the parameters and boundaries that define what it means to love Yah and our neighbors. The Torah and its law taught redeemed, unregenerated people how to walk out the Ten Commandments. The apostolic writings teach regenerated people how to fulfill the intent of the Torah, which keeps them within the parameters and boundaries of the Ten Commandments, which is why Yeshua said that the Torah and the Prophets hung on two commandments.[376] The first is "Thou shalt love the Lord thy God with all thy heart, and with all thy soul, and with all thy mind" (a summary of commandments one through five). The second is "Thou shalt love thy neighbor as thyself" (a summary of commandments six through ten).

Yah built the apostolic writings on the foundation of the Torah, and He built the Torah on the foundation of the Ten Commandments (the Ten Words). Therefore, the theologians who say or even imply that the apostolic writings oppose the Torah, or the Ten Words, are wrong.

Yah is love. As Yah's Spirit leads us, love leads us. Yah's Spirit wrote the Ten Words, Torah, and apostolic writings and set parameters for Himself, so His writings tell us how to love Him, our neighbors, and ourselves. There were instructions in the Torah for unregenerated people who related to Yah and their neighbors through the parameters of the law that Yeshua's Spirit implements in regenerated people. Consequently, Yeshua released us from the custodianship of the law, but this does not mean that the law, the Torah, and the Ten Words do not apply to us.

The Torah is Yah's teachings and instructions. The Mosaic covenant linked the Torah to a legal code, and as the saints kept it, they sanctified themselves, and Yahweh cleansed them when they sinned. The new covenant links the Torah to Yah's Spirit. Yah's Spirit lives in us and changes our nature in order to sanctify us. Yah's Spirit empowers us to fulfill the intent of the Torah and cleanses our conscience as we confess our sins; thus the law no longer functions as our *custodian*.

Excursus

The Operation of the Covenants

Yahweh began teaching and instructing man in the Garden of Eden. Hence the Torah originated in the Garden of Eden. Yahweh added new teachings and instructions as He prepared to implement the phases of His plan. In about 2000 BC, Yahweh's plan took a major step forward as He cut a covenant with Abram. Yah preached the gospel to Abram, and he believed that his Seed (the Promised Seed) would bless the nations. Yahweh declared Abram righteous and placed His Spirit on him to transform him into Abraham. Yahweh's Spirit helped Abraham obey the Torah (His teachings and instructions), and he taught his children to obey them as well.

---

[376] *The Hebrew-Greek Key Word Study Bible*, KJV, Matthew 22:37–40.

Abraham's children disobeyed Yah and mixed with the Canaanites, so Yah took them to Egypt to mold them into a distinct people. Abraham's children prospered and became a distinct people that threatened the security of Egypt, so Pharaoh enslaved them and they started worshiping his gods. Yah called Abraham's children to repentance, and they believed Him, repented, and put their faith in the blood of the Passover lamb. Yah redeemed Abraham's children and justified them, just as He had justified Abraham.

Abraham's children entered the Abrahamic covenant by faith and partook of Yah's grace. There was a problem, however. They thought and acted like Egyptians, so Yah took them to Sinai, where He reiterated all His past teachings and instructions and added some new ones to implement the next phase of His plan. The key component that Yahweh put in place to implement the next phase of His plan was the law.

Yahweh's legal code (the law) called for blessings for obeying the Torah and curses for disobeying it. The law contained a sacrificial system that allowed Yah to forgive His people whenever they sinned. This permitted Yahweh to continue fellowshiping with His people without compromising His righteousness. At Sinai, Yah described the institutions and protocols that He needed to put in place in order to implement the law and invited Israel to have a relationship with Him through the law. Israel accepted Yah's proposal, and Moses sealed the covenant between Yah and Israel in blood; hence we call this covenant the Mosaic covenant.

The Abrahamic covenant was the covenant of redemption. The Mosaic covenant was the covenant of sanctification. Yah cut the Mosaic covenant in order to hold the Abrahamic covenant in place until Yeshua could come to the earth and fulfill the Abrahamic covenant. This is how the older covenants worked: Yah's Spirit gave grace to people so that they could circumcise their hearts by choosing to love Him, believe His promises about the Seed, and put their trust in Him. Yah took them off the serpent's slave market and declared them righteous (nailed their justification ledger to the execution stake with Yeshua). Since Yah's saints still had a fallen nature to overcome, He related to them through the law. Yahweh watched over their sanctification ledger and blessed the saints when they obeyed Him and cursed them when they did not.

Since Yah had redeemed the saints' spirits from the serpent's slave market, the saints' spirits wanted to obey His Torah, but they lacked the authority and the power to force their souls and bodies to obey. John 14:17 tells us that Yah's Spirit lived *with* the saints, not *in* them. As saints prayed, fasted, and worshiped Yahweh, from time to time His Spirit would come on them and give their spirits the power to bring their souls and bodies into submission so that they could do Yah's will. When saints sinned and Yah's Spirit or their conscience brought it to their attention, they took sacrifices to the temple, and the priests offered them to Yah so that He would remove the blot from their record (sanctification ledger) and silence their conscience so they could resume their fellowship with Him.

After Yahweh had forgiven and cleansed a saint, he could fellowship with Him, and from time to time His Spirit would come on him to help him do His will. But the saint still possessed a prideful fallen nature that strove for self-sufficiency, so he would sin again. Afterwards, the saint would realize that there was a break in his fellowship with Yah, and His Spirit or the saint's conscience would point this out. Then the saint took another offering to the temple so the priests could offer it to Yah. The sacrifice made it possible for Yah to erase the sin from the saint's record and cleanse his conscience without compromising His righteousness.

The cycle of fellowship, sin, broken fellowship, repentance, offering, and restored fellowship never ended. Yah dealt with the sin that the fallen nature produced; that is, He forgave the saints and cleansed their conscience, but He left the fallen nature in place. The saints' struggle with the fallen nature produced the cycle that called for more sin offerings and built a sin consciousness in them. Hence the saints were painfully aware of the "leprosy" that was eating away at them, and they longed for the Seed. Thus the law pointed the saints to the Seed.

About three centuries before Yeshua was born, Alexander marched across the Middle East, conquering every nation in it. Alexander forced the nations to adopt his ways. Hellenism threatened to absorb Israel's culture and destroy her. Israel's religious rulers did not humble themselves and seek their divine general's battle plans and follow Him as loyal soldiers obeying His commands. The sages tried to protect their offices and save their nation by systematizing the traditions of the elders (the oral Torah) and developing a strict legal halachah. If a person kept the Torah and its law by obeying the oral Torah and halachah, the sages conferred Jewish legal status on him, which entitled him to share in the Abrahamic covenant and the age to come.

The sages' plan of salvation opposed Yahweh's plan of salvation. In essence, the sages put the Mosaic covenant above the Abrahamic covenant by teaching that if a person kept the Mosaic covenant (their way), then he was in the Abrahamic covenant. This is the problem: Yah did not design the Mosaic covenant to justify anyone; He designed it to sanctify those who were already justified. Hence Yah has never justified anyone for keeping the Torah and its law!

The sages' plan appealed to prideful fallen man because he thought he could keep the commandments and overcome his evil inclination (fallen nature) so that Yahweh would bring him into the Abrahamic covenant and the age to come. The sages loved the Torah and its law because they could use it to exalt themselves. The sages were fanatical over the Torah and its law, meticulously keeping every jot and tittle of it. However, since they did not believe Yah's promises and trust Him, they were not in the Abrahamic covenant, and no amount of Torah observance or law keeping could change that. Sadly, the sacrifices the sages offered were ineffectual, so they lived under the condemnation of the law that they were so fanatical about!

The sages did not believe Yahweh's promises and did not put their faith in the Seed so that He could justify them. Hence the Holy Spirit did not come on them and help them subdue their souls and bodies so that they could do Yah's will. The sages did what the Torah said and complied with its law, but they did it to establish their own righteousness. When the sages sinned, it wounded their *pride*, and they took a sacrifice to the temple and got the priests to offer it to Yah to repair their own righteousness (pride). Yah did not accept their sacrifice, forgive them, and cleanse their conscience, because they were trusting in their own works, not the works of the Seed.

The sages were under the condemnation, guilt, and shame that the law generated, but, like Adam, they covered it up with the fig leaves of religion. Israel chose to follow the sages, but Yah poured out His grace on a remnant so that He could keep His tree connected to its roots. Yahweh empowered the remnant to keep the faith and rise above the condemnation of the law so that His tree could bring forth the fruit of Yeshua. (Whoever eats this fruit will never die!)

Yeshua came to accomplish three things: (1) Yeshua exposed the apostate sages' religion of works and renewed the principle of redemption, justification, and salvation by faith in order to save the lost sheep of the house of Israel by bringing them into the righteous remnant. (2) Yeshua transformed the institutions, protocols, and rituals of the Mosaic covenant, which decentralized the process of sanctification and made it impossible for men to shut up Yahweh's kingdom and use their positions to lord over others and abuse them spiritually, which allowed Him to expand Israel into a global commonwealth. (3) Yeshua redeemed the righteous remnant from the law's custodianship, condemnation, and curses, regenerating them and uniting them with His Spirit and writing the Torah on their hearts, which gave their spirits the power to force their souls and bodies to comply with the desire to serve Yahweh and bring His will to pass.

After Yeshua cut the new covenant, He returned to heaven to sit at Yah's right hand. Yah and Yeshua commissioned the Spirit to begin His ministry of baptizing fallen spirits into His spiritual body so that they could die in Him; then He could resurrect them as sinless spirits and become one with them in order to make them righteous, holy, above blame, and beyond reproach. In the new covenant, a saint is not under the custodianship of the Torah and its law that Yahweh wrote on stone tablets. The reborn spirit is under the custodianship of the Holy Spirit, and He writes the Torah on his heart and serves as the law that constrains him from sin. A regenerated person obeys the Torah that Yah writes on his heart, and if he does not, his *heart* condemns him. Yahweh nails our justification ledger to the execution stake with Yeshua, and turns the sanctification ledger over to our heart so that our heart can watch over it.

A regenerated person is not under the custodianship of the Mosaic law, but he is not a lawless person. A regenerated person is under the custodianship of the law of Messiah, which is Messiah in him restraining him from sin and compelling him to keep the Torah that He writes on his heart. How does Yah's Spirit write the Torah on our heart? As we renew our mind with the Scriptures, Yah's Spirit writes His commands on our heart. What happens if we disobey? When we disobey a command that Yah has written on our heart, *our heart* condemns us. If we repent, confess, and embrace the forgiveness that Yeshua has given us, we submit to His Spirit so that He can flood our heart with love and silence its condemning voice. However, if we continue to sin and ignore our conscience, we will grieve the Spirit. If we keep on grieving the Spirit, we will quench Him. However, if we repent, confess, and embrace the forgiveness that Yeshua has given us, His Spirit will flood our heart with love so that we can enjoy our relationship with Him again.

Yah has not yoked the regenerated person to Himself through the Mosaic law; He has yoked the regenerated person to Himself through His Spirit, who implements the law of Messiah in him.[377] If we disobey Yah's Spirit; that is, violate the law of Messiah (the royal law of love), He prompts us to confess, repent, and embrace the forgiveness that Yeshua has given us to cleanse our conscience. If we refuse to submit to Yah's Spirit, then, by default, we submit to HaSatan. Yah has set us free from the *Mosaic law* and the *curses* that come from violating it. Moreover, since we are in Christ, Yah treats us as if we have kept the Mosaic law perfectly. Yah has given us all the blessings in the covenant, but if we do not obey His Spirit or refuse to repent, confess, and cleanse our conscience, we give HaSatan an opportunity to steal them.

Yeshua did not do away with the law; He transformed it. The law is no longer an external set of rules that are contrary to our nature. It is the One who wrote the law living in us, giving us His nature and writing the law on our heart so we can obey and live the abundant life!

End of Excursus

---

[377] Ibid., Galatians 6:2; John 13:34; James 2:8; 1 John 4:21.

Chapter 49

Romans 12 And 13

Verses 12:1–2

In these verses, Paul tells us how to walk in the Spirit. Paul has already told us that the Spirit lives in us and is trying to get us to follow Him. The Spirit wants to sanctify our lives and manifest the blessings in them. On the other hand, the soul and body conspire together to get us to follow them. If we follow the corrupt duo, we will give HaSatan a chance to steal our blessings. In Galatians 5:17, Paul sums it up by saying the Spirit pulls us one way, but the flesh; that is, the desires of the unrenewed mind and the lusts of the unredeemed body, pulls us the other way.

Paul says that the first step to walking in the Spirit is to present our body as a living sacrifice. Yahweh said that His people were to offer Him sacrifices at an altar. An altar is a place where something dies. Yeshua died on an execution stake and transformed it into our altar. Yeshua said that those who follow Him must take up their stake and follow Him. Paul is simply repeating Yeshua's instructions when he tells us that the first thing to do is to get on the stake. Yahweh has not redeemed the body, so its passions and desires are out of alignment with His will. Each day we must choose to get on the execution stake and put the body's desires and passions to death. This is painful because the body is used to getting whatever it wants.

Paul says that the second step to walking in the Spirit is renewing the mind. A person's mind is the thoughts and intents of his immaterial spirit. A person's immaterial mind becomes functional in the material realm as it materializes in the brain's neuronal circuits, burning electrochemical pathways in the cortex and in the limbic, endocrine, and nervous systems that generate and regulate emotions. After a person emerges from his mother's womb with Adam's nature, HaSatan takes his spirit captive. HaSatan plants his thoughts and intents in the spirit, and the spirit programs the cortex and the limbic, endocrine, and nervous systems with them. These circuits and pathways project HaSatan's image and derive pleasure from satisfying the body.[xiv]

As Yahweh's Spirit puts a person's spirit to death on the stake, resurrects him as a new spirit, and becomes one with him, his thoughts and intents change. However, the self (HaSatan's proxy personality), which is the composite image that is formed by the neuronal circuits and the limbic, endocrine, and nervous systems, does not. Thus after Yah saves a person, there is a conflict between his spirit and the self; his spirit wants to exalt Yah and Yeshua by following the Spirit, but the self wants to exalt itself and anesthetize its pain by bathing in the chemical messengers that the body releases as it gets what it desires. Man's spirit yields either to Yah's Spirit or to the self.

Paul tells us to offer our body as a living sacrifice because this takes the body out of the fight. However, after we take the body out of the fight, the self tries to activate the neuronal circuits and the limbic, endocrine, and nervous systems' pathways in order to draw the body back into the fight. This means that we have to weaken the self in order to win the fight and walk in the Spirit.

HaSatan holds the self together with strongholds. HaSatan builds strongholds by guiding our thoughts and shaping our intents in order to burn deep patterns in our neuronal circuits and limbic, endocrine, and nervous systems. Paul says that we need to renew our mind and allow the Spirit to write His commands on our heart and give us the desire to obey them so that we can build new neuronal circuits and burn new patterns in the limbic, endocrine, and nervous systems.

As we suffer and die on the stake with Yeshua; that is, as we let the lusts of the body go unfulfilled, the old neuronal circuits shut down and fade into the background along with the old patterns in the limbic, endocrine, and nervous systems. As we renew our mind, the Spirit writes the Torah on our heart and gives us a strong desire to obey it. As we yield to the thoughts and intents of the Holy Spirit and follow Him, our spirit interacts with our biology, creating new neuronal circuits and burning new electrochemical pathways in the limbic, endocrine, and nervous systems. The new neuronal circuits and the limbic, endocrine, and nervous systems' pathways manifest Yahweh's peace in us, and His peace keeps us at perfect peace. As our spirit follows the Holy Spirit, we tear down HaSatan's strongholds and break up the concrete that holds the self together. This takes the self out of the fight and enables us to keep the body out of the fight so that we can walk in the Spirit and let Him re-form us in Yeshua's image and change our life.

Romans 13:14

In this verse, Paul tells us to put on the Lord Yeshua Messiah and make no provision for the flesh in order to fulfill its lust. The unredeemed flesh is weak. Hence a regenerated person should not put himself in a situation that could stimulate the latent neuronal pathways or their support patterns that HaSatan has burned into his limbic, endocrine, and nervous systems. These circuits and pathways may have been inactive for years, but if we reactivate them, they will reinvigorate the self. The self will flood the heart with thoughts, imaginations, and emotions that will drown out the voice of the spirit, and we will fulfill the desires of the self and the lusts of our vile body.

A regenerated person's spirit wants to please Yahweh, but HaSatan has programmed his soul to think as he thinks and to derive pleasure from fulfilling the body's lusts. Every regenerated person has days when he perceives the presence of the Spirit and His power infusing him so that he can subdue the rebellious soul and the vile body. On these days, a regenerated person has the self in submission and the vile body securely nailed to the stake. Unfortunately, however, every regenerated person also has days when it seems as if the Spirit has abandoned him. On these days, the spirit struggles to keep the rebellious soul and vile body in submission.

On the days that a regenerated person is strong in the Holy Spirit, he should go through his home and trash anything that could make him stumble when he is weak in the Spirit. If there are people in our lives who are not endeavoring to walk in the Spirit and overcome the lusts of the flesh, we must cut them off. If a place triggers old memories and emotions that refresh the self and cause us to stumble, we must stay away from that place. In order to be victorious, we must trash everything and avoid every person and every place that could make us stumble, because the devil and his crew are in the atmosphere waiting for us to give place to them so that they can get a foothold in our soul and build (or reactivate) a stronghold that they can use to destroy us.

People focus on the devil and the demons, but this is a mistake. Yeshua has defeated the devil and his crew. Yahweh's Spirit has hidden our spirit in Yeshua, and Yeshua is in Yahweh. Consequently, Yeshua has seated us in heavenly places far above the devil and his crew. This means that the devil and his crew cannot touch us if we keep our soul in submission and our body nailed to the tree![378] Yeshua has defeated the devil and his crew and executed our spirit, which was once subject to them, and we have buried it in the baptismal waters with Him. Focus on Yeshua's Spirit and keeping your soul in submission and your body nailed to the tree.

Casting Out Demons

Yeshua cast out demons from unbelievers in order to prove that the kingdom He was in (Yahweh's kingdom) could overpower the kingdom that ruled over them (HaSatan's kingdom). Yeshua told the unbelievers who had to see a sign before they would believe that they were an evil and adulterous generation, and the only sign that He was going to give

---

[378] *The Hebrew-Greek Key Word Study Bible*, KJV, Colossians 3:3; Ephesians 1:20–21; 2:6; 1 John 5:18.

them was the sign of His resurrection. Yeshua told these unbelievers that if He were to cast out a demon from them, it would return and bring seven more with it, and their latter state would be worse than their former one. Yeshua knew that these unbelievers had hardened their hearts, and even if He showed them a sign, they would not repent so that He could redeem them. Consequently, these people would remain in HaSatan's kingdom, and the demon would return to its home with seven associates. Yeshua cast out demons from the unbelievers who would repent so that He could take them out of HaSatan's kingdom and bring them into His kingdom where His Spirit could protect them.

In the older covenants, Yah redeemed people (rescued them from HaSatan's kingdom), but His Spirit did not become one with their spirit and change their nature and empower them to obey (He did not regenerate them). In the new covenant, Yahweh redeems us (rescues us from HaSatan's kingdom), and His Spirit becomes one with our spirit. Yahweh's Spirit establishes His kingdom in us. As we submit to Yah's Spirit, He empowers us to tear down HaSatan's strongholds in our soul so that it will submit to Him and He can re-form it in His image.

In the new covenant, Yah takes a person's spirit off the serpent's slave market and delivers it from HaSatan's kingdom and brings it into His kingdom, and the demons that were in it are evicted and cannot return because His Spirit has transformed their old house into His temple. However, demons can work through the strongholds that are in a saint's soul. After Yahweh regenerates a person, the demons that are *flowing through* the strongholds in that person's soul can manifest (make themselves known), but we can use His authority to command them to leave. If, however, a saint does not cooperate with the Holy Spirit and tear down the strongholds in his soul, the demons that are cast out will have an open door that they can flow through in order to influence the saint again. Casting out demons without tearing down the strongholds that gave them access to a saint's soul is a temporary solution. The lasting solution is to tear down the strongholds in a saint's soul so that demons cannot plant their thoughts and intents in the saint.

In Ephesians 6:12, Paul says that we do not wrestle with flesh and blood, but with principalities, powers, rulers of darkness, and spiritual wickedness in high places. Paul is telling us that the devil and his crew try to get us to yield to the desires of the self and the lusts of the body so that they can gain a foothold and build (or reactivate) a stronghold in us that they can use in order to bring us into bondage. However, 1 John 5:18 says that if we keep ourselves, they cannot. Demons control unregenerated people and can control a saint who yields to the soul and body. However, these people are not our enemies. The demons are. We must pray for and bless the people who do evil things to us and come against the demons who are controlling them.

Yeshua cast out demons from *unbelievers*. Paul cast out demons from *unbelievers*. Paul tells *believers* to take off the old man with its desires and put on the new man with its desires. In essence, Paul tells *believers* to cooperate with the Spirit in order to tear down the strongholds in the soul, bringing it into submission, re-forming it in Yeshua's image.

In 1 Corinthians 5, Paul corrects a *believer* who was sleeping with his stepmother. If there was ever a time to cast out a demon from a believer, this was it! Paul, however, did not tell the leaders to cast out a demon; he told them to turn the man over to HaSatan for the destruction of *the flesh* (the desires of the self and lusts of the body) to work out his salvation. Let us follow Paul as he followed Yeshua.

Chapter 50

Romans 14:1–20

Background

In chapters 1–11, Paul built a theological foundation that prepared the people in the Roman ekklesia to receive the correction he was about to give in chapter 14. In chapter 14, Paul identified some behaviors that had been dividing the Roman ekklesia and sought to change them so that the Jews and Gentiles could come together to manifest the one new man.

This is the key to understanding Romans 14. The Roman congregation (like every other congregation) was a dynamic institution; periodically, people joined the congregation and people left it. Hence there were two groups of Gentiles in the Roman congregation: (1) a group of mature Gentiles who were strong in the faith and (2) a group of immature Gentiles who had just recently repented from paganism in order to join the congregation and were weak in the faith.

After the government permitted the Jews to return to Rome, the messianic Jews located the houses where the Gentile believers were worshiping and joined them. Many of the messianic Jews had worshiped Yeshua in the synagogues and instructed the Gentile believers before the government expelled them from the city. These messianic Jews were mature believers. From time to time, new Jews would believe that Yeshua was Messiah and join the Roman ekklesia. As new believers, these Jews were immature and weak in the faith. Thus the Roman ekklesia contained two groups of Jews: (1) a group that was strong in the faith and (2) a group that was weak in the faith. So when Paul speaks of those who are strong in the faith, he is speaking of Jews and Gentiles who were mature and strong in the faith; conversely, when he speaks of those who are weak in the faith, he is speaking of Jews and Gentiles who were immature and weak in the faith.

Most Gentile commentators say that the Jews were weak in the faith and that the Gentiles were strong in the faith. These commentators say that Jews were trying to bring Gentiles into bondage to the Torah and its law. Hence, they say, Paul was writing to rebuke the Jews and straighten them out. This interpretation, however, is a product of the old Roman mind-set that Paul was trying to correct.

This is what we need to remember: The Jews were the first people to accept Yeshua. As large numbers of Gentiles began to accept Yeshua, Jewish apostles instructed them to obey a few key principles of the Torah *so that they could join the community of faith and learn the rest of it*. The messianic Jews were the fathers of the faith who were supposed to teach their sons in the faith (the Gentiles) the Torah and watch over them, helping them transition from paganism to the worship of Yahweh. The Jews' divine assignment was to teach the Torah to the Gentiles.[379]

As the messianic Jews returned to the Roman ekklesia, the mature Gentiles embraced them as sons and began to move back to their Hebrew roots. However, the immature Gentiles resisted this movement back to the Hebrew roots. The immature Gentiles were afraid that the Jews were trying to yoke them to the Mosaic law or entangle them in the legalism of the oral Torah and halachah. This is why Paul spent so much time explaining that the written Torah was holy, but that Yah no longer used its law as the primary agent of sanctification. Now Yahweh's Spirit regenerated people and indwelt them in order to function as the primary agent of sanctification.

In the older covenants, Yahweh said that if a man who was not born in the camp put his faith in the blood of a Passover lamb, then the people who were born in the camp were supposed to treat him as if he had been born in the camp. Yahweh said that there was one Torah for His people, whether they were born in the camp or He joined them to it (whether they were Jew or Gentile).[380] Paul let the Gentiles know that when they put their faith in Yeshua, Yahweh grafted them onto Israel's righteous remnant to build a global commonwealth that His Spirit governs. The Torah (and its law) did not fade away. The Torah (and its law) became a Person who lived out its intent and submitted to death so that Yahweh could put His Spirit in us to empower us to fulfill its intent.

In the new covenant, there is one Torah for Yahweh's people. It does not matter whether we were born on Yahweh's tree, or He grafted us onto it. Yahweh's Spirit writes the Torah on our heart, changes our desires, gives us the power to obey, restrains us from sin, and cleanses us as we fail so that we can live the abundant life. Yeshua said it this way: "Think not that I am come to destroy the law, or the prophets: I am not come to destroy, but to fulfill."[381]

---

[379] *The Hebrew-Greek Key Word Study Bible*, KJV, Isaiah 42:4; Matthew 28:20; Acts 15:21; Romans 7:12.

[380] Ibid., Exodus 12:48–49; Numbers 9:14; 15:13–16; Galatians 3:28.

[381] Ibid., Matthew 5:17.

Verse 14:1

In this verse, Paul says, "You must continually take to yourselves the one who is weak in faith, yet do not get into quarrels about opinions."[382] Paul exhorts the people who are strong in the faith to embrace the people who are weak in the faith without fighting over opinions. As we read Paul's words, we need to keep in mind that the Torah is not "opinions." The Torah is Yah's teachings and instructions that constitute the foundational revelation of who He is and His plan for man. Hence the Prophets and the Writings, as well as the apostolic writings, had to line up with the Torah.

The Jewish believers knew the Torah, the Prophets, and the Writings, so they realized that the new covenant accomplished what the Mosaic covenant could not. In the new covenant, Yah dealt with the weak link that caused the Mosaic covenant to fail. Yah puts man's fallen spirit to death, resurrects him, and becomes one with him to change his nature. Yah's Spirit writes the Torah on man's heart, which gives him the desire and the ability to fulfill its intent so that he can live the abundant life.[383] Jewish believers knew that the Torah still applied to them.

The Gentiles did not know the Torah, the Prophets, and the Writings. So when the Gentiles began accepting Yeshua and coming into His ekklesia, Yahweh's Spirit spoke through the Jewish apostles on the Jerusalem Council and commanded the Gentiles to abstain from idols, fornication, blood, and things strangled. Yahweh wanted the Gentiles to obey the basic precepts of the Torah so that they could assemble with His people on the Sabbath to learn the rest of it. As the Gentiles studied the written Torah, Yahweh's Spirit wrote it on their hearts, changed their desires, and empowered them to walk out its intent so that they could live the abundant life. Hence the Gentiles knew that Yahweh expected them to study the written Torah so that His Spirit could write it on their hearts and empower them to walk it out and fulfill its intent.

In verse 1, Paul is not writing about conflicting opinions between Jews and Gentiles over whether the Torah applied to Yeshua's ekklesia. At the time Paul penned these words, the Torah, the Prophets, and the Writings were the *only* Scriptures that existed. Hence it would be utterly bizarre for *anyone* in Yeshua's ekklesia to think that His Torah no longer applied to him!

Verses 2–4

In verse 2, Paul says that the people who were strong in the faith believed that they could eat anything (that is, anything the Torah *permitted,* because Yahweh sanctified these

---

[382] William Morford, *The Power New Testament*, Lexington, SC, Shalom Ministries, Inc., 2004, p. 224.

[383] *The Hebrew-Greek Key Word Study Bible*, KJV, Ezekiel 36:24–29.

things), but the people who were weak in the faith ate only vegetables. The Gentiles who were weak in the faith were afraid pagans might have sacrificed animals to their gods and sold the meat to the local market. The weak Gentiles believed that the pagan gods defiled the meat that Yahweh had sanctified and thus made it impure, so if they were to eat it, they would become impure. In order to avoid becoming impure, they were of the *opinion* that everyone in the congregation should eat only vegetables.[xv] The Gentiles who were mature knew that if Yah had sanctified meat for them to eat, then no idol or spirit could defile it and make it impure, so they did not worry about where meat came from.

The Jews in the Roman ekklesia had come out of a religion that built a high fence around the Torah to ensure that no one violated it. The high fence (the oral Torah and the legal halachah) was a heavy burden that oppressed them with thousands of rules, regulations, and laws. The Jews were used to keeping these rules, regulations, and laws in order to walk out the written Torah, so it was hard for them to unshackle themselves from this oppressive system. The Jews who were weak in the faith had trouble breaking free from the sages' teachings that said that a permitted meat became impure if anyone mishandled it or a pagan touched it. So to avoid eating impure meat, they were of the *opinion* that the congregation should eat only vegetables.[xvi] (See endnote.)

The Jews who were mature had learned to follow the Holy Spirit as He showed them how to walk out the written Torah and fulfill its intent. The Jews who were strong in the faith knew that if Yah sanctified a particular kind of meat, then no demon spirit could make it impure. The mature Jews did not worry about where their permitted meat came from. Paul told the strong people in the congregation not to despise the weak and the weak people not to judge the strong.

Verses 5–13

In verse 5, Paul says that one person esteems one day above another and one person esteems every day. Some commentators use this verse to free New Testament saints from the Sabbath, but Paul was not talking about the weekly feast (the Sabbath) or the seasonal feasts. These feasts occur on set days, not on a day of our choosing. There were, however, differing *opinions* on what the term *the morrow after the Sabbath* meant. A person's interpretation of this phrase determined when the Omer count began and when it ended to signify that the day of Pentecost had fully come. Again, this does not fit in with Paul's statement that some esteemed every day, because the Sabbath and the other feasts were set days that could not occur every day.

What is Paul talking about in verse 5? The subject of the previous verse was food, and the verse that follows this one connects food with days, which suggests that the subject of this verse is fast days. Tim Hegg points out that the ancient fathers believed this verse was referring to fast days[384] and that during the intertestamental period, there was an increased emphasis put on fasting.[385] Here is the key to interpreting this verse: The sages determined the fast days for the people in the synagogues. The pagan priests determined the fast days for the people in their temples. Hence, when the people in the synagogues and pagan temples repented and joined Yeshua's ekklesia, they each had their own *opinion* about which day was the right day to fast.

Hegg makes an observation that supports this reasoning. The Didache[xvii] describes a controversy that was raging around the turn of the first century over the ekklesia's fast days. The rabbis prohibited fasting on the Sabbath and the other festival days, and since the synagogues fasted on Mondays and Thursdays, Wednesdays and Fridays seemed like the preferred days for those in the ekklesia to fast.[386] Since the fathers wrote the Didache twenty to fifty years after Paul wrote his letter to the Romans, it is reasonable to assume that this controversy existed in the Roman congregation. So Paul told the Romans that if they selected a day to fast, then they were to fast unto the Lord; and if they chose to eat on a particular day, then they were to eat unto the Lord. In other words, there was no right answer because the written Torah was silent on this issue. Paul told the people in the Roman assembly to stop judging each other because they would all stand before the bema seat.

Verses 14–20

In Genesis, Yahweh looked at His creation and saw that it was good. Yahweh did not create anything that was intrinsically impure. After the fall, however, some animals acquired attributes and behaviors that were inconsistent with Yahweh's nature. Yahweh permitted His people to eat the animals that were consistent with His nature. Conversely, Yahweh forbade His people to eat the animals that were not consistent with His nature. We call these laws the *kosher laws*.

Yahweh also gave His people the laws of "pure" and "impure" ("clean" and "unclean"). For example, death is not consistent with Yahweh's nature. If a saint touched a corpse, he was unclean and could not enter the temple to draw near to Yahweh. If an unclean saint were to enter the temple, he would defile it, and Yah would cut him off from Israel.[387] However, if he purified himself by baptism on the *third day* after his defilement, he would be clean on the *seventh day*.

If a saint was in an impure state, he could not enter the temple to fellowship with Yah until he went through the cleansing rituals that pointed to the Seed. The system of pure

---

[384] Tim Hegg, *Paul's Epistle to the Romans*, Tacoma, WA, TorahResource, 2005, p. 412.

[385] Ibid., p. 416.

[386] Ibid., p. 416.

[387] *The Hebrew-Greek Key Word Study Bible*, KJV, Numbers 19:11–13.

and impure revealed the condition of a person's heart. A person with a circumcised heart avoided impurities, and if he became impure, he submitted to the cleansing ritual focusing on the Seed. A person with an uncircumcised heart kept the rules in order to establish his own righteousness.

Yahweh wanted His people to reflect His nature. Hence Yah wanted His people to avoid the things that were not consistent with His nature. However, since Yahweh's people possessed fallen natures and lived in a fallen world, He provided remedies for those times when they failed to reflect His nature, and these remedies pointed to the Seed. Yahweh's system of pure and impure showed how easily the things of the world could defile fallen people, while emphasizing that the Seed was the only remedy for man's problem. Yah's system of pure and impure contrasted His holiness with man's nature so that man would recognize his need for the Seed and pine for Him.

In verse 14, Paul says that nothing is impure of itself, but if a person thinks something is impure, he must avoid it. If he does not, his heart will condemn him, and his conscience will separate him from Yah. Paul tells the strong to walk in love by abstaining from meat that might cause the weak to withdraw from fellowship, because that could give HaSatan an opportunity to harm them. Paul reminds us that Yahweh's Spirit manifests the kingdom through righteousness, peace, and joy, not food and drink. In verse 20, Paul says that all *food* is pure (everything that Yahweh sanctified for food is pure), but it is evil to offend others by what we eat.

Chapter 51

Romans 14:21–16:27

Paul's Closing Remarks

In verse 21, Paul says saints should not eat meat or drink wine if it makes a brother stumble. If they have the faith to eat meat or drink wine that pagans might have used to worship their gods, they should do it alone in the presence of Yah and enjoy the blessing that comes from not condemning themselves in the things they allow. (Note: They allowed it because Yahweh permitted it in the Torah, and it would not bring them into bondage. Paul put it this way in 1 Corinthians 10:23: all things that were lawful in the Torah were lawful for him, but not all things edified).[xviii] If, however, saints doubt whether meat is pure and eat it anyway, their hearts will condemn them and separate them from Yah; for them, therefore, it is sin, because sin is anything that separates us from Yah.

Paul is talking about *permitted* meat that a pagan may have offered to an idol. He says if saints think that a demon or a sage's decree has turned a permitted meat into a forbidden meat, they should avoid it. If Paul believed that Yeshua abolished the kosher laws, then this whole discourse was pointless. The fact that he teaches that for some people, some things fall into the questionable category proves that there is a nonquestionable category. It is clear that Paul believed that the Torah and its laws of permitted and forbidden meats still applied to believers, which is why he kept it and was able to say that he had never walked contrary to the customs of the fathers.[388]

---

[388] *The Hebrew-Greek Key Word Study Bible*, KJV, Acts 28:17.

Excursus

Did Yeshua Fulfill the Law or Abolish it?

Sin Becomes a Criminal Matter

Adam rebelled against Yah, and HaSatan altered his HSC so he could rule over him. Adam's children possessed the corrupted HSC, and it allowed HaSatan to rule over them. Man's sin separated him from Yah, and it had other consequences, but Yah did not treat his sin as a criminal matter and punish it. Later Yah cut a covenant with Abram and promised that his Seed would be the agent through which He would reconcile the world to Himself. Four hundred years later, Yah redeemed Abraham's seed, along with a group of Gentiles, and took them to Sinai, where He reiterated His Torah and attached a legal code to it that criminalized sin and prescribed penalties for it to dissuade them from sinning so they could project His image and live the abundant life.

At Mount Sinai, the children of Israel (a core group of Hebrews and the Gentiles who had attached themselves to this core) agreed to let the Torah and its law function as a custodian over their relationship with Yahweh. We call this agreement the Mosaic covenant. The heart of the Mosaic covenant was the law. The law set forth blessings for obeying the Torah and curses for disobeying it. Yahweh sanctified Israel through the agency of the written Torah and its law.

In Romans 3:19, Paul said that Yahweh gave the law to Israel so that she would realize that she possessed a corrupted nature and put her faith in His promises. In turn, Israel was supposed to teach the people of the nations (the Gentiles) that they stood guilty before Yahweh because of their unredeemed corrupted nature. Israel's assignment was to teach the nations the Torah and its law so that all people on earth would know they possessed a fallen nature that separated them from Yahweh forever. This may seem unfair, but it is not. Remember, Yahweh told Adam that if he ate the illicit fruit, he would die. Adam ate the fruit, and he died spiritually. Afterwards, Adam and Eve produced children who were also spiritually dead. We are all born spiritually dead, and when Yahweh gave the law to Israel, He was making sure that we knew it.

The only way a person could reconcile with Yah and escape condemnation was to join himself to Israel by believing Yah and putting his trust in His promises. When a person put his faith in Yahweh, submitted to circumcision, and kept the Passover, Yah redeemed and justified him and attached him to Israel. After this, the saint yoked himself to the Torah so he could learn how to walk out his faith and obtain forgiveness and cleansing when he missed the mark.

In the Mosaic covenant, the law was the custodian of a saint's relationship with Yahweh. Yahweh placed a blot on the saint's record when he sinned. The sins that Yah imputed to the saint's account interrupted his fellowship and opened him to the curses. The saint had to do the works that the law called for while looking towards the Seed before Yah would remove the blot from his record. As a saint complied with the law, Yah forgave his sins, cleansed his conscience, wiped the blot from his record, restored him to fellowship, and blessed him. The Mosaic law restrained a saint from sin and cleansed him when he did sin so he could live the abundant life.

The Abrahamic covenant was the covenant of redemption that people accessed by faith. The Mosaic covenant was the covenant of sanctification that showed the redeemed how to walk out their faith. When a saint violated the Torah, the law compelled Yah to place a blot on his account, which separated him from fellowship with Yah and opened an avenue for the curses, but this did not mean that he was no longer a saint. Sin affected a saint's sanctification (the image he projected and the quality of his life), not his redemption. In other words, Yah placed a blot on a saint's sanctification ledger; He did not impute sin to his justification ledger. People could not enter the Abrahamic covenant by keeping the Torah, nor could they lose their position in the Abrahamic covenant by violating the Torah. However, if people refused to comply with the Torah's legal code, Yahweh cut them off from Israel until they either repented or died in isolation.

Fifteen hundred years later, Yahweh cut the new covenant with Israel. Yeshua, the mediator of the new covenant, sealed the covenant with His own blood. As a person believes the gospel and bows to Yeshua, he partakes of the Passover Lamb. Yah brings this person into the Abrahamic covenant and Israel's righteous remnant. Yahweh's Spirit becomes one with this person, writing the Torah on his heart, circumcising his heart, changing his desires, restraining him from sin, and cleansing him when he does sin, which empowers him to project Yeshua's image and live the abundant life. In short, Yeshua's Spirit implements the Mosaic covenant in this person and prompts him to walk in love towards Yahweh and man and fulfill the intent of the Torah.

Since Yeshua's Spirit is one with our regenerated spirit, His righteousness is our righteousness! The "old man," who was under the condemnation of the law, is dead. Yeshua's Spirit is the custodian of our relationship with Yahweh, and when we sin, His blood cleanses us. Since Yeshua is one with us, we possess His nature, and when we touch or eat something impure, it does not defile us. There is no need for us to go through the Mosaic covenant's cleansing rituals that pointed to the Seed because He is in us and fulfills those cleansing rituals! Through Yeshua, Yah has sanctified us and made us pure by faith, not by the works of the law.

Yahweh Decriminalizes Sin

In the new covenant, Yahweh has fulfilled the law and decriminalized the transgression of the Torah (sin). So shall we disregard the Torah and live as we wish? Yahweh forbid! In the new covenant, Yahweh has put our old nature to death and rebirthed us with His nature. So shall we partake of the things that Yah said were not consistent with His nature? Yahweh forbid!

Is the written Torah relevant for Yahweh's people? Yes! Are Yahweh's definitions of what is and what is not consistent with His nature relevant for His people? Yes! Is the Mosaic law relevant for Yahweh's people? Yes! However, Yeshua's perfect life, absolute submission, and death, burial, and resurrection transformed the Mosaic law. Yeshua's Spirit indwells us so that He can implement the Mosaic law in us to restrain us from sin, cleanse us as we sin, and prompt us to walk in accordance to the royal law of love, thus fulfilling the *intent* of the written Torah. Yah has not changed, and He has not changed the Torah or its law.[xix] Yahweh has not changed His mind about what is and what is not consistent with His nature. Yahweh has not abolished the kosher laws. *The only thing that has changed is the location of the written Torah and its law.*

Location, Location, Location

At Mount Sinai, Yahweh fashioned two stone tablets and wrote a condensed form of the Torah on them. However, before Moses could get back down the mountain, Yah's people had rebelled. Moses got angry and broke the stone tablets, and Yah told him to fashion two more tablets and bring them up to Him so that He could write the Torah on them. This is a picture of Yahweh cutting the Mosaic covenant with Israel by writing the Torah on stone tablets, and her breaking of the covenant and His cutting of a new covenant by writing the Torah on new tablets. In the new covenant, a person brings the tablets of his heart to Yahweh, and He writes the Torah on them and changes his heart and his nature so that he will obey Yahweh and live the abundant life.

Yahweh shares His nature with His people, and *since they are partakers of His nature*, they shun sin and the things that are not consistent with His nature. If a saint eats something that is inconsistent with Yahweh's nature, it does not affect his redemption (his salvation); it affects his sanctification (the image he projects and the quality of his life). Thus, if a regenerated person does not follow the promptings of the Spirit in order to fulfill the intent of the Torah and avoid the things that are inconsistent with Yahweh's nature, he will not enjoy the full measure of the abundant life. However, a saint's actions will not defile his spirit and make him impure. Yeshua's Spirit lives in the saint, fulfilling the Mosaic covenant's animal sacrifices and cleansing rituals in him. *Hence, Yeshua did not abolish the Mosaic law; He fulfilled its requirements and intent in us.*

End of Excursus

In Romans 15, verses 1–3, the apostle Paul exhorts the strong to bear with the weak instead of pleasing themselves, and he exhorts everyone to follow Yeshua's example. Paul reminds us that Yeshua kept the written Torah and deserved to enjoy the covenant blessings, but instead of pleasing Himself, enjoying what He was entitled to, He took the covenant curses for those who dishonored Yah so they could enjoy His blessings. In verse 14, Paul begins to wrap up his letter by discussing his ministry plans. In chapter 16, Paul ends by saying his good-byes.

Chapter 52

Keeping It Between The Bookends

Has Yahweh Said?

*T*he bookend epistles tell us that Yahweh has not done away with the written Torah or changed it. However, most Gentile commentators say that Yeshua changed the Torah and released us from its dietary guidelines. Is this what Yahweh said? Let us look at the scriptures that these Gentile commentators use to support this idea and see if this idea is valid or if this idea is a product of the old Roman mind-set that despised everything Jewish. Remember, Galatians and Romans are bookends that hold the other books of the New Testament in their proper places. This means that we must keep our interpretation of the New Testament books *between* these two bookends.

Commentators use Mark 7, Acts 10, Acts 15, Galatians 2, 1 Timothy 4:1–5, Romans 14, and 1 Corinthians 8 to support the idea that Yahweh has abolished His dietary guidelines and declared everything clean for those who are in Yeshua's ekklesia. So in this chapter, we will examine these passages and determine whether Yah has changed the Torah and said that the people who attach themselves to Israel do not have to live like Israel, or whether we have inherited lies.

Surely, We Have Inherited Lies

In Jeremiah 16:19, Yahweh says that after He gathers His people back to their land, the Gentiles will come to them for truth because they will realize that they have inherited lies. Yah began bringing the Jews back to Israel in 1948. In 1967, Yah began removing the blinders from their eyes so that they could see Yeshua and return to the ekklesia. Since 1967, the Jews have pointed out some flaws in the Gentiles' understanding of Scripture. Remember, this is what prompted Paul to write Romans in the first place. This means that it is time to apply Paul's correction in the ekklesia so Jew and Gentile can come together to form the one new man.

As Gentiles, we possess a skewed understanding of the Torah and its law, which causes us to project an image of Yah that Jews do not recognize; thus the Jews think we are worshiping another god. One area of our life that does not project Yahweh's image is in what we eat. We think that it is fine to eat forbidden meat, but what understanding do the Jews bring to the table?

Jews know that Yahweh's teachings and instructions bless and protect us.[389] How does Yahweh's system of permitted and forbidden meats bless and protect us? After the fall, some animals started eating dead things, but because they were not equipped to eliminate the toxins in the rotting flesh, these poisons accumulated in their flesh. If we eat these scavengers, our bodies will not know how to deal with the toxins, and they will clog our arteries or provoke other inflammatory responses that will cause diseases like arthritis.[390] If a person eats swine flesh, it will not affect his salvation, but it will affect his sanctification. Yah's Torah sanctifies us; that is, it sets us apart from the world, lack, bondage, and disease. The Torah says that swine flesh is not consistent with Yah's nature, which means that there is death in it; and if we eat it, we are choosing death.

Mark 7 (King James Version)

At Sinai, Yahweh set life and death before His people. Yah encouraged His people to choose life by obeying the Torah. Commentators say that the Torah's dietary instructions no longer apply and that we can eat whatever we want without consequence. What has Yahweh said?

In Mark 7, Yeshua rebukes Israel's religious leaders for exalting their traditions above the Torah. The Pharisees were an extremely strict sect of religious rulers who believed everyone should live like priests. Yah said that Israel was a nation of priests who would bring the nations into the covenant, and the Pharisees took these words literally. The Pharisees kept the written Torah by keeping the rules, regulations, and laws of the oral Torah and legal halachah (the whole Torah). The whole Torah said that people had to wash their pots, plates, cups, and hands before eating, or they would defile themselves and make themselves impure. If they were impure, they would have to go through a cleansing ritual before they could enter the temple to worship Yah.

The Pharisees saw Yeshua and His disciples enjoying a meal. Yeshua and His disciples were eating *permitted* food, but they were not following the rules in the oral Torah and halachah. The Pharisees condemned Yeshua and His disciples for disobeying the Torah. The

---

[389] *The Hebrew-Greek Key Word Study Bible*, KJV, Exodus 15:26; Joshua 1:8; Psalm 1:2–3; 119:24, 77, 92.

[390] http://www.kyrieology.com/drupal/wwje/adverseinfluenceofpork. [06/2011]

Pharisees said if a person's pot, plate, cup, or hands accidentally touched an impure person or something a pagan had used to worship his gods, then the pot, plate, cup, or hand would transmit impurity to the *permitted* food and defile it and make it *forbidden*. Thus a person had to wash his pot, plate, cup, and hands before he ate. According to the Pharisees, if a person did not follow their rules, his permitted food was impure, and if he ate it, it would defile him and make him impure.

Yeshua scolded the Pharisees for setting the Torah aside in order to keep their own traditions. Yeshua cited an example of how they were destroying the Torah. The written Torah said that a person must honor his parents if he wanted to live long and prosper on the earth. A person honored his parents by taking care of them when they were too old to work. However, the Pharisees said a person could give his money to the temple instead of giving it to his parents.

It was the same situation with the written Torah's dietary laws. The written Torah spelled out which animals were fit to eat and which animals were not fit to eat. However, the Pharisees said that the things that Yahweh said a person could eat and freely enjoy were not fit to eat unless a person followed their rules. The Pharisees placed their teachings and traditions above the written Torah and made it to none effect. In other words, they destroyed the Torah.

Yeshua said that *food* (what Yah sanctified) does not defile a man because it does not enter his heart; it enters his belly and goes out into the toilet, *purging all food from the body*. In effect, Yeshua said that a man's heart generates the desires that drive his behavior, and behavior that violates the letter or the spirit of the Torah is what defiles him. The *food* that a person eats does not change his heart, for the better or for the worse, but the Pharisees thought that they could overcome their evil inclination by keeping the written Torah the way the traditions of the elders (oral Torah) and the sages' legal rulings (halachah) specified and take on Yahweh's image.

Commentators say that Yeshua permitted all animals and destroyed the Torah's dietary guidelines. However, Yeshua tells us not to think that He came to destroy the Torah; He did not come to destroy it, but to fulfill it,[xx] and Paul says that our faith in Yeshua establishes the Torah. *Yeshua did not cleanse all the animals and permit us to eat them*. Yeshua upheld the written Torah and its dietary laws, but the Pharisees set the written Torah and its dietary guidelines aside for their own teachings and traditions. Consequently, Yeshua said that the Pharisees were worshiping Yahweh in vain. Sadly, most commentators have followed in the footsteps of the Pharisees, setting the Torah's dietary guidelines aside for their own teachings and traditions.

Acts 10

In this section, Peter went into a trance and saw a large sheet of unclean animals.[xxi] Peter heard a voice tell him to rise, kill, and eat. Peter assumed that the voice was Yeshua's voice. Peter told Yeshua that he had never eaten anything unclean. The voice told Peter not to call anything unclean that Yahweh had cleansed. Peter could not understand the trance and doubted whether it was from Yeshua. Peter had walked with Yeshua for three years, and He had never eaten anything unclean or taught anyone to. Peter knew that Yeshua did not change the written Torah!

Peter knew the Torah, the Prophets, and the Writings. Peter recalled the scriptures that told of Yahweh testing Ezekiel by telling him to cook his bread over dried human dung. Ezekiel knew that the Torah instructed Yah's people to relieve themselves outside the camp and bury their excrement so that He could walk in their midst and fight for them.[391] Hence Ezekiel protested against Yah's instructions and said he had never polluted his soul by eating anything unclean. Yahweh was testing Ezekiel to see whether he would obey the Torah or follow a spirit that asked him to violate it. Ezekiel passed the test, and Yahweh told him to use cow dung to cook his food.[392]

Peter knew that if a spirit asked him to violate the Torah, it was not of Yahweh. Like Ezekiel, Peter protested and waited for a response. Yah's Spirit spoke to Peter and told him that there were three men at his door, and he was to go with them because He had sent them. Peter saw that the men were Gentiles, and he knew what the meaning of the vision was. The sages said Gentiles were unclean, and Jews were not to enter their homes or eat with them because it would defile them. The Torah did not say this, however. Yah was telling him to call no man unclean! Yah confirmed this as Peter preached the gospel to the men. Yah's Spirit cleansed these men of their sins, filled them, and empowered them to speak in tongues. Yah was using the imagery of unclean animals to represent the Gentiles. *Yahweh did not declare all things clean.*

Acts 15

In this section, Judaizers were telling Gentiles they must submit to circumcision and keep the law before Yah would save them. The Jerusalem Council met to rule on this and decided not to burden Gentiles with circumcision because it was the outward sign that showed that a man had circumcised his heart by believing Yah and His promises and had entered the Abrahamic covenant.

---

[391] *The Hebrew-Greek Key Word Study Bible*, KJV, Deuteronomy 23:13.

[392] Ibid., Ezekiel 4:1–17.

The apostles said that the presence of Yeshua's Spirit in Gentiles was the sign that they were in the covenant. The ritual of circumcision pointed to the Seed, and since His Spirit was in Gentiles, cutting the flesh from the hearts so that they could leave their former lifestyles behind, it was not necessary for them to cut the flesh from their penises. If Gentiles adhered to a few key precepts of the Torah, they could meet with Yah's people on the Sabbath and learn the rest of it.

For the apostles, obeying the Torah was a sign that a Gentile was in the covenant. Most commentators say that the apostles gave the Gentiles four commandments: to abstain from the pollutions of idols, fornication, things strangled, and blood. Hence the Torah and its dietary rules did not apply to Gentiles. But the four commands deal with things that went on in pagan temples where Gentiles worshiped devils and specifies what Gentiles had to repent of in order to show that the Spirit's invisible circumcision was in place and that they were in the covenant.

Galatians 2

In this section, Peter and Paul were eating with some Gentile brothers. Peter saw a group of Jewish religious officials approaching and withdrew from the table. Paul rebuked Peter. In that culture, eating with a person was a covenant act, which meant that you were at peace with him. For example, the Passover was a covenant meal between Yah and man that signified that they were at peace with each other, which is why a person who was in the covenant could eat it, but a person who was not in the covenant could not. The peace offering was also a covenant meal between Yah and man. Man ate a portion of the peace offering and burned a portion on the altar for Yahweh.

Peter's withdrawal from fellowship indicated that he believed the Gentiles held an inferior position in the covenant or were not in it at all! In essence, Peter came into agreement with those who were of "the circumcision" because they were in power in Jerusalem. (*The circumcision* is shorthand for those who relied on circumcision as an ethnic marker that defined who was in the covenant.) Remember, the sages taught that a Jew (a covenant member) was a person who submitted to circumcision, baptized himself, offered a sacrifice, and kept the written Torah by obeying the rules, regulations, and laws of the oral Torah and legal halachah. In this context, to live like a "Jew" was to follow the rules of *the circumcision for covenant inclusion*. Peter did not live like a Jew (like those of the circumcision), so Paul rebuked him and asked him why he wanted Gentiles to live like Jews (like those of the circumcision), when he did not.

Essentially, Paul asked Peter why he would withdraw from table fellowship with the Gentiles and lead them to believe they needed to submit to circumcision and follow the oral Torah and legal halachah to be covenant members. Clearly, these verses are about table fellowship, covenant inclusion, and the unity of the ekklesia. Paul was trying to make sure the ekklesia was not divided along ethnic lines so that the one new man, whom Messiah came to make by tearing down the middle wall of separation (the man-made rules that separated Jews and Gentiles), could come forth and the Abrahamic covenant be fulfilled. Paul reminded Peter that the sages were wrong because covenant inclusion came by faith in Yeshua and not by the works of the Torah. *These passages have nothing to do with changing the Torah's dietary guidelines.*

1 Timothy 4:1–5

In these verses, Paul says that in the last days, people will fall away from the faith and listen to seducing spirits and demons who teach them not to marry or eat food [xxii] that Yahweh created to be received with thanksgiving because it is sanctified by His Word and prayer. Is Paul referring to the Torah and people who teach that its dietary guidelines apply to believers? In Romans, Paul says the Torah is spiritual, good, and holy. After Paul became a believer, he kept the Torah. Paul kept Yah's feasts and offered a sacrifice in the temple. When Paul was on trial in Rome, he swore that he had never walked contrary to the traditions of the fathers (who kept the dietary guidelines). Either Paul kept the dietary guidelines, or he is a liar who cannot be trusted.

Clearly, Paul kept the Torah and its dietary guidelines and taught others to do so. How could Paul possibly tell Timothy that the Torah's dietary guidelines were doctrines of devils? Paul is not referring to the Torah or some misuse of it. The Torah does not forbid anyone to marry; it commands us to marry and produce children. Paul said that every creature was good and that saints did not have to abstain from the ones Yah said were fit for food, *because His Word has sanctified them.* Yah told His people to enjoy food and thank Him with a prayer of thanksgiving. Hence, Yah's Word, along with a saint's prayer that reflects a thankful heart, sanctifies food.[xxiii]

In order to conclude that a believer can pray over something that Yahweh has said is not fit for food and turn it into something that is fit for food, we have to do six things: (1) Isolate these verses from the context of the Torah, the Prophets, and the Writings, which was the only Scripture that people had when Paul wrote this letter. (2) Disregard Paul's Torah-observant lifestyle and his clear teachings. (3) Affirm that Yeshua transformed the Torah's dietary guidelines into doctrines of demons and that those who promote them have been drawn away from the faith and are drawing us away. (4) Affirm that we are not in the new covenant that empowers people to obey the Torah. (5) Affirm that we are under grace and that everything is lawful for us, or in other words, we are lawless. (6) Affirm that our faith in Yeshua delivers us from the penalty of sin and transforms us into a new man that is free to ignore Yah's instructions and do as he pleases.

Romans 14 and 1 Corinthians 8

In these sections, Paul lets his readers know that once Yahweh declares a food clean, nothing can make it unclean. Paul says if a pagan touches or offers clean meat to an idol, the spirit behind the idol cannot defile it and make it unclean. The strong have come to this understanding. The weak are not there yet. The weak believe that a spirit can make clean meat unclean. Since they are not convinced of their liberty in Messiah, if they eat, their heart will condemn them; and they will need to confess their actions as sin in order to silence their conscience. Paul tells the strong to have consideration for the weak and the weak not to judge the strong.

If Yahweh had changed His mind about the designations of clean and unclean, then Paul would have said something like, "Relax, because nothing is unclean anymore." This is not what Paul said, however. Paul knew that if a believer ate swine flesh, it did not defile him and prevent him from fellowshiping with Yahweh until he went through some cleansing ritual. However, Paul also knew that if a believer renewed his mind; that is, studied the Torah and accepted it as truth that applied to him, the Holy Spirit would write it on his heart. If this believer ate swine flesh, his heart would know that his actions violated the Torah, and his heart would condemn him and separate him from Yahweh until he confessed his sin and silenced its voice. Moreover, Paul knew that if a weak person thought that a pagan had killed a choice calf as an offering to an idol, defiling its meat and making it unclean, then for him there would be no difference between eating it and eating swine flesh, because his unrenewed mind and his heart would condemn him.

In sum, Yah's Spirit puts a person's fallen spirit, which related to Him through the law, to death on the stake, resurrects it, and becomes one with it. In doing so, Yeshua redeems this person from the law, and when he sins, Yah does not impute his sin to him. This person's spirit is now one with Yah's Spirit. Thus, if this person touches or eats something that is inconsistent with Yah's nature, it does not defile him and make him unclean. This person has passed from a judicial relationship with Yah into a relationship with Him based solely on love. A saint's heart seeks to obey Yahweh's Spirit and to walk out the intent of the Torah. If a saint does not follow Yah's Spirit in order to walk out the intent of the Torah, or if he thinks he is not yielding to His Spirit in order to walk out the intent of the Torah, his heart condemns him until he confesses.

The writings of the apostles do not say that Yeshua made all things clean; they say that nothing Yahweh sanctified in the Torah can become unclean, and unclean things do not defile us and make us unclean. [xxiv] In the Garden of Eden, Yahweh defined food and non-food. Adam and Eve chose to be their own god and ate the non-food. At Mount Sinai, Yah codified His teachings and instructions that defined food and non-food. Whom will you obey: Yahweh or man?

Part 15

The Final Analysis

Summary

Marring the Image

Yahweh created man in His own image and likeness so that He could have a relationship with him. Yahweh also gave man a free will so that he could choose whether he wanted to have a relationship with Him. Some people choose to love, obey, and cooperate with Yahweh in order to bring His plan to pass on the earth. Other people attempt to take a neutral position and do their own will without cooperating with or fighting against Yah's plan. A few people actually choose to reject, disobey, and fight against Yah and His plan. In the end, Yah's plan separates the people who want to love and obey Him from those who want to do their own will or reject Him or fight against Him. In biblical language, in the final dispensation, Yahweh will separate His sheep from the rebellious goats and restore man and the creation to their original conditions.

A prideful angel named Lucifer was the first to rebel against Yahweh. Lucifer rebelled and persuaded some other angels to follow him. Yahweh kicked all of them out of heaven. The earth was the only other place that was habitable, so Lucifer and the other fallen angels set up a kingdom on it. Then Yah came to the earth and created humans. Yah breathed His Spirit into the humans and gave them dominion over the earth. Yah set a boundary around their dominion by giving them a law that commanded them not to eat of a corrupt tree the enemy had planted.

Unfortunately, the law gave the serpent a platform to stand on so that he could separate man from Yah, enslave him, and control him in order to keep his earthly kingdom intact. The serpent tricked Eve, and then Adam chose to turn his back on Yah in order to follow his wife. Adam's rebellion separated him from Yahweh's Spirit. Then the serpent took him captive and began to rule over him. In sum, Yahweh created man in His image, and he marred His image.

The Change

Before Yeshua created the heavens and the earth, He knew that man would rebel and mar His image, so He devised a plan to restore His image in man. Yeshua agreed to take the sin of man into Himself and suffer the penalty that he deserved so that He could restore the ones who wanted to love, obey, and cooperate with Him. The Holy Trinity is omnipotent and omniscient, so when Yeshua agreed to die on the execution stake, it was a done deal. Therefore, Yeshua died on the execution stake before He created the earth. However, in order for Yeshua's work to be fully effective for humans who live on the earth in the stream of time, He would have to enter the stream of time and manifest Himself on the earth in order to make His sacrifice real to man. Hence Yahweh began to set the stage so that Yeshua could manifest His finished work to man.

The first humans broke Yahweh's law, and this precipitated a configuration change in them. This configuration change isolated them from Yahweh's Spirit and gave HaSatan the ability to build strongholds in them so that he could rule them and bring bondage, sickness, and death upon them. We call this configuration the "body of death," the "body of sin," or the "Adamic nature." The Adamic nature produces compulsions, obsessions, and addictions. Thus we have to deal with the Adamic nature in order to be free of our compulsions, obsessions, and addictions. There is a problem, however. We do not have the ability to put off the Adamic nature and put on Yah's image to free ourselves from compulsions, obsessions, and addictions.

Restoring the Image

If we have to put off our Adamic nature in order to free ourselves from our compulsions, obsessions, and addictions, but we do not have the ability to put off our Adamic nature, then obviously, we need Yah's help. However, before a creature with free will can receive help, it has to realize that it needs help, desire it, and ask for it. This is problematic, though, because the serpent lied to us, and we believed we could be gods and determine what is good and evil for ourselves in order to produce the abundant life. HaSatan has blinded our hearts and minds and built strongholds of pride in us. Hence we will not humble ourselves and ask for Yah's help.

There is another thing that prevents us from surrendering to Yah and asking for His help. After man fell, he picked some fig leaves and tried to cover his new nature so that he could fellowship with Yah; that is, man created religion so that he could work his way back to Yahweh. Thankfully, however, Yah showed up and pronounced the curses, announced the gospel of the Promised Seed, and killed an innocent lamb that (from our perspective) prefigured His sacrifice.

Summary

Yahweh showed man the pathway to restoration by shedding the blood of an innocent lamb and clothing him in its covering. Yah redeemed the people who believed Him and put their faith in the Promised Seed; that is, Yahweh took these people out of HaSatan's kingdom and placed them in His kingdom. The blood of the lamb connected man to Yeshua and His work that He had finished before creating the earth, and this allowed Yahweh to save those who trusted Him.

Two Ways

The serpent separated Adam from Yahweh, and this changed his nature. The serpent deceived Adam into thinking that he could fix himself up in order to restore his fellowship with Yah. However, Yah exposed HaSatan's lie by killing a lamb and covering Adam in its sinless fur to restore their fellowship. The killing of the lamb prefigured and *drew upon* the finished work of Yeshua and set the pattern of how Yah would permit man to partake of His grace until Yeshua could manifest Himself in the stream of time to manifest the fullness of His grace.

Abel chose Yah's pathway to redemption. Abel offered the life of an innocent lamb in place of his own, and Yah declared him righteous.[393] Cain chose the serpent's way.[394] Yah sent Cain into the land of Nod so that he would recognize his fallen condition, repent, and offer an innocent lamb for his sins. Yahweh would have forgiven Cain and declared him righteous, but sadly, he invented a religion so he could be comfortable in the land of Nod and never repented.

There are two ways to seek reconciliation with Yahweh: (1) His way or (2) the way of Cain.[395] Yah decided to bring redemption and restoration into the stream of time and manifest it on earth over a period of seven thousand years. Hence each person does not receive the same revelation of Yah's plan, but if each person believes the revelation that Yah gives him and puts his trust in it, then He redeems him from HaSatan's kingdom. If, however, people reject the revelation that Yahweh gives them (like Cain), they will remain in HaSatan's earthly kingdom and go to a prison called hell to be held there until their trial at the great white throne, where they will be found guilty and thrown into the lake of fire and enter HaSatan's eternal kingdom to be tormented forever.

---

[393] *The Hebrew-Greek Key Word Study Bible*, KJV, Hebrews 11:4.

[394] Ibid., 1 John 3:12.

[395] Ibid., Jude 1:11.

We Have No Excuse

Yahweh loves us. Yahweh does everything that He can do to get us to realize that we have fallen, and we need to believe the revelation that He has given us and trust Him and the Seed who will redeem and restore us so we can live the abundant life. However, HaSatan, who is the god of this world system, does everything he can do to make us think that there is no God, or that we are gods, or that we are like God and just need to fix ourselves up a little so we can fellowship with Him. Yahweh is more powerful and much wiser than HaSatan. Yahweh reveals truth on many different levels; consequently, there is no excuse for making the wrong decision.

Yah reveals Himself to everyone who comes into the earth.[396] Yah wrote the gospel in the heavens to reveal His glory.[397] We see Yah in His creation.[398] Yah's Spirit strives with us in an effort to bring us to repentance.[399] Yah revealed His plan in Eden.[400] Yah revealed His plan to Israel in the Torah, the Prophets, and the Writings.[401] Yah put on flesh so that He could speak with man face-to-face and perform the works that were necessary to bring His plan into the stream of time, and His disciples wrote about His life, teachings, and works.[402] Yah returned to heaven and spoke to His apostles, telling them how to apply His victory in their lives to destroy the works of HaSatan, and they wrote to show us how to do the same.[403] We have no excuse.

The Stream of Time

Yah gives different generations different revelations of His plan. Yah's revelations are currents that converge to form the stream of time. We have given these currents (ages) names that describe the tone of the revelation that Yah released to form them. Yah deals with those who live during an age according to how they respond to the revelation He gave during that age.

The first age was the Age of Innocence. In this age, humans were innocent; that is, they did not know good or evil. Yahweh wanted humans to simply trust and obey Him. Yah

---

[396] Ibid., John 1:9; Romans 1:19.

[397] Ibid., Psalm 19:1.

[398] Ibid., Romans 1:20; Job 12:7–9.

[399] Ibid., Genesis 6:3; John 6:65; 15:26.

[400] Ibid., Genesis 3:15.

[401] Ibid., 2 Timothy 3:16.

[402] Ibid., John 1:14; Hebrews 1:1–3.

[403] Ibid., Romans 1:1–6; Hebrews 2:3.

revealed His teachings and instructions to humans and attached a law to it. The serpent got the humans to question Yah's motives and disobey Him. The humans stepped over the fence that Yahweh had put up to protect them, and there were consequences. As they ate of the illicit fruit, their spirit separated from Yahweh's Spirit, their conscience came to life, and they knew good and evil.

The second age was the Age of Conscience. Yah promised man that He would send the Seed to redeem him and showed him how he could draw near to Him through a veil of innocent blood; and when he heard Yah's word, it burned itself into his conscience. Yahweh's Spirit tried to get man to obey his conscience and come to an altar with innocent blood. Man refused, however. Yah poured out grace on a remnant. The remnant believed Yah and offered innocent blood on an altar. Yahweh made the remnant righteous, and His Spirit helped them obey their conscience.[404]

The people on the earth grew so vile that Yahweh decided to pour out His wrath on them and destroy them. Yah spared the *righteous remnant*, however. Shortly before Yahweh poured out His wrath on the earth, He raptured some of the people in His kingdom (Enoch), but left others behind in order to keep His promise to Eve and fulfill His prophecies. Yahweh chose an elect group (Noah and his family) and their descendants to bring the Promised Seed into the earth, so they had to go through His wrath; but He protected them from His wrath and saved them.

During the Age of Conscience, if a person yielded to the Holy Spirit and put his faith in Yahweh's promise to send the Seed, then He declared that person righteous. Since they were righteous, these people met with Yahweh at an altar soaked in innocent blood, and His Spirit helped them obey their conscience so that they could obey His teachings and instructions. On the other hand, if a person ignored the wooing of Yah's Spirit and the principles of His Torah; that is, the principles behind His teachings and instructions (his conscience), he perished.

Starting Over

The third age was the Age of Human Government. In this age, Yahweh gave man some principles of government that he could use to restrain the masses from becoming exceedingly wicked again. Once a man heard the principles of government and accepted them as truth, they burned themselves into his conscience. The Spirit used man's conscience to woo him to an altar with an innocent sacrifice and inspire him to obey His Torah and govern the masses by His principles of human government. Sadly, man ignored Yahweh, and HaSatan lured him to the plains of Shinar. On the plains of Shinar, man built a city; that is, a government, economy, and religion. The people of the earth built a tower to reach the gods, and

---

[404] Ibid., Hebrews 11:5, 7.

they made a name (a *shem*) for themselves; that is, they developed a religion that revolved around a counterfeit seed. So Yah confused their language and dispersed them to the ends of the earth in order to form the nations.

The fourth age was the Age of Promise. All the nations of the earth had shut themselves up in disobedience and estranged themselves from Yahweh. Nevertheless, Yahweh had to keep His promise to Eve and Shem, so He poured out His grace on a man in Ur. Yah's Spirit called Abram and promised to prosper him, make his name great, and bring a nation out of his loins. Yah promised to use Abram's seed to bless all the families of the earth, and he realized that He was promising to bring the Seed through his loins![405] Abram repented and believed Yah and put his faith in the Seed. Yah declared Abram righteous, and since he was righteous, he obeyed His Spirit as He prompted him to obey the Torah and live by the principles of human government.[406]

As Abraham's children heard the promises and accepted them as truth, their conscience incorporated them into their databanks. Then Yah's Spirit used their conscience to woo them to an altar with a sacrifice and prompted them to trust in the promises, obey the Torah, and live by His principles of government. Unfortunately, Abraham's children ignored Yah's Spirit, the Torah, and its principles, along with their conscience, and did not trust in the promises, so He sent a famine.

Yah poured out His grace on Joseph and indwelt him so that he could obtain favor to become the vice regent of Egypt and save his brothers.[407] Abraham's children turned to the world for provision and prospered. However, there arose a pharaoh who did not know Joseph, and he enslaved Abraham's children until they were ready to believe Yah and trust in His promises.

Out of Egypt

The fifth age was the Age of the Written Torah. The Age of the Written Torah began with Yahweh putting pressure on Pharaoh to make him free his Hebrew slaves. Yahweh overpowered Pharaoh's gods, but he would not release his Hebrew captives. Pharaoh believed that he was the god of the world system and that his firstborn son would inherit his position after he took his position in heaven with the other gods. Yah's final judgment threatened to destroy Pharaoh's plan. Yah judged the people of Egypt, found them guilty, and sentenced their firstborn to death. Was Yah heartless? No, because Yah said that if a man killed a lamb and put its blood on his doorposts, He would accept the lamb's blood in the place of the blood of the firstborn of that household.

---

[405] Ibid., John 8:56; Galatians 3:8.

[406] Ibid., Genesis 26:5.

[407] Ibid., Genesis 41:38; Acts 7:9–10.

Yahweh did not want anyone to perish; He takes no pleasure in the death of the wicked. Before He released His wrath on the firstborn, Yah sent His Spirit into Egypt to offer grace and forgiveness through the blood of the lamb. Yahweh's Spirit wooed people by appealing to their conscience, but most people ignored their conscience and shut out His voice. Yah redeemed the Hebrews and Gentiles who yielded to the Spirit, believed Him, and put their faith in the blood. Yahweh took these people off Pharaoh's slave market and put His Spirit upon His shepherd (Moses), and the flock of the redeemed followed him through the Red Sea. As the flock of the redeemed followed Moses through the sea, Yahweh baptized them into his body.[408] Yahweh delivered the Hebrews and Gentiles who believed Him, trusted in the lamb's blood, and passed through the baptismal waters with Moses, but He put Pharaoh and his army to an open shame.

A New Life

Yahweh was in heaven, but He placed His Spirit upon Moses, who was on the earth. Yah put His Spirit on Moses so that He could lead him, and in turn, he could lead His ekklesia. Yah wanted to manifest Himself on the earth through Moses' ekklesia. There was a problem, however. The Hebrews had been in Egypt so long that they had forgotten Yah's Torah and His principles of government, and the Gentiles who came out with them had never known Him, His Torah, or His principles of government. So Yah needed to sanctify His redeemed flock; that is, He needed to get them to stop doing the things that they had done in Egypt and start doing things His way so that He could bless all the families of the earth through them and fulfill the Abrahamic covenant.

At Mount Sinai, Yahweh reiterated His teachings, instructions, and principles of human government and gave some new teachings, instructions, and principles of government. Yahweh linked these teachings, instructions, and principles of government to a legal code that rewarded obedience and punished disobedience. As the people in the redeemed flock meditated on the teachings, instructions, principles of government, and legal code with its blessings and curses, this information burned itself into their conscience. Yahweh's Spirit dwelt in the midst of the ekklesia of Moses,[409] and now He had a new tool to restrain sin. However, this new tool (the law) was weak, because although Yah had redeemed people, He had not changed their nature. A saint's nature was in conflict with the nature of the Torah and its law. Hence Yah's new tool highlighted the fallen nature and pointed to the Seed who would come to heal His people of the spiritual leprosy that was disfiguring them and sucking the life out of them, and to restore all things.

---

[408] Ibid., Numbers 11:17, 25; Nehemiah 9:20; 1 Corinthians 10:2.

[409] David Stern, *Complete Jewish Bible*, Clarksville, MD, Jewish New Testament Publications Inc., 1998, p. 537.

False Religion or True Faith?

During the Age of the Written Torah, the Spirit used the conscience to try to get the people who were born in Israel to put their faith in Yah and the Seed. Sadly, most of these people believed that since they were born in Israel, they were automatically in the Abrahamic covenant; and if they obeyed the Torah and complied with its law, they believed they would remain in it and inherit a place in the world to come. These people took pride in the works of righteousness that supposedly kept them in the covenant and would not humble themselves and put their faith in the Promised Seed. In reality, these people were never in the Abrahamic covenant because their faith was not in Yahweh and His promises; their faith was in the teachings and traditions of their religious leaders.

The Scriptures say that Abram put his faith in Yahweh and the Promised Seed. After this, Yahweh cut a covenant with Abram and changed his name to Abraham. This tells us that Yah put His Spirit on Abraham to help him obey His teachings and instructions. The Scriptures say that Abraham had two boys. Ishmael was born of the flesh; hence he trusted in the flesh and did not enter the covenant. Isaac was born of Yahweh's Spirit; hence he trusted in the Spirit and entered the covenant. The Scriptures say that both boys submitted to circumcision; hence the Scriptures say that being born in Israel and submitting to circumcision did not bring a person into the covenant. A person had to put his faith in Yah and the Seed in order to enter the Abrahamic covenant. Once a person was in the covenant, Yah's Spirit helped him keep the Torah so that he could live the abundant life; that is, avoid the curses of the Mosaic covenant and obtain its blessings.

Under the Law or Partakers of Grace?

During the Age of the Written Torah, the Holy Spirit used the conscience to invite people to put their faith in the Promised Seed. Most people ignored their conscience and the wooing of the Spirit, however, and joined a religion that taught that they were born into the covenant. This religion said that a person had to keep the written Torah and comply with its law by keeping the oral Torah and legal halachah in order to overcome their evil inclination (fallen nature) and remain in the covenant. Sadly, these people were never in the covenant, and it did not matter how many rules or commandments they kept or how perfectly they complied with the legal code. It did not change their nature, for it is written, "Can the Ethiopian change his skin or the leopard his spots?"[410]

The law highlighted the fallen nature and condemned it. The law also allowed a saint to put his sins on an animal so it could "pay" for them, but since the rebellion of Yahweh's son (Adam) gave birth to the fallen nature, ultimately Yahweh's Son (Yeshua) had to pay

---

[410] *The Hebrew-Greek Key Word Study Bible*, KJV, Jeremiah 13:23.

for the sins of the fallen nature. Hence a person who sinned had to put his faith in the Promised Seed as a priest offered his sacrifice to Yahweh in order for Him to forgive him and release him from condemnation. Thus Yahweh did not forgive the people in the sages' religion and release them from condemnation. These people lived "under the law" (under the law's condemnation).

Thankfully, Yahweh poured out grace on a remnant. These people yielded to Yahweh's Spirit and put their faith in the Promised Seed so He could declare them righteous and help them do His will. As these people violated the written Torah and the law condemned them, they offered a sacrifice to Yahweh, and He forgave them, freeing them from condemnation. Therefore, these people were not under the law; they were partakers of Yahweh's grace.[411]

A Sin Consciousness

In the Age of the Written Torah, there were people who were under the law and people who were partakers of grace. The people who were under the law tried to keep the law without faith, and Yah did not forgive them and release them from condemnation. The people who were partakers of grace believed Yah's promises about the Seed, trusted in His righteousness, and kept the law in faith. Yahweh forgave these people and released them from condemnation.

The sacrifices in the Mosaic covenant took away the law's condemnation, but they did not take away what caused it; that is, the fallen nature. Thus each year on the Day of Atonement, the high priest had to offer innocent animals to Yahweh in order to sanctify Israel, and each day the Levitical priests had to offer innocent animals on behalf of the Israelites in order to maintain their fellowship with Him.

In the Mosaic covenant, people were always offering sacrifices. This was a constant reminder of their sin nature. Hence this covenant fostered a sin consciousness in Yah's people. In the Mosaic covenant, Yahweh's Spirit would visit a person and empower him to rise above his sin nature and destroy the works of the devil. However, Samson's life shows that when Yahweh's Spirit lifted from a person, he was alone with his sin nature again, and it rose up to rule him. Saul's life reveals the most terrifying aspect of the Mosaic covenant. In this covenant, if Yahweh's Spirit visited a person and gave him the power to rise above his sin nature and obey His directions, but the person continued to yield to the sin nature, the Spirit could leave and not return!

---

[411] Ibid., Genesis 6:8; 19:19; Exodus 33:12–17; Psalm 32:1–11; 84:11; Proverbs 3:34; Romans 4:1–8.

A Change in the Holy Spirit's Ministry

The sixth age is the Age of Grace. In this age, Yeshua revealed the grace that Yahweh had hidden in the types and shadows of the previous ages. Yeshua proclaimed repeatedly that He was the Messiah that everyone was waiting for.[412] Yeshua expounded upon the Torah and its law. Yeshua went beyond the letter of the written Torah and its law, living out its intent in order to reveal it to man. Yah's Spirit used Yeshua's words and deeds to bear witness with the truth that the righteous remnant had programmed into their conscience,[413] and since their trust and hope was in the Promised Seed, they accepted their Messiah. However, the people in the sages' religion had programmed their conscience with error,[414] so they rejected their Messiah and wanted to kill Him; but Yahweh's Spirit pricked their conscience, and some of them repented.

Yeshua fulfilled the Torah and its law by perfectly living out its *intent*. At the appointed time, Yeshua willingly got on the execution stake so that the Romans could put Him to death. Three days later, Yeshua rose from the dead. Yeshua walked and talked with His disciples for forty days and returned to heaven to take His place at the right hand of the Father. After ten days had elapsed on earth, it was the day of Pentecost, and the Godhead charged the Holy Spirit with the task of *sealing everyone* on earth who put his trust in Yeshua. For the most part, up to this point, the Holy Spirit had temporarily come on people in order to empower them to do the will of the Father on the earth. However, from this day forward, the Holy Spirit would indwell each believer and place a seal on him that marked him as Yahweh's property.[415]

A New Creature

In the Age of Grace, the Holy Spirit began an important phase of His earthly ministry. The Spirit began sealing everyone who repents and puts his trust in Yeshua for salvation. What does this mean? It means that a measure of the Spirit comes to live in us and becomes one with our spirit, which guarantees that one day we will receive the full measure of the Spirit, which will bring our body back to life and glorify it so that we can live with Yeshua forever.[416]

---

[412] Ibid., John 1:51; 4:26, 5:30; 6:35, 44, 48; 7:29; 8:24, 42, 58; 10:7, 14, 30.

[413] Ibid., John 5:46; 7:17; 8:19; 8:47a.

[414] Ibid., John 5:47; 7:19; 8:37; 8:47b.

[415] Ibid., John 7:39; Ephesians 1:13; 4:30; 2 Corinthians 1:22.

[416] Ibid., Ephesians 1:13; Romans 8:23; Philippians 3:21; Colossians 3:4; Revelation 22:5.

As a person, repents, believes Yahweh, and puts his trust in Yeshua's payment on the execution stake for the remission of his sins, bowing his knee to Him in order to follow Him, the Holy Spirit baptizes his spirit into His body and puts his spirit to death "in Him" and resurrects it "in Him." Yahweh's Spirit becomes one with this person's spirit, which is the seal that marks him as Yah's property.[417] After Yahweh's Spirit places His seal on a person, his life is not his own because he has been taken off the serpent's slave market with something more precious than silver or gold—Yeshua's blood. Hence he, too, can say, "I am crucified with Christ: nevertheless I live; yet not I, but Christ liveth in me: and the life which I now live in the flesh I live by the faith of the Son of God, who loved me, and gave himself for me."[418]

Gradual Manifestation

The reborn spirit is one with Yahweh's Spirit. The Spirit comes from the Father and the Son. The Holy Spirit hides the reborn spirit in the Son and the Son in the Father. Consequently, the new spirit is safe because nothing can pluck him out of Yahweh, and He has promised never to leave or forsake him.[419] This new creature (reborn spirit) is safe, and what is true of Yeshua is now true of him.[420] Yeshua is righteous because He kept the Torah and complied with its law perfectly, so the new creature is righteous.[421] Moreover, since Yahweh has declared this spirit righteous, the person will become righteous in order to uphold Yahweh's righteousness.[422]

It is the Spirit's job to uphold Yahweh's righteousness. Yahweh's Spirit is one with our spirit, and He gives us the desire and the ability to live righteously to uphold His righteousness.[423] It is our job to cooperate with the Spirit as He labors in us to accomplish His will.[424] As we do, Yeshua rebuilds our soul structure to ensure that we take on His image and live the abundant life.[425] Yah is serious about upholding His righteousness, serious enough to set aside His glory, take on flesh, and die on a tree so that He could give us His

---

[417] Ibid., Romans 10:9; 2 Corinthians 5:17.

[418] Ibid., Galatians 2:20.

[419] Ibid., John 15:26; Galatians 4:6; Colossians 3:3; John 10:28–30; Hebrews 13:5.

[420] Ibid., 1 John 4:17.

[421] Ibid., 1 Peter 2:22; Romans 5:19; 2 Corinthians 5:21.

[422] Ibid., 1 John 2:1, 6, 29; 3:3, 24; 5:18; Ephesians 4:17–5:20; Romans 1:17.

[423] Ibid., Romans 8:2, 14; 1 Peter 1:22.

[424] Ibid., Romans 8:5; Galatians 5:16, 24, 25.

[425] Ibid., 2 Corinthians 3:18; Romans 8:29; 12:1–2; John 10:10.

Spirit.[426] So do not be deceived. If Yahweh declares a person righteous, then that person will manifest righteousness in his life.[427]

Right Now

Right now, I live in a fallen world in a vile body, interacting with the material realm through a soul that is predisposed to pride, and I will not manifest the righteousness that I became in Messiah in the entirety of my being until I receive the full measure of His Spirit. Right now, Yah's Spirit has freed my spirit from the confines of the corrupt realm and remade it in His image. Right now, Yah's Spirit is freeing my soul from the confines of the corrupt realm and transforming it into His image. Right now, Yah has confined my body to the corrupt realm.

Right now, my spirit sits at the right hand of the Father, drawing nutrients from Him.[428] Right now, my soul spends some of its time in the spirit realm and some of its time in the corrupt realm, drawing nutrients from each.[429] Right now, the Spirit is trying to get my soul to turn away from the nutrients in the corrupt realm and feed upon the nutrients in His realm so that He can manifest Yah's righteousness through me.[430] Right now, my body lives in the corrupt realm, drawing nutrients from it. Right now, I look forward to the glorious day when I will receive the full measure of Yahweh's Spirit; then my soul will be fully conformed to His, and His glory will replace the blood in my body, and it will disconnect from the corrupt realm and connect to His realm and draw its nutrients from Him.[431] Hence, right now, I am in the process of becoming.[432]

The Process Begins

I was born "in Adam," so my spirit came into this world infused with his iniquities and the iniquities of the other men in my bloodline, and this iniquity separated me from Yahweh.[433] HaSatan enslaved my spirit and built strongholds in my soul so that he could control me and get me to build up his kingdom on earth, and as my spirit languished in slavery,

---

[426] Ibid., Isaiah 7:14; 53:11; Romans 3:21–26; 1 Peter 2:23–24.

[427] Ibid., Romans 8:4, 5, 10, 14, 29; 1 Corinthians 6:11; James 2:17; 2 Corinthians 7:1; Galatians 5:24, 25.

[428] Ibid., Ephesians 1:20; 2:6.

[429] Ibid., Romans 8:5; Galatians 6:8.

[430] Ibid., Romans 8:14; Galatians 5:16–23.

[431] Ibid., Romans 8:23; 1 Corinthians 15:50; Philippians 3:21.

[432] Ibid., Romans 8:29; 2 Corinthians 3:18; Colossians 3:4; Ephesians 4:22–24; 1 Corinthians 15:51; 1 John 3:2.

[433] Ibid., Genesis 5:3; Exodus 20:5; Isaiah 59:2.

my soul gorged on the nutrients in his kingdom.[434] However, the Holy Spirit offered me the gift of repentance and gave me the faith to accept it and the power to get off the throne and invite Yeshua to sit on it. Thankfully, I accepted the gift, and the Spirit baptized me into Yeshua, putting my iniquitous spirit to death on the execution stake and resurrecting it as a spirit that was in union with Him.[435]

My old spirit, which was a slave to sin, died, and my new spirit, which is free to serve Yahweh, was born. Sin no longer separates my spirit from Yah's Spirit, so my spirit is able to fellowship with His Spirit. As my new spirit gives my old soul its new marching orders, two things happen: (1) The Spirit's presence strengthens my spirit so it can pull down the weak strongholds that control some areas of my soul so that I can be obedient in those areas. (2) The presence of the Spirit does not strengthen my spirit enough so that it can pull down the well-fortified strongholds that control other areas of my soul, so I cannot always be obedient in those areas. Hence when I was born again, some areas of my life changed instantly, but others did not. However, as my spirit matures in Christ, it is able to force the stubborn areas of my soul to submit to Yah's will.

The Process of Becoming

Yah did not regenerate the believers who lived in the previous ages. Primarily, Yah dealt with these people in the physical realm. However, Yah regenerates the believers who live in this age, and He deals with us primarily in the spiritual realm. There is a problem, however. It is hard for us to see into the spirit realm. To help us, Yahweh recorded His interactions that took place in the physical realm with the believers of the previous ages to show us how He interacts with us in the spirit realm. Yah recorded this information in the Old Testament, and He expects us to study it to learn how to interact with Him.[436] What follows is an application of this truth.

Israel is Yah's son; I am Yah's son. Thus I need to look at how Israel cooperated with Yah in order to allow Him to establish His kingdom in their midst to see how I must cooperate with Him so that He can establish His kingdom in me. Israel came out of Egypt (the kingdom of darkness) by the blood of Paschal lambs. I came out of the kingdom of darkness by the blood of the Paschal Lamb. Yah baptized Israel in the Red Sea, where she passed from a life of slavery to a life of freedom. Yah baptized me in water, where I passed from slavery to sin to freedom from sin. Yah took Israel to Sinai, where He wrote the Torah on stone tablets to show her how to live the abundant life. Yah came to live in me and wrote the Torah on my heart to empower me to live the abundant life. Israel almost died in the

---

[434] Ibid., Psalm 51:5; Ephesians 2:2; Colossians 1:21a.
[435] Ibid., Acts 11:18; 2 Timothy 2:25; 1 Corinthians 12:13; 6:17.
[436] Ibid., Romans 15:4; 1 Corinthians 10:11; Hebrews 3:8–19.

wilderness because she would not believe Yah, obey His Torah, and cooperate with His Spirit. I almost died in the wilderness of addiction because I would not believe Yahweh, obey His Torah, or cooperate with His Spirit. In short, Israel was supposed to worship Yah, but she refused. I was supposed to worship Yah, but I refused.

After His people spent forty years in the wilderness, Yah led a remnant of Israel to Gilgal, where Joshua circumcised them. Here they took hold of the covenant, baptizing themselves in the Jordan River as Yah parted the waters so that they could enter Canaan. After I spent forty years in the wilderness of life, Yah led a remnant of my former self to Gilgal, where Yeshua circumcised my heart. Here I took hold of the covenant, baptizing myself as He parted the waters so that I could enter Canaan.

After Israel had entered Canaan, Yah told her to drive out its inhabitants so that He could establish His kingdom in it and she could live in peace. As Israel went through Canaan with the ark of the covenant (Yahweh's presence), some of the inhabitants were so terrified that they abandoned their strongholds.[437] As Israel obeyed the Torah and followed the Spirit, some of the remaining strongholds fell without much of a fight.[438] Israel, however, had to fight long and hard to tear down the fortified strongholds and slay the giants so that she could live in peace.[439]

After I had entered Canaan, Yah told me to drive out the inhabitants of my soul so that He could establish His kingdom in it and I could live in peace. As I went through my soul with Yah's presence, some of its inhabitants abandoned their strongholds and fled in terror. Some of the inhabitants of my soul remained in their strongholds, but as I obeyed the Torah and followed the Spirit, we drove them out without much of a fight. However, there were strongholds in my soul that were well fortified and well supplied, and it took a long time to tear those down and starve out their inhabitants. Moreover, there were giants who ruled over certain parts of my soul that Yahweh and I had to slay so that He could establish His kingdom in those parts of my soul and I could prosper and manifest His righteousness to the people around me and live in peace.

Two Covenants, One Purpose

The Scriptures are one continuous, contiguous, progressive revelation of Yahweh's eternal, unchangeable plan for redeeming His creation. Yah put this plan into place before He laid the foundations of the earth. This means that the new covenant is not the polar opposite of, or adversarial to, the Mosaic covenant. The two covenants perform many of the same functions because they are both covenants of sanctification. Yahweh uses the

---

[437] Ibid., Joshua 2:9; 5:1; 11:19; 24:12.

[438] Ibid., Joshua 6:16.

[439] Ibid., Joshua 11:18; 13:1; 13:12; 1 Samuel 17:1–58; 2 Samuel 21:15–22.

covenants of sanctification to fulfill the covenant of redemption. The mechanisms that sanctified Yah's saints are different in each covenant, but these differences are primarily qualitative and not quantitative in nature.

Galatians 3:19 tells us that Yahweh put the Mosaic covenant in place to deal with the sin that the sin nature produced so that He could bless the redeemed and preserve Israel until Yeshua came to cut a better covenant. Yeshua cut the new covenant, and through it Yahweh dealt with the sin nature in order to deal with sin so that He could bless His people and keep His promises to Abraham. Yahweh used the Mosaic covenant and the new covenant to sanctify the people He declared righteous in order to uphold His righteousness and manifest it to all the families of the earth in order to draw them into a relationship with Him and fulfill the Abrahamic covenant.

Servants or Sons?

In the Mosaic covenant, when a saint (a person whom Yahweh declared righteous) transgressed the Torah, the law generated a judicial breach between Yah and him. The saint had to offer a sacrifice to Yah to bridge the judicial breach between Yah and him. The sacrifice restored the saint's fellowship with Yah and took away His Spirit's conviction that carried with it the curses of the law. If it was possible for a saint to travel to the temple and offer the sacrifice that the law called for (with the right heart attitude), but he refused, Yah put the curses on him until he repented.

In the new covenant, Yeshua's sacrifice of Himself on the tree satisfied Yah and met the requirements of the law. Yeshua's Spirit baptizes a saint into His body and releases him from the law's custodianship. Thus when a saint transgresses the Torah *that Yah has written on his heart*, the Spirit does not convict him of sin, because Yeshua has met the requirements of the law; and since He became a curse on the tree, Yah does not curse the saint for disobedience.

In the new covenant, as a saint studies the Torah, the Spirit writes it on his heart. If a saint refuses to govern himself by the Torah that Yah has written on his heart, *his heart will condemn him*; thus he will not have the confidence to approach Him to ask Him for what he needs. In other words, his conscience will separate him from Yah. If a saint does not bridge the relational breach with the Spirit by confessing his sin and appropriating the grace Yeshua has given him, he will give HaSatan an opportunity to kill, steal, and destroy in his life until he does.

In the Mosaic covenant, Yahweh treated His saints like servants, rewarding them for obedience and punishing them for disobedience. In the new covenant, Yahweh treats His saints like sons, giving them free access to everything that He possesses. *In the new covenant, the consequences of sin are relational and not judicial.*

Yah is our Father, and Yeshua is our elder brother. Yahweh's Spirit has interwoven His life with ours. Hence when we disobey Yah, our heart condemns us. If we continue to disobey Yah, we will grieve Him; and if we refuse to make things right with Him, we will quench Him, and He will withdraw from fellowship with us. Our Father and our elder brother will always be there for us, however, and if we humble ourselves, repent, confess our sin, and take advantage of the grace He has given us, He will draw near to us.

The Transformation of the Mosaic Covenant

Yeshua brought the Torah to life, living it out perfectly. When Yeshua returned to heaven, He sent His Spirit back to enable His disciples to live out the Torah. Yeshua's Spirit transformed the Torah of the old covenant, which He had written in lifeless letters on lifeless stone, into the Torah of the new covenant by writing it in spiritual letters on living hearts. The objectives of the two covenants are the same, but Yeshua's Spirit transformed the mechanisms that implement the covenants, which transformed a covenant that overlooked man's sin nature and dealt with its effects (sin) into a covenant that replaced the sin nature with His nature in order to deal with the sin problem. Thus there were changes in the way Yahweh's people were to walk out the covenant.

Yeshua transformed the Mosaic covenant into the new covenant by transforming the temple, priesthood, and the sacrificial system. Yeshua's Spirit came to live in the hearts of those who put their faith in Him, and He fulfilled the sacrifices, clothed them in His righteousness, made them priests, and created a temple in them that connected them to the heavenly temple. The saints could now fellowship with Yahweh in the temple without traveling to Jerusalem.

The worship of Yahweh is no longer dependent on an earthly temple, a human priesthood, or animal sacrifices because the Spirit who lives in us now performs the functions that they performed in the previous ages. Most of Israel's religious rulers would not turn away from their contrived religion and embrace the new covenant of sanctification because they would lose their influence, power, and income. Therefore, in AD 70, Yahweh sent the Roman army to destroy His earthly temple. After that, there was no place for the priests to offer sacrifices. Thus, by divine design, it is now impossible for us to obey the literal teachings and instructions that pertain to the temple, priesthood, sacrifices, and the support systems that sustained them.

Rightly Dividing the Word

A portion of the Torah is teachings and instructions on how to live in Yahweh's earthly kingdom, but since we do not live in His earthly kingdom, we cannot obey these teachings and instructions literally. However, Yeshua's Spirit is in us, fulfilling the teachings and instructions that pertain to the temple, priesthood, and sacrifices in order to establish His kingdom in us. Yeshua's Spirit will never lead us to do anything that violates the intent or principles behind these teachings and instructions. Hence we should study the Torah and ask the Spirit to show us the principles behind these teachings and instructions so that we can be more sensitive to Him.

At Mount Sinai, Yahweh gave His people 613 commandments. Fifteen hundred years later, Yeshua's Spirit transformed the temple, priesthood, sacrifices, and kingdom, which means that it is now impossible to literally keep the commandments that relate to these institutions. Moreover, some of Yah's commandments apply to women and not men. Conversely, some commandments apply to men and not women. This leaves the teachings and instructions about what to eat, what holidays to celebrate, and a few others that we are able to obey. Remember, we are not under the Mosaic law, so there is no judicial condemnation or curse put on us for neglecting these teachings and instructions. However, since we are in an intimate love relationship with Yah and His Son by way of the Spirit who indwells us, we want to follow His instructions; and when we do, we reap many benefits because His instructions are a hedge that protects us from the enemy. If we follow the Holy Spirit and eat what Yah sanctified as food, delight in His Sabbath, observe His holidays, and live according to the principles behind the commands that are impossible to keep literally, then we will stay within His protective fence and not give place to HaSatan.

The Devil's Field Day

Our Creator wants us to submit to Him by believing what He has revealed to us and obeying His commands to show that we trust Him. In this age, we submit to Yah by believing that Yeshua is the Messiah and obeying His teaching and instructions to show that we trust Him. Most commentators say that Yeshua's teachings and instructions are different from the teachings and instructions that Yah gave at Mount Sinai. However, these same men say that Yeshua was Yah clothed in human flesh. So did Yahweh give two different sets of teachings and instructions?

No, Yeshua is the Creator, and His teachings and instructions are the same ones that He gave at Sinai. Yeshua walked out the commands that He gave at Sinai, revealing His intent for giving them. Yeshua sent His Spirit to live in us in order to enable us to walk out His commands by following His promptings. Yeshua is our foundation. Yeshua is the living Torah, and if we follow the Spirit of the living Torah, we will walk out the intent of the written Torah. Sadly, men have told us that the Torah does not apply to us, so we do not study it and allow the Spirit to write it on our hearts. Thus we do not recognize the Spirit's promptings to walk out the Torah's intent, and it does not bother us when we live contrary to it. As a result, the devil is having a field day!

Destroying the Torah

How did we destroy the Torah? Yahweh established a relationship with Israel based on her faith in the blood of the Passover lamb. Yah *declared His people righteous*, and at Sinai He told them how to walk out their faith. Sadly, the sages turned Israel's relationship with Yah into a religion that deceived people into trying to establish their own righteousness by keeping the Torah. Paul spent a great deal of time refuting this religion and restoring the knowledge of how to have a relationship with Yah. Gentiles misinterpreted Paul to say that it was Yah's plan for the saints in the Old Testament to work for salvation by keeping the Torah, but that Yeshua came to fix this.

The ekklesia's Gentile leaders said Yeshua introduced a new system that brought people into right relationship with Yah by faith through grace, and that this new system was adversarial to His old system. In the new system, the New Testament replaced the Old Testament, the Spirit's leadings replaced the Torah, and the church replaced Israel! Under the leadership of Gentiles, Yeshua's ekklesia followed in the footsteps of the Jewish leaders of Moses' ekklesia, inventing a religion that gave them position, power, and income.

To their own peril, the Gentiles ignored Paul's warning not to become proud and boast against the natural branches. The proud Gentiles taught that belief replaced repentance, grace replaced obedience, the Spirit replaced the Torah, and the church replaced Israel. These pied pipers played their magic flutes and created pleasing theological melodies that tickled the ears of the masses, and they followed them into the fiery lake!

Yeshua sent His Spirit to regenerate us, which required Him to transform the institutions that implemented the law, but the Jewish rulers refused to leave the old institutions because they would lose their position, power, and income. Yah destroyed the old institutions to get them to embrace the new ones by making it impossible to keep the commands that pertain to the old institutions. It may look like Yeshua did away with the law, but He did not; His Spirit writes the law on our hearts and fulfills its requirements while prompting us to keep the Torah and live by its principles.

After Paul became a believer, Yahweh had him worship in the temple and offer a sacrifice to fulfill a vow. This proves that the Torah and its law apply to believers, and if kept with the right heart, neither detracts from Yeshua. Yeshua did not destroy the Torah—we did.

The New Testament Believer

Paul honored the Torah and never taught against it. Paul kept the literal commandments and told us to follow him as he followed Messiah, who also kept the literal commandments. So obviously, Yeshua and Paul want us to keep the commandments or the principles behind them whenever it is possible to do so. However, this is unthinkable to those who have bought into man's contrived system. Well-intentioned teachers have convinced these people of the "fact" that the Torah does not apply to them because they are not under the law, but under grace.

However, the grace Yeshua poured out as He sent His Spirit to transform the Mosaic covenant into the new covenant did one thing: it changed our nature to ensure that there would not be any enmity between the Torah and us so that Yah could write it on our hearts to change our desires and empower us to obey it. When Paul said that we were not under the Torah's law, this meant that we had died to the law, and it could not condemn us. Most people think that Paul meant the Torah and its law no longer apply to us. This is what Paul meant: the Torah still illuminates the pathway to righteousness and blessings, or sin and curses, but its law no longer condemns us.[440]

Most New Testament believers fail to realize that the Spirit gives us grace to empower us to obey the apostles' teachings and instructions. They also fail to realize that the Spirit spoke to the apostles and told them how to apply the principles behind the written Torah's commands that pertained to the old institutions in order to fulfill the covenants and implement Yah's plan. A New Testament believer who is obeying the apostolic writings and following the promptings of the Spirit is living by the principles behind the commands that pertain to the old institutions, but since our teachers have misinterpreted Galatians and said that the Torah does not apply to us, we have neglected aspects of our sanctification and are not walking in the fullness of the blessing.

Elohim or Elohims?

Yahweh told man that the Tree of the Knowledge of Good and Evil was evil. The serpent told man that the Tree of the Knowledge of Good and evil was good. Man believed the serpent so he could know for himself what good and evil were. Essentially, man chose not to trust Yah's definition of good and evil and trust in his own ability to determine good and evil. Man shunned Yahweh's Tree of Life and ate from the serpent's tree so that he could be his own *elohim* (god).

In every age, man has twisted Yahweh's word (His definition of good and evil) to fulfill his own lusts and has tried to return to Eden by building a religion, government, and economy that enable him to live the abundant life. However, the painful journey from Eden to the new earth proves that the serpent lied, because in every age we have tried to be our own elohim and failed.

Each person has to choose whether to listen to the serpent and trust in his own ability to define good and evil, govern his own life, and produce his own prosperity, or to believe Yahweh and trust in His definitions of good and evil, submitting to His lordship so that

---

[440] Ibid., Romans 3:20; 6:16; 7:12; 1 Timothy 1:8.

He can prosper him. The Torah tells us what is good and evil by identifying the rebellious desires of the soul and the corrupt lusts of the body. The Holy Spirit empowers our spirit to rise above the desires of our rebellious soul and the lusts of the vile body so we can worship and serve Yah. If we embrace the written Torah and yield to the Spirit's promptings, we will fulfill the intent of the Torah, which is to love Yah with all our heart, soul, and strength and love our neighbors as ourselves.

The Falling Away

The Imperial Cult held the Roman Empire together. However, the Jews lived by the Torah and refused to participate in the universal political religion. The Romans tolerated the Jews, but hated them and sometimes expelled them in order to stabilize Rome. After the apostle Paul had written his letter to the Roman congregation, the Jews and Gentiles set aside their differences and became a one-new-man congregation that honored the Torah and its principles. Like the synagogue, the one-new-man congregation refused to participate in the empire's political religion, but unlike the synagogue, the one new man spread across the empire like wildfire.

In the fourth century, a Roman emperor took control of the ekklesia and forced the saints to forsake their Jewish traditions.[441] Constantine made it a crime that was punishable by death for a person to limit his diet to Yah's menu, rest on His Sabbath, celebrate His holidays, or wear fringes on his garments to remind himself of Yah's commands.[442] The proud Gentile emperor exalted himself as the head of Yeshua's ekklesia and built a religion that served as the empire's new universal political religion. The Roman emperor and his cohorts set the Torah aside and invented an institution called "the Church" that was separate from Israel and her covenants. They invented a Yeshua who embraced pagans without repentance, and they integrated their doctrines and traditions into the faith that was once delivered unto the saints, thus creating a religion of works.[443]

The End of the Age of Grace

In the sixteenth century, the righteous remnant began to do what it was designed to do; that is, it started drawing people out of the Roman religion of works into a relationship with Yeshua. A man in the righteous remnant influenced Luther, and he protested against the doctrines of the Roman religion of works and proclaimed salvation by faith through

---

[441] Dr. Robert Heidler, *The Messianic Church Arising!*, Denton, TX, Glory of Zion International Ministries, 2006, p. 45.

[442] Ibid., p. 46.

[443] Raymond Fisher, *The Children of God*, Tiberias, Israel, Olim Publications, 2000, pp. 147–148.

grace alone. The daughters of Rome abandoned the harlot that claimed to be their mother, but they held on to some of her doctrines and traditions. In these last days, we need to flush this poison out of our system so that our strength will return and we can rejoice with our real mother, who is the New Jerusalem.

The bride set her glory aside as she set the teachings and instructions of her groom aside. Yahweh's teachings and instructions are a tree of life, and like Eve, the bride shunned His tree and ate the illicit fruit of paganism, power, and wealth. It is time for the bride to start living by the Torah's principles again. Though she preaches about the glory of her groom, He is unable to manifest much of it through her, so the world does not believe her testimony about Him.

Yeshua is Yahweh clothed in human flesh. Yeshua told us to keep His commands in order to show our love for Him. What commands? Well, since Yahweh had not yet written the New Testament, the only commands that He could have been talking about were the commands in the written Torah! When the bride returns to the Torah's commands, she will make the Jews jealous. The jealous Jews will return to the bride, and the groom will manifest Himself in her through the one new man, glorifying her. Then the world will believe her testimony about Yeshua and have to choose to either bow to Him or reject Him, and Yah will end the Age of Grace.[444]

The Millennial Age

The seventh age is the Millennial Age. Around 1000 BC, Yahweh promised King David that *his seed* would sit on his throne and rule the kingdom forever. Yah promised David that He would give His people a permanent place to live and that the children of the wicked would no longer torment them and drive them from their land. Yah promised David that his seed would be His Son and that He would chasten Him for sin, but His mercy would never depart from Him. The Hebrew word *zar* (seed) connects Yahweh's promise to David with the promise He made to Abraham. The fulfillment of the promise to David would lead to the fulfillment of the promise to Abraham. Yahweh reminded David that Eve's seed would come through Shem's line, through the tribe of Judah, through his house, to crush the serpent's head, redeem man, and restore the earth. So once again, Israel began to look for the appearance of the victorious conqueror.

One thousand years later, the victorious conqueror showed up as a lowly servant. The lowly servant took the sins of the world into Himself, and Yahweh chastised Him for them, crushing the serpent's head. The victorious conqueror crushed HaSatan's head and made it possible for anyone anywhere to enter the process of redemption, sanctification, and restoration. At the end of the Age of Grace, Yahweh will give His saints the full measure

---

[444] *The Hebrew-Greek Key Word Study Bible*, KJV, John 17:20–21; Romans 11:13–15; Ephesians 5:27.

of His Spirit, and their bodies will be glorified and resurrected from the grave or raptured. Then the saints will be righteous, spirit, soul, and body, and fully conformed to Yeshua's image. So ultimately Yahweh is going to make us 100 percent righteous—body, soul, and spirit—in order to uphold His righteousness in respect to His decision to declare us righteous before we were in fact righteous.

Now obviously, Yahweh's righteousness does not depend on how well we cooperate with Him in the sanctification process in order to manifest the righteousness that He made us when we bowed to Him as Lord. However, after Yeshua resurrects or raptures us, we will stand before His bema seat so that He can evaluate how we ran the race on earth; that is, how we cooperated with His Spirit in the process of sanctification and restoration in order to accomplish His will, thereby manifesting His righteousness to the world. Based on how we ran our race, Yeshua will reward us with a position in the millennial kingdom where we will rule and reign with Him for one thousand years. This is one more reason why we should cooperate with the Holy Spirit!

The New Heaven and the New Earth

The eighth age is the Age of Restoration. After we have ruled with Yeshua for a thousand years on earth, He will release HaSatan from the pit so that he can gather all the people who want to rebel against Yeshua and overthrow His kingdom. After Yeshua destroys these people and throws HaSatan into the lake of fire where he will suffer day and night forever, He will resurrect the wicked people of every age and take them to the great white throne. At the great white throne, Yeshua will open the books, and if He does not find a person's name in the Book of Life (which He will not), He will throw him into the fiery lake with HaSatan and his crew.

After every evil angel, person, and demon is in the lake of fire, Yeshua will transport His saints to the heavenly Jerusalem, destroy the earth with fire, and create a brand-new one. Once Yeshua has re-created the earth and imprisoned the rebellious creatures who would sin again and mess up the new earth, He will command the heavenly Jerusalem, which is home to the saints, to descend to the earth as a bride prepared for her groom, and we will live with Yeshua forever. As you can see, the process of redemption, sanctification, and restoration is a very long one.

Conclusion

A Journey to Wholeness

Adam rebelled against Yahweh. Adam's decision to rebel opened a door for HaSatan. HaSatan walked through the open door and corrupted the human system configuration so that he could rule over man and force him to build his vile kingdom on earth. Man devolved because he lost the connection with Yahweh that enabled him to take dominion over his soul and body, which allowed him to take dominion over the earth and spread His kingdom throughout it. [xxv]

Paul called the corrupted HSC the "body of death," or "body of sin," because HaSatan uses it to control us with compulsions, obsessions, and addictions (sin) that lead to death. As people struggle with a serious compulsion, obsession, or addiction, at some point it becomes clear that they need help from an outside source, which indicates that they are not whole. Hence people who struggle with serious compulsions, obsessions, and addictions seek wholeness because on some level they know that if they were whole, they could control themselves to live a good life.

It is the nature of the corrupted HSC to try to become whole through its own efforts, and this birthed psychology. The corrupted HSC also tries to reconcile itself with God, and this birthed religion. In these last days, HaSatan has combined psychology, religion, and the New Age concept of spiritual evolution to produce a deceptive movement that promotes his end-time agenda and keeps people separated from Yahweh. Today the recovery movement's Twelve-Step programs are helping HaSatan keep people separated from Yeshua and His recovery plan as they implement HaSatan's end-times ecumenical plan to usher in the kingdom of the anti-Messiah.

The book of Romans explains what causes compulsions, obsessions, and addictions. It also explains how to take advantage of Yah's recovery plan in order to get free. Most people, however, turn to the recovery movement to learn how to overcome their compulsions, obsessions, and addictions. What is the difference? Yah's recovery plan restores the corrupted HSC to its original state and teaches us how to operate it; the recovery movement's Twelve Steps do not.

Paul says there are two things that cause compulsions, obsessions, and addictions. The first thing that causes compulsions, obsessions, and addictions is a corrupted HSC. The second thing that causes compulsions, obsessions, and addictions is the misuse of a restored HSC.

Thus believing Yahweh, repenting, and putting our faith in Yeshua so that He can restore our HSC to its original state and teach us how to use it is the only real cure for compulsions, obsessions, and addictions.

After Yeshua restores a person's HSC to its original state, His Spirit prompts him to follow Him so that together they can tear down the strongholds that cement the Adamic soul structure together and keep it strong. If a person cooperates with Yeshua's Spirit and His Word, together they tear down the Adamic soul structure and replace it with a messianic soul structure. As we cooperate with Yeshua's Spirit and Word in order to construct a messianic soul structure, our compulsions, obsessions, and addictions disappear, and the abundant life materializes.

I encourage you to bow your knee to Yeshua and confess Him as Lord, so that His Spirit can enter your heart, and you can enter His Body. After you take your position "in Christ," I encourage you to embrace your Hebrew Roots and take your position in the "One New Man."

Why is it important for you to take your position in the "One New Man"? Remember, Abraham was the first Hebrew. Abraham brought Gentiles into his camp to serve Yahweh and built the One New Man. Then, famine and conflict separated the Hebrews from the Gentiles, and the Hebrews became slaves. Afterwards, Moses led a mixed multitude of Hebrews and Gentiles (the One New Man) out of Egypt. Later, Joshua (a Hebrew) and Caleb (a Gentile) united as the One New Man and entered the Promise Land to live the abundant life. Then, the Hebrews built a theological wall to separate from the Gentiles, and the Hebrews became religious slaves. Afterwards, Yeshua tore down the Hebrew's wall and released them from religious slavery, and reunited them with the Gentiles to rebuild the One New Man. Then, Yeshua's ekklesia walked in power and reflected His glory. Later, the Gentiles built a theological wall to separate from the Hebrews, and the Gentiles became religious slaves.

Do you see the pattern? HaSatan separates Hebrew and Gentile believers (cripples the One New Man) so that he can enslave the ekklesia and take away her power. However, Yeshua said that the gates of hell would not prevail over His ekklesia, which is why the Holy Spirit is revealing the Hebrew Roots of Christianity to Gentiles and releasing them from religious slavery. Today, the Holy Spirit is reuniting Gentiles with Hebrews and rebuilding the One New Man. The Holy Spirit is bringing the ekklesia back to life, that is, He is glorifying her; consequently, when you take your position "in Christ" and the "One New Man," the Holy Spirit gives you the power to break free from bondage so that you can live the abundant life and reflect His glory!

In this volume of Recovery in Christ, we have looked at the theology of addiction and recovery so that we can understand Yahweh's plan. In the next volume, we will look at how HaSatan uses our human spirit to establish the biological, neurological, and psychological conditions that we associate with compulsions, obsessions, and addictions. In the final volume, we will apply this information and tear down the Adamic soul structure, which will free us from our compulsions, obsessions, and addictions and cause the abundant life to materialize before us.

Bibliography

Bibliography Of Works Cited

Alcoholics Anonymous. Alcoholics Anonymous World Services, Inc. New York, 1976.

Bobgan, Martin and Deidre. *12 Steps to Destruction*. Santa Barbara, CA: EastGate Publishers, 1991.

Carson, D. A. *Exegetical Fallacies*. Grand Rapids, MI: Baker Book House, 1993.

Carson, D. A. *New Bible Commentary*, 4th ed. Downers Grove, IL: InterVarsity Press, 1994.*

Cloud, Bill. *Enmity Between the Seeds*. Cleveland, TN: Shoreshim Resources, 2004.

Concordant Literal New Testament. Canyon Country, CA: Concordant Publishing Concern, 1983.

Congdon, Robert R. *The European Union and the Supra-Religion*. Maitland, FL: Xulon Press, USA, 2007.

Dake, Finis. *God's Plan for Man*. Lawrenceville, GA: Finis Publishing, 2004, c1949.

Davis, John J. *Moses and the Gods of Egypt*. Winona Lake, IN: BMH Books, 2006.

De Coulanges, Fustel. *The Ancient City*. Garden City, NY: Doubleday Anchor Books, 1873.

Edersheim, Alfred. *Bible History: Old Testament*. Oak Harbor, WA: Logos Research Systems, Inc.,1997.*

Edersheim, Alfred. *The Temple, Its Ministry and Services as They Were at the Time of Christ*. Grand Rapids, MI: WM. B. Eerdmans Publishing Company, 1958.

Edmundson, George. *The Church in Rome in the First Century*. London: Longmans, Green and Co., 1913.

Enns, Paul P. *The Moody Handbook of Theology*. Chicago, IL: Moody Press, 1997, c1989.*

Ferguson, Everett. *Backgrounds of Early Christianity*. Grand Rapids, MI: Eerdmans Publishing, 2003.

Ferguson, Marilyn. *The Aquarian Conspiracy*. Los Angeles, CA: T. P. Tarcher, Inc., 1980.

Fischer, John. *The Olive Tree Connection*. Downers Grove, IL: InterVarsity Press, 1983.

Fisher, Raymond. *The Children of God*. Tiberias, Israel: Olim Publications, 2000.

Fitzgerald, Robert. *The Soul of Sponsorship*. Center City, MN: Hazelden, 1995.

Freeman, James M., and Harold J. Chadwick. *Manners and Customs of the Bible*, rev. ed. North Brunswick, NJ: Bridge-Logos Publishers, 1998.*

Fuller, Daniel P. *Gospel and Law: Contrast or Continuum?* Pasadena, CA: Fuller Seminary Press, 1982.

Garr, John D. *Bless You!* Atlanta, GA: Restoration Foundation, 2003.

Goodman, Martin. *Rome and Jerusalem: The Clash of Ancient Civilizations*. New York, NY: Random House, 2007.

Grant, Michael. *Tacitus: Annals*. London: Penguin Books, 1956.

Green, Arthur. *These Are the Words*. Woodstock, VT: Jewish Lights Publishing, 1999.

Gruber, Daniel. *The Separation of Church and Faith, Volume 1: Copernicus and the Jews*. Hanover, NH: Elijah Publishing, 2005.

Halliday, William. *History of Roman Religion*. Liverpool, UK,: University Press of Liverpool, 1922.

Harris, R. Laird, Gleason Leonard Archer, and Bruce K. Waltke. *Theological Wordbook of the Old Testament*, electronic ed. Chicago, IL: Moody Press, 1999, c1980.*

Hegg, Tim. *Fellow Heirs*. Littleton, CO: First Fruits of Zion, 2003.

Hegg, Tim. *Paul's Epistle to the Galatians,* 1st ed. Tacoma, WA: TorahResource, 2010.

Hegg, Tim. *Paul's Epistle to the Romans*. Tacoma, WA: TorahResource, 2005.

Hegg, Tim. *The Letter Writer*, 2nd ed. Tacoma WA: TorahResource, 2008.

Heidler, Robert. *The Messianic Church Arising!* Denton, TX: Glory of Zion International Ministries, 2006.

Henry, Matthew. *Matthew Henry's Commentary on the Whole Bible*. Peabody, MA: Hendrickson, 1996, c1991.*

Hodge, Charles. *Systematic Theology*. Oak Harbor, WA: Logos Research Systems, Inc., 1997.*

Hughes, Robert B., and J. Carl Laney. *Tyndale Concise Bible Commentary. The Tyndale Reference Library*. Wheaton, IL: Tyndale House Publishers, 2001.*

Irvine, William. *Heresies Exposed*. Neptune, NJ: Loizeaux Brothers, Inc., 1980.

Jones, Peter. *Spirit Wars*. Mukilteo, WA: WinePress Publishing, 1997.

Josephus, Flavius. *The Works of Josephus*. Peabody, MA: Hendrickson Publishers Inc., 1987.

Kaiser, Walter C. *The Messiah in the Old Testament*. Grand Rapids, MI: Zondervan Publishing House, 1995.

Kasemann, Ernst. *Commentary on Romans*. Grand Rapids, MI: Eerdmans Publishing, 1980.

Kimble, Gregory, and Michael Wertheimer. *Portraits of Pioneers in Psychology*, Volume 3. Washington, DC: American Psychological Association, 1998.

Klein, John, and Adam Spears. *Devils and Demons and the Return of the Nephilim*. Maitland, FL: Xulon Press, 2005.

Lancaster, D. Thomas. *Grafted In*, 2nd ed. Marshfield, MO: First Fruits of Zion, 2009.

Maier, Paul. *Eusebius: The Church History*. Grand Rapids, MI: Kregel Publications, 1999.

Matrisciana, Caryl. *Gods of the New Age*. Eugene, OR: Harvest House Publishers, 1985.

Moo, Douglas. *The Epistle to the Romans*. Grand Rapids, MI: Eerdmans Publishing Co., 1996.

Morford, William. *The Power New Testament*. Lexington, SC: Shalom Ministries, 2003.

Mounce, R. H. *The New American Commentary*, Volume 27. Nashville, TN: Broadman & Holman, 2001.

O'Brien, Cormac. *The Fall of Empires*. New York, NY: Fall River Press, 2009.

Paschall, F., and H. Hobbs. *The Teacher's Bible Commentary*. Nashville, TN: Broadman & Holman, 1972.*

Pass It On: The Story of Bill Wilson and How the A.A. Message Reached the World. New York, NY: Alcoholics Anonymous World Services, Inc., 1984.

Bibliography Of Works Cited

Prasch, James. *Israel, the Church and the Jews.* Springfield, MO: 21st Century Press, 2008.

Price, S. R. F. *Rituals and Power.* Cambridge, UK: Cambridge University Press, 1984.

Restore! Issue 16, Winter 2000. Atlanta, GA: Restoration Foundation.

Robertson, AT. *Word Pictures in the New Testament.* Nashville, TN: Broadman & Holman, 2000.*

Roth, Sid. *The Incomplete Church.* Shippensburg, PA: Destiny Image Publishers Inc., 2007.

Rothschild, Fritz. *Between God and Man.* New York, NY: Free Press Paperbacks, 1997.

Schaff, Philip. *History of the Christian Church, Volume 1: Apostolic Christianity.* Oak Harbor, WA: Logos Research Systems Inc., 1997.*

Shulam, Joseph. *A Commentary on the Jewish Roots of Romans.* Baltimore, MD: Lederer Books, 1997.

Smith, George. *The Gentile Nations.* New York, NY: Carlton & Porter, 1854.

Smith, James E. *The Pentateuch*, 2nd ed., Joplin, MO: College Press Publishing Company, 1993.

Stern, David. *Complete Jewish Bible.* Clarksville, MD: Jewish New Testament Publications, 1998.

Stern, David. *Jewish New Testament Commentary.* Clarksville, MD: Jewish New Testament Publications, 1992.

Stott, John. *Romans.* Downers Grove, IL: InterVarsity Press, 1994.

Sudduth, William. *What's Behind the Ink?* Downers Grove, IL: RAM Inc., 2008.

Thatcher, Tom. *Greater Than Caesar.* Minneapolis, MN: Fortress Press, 2009.

The Bible Knowledge Commentary, Wheaton, IL: Victor Books, 1983.*

The Hebrew-Greek Key Study Bible, KJV. Chattanooga, TN: AMG International, Inc., 1991.

The Holman New Testament Commentary. Nashville, TN: Broadman & Holman, 2000.

The Pulpit Commentary. Bellingham, WA: Logos Research Systems, Inc., 2004.*

The Tanach, Stone Edition. Brooklyn, NY: Mesorah Publications, 1996.

Unger, Merrill. *The New Unger's Bible Dictionary*. Chicago, IL: Moody Press, 1966.*

Ussher, James. *The Timechart of Biblical History*. Chippenham, England: Third Millennium Press, Ltd., 2002.

Vitz, Paul C. *Psychology as Religion*. Grand Rapids, MI: Eerdmans Publishing Co.,1977.

Whiston, William. *The Works of Josephus*. Peabody, MA: Hendrickson Publishers, Inc., 1987.

Wiersbe, W. Warren. *The Bible Exposition Commentary*. Wheaton, IL: Victor Books,1996.*

Wiersbe, W. Warren. *Wiersbe's Expository Outlines on the New Testament*. Wheaton, IL: Victor Books, 1997.*

Wilken, Robert. *The Christians as The Romans Saw Them*: London: Yale University Press, 1984.

Wilson, William (Bill). *The Language of the Heart*. Published posthumously. New York, NY: AA Grapevine, 1988.

Witherington, Ben. *Paul's Letter to the Romans*. Grand Rapids, MI: Eerdmans Publishing Co., 2004.

Bibliography Of Works Cited

Marshall, Howard. *New Bible Dictionary*, 3rd ed. Downers Grove, IL: InterVarsity Press, 1996.*

Wuest, K. S. *Wuest's Word Studies from the Greek New Testament*. Grand Rapids, MI: Eerdmans Publishing Co., 1997.*

Young, Robert. *Young's Literal Translation of the Holy Bible*. Lafayette, IN: Greater Truth Publishers, 2004

* This resource was an electronic edition from LOGOS Bible Software, LOGOS Research Systems, Inc., Bellingham, WA 98225-4307.

Internet Sources

http://www.britannica.com/EBchecked/topic/88114/Julius-Caesar

http://www.flowofhistory.com/units/birth/4/FC30

http://www.graceandknowledge.faithweb.com/cain.html

http://historion.net/american-encyclopedia-history-i/triumvirate-caesars-gallic-wars-war-between-caesar-and-pompey

http://historion.net/american-encyclopedia-history-i/dictatorship-and-death-caesar-second-triumvirate-civil-wars-mark-ant

http://www.kyrieology.com/drupal/wwje/adverseinfluenceofpork

http://www.lesfeldick.org (Les Feldick's *Through the Bible* television series)

http://www.livius.org/am-ao/antisemitism/antisemitism01.html#agrippa

http://www.philipharland.com/publications/articleAHB.html; p. 103

http://www.roman-emperors.org/auggie.htm; p. 20., Fagan, G., Garrett, Pennsylvania State University

http://www.roman-emperors.org/auggie.htm; p. 12

http://www.roman-empire.net/diverse/faq.html#romerise

Internet Sources

http://www.roman-empire.net/kings/kings-index.html

http://www.skipmoen.com (*Today's Word*)

http://www.theancientworld.net/civ/roman_republic.html

http://www.unrv.com/fall-republic/gaius-julius-caesar.php

http://www.unrv.com/fall-republic/caesar-the-god.php

http://www.unrv.com/fall-republic/death-antony-cleopatra.php

http://www.unrv.com/early-empire/augustus-empire.php

http://www.jungcircle.com/fish.html

Scripture Index

Scripture Index

Genesis
  2:17, 109
  3:14, 131
  3:15, 51, 302, 350
  5:3, 358
  6:3, 96, 350
  6:8, 355
  11:2, 101
  12:2, 102
  12:3, 162, 175, 302
  12:5, 125
  12:7, 86
  15:13-15, 123
  17:4-6, 175
  17:6, 162
  17:7, 86
  17:23, 135
  19:19, 355
  21:8-14, 175
  24:4, 135
  26:5, 352
  38:1-30, 135
  38:2, 120
  41:38, 352
  41:45, 135

Exodus
  2:21, 136
  4:22, 104
  8:22-23, 78
  11:8, 81
  12:38, 136
  12:48, 81
  12:48-49, 137, 327
  15:26, 338
  19:3-6, 122
  20:5, 358
  20:14, 242
  24:7, 88
  28:3, 262
  31:3, 269
  31:13, 262
  32, 87
  32:4, 88
  33:12-17, 355
  35:30-31, 160
  35:31, 269

Leviticus
  17:11, 109
  19:18, 147
  20:10, 242
  25:47, 131

Numbers
  5:11-31, 88
  9:14, 327
  11:17, 262, 353
  11:25, 269, 353
  15:13-16, 327
  15:16, 137
  15:17-21, 310
  19:11-13, 330

Deuteronomy
  4:5-8, 121
  5:15, 103
  5:18, 242
  6:1-5, 147
  8:3, 73
  10:12, 268
  10:16, 132, 268
  10:12-13, 256
  13:5, 170, 260
  18:15-19, 153, 180
  23:3, 137
  23:13, 340
  28:1-14, 85
  29:1-10, 308
  30:6, 159, 269
  34:9, 262

Joshua
  1:8, 338
  2:9, 360
  2:18-19, 136
  5:1, 360

5:5, 81, 82
5:9, 83
6:16, 360
11:18, 360
11:19, 360
13:1, 360
13:12, 360
14:6, 136
24:12, 360
24:14, 86

Judges
6:34, 262, 269
14:6, 269
14:19, 269
15:14, 262, 269

Ruth
4:10, 136
4:17, 137

1 Samuel
10:10, 269
11:6, 269
16:13, 242, 257, 262, 269
17:1-58, 360

2 Samuel
7:12-17, 162, 242
8:1-14, 162
12:1-20, 257
12:9, 242
12:13, 242
21:15-22, 360

1 Kings
9:4, 159
14:21, 136, 137

1 Chronicles
3:2, 136
12:18, 269

2 Chronicles
24:20, 269

Ezra
6:21, 136

Nehemiah
9:14-20, 262
9:20, 353
10:28, 136

Esther
8:17, 136

Job
1:1, 159
4:19, 52
10:11, 52
12:7-9, 350

Psalm
1:1-3, 144
1:2-3, 338
8:5, 93
19:1, 350
19:7-8, 144
19:8, 89
32:1-11, 355
32:3, 257
32:5, 242
51:3, 242
51:5, 359
51:16-17, 257
51:16-19, 257
69:21-28, 308

84:11, 355
89:26, 242
110, 242
119:24, 338
119:77, 338
119:92, 338

Proverbs
3:34, 355

Isaiah
1:11-17, 257
5:5-7, 153
7:14, 358
9:6-7, 153
29:9-24, 308
42:1-9, 102
42:4, 327
49:6, 121
53:1-12, 153
53:11, 358
54:5-8, 121
59:2, 358
66:2-3, 257

Jeremiah
2:1-3, 121
4:4, 132
6:19-20, 257
11:16-17, 310
13:23, 354
14:10-11, 153
16:19, 337
31:33-34, 148
32:37-42, 159
51:7, 61, 94, 101

Ezekiel
2:2, 269

Scripture Index

3:24, 269
4:1-17, 340
11:5, 269
11:17-20, 159
11:19-20, 148
14:14, 257
18:4, 109
20:5-9, 121
20:5-11, 261
20:6-8, 88
20:7-9, 78
20:12, 262
24:21-23, 153
34:2-15, 159
36:24-30, 304, 328
36:26-27, 148

Daniel
  2:44, 153
  8:24-25, 56
  8:25, 117
  9:24, 153
  11:21, 117
  11:23, 117
  11:24, 117

Amos
  5:21-27, 257
  9:11-15, 309

Micah
  6:6-8, 257

Habakkuk
  3:7, 136

Zechariah
  8:23, xxiv
  12:10, 309

Malachi
  3:6, xxii

Matthew
  1:19, 159
  4:17, 155
  5:1-7:29, 154
  5:17, xxii, 170, 260, 327
  5:20, 154
  6:33, 155
  7:21, 133
  13:24-30, 311
  13:30, 158
  16:18, 159
  16:19, 159
  17:1-13, 180
  20:28, 155
  21:33-46, 159
  22:36-38, 147
  22:37-40, 316
  22:39, 147
  22:40, 147
  22:41-46, 154
  23:13, 159
  23:13-15, 154
  23:28, 272
  26:40, 107
  26:41, 107
  28:20, 327

Mark
  7:7-13, 154
  12:36-37, 154

Luke
  1:6, 159
  2:25, 159
  2:37, 159
  4:4, 73
  5:20-21, 154

18:31-33, 155
20:41-44, 154
22:20, 155

John
  1:1, xxii
  1:9, 350
  1:14, 350
  1:51, 356
  3:6, 128
  3:7, 289
  3:18, 119
  4:26, 356
  5:30, 356
  5:46, 356
  5:47, 356
  6:35, 356
  6:44, 133, 356
  6:48, 356
  6:63, 74
  6:65, 350
  7:17, 356
  7:19, 356
  7:29, 356
  7:39, 356
  8:24, 154, 356
  8:37, 356
  8:42, 356
  8:47, 356
  8:56, 71, 86, 126, 302, 352
  8:58, 154, 356
  10:7, 356
  10:10, 357
  10:14, 356
  10:16, 171
  10:28-30, 357
  10:30, 356
  13:34, 320

14:20, 154
15:26, 350, 357
17:5, 154
17:20-21, 171, 367
17:20-22, 218
20:28-29, 154

Acts
3:25, 302
7:9-10, 352
7:38, 157
11:18, 359
13:22, 257
15:21, 327
17:10-12, 171
18:2, 212
28:17, 332
28:22, 213

Romans
1:1-6, 350
1:16, 169
1:17, 357
1:19, 350
1:20, 350
2:1, 232
2:25, 133
2:25-29, 74
2:29, 130
3:20, 107, 365
3:21-26, 358
3:25, 111
4:1-8, 355
5:19, 357
5:20, 108, 110
6:1, 272
6:14, 89
6:16, 365
7:5, 89, 108, 144

7:8, 108
7:11, 144
7:12, 144, 327, 365
7:15, 89, 147
7:16, 147
7:18:144
7:22, 147
7:24, 148
8:2, 357
8:4, 358
8:5, 357, 358
8:10, 358
8:14, 357, 358
8:23, 356, 358
8:29, 357, 358
9:6, 127
9:7, 127, 130
9:31-32, 256
10:4, 170
10:9, 284, 357
11:13-15, 218, 367
11:26, 269
11:32, 101
12:1-2, 357
15:4, 359

1 Corinthians
3:9, 160
3:16, 160
5, 325
6:11, 358
6:17, 359
7:14, 133
10:1-4, 80
10:2, 104, 353
10:11, 359
11:25, 305
12:13, 284, 359
14:4, 294

15:50, 358
15:51, 358

2 Corinthians
1:22, 356
3:3, 148
3:6, 305
3:6-7, 143
3:18, 357, 358
5:17, 289, 357
5:21, 357
7:1, 358

Galatians
2:20, 357
3:6-8, 242
3:6-9, 175
3:8, 126, 302, 352
3:16, 86, 130
3:19, 83, 86, 87, 262
3:24, 107, 143, 248
3:28, 171, 327
3:29, 175
4:6, 357
4:7-11, 175
4:21-31, 175
4:23, 130
5:2-4, 220
5:16, 133, 357
5:16-23, 358
5:24, 357, 358
5:25, 290, 357, 358
6:2, 320
6:8, 358
6:16, 127

Ephesians
1:13, 104, 356
1:20, 358

1:20-21, 323
2:2, 359
2:6, 323, 358
2:8-9, 284
2:14-15, 171
2:15-16, 225
2:19-22, 160
3:9, 99
4:17-5:20, 357
4:22-24, 358
4:30, 356
5:26, 218
5:27, 218, 367
6:12, 324

Philippians
  3:21, 356, 358

Colossians
  1:21, 359
  3:3, 323, 357
  3:4, 356, 358

2 Thessalonians
  2:8-12, 56

1 Timothy
  1:8, 144, 365
  1:9-11, 248
  4:1-5, 342

2 Timothy
  1:9, 99
  2:25, 359
  3:16, 350

Titus
  1:2, 99

Hebrews
  1:1-3, 350
  2:3, 350
  2:14, 131
  2:15, 131
  3:8-19, 359
  8:10, 148
  9:22, 109
  10:1, 148
  10:4, 110
  10:6, 257
  10:8, 257
  10:16, 148
  11:4, 349
  11:4-7, 99
  11:5, 351
  11:7, 351
  11:31, 136
  13:5, 357
  13:8, xxii

James
  2:8, 320
  2:17, 358
  2:18, 133, 261
  2:21, 241
  2:24, 261
  2:26, 261

1 Peter
  1:11, 262
  1:20, 99
  1:22, 357
  2:3-5, 160
  2:22, 357
  2:23-24, 358
  5:13, 182

2 Peter
  3:16, 177

1 John
  2:1, 357
  2:6, 357
  2:29, 357
  3:2, 358
  3:3, 357
  3:4, 95
  3:12, 349
  3:24, 357
  4:17, 357
  4:21, 320
  5:18, 323, 324, 357

Jude
  1:11, 349

Revelation
  13:7, 56
  13:8, xxii, 99
  13:11-14, 118
  13:12, 118
  13:15-17, 118
  13:15-18, 56
  14:8, 94
  17:5, 94, 182
  19:20, 118
  20:15, 119
  22:5, 356

Subject Index

Subject Index

A

AA. See Alcoholics Anonymous (AA)
Abraham, 72–73, 75–79, 81–84, 86–87
    natural seed and spiritual seed, 133–134
    seed, 50, 53, 69, 73, 130, 162, 367
Abrahamic covenant, 104, 106–107, 129, 130, 141
    redemption in, 261–262
    sign of, 130
Abram, 71–73
Abram's spirit versus Abraham's spirit, 132
Adam and Eve
    conscience, 54
    curse, 45
    God's love for, 47
    loss of authority, 54
    rebellion, 93–94
    submission, 93, 95
    testing, 40–41
Addiction, xxv–xxvi, xxx, 49
    environment of, 60
    biochemistry leading to, 50
Age of Aquarius, 57–59
Age of Conscience, 96–97, 98–100, 351
Age of Human Government, 100–101, 351
Age of Promise, 102–103, 106, 352
Age of the Written Torah, 103–104, 106, 111, 256, 352
Alcoholics Anonymous (AA), 62, 63, 64, 306
Alexander the Great, 149, 187, 205, 318

Antiochus, 149
Assyrians, 163

B
Babylon, 61, 70, 75
Babylonian mystery religion. See Mystery Babylon
Babylonians, 57, 149
Biochemistry
    sin and, 54, 95, 110
    spirit and, 50, 108, 143
Body of sin, 251–253, 348, 369
Buchman, Frank, 61

C
Cain, 60, 115, 140, 199–200, 349
Cain's kingdom, 115–116
Calvary, xv, 110
Calvin, John, 302–304
Canaan, 70, 75, 360
Circumcision, 73, 81, 87, 128, 133–134, 163–164, 177, 243, 354
Collective conscience, 62-63
Collective consciousness, 63
Congregation of Moses, 80–84, 85
Conscience, 54, 95, 258, 320, 351
    operation of, 98–99
Covenant, xxiv, 71, 147. See also Abrahamic covenant; Mosaic covenant

D
Daniel, 257
Darby, John, 302, 304
Darwin, Charles, 37–38, 55, 61
David, 136, 140, 162, 242, 257, 308, 367
De-evolution, 47–51, 64
Dope sickness, xxvi

E
Egypt
    captivity in, 75, 105
    gentiles in, 82

       judgment of, 76
       plagues, 77, 78
       religious system, 78
       separatism, 120
Ekklesia, 99, 157–161, 217
Elite liberal intellectual gospel, 57
Emergents, theology of, 59–60
Evolution, 37, 55, 58–59, 61
External motivational system, 107, 108

F

Fall, 49, 115, 232, 267, 330, 338
Fall, before, 48
Fallen nature, 44, 50, 70, 87, 105, 221, 261–262, 274, 278-279, 355
False Prophet, 118
Fig leaf suit
       worldview metaphor, 50, 54–55
Foreigner, etymology, 138

G

Galatians, Book of
       bookend epistle, 180
       covenant inclusion, 177–178
       historical perspective, 174–175
       Paul's letter to, 172, 175–177
       purpose, 217–218
       situation in, 172–173
Garden of Eden, 40, 89
Gentiles, 121–124, 136–138, 148–151, 164–165
       grafted into the righteous remnant, 160–161, 172, 220
Global socialist economic systems, 118
Golden calf incident, 87–89
Golden plank, xxiii–xxv
Grace, 80, 85, 99–103, 108–110, 143–144, 236, 243, 249, 354, 356

H

Halachah, 150, 165, 171, 224, 315, 354
HaSatan
       addiction and, 60

conquering strategies, 117–119
deception of Babylonians, 70
corruption of gene pool, 69
deception of, 47
enslavement of men, 99
etymology, 39
image projected, 131
motivation, 39
worship of, 101

HSC. See Human system configuration (HSC)
Hebrews, v, 71, 80, 370
Holy Spirit, 285–286
Human system configuration (HSC), 52, 107, 252, 267, 369-370

I
Inheritance, saints, 140–144
Isaac and Ishmael, 128–129
Israel
    as adopted son, 121, 122
    birth of, 120–124
    creation of, 115
    foundations, 125–126
    founders, 135–136, 407t
    and Gentiles, 137–139, 141
    of God, 126–127
    nation of, 126–127
    native born versus the stranger, 137
    Torah as constitution, 122
    as wife, 121, 122

J
Jerusalem Council, 163–164

K

L
Law
    condemnation by, 319
    dual role of, 244–245

Subject Index

    faith and, 238
    letter of, 142–144
    Mosaic, 248, 257, 273, 302, 319, 335, 363
    Roman, 273
    spirit, 286–287
    Torah's, 85, 141, 160, 220, 274, 333, 351
    transformation of, 320
    under, 220–222
    works of, 220–222, 238
Lucifer
    etymology, 39. See HaSatan

M

Messianic Jews, 163, 218, 326
Mark of the covenant, 73-74
Mosaic covenant, 85–86, 107, 148, 156
    God's grace in, 108
    operation of 255–258
    problems with, 142
    righteousness standard, 261–262
Moses, 76–78, 80–84, 152, 153–155
Mount Sinai, 82–84
Mystery Babylon, 70–71, 94-95, 101-104, 152, 181

N

Negative emotions, and spiritual disposition, 44
New Age system, 57–59, 62, 64, 369
New covenant, 258
Nimrod, 60, 64, 70, 116-117, 119, 180, 199, 203
Noah, 69, 100, 351
Noah's descendants, 101
Noah's flood, 105, 116

O

O.G. See Oxford Group (O.G.)
Oxford Group (O.G.), 61–64

P

Passover meal, 82

Paul
- background, 169
- experiences under the law, 270–272
- illuminated by Holy Spirit, 171
- letters, 171–172
- message, 172
- presuppositions of, 171–172
- scholarship of, 170–171
- situation in Galatia, 172–173
- spiritual blindness, 269

Pentecost, 155, 160, 244, 329, 356
Pharisees, 158, 163–166
Pharaoh, 76–77, 147
Praying in tongues, 294
Primitive atonement, 42–43
Progressive revelation, xxiii, 302, 360
Promised Seed, 69, 86–87, 99, 100, 110-111, 268–269, 301, 354

Q

R

Rebellion, 39, 42, 48, 71, 96, 120, 267, 347, 354
Recovery, xxix, 49, 223, 253, 369
Recovery movement, xxxi, 60, 62–63, 369
Redemption, 80, 106, 131, 176, 261–262, 349, 368
Regeneration, 49, 256, 276–277
Rehabilitation, xxviii
Religion, 60, 94, 118, 180, 244, 348, 369
Renaissance, 61
Renewal of mind, v, xxii, 62, 253, 295, 322, 343
Repentance, 50, 131, 152-155, 256, 305, 350, 366
Responsibility, 46
Righteous remnant, xxiv, 71, 99, 159-160, 244, 309, 356, 366
Roman Empire
- Augustus, 195, 197–198, 206
- expanse of, 198–199
- image of, 198-199, 203
- imperial cult, 205–206
- loyalty to, 203–204

Subject Index

Pax Romana, 206–207
Pontifex Maximus, 202–203
religion of Romulus and Remus, 202–207
rise of, 192–196
Romans, Book of
    Adam's sin and its consequences, 247
    background, 223
    belief, 242–243, 252–254
    believers versus unbelievers, spiritual response to, 324–325
    born again, 249, 259, 277, 289, 319, 357
    condemnation, 246, 274–275
    confessing Yeshua is Lord, 305–306
    context of, 208–213
    disorder in the universe, 293
    election of Israel, 301–302, 308
    equality of Jew and Gentile, 234–235
    escape from condemnation, 283
    faith in Yeshua, 236–237
    fall of man, 232
    Gentiles and, 225–227
    grace, 250, 283–284
    grafting of Gentiles to Jews, 310–312
    Holy Spirit, 285-287, 288, 289–292
    hope, 293
    inherited nature, 247
    Israel, 234, 244, 286, 295–296, 301–302, 306
    justification by faith or works, 241–243
    justification by Yeshua's death, 246–247, 254
    law and, 224
    law of the spirit, 286–287
    Mosaic covenant, 255–259
    old covenant, 304–305
    old nature, 289
    paganism and, 224
    Paul's credentials, 231
    presentation of bodies as living sacrifice, 321, 322
    rapture/resurrection, 309
    regeneration, 276–277, 288, 290, 323
    release from law, 275

religious Jews, 233
remnant, 307–308
renewing mind, 321–322
righteousness, 237–238, 294
sacrifices of Mosaic covenant, 236
sacrificial death of Yeshua, 251
salvation, 279–280, 312
sovereignty of Yahweh, 301
Torah and, 260–264, 303–304
unredeemed flesh, 322–323
walking in the Spirit, 315–316
works of Adam and works of Yeshua contrasted, 248–249
Yah's purpose for the nation of Israel, 234
Yah's wrath, 232

Rome
    birth of, 187–188
    classes, 188–189
    death spiral, 190–191
    evolution, 189
    near destruction, 189
    political and social dynamics, 296
    tipping point, 189–190

Romulus and Remus, 200–201, 202–207
Royal grant treaty, 86

S

Sacrifice
    blood, 110, 111
    etymology, 109

Sadducees, 158
Salvation, 61, 85, 99, 123, 151, 271, 279–280, 318
Sanctification, 49, 262
Secondary planks, xxv
Second law of thermodynamics, 48
Shem's line, 116
Sin, 48
    consequences of, 94–95
    rationalization of, 54

Soul, design of, 52–53

Sovereignty versus free will, 295
Spirit, xxii
    authority and power, lack of, 106
    biochemistry and, 50
    fallen man's, 50
Spiritual de-evolution, 47–49
Spiritual disposition, 44
Spiritual evolution, naturalistic, 55–56
Spiritual exodus, 153–156
Spiritual re-evolution, 49
Submission, xxix, 47
Suzerain-vassal treaty, 86

T
Tabernacle of David, 162–166
Torah, 61, 83–84, 85–86, 90, 106, 150, 165
    and circumcision, 219–220
    constitution of Israel, 122
    and grace, 109
    legal code, 260–264, 317
    messianic paradigm, 272
    older covenants, 141–142
    origination of, 316
    preserving agent, 218
Tower of Babel, 105, 180
Two-edged spiritual sword, 89

U

V

W
Wilson, Bill, 62–63
World Christian Fundamentals Association, 62
Worldview, xxi–xxiii

X

Y

Yah
- creator, 38
- outside of time, 131
- qualities of, 43–44
- uncaused cause, 38

Yahweh, etymology of, 72

Yeshua, xxi, xxx–xxxii, 37–38, 49, 59, 62–64, 80–82, 89, 99, 131, 153–156

Yeshua's Ekklesia, 181

Yeshua's plan, 319

Z

Glossary

Glossary

Ancient city: The first cities were religious institutions that used political and economic systems to control their citizens and build up the wealth and power of their founders, who were the rulers and the great high priests of the institutions.

Body: The dirt house that our spirit lives in during its time on the earth.

Dynamics of the HSC: How the spirit, soul, and body interact with each other.

Ecumenical organization: An organization that brings all the religions of the earth together.

Egalitarian society: A society in which everyone is equal, politically, socially, and economically.

Ekklesia: Greek for group of citizens summoned by a town crier to a legislative assembly. By implication, ekklesia means an assembly called together by the Holy Spirit. The Romans translated *ekklesia* as "church," which comes from the Greek word *kyriakon*, which means "pertaining to the Lord" (the Lord's house). The Romans changed the meaning of this word from an assembly of people (which they could not control) to a place of worship (which they could control). The word *church* caries a great deal of baggage, so I prefer the word *ekklesia*.

Elohim: Hebrew for "the divine ruler and judge," or "God."

Execution stake: The tree, or the cross, that Yeshua was put to death on.

HaSatan: Hebrew for "the adversary."

Human system configuration (HSC): The arrangement of the spirit, soul, and body.

Legal halachah: The sages' legal rulings that defined how the written Torah and the oral Torah were to be lived out or, more accurately, how they were to be walked out.

Messiah: An English transliteration of the Hebrew word *mashiah*, which means "anointed one." Messiah is translated into Greek as *khristós,* which translates into English as "Christ."

Oral Torah: The sages' interpretations and additions to the written Torah.

Self-actualization: Becoming fully human (reaching the fullest human potential) by removing the obstacles that prevent the true self (the divine self) from emerging.

Serpent's slave market: HaSatan's collection of slaves that he uses to build up his kingdom on the earth. HaSatan visits his slave market and selects certain people for certain jobs, and then he grooms them and equips them so that they can do the jobs assigned to them. But when a person bows his knee to Yeshua and puts his trust in Him, then His blood pays the redemption price that takes that person off the serpent's slave market. This is what it means to be redeemed.

Soul: The biological organism that expresses the thoughts and intents of the spirit on earth.

Spirit: The essence of man.

Spiritual evolution: The process of the human spirit becoming one with its Creator.

Tanakh: The Hebrew Scriptures; that is, the Torah, the Prophets, and the Writings, or what is more commonly called the Old Testament.

Written Torah: The five books of Moses (the first five books of the Bible), or Yahweh's teachings and instructions that He codified at Mount Sinai and gave to Israel.

Yahweh: The Creator's personal name.

Yah: The shortened form of Yahweh, as in *hallelujah* ("praise Yah").

Yeshua: Hebrew for "salvation," or "Jesus" in English.

Yeshua Ha Mashiach: Hebrew for "Jesus the Christ" or "Jesus the Messiah."

Figures And Tables

Israel

Natural Seed	Abram	Spiritual Seed
Abram		The Souls from Haran
Abraham		The Camp
Isaac		Rebekah (Syrian)
Jacob		Leah, Rachel, Bilhah, Zilpah (Syrians)
Judah		Shuah, Tamar (Canaanites)
Joseph		Asenath (Mitsrite)
Moses		Zipporah, the Cushite (Midianite) (Ethiopian)
The Twelve Tribes		The Mixed Multitude
Joshua		Caleb (Kenizzite)
The Spies		Rahab (Canaanite)**
David		Maachah (Geshurite)
Solomon		Naamah (Ammonite) *
The Remnant from Babylon		The People of the Lands
Mordecai		The Persian Believers
Boaz		Ruth (Moabite) **

* The mother of a king of Israel.

**The mother of a king of Israel who was also in Yeshua's line.

Table # 1

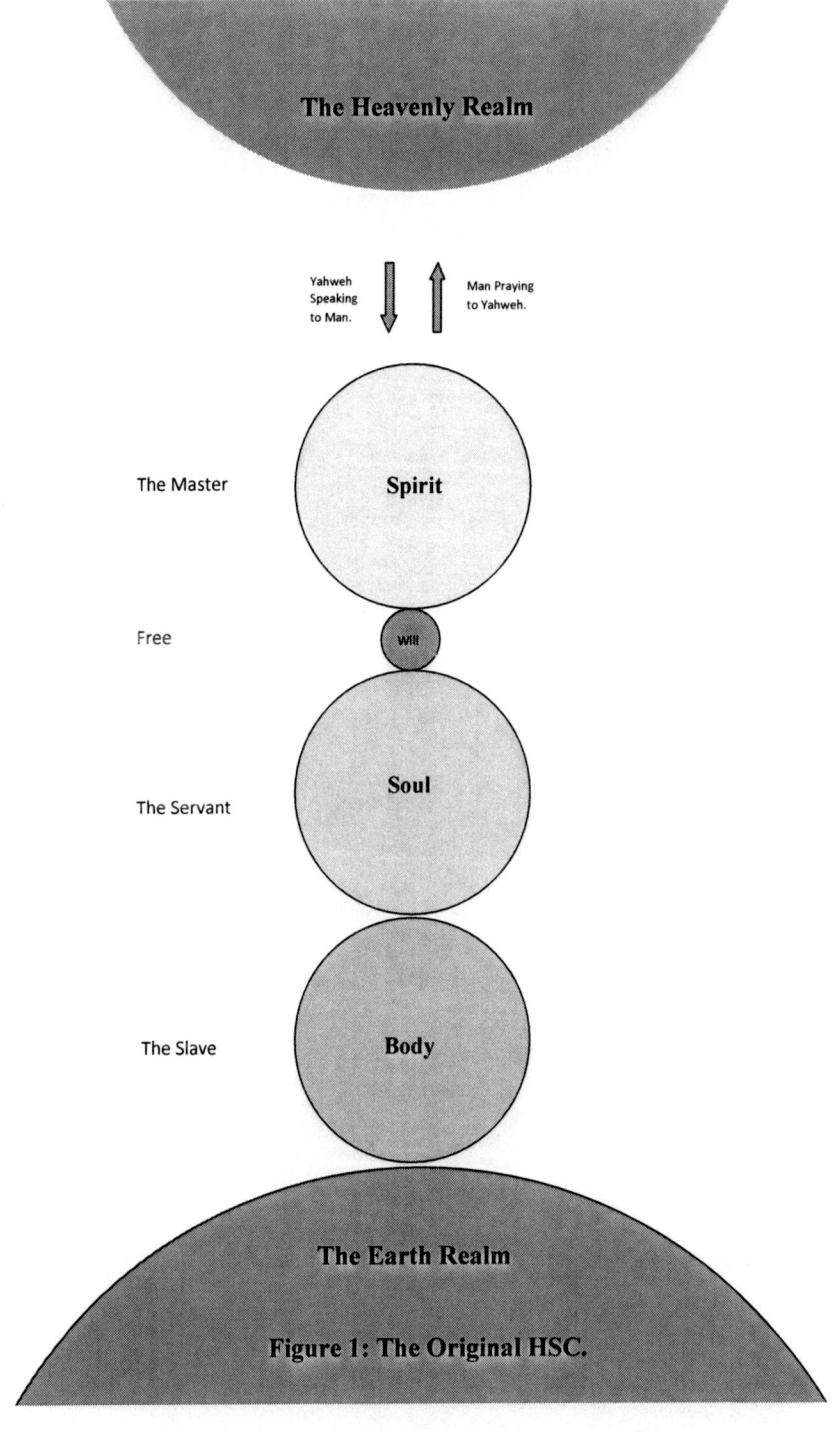

Figure 1: The Original HSC.

Figures And Tables

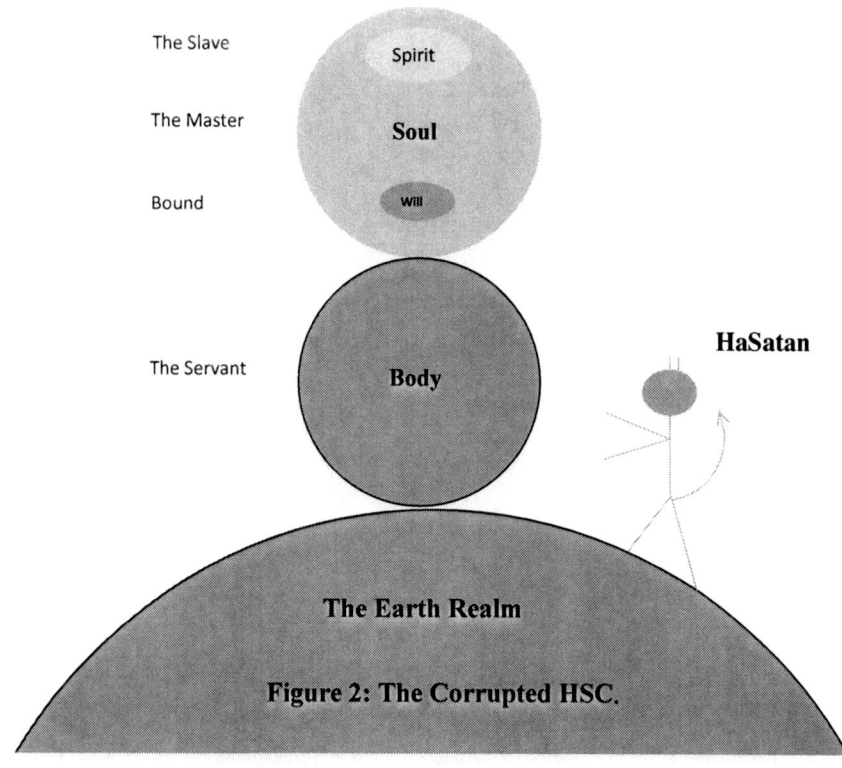

Figure 2: The Corrupted HSC.

Endnotes

[i]Maureen B. Roberts, Ph.D., says it this way:

The age of Aquarius is indeed dawning. The celestial water-bearer is about to pour out onto our parched Earth a new vision of our human potential and our place in the Cosmos. Uranus, as planetary co-ruler of Aquarius, personifies sky, stars, the Heavens, a breaking free of mind and spirit from the Piscean bondage to the blurring undersea realm of the Neptunian unconscious. Briefly, in astrology different "ages" correspond to different signs of the Zodiac, running backwards from Pisces to Aries. Based on the precession of the equinoxes, each age lasts for roughly 2000 years and the complete cycle, known as the "Great Year," spans 25,000 years.

The Piscean Age began around the time of Christ and lasts until approximately 200 A.D. when we transit through the Pisces/Aquarius cusp into Aquarius. From a holistic psychological perspective, we can view the entire Zodiacal cycle as a paradigm of the collective unconscious, the two forming a mirroring synchronicity of macrocosm (Cosmos) and microcosm (the human psyche). Broadly speaking, the ages are dominated by the qualities of their ruling archetype and by the character of their ruling planet(s).

The Piscean Age, ruled by Neptune and symbolized by the twin fish swimming in opposite directions, has accordingly been dominated by dualistic thinking in the form of an endless array of irreconcilable polarities. Key dualisms such as God/human, good/evil/spirit/matter, inner/outer, male/female, science/religion, reinforced in Western culture by Christian dogma, gave rise to hierarchical thinking which inevitably privileged one pole of the duality at the expense of the other. Hence, the Medieval model of an ascending ladder or chain of command reaching back to God is a feature of Piscean vertical thinking, which remains attracted by the desirability of escaping the earthly realm into the spiritual beyond.

Meanwhile, reluctantly confined to the physical plane, the "shepherd versus flock" hierarchy translated into the blind belief and obedience of dependent followers, unquestioning faith and the idea of an authoritarian God "out there"; into seeing spirit/above as superior to matter/below, male as superior to female ("matter" comes from L. "mater" meaning "mother") and good as supreme over evil. In Piscean mode, homogeneous flocks and shoal-like tendencies prevail; masses rely on spiritual or political leaders, and the individual is repressed by Church and State.

The Aquarian age, in contrast, symbolized by a celestial human wielding the pitcher of divine water, not only privileges the individual as divine but is dominated by the less mystical, more focused, incisive and pragmatic planets, Saturn and Uranus. Saturn presides over penetrating critical scrutiny, science, discipline and methodical questioning rather than blind belief. Co-ruler Uranus is the revolutionary magician who stands for independence, humanitarianism, scientific inventiveness and futuristic ideas. An intriguing duo! But most importantly, the shift into Aquarius will profoundly affect the way we relate to and understand "God," for we ceaselessly make and remake God in our image.

Two astrological ages ago, before the Divine descended to become the Piscean God in human form, God reflected the egotistical, childish and warlike age of Aries, Zeus and the Old Testament. Now the God-image, formerly polarized as male/spiritual, is being subsumed by the Aquarian vision of complementarity, the latter implying that each pole of a duality is in reality one end of a holistic continuum rather than a separate opposite. Hence, as a reflection of the human divine Self, the Aquarian God-image as matter, female and human can be understood as one pole of the continuous "light spectrum" of the collective unconscious, which merges into spirit, male and divine at the other end. Similarly, science and mysticism, formerly at dualistic odds with each other, are now being seen increasingly as two faces of the same holistic coin. If light is the privileged metaphor of mystical holism, in physics, too, light's wave-particle complementarity subverts at the most basic level of existence the former dualism of energy and matter.

In the realm of religion, the old metaphysical dualism of good versus evil is superseded in Aquarian thought by the psychological complementarity of "light" and "dark;" hence a key ingredient in moving on to a more mature level of awareness and God-like responsibility is that the shadow side of life must no longer be denied, repressed, hated or projected elsewhere (e.g., onto "evil forces" or other people and races) but must be dealt with first and foremost within ourselves. All this implies that as a divine humanity we can no longer appeal to outside deities, gurus or messiahs to conveniently hand us doctrines or religions to believe in, for belief can only ever be a substitute for the direct knowledge and experience which can only come from within— from openness to and trust in the inner Self as experientially indistinguishable from God. In part this means recognizing the close proximity, if not identity, of what was dark or hidden in human nature with what contains the seeds of the divine.

When God descends from an unreachable throne on high to a place within our individual hearts, so we as individuals become all powerful—and we soberly need to be reminded that we can use that power either to heal, create and understand—or to destroy. The choice is ours. One thing is certain: we are entering the first age in history in which the ball has stopped in our court in the sense that we can never again hand it back to a cosmic savior or scapegoat. We are now the forgers of our own destiny as we create and watch unfold the continuing evolution of consciousness and Cosmos. On, then, to grounded details: given that the key words for Aquarian thinking will be holism and relatedness, what kinds of changes will take place in our day-to-day transactions and interactions? In follow-up discussions and in the context of some of Jung's ideas, we could perhaps explore some anticipated future changes in how we relate to ourselves, to one another, to our world, to the Cosmos—and to the God we are once again remaking in our image.

I obtained this excerpt at http://www.jungcircle.com/fish.html. [03/2010] In this excerpt, we see the merging of Jung's psychology, humanism, and transformational evolution to produce a New Age religious worldview.

[ii] New Agers have not systematized their theology. Thus New Agers express their beliefs in different ways. For instance, the doctrine of spiritual evolution is central in New Age theology, but some New Agers express spiritual evolution in individualistic terms, and some express it in more universal terms.

The New Agers who express the principle of spiritual evolution in universal terms use the language and concepts that I have used in this book. These New Agers express the doctrine of spiritual evolution through the concept of the cosmic field driving humanity's spiritual evolution. In this system, a person's spiritual evolution is directly proportional to his efforts to cleanse his soul of negative attitudes and emotions that block the cosmic field and prevent it from nourishing his spirit. The New Agers who express the doctrine of spiritual evolution in individualistic terms use the concept of reincarnation. In this system, a person tries to live "right" by cleansing his spirit and soul of negative attitudes and emotions so that he can live a better life. In this system, when a person dies, his spirit leaves his body and enters the womb of a woman so that she can birth the person into the earth realm again.

The people who cooperate with this cycle of death and rebirth by cleansing themselves of all their negative attitudes and emotions will evolve spiritually and live a better life.

In addition, the people who cooperate with the cycle of death and rebirth will eventually progress to a state of godhood.

The mechanics of the two systems are a little different, but the two systems produce the same result. In each system, a person has to cleanse himself from resentment, bitterness, anger, hatred, lust, and greed and put the intolerant, divisive doctrines of religion away so that he can evolve spiritually. The goal is for everyone to evolve spiritually to godhood and come together to build a global egalitarian society.

[iii] Please understand that I am not against the people who go to AA; I am against AA as a belief system. Yeshua's ekklesia has failed alcoholics and addicts. We introduce alcoholics and addicts to Yeshua, but then we do not support them in their struggle to get free and remain that way. A few alcoholics and addicts meet Yeshua and never use mind-altering substances again. However, most alcoholics and addicts have to grow spiritually to gain the strength to shun mind-altering substances. The people who are struggling with a mind-altering substance are in a spiritual struggle that has soulish and bodily consequences. Consequently, these people need spiritual, soulish, and physical support.

Yeshua's ekklesia offers spiritual support on Wednesdays and Sundays for one hour. A few assemblies even offer spiritual, soulish, and physical support on one other night of the week. Here is the problem: a person who is in a life-or-death struggle with mind-altering substances needs daily spiritual, soulish, and physical support. The alcoholic or addict needs to meet daily with people whom Yahweh has re-created spiritually so that he can learn how to deal with life and develop a positive habit.

Since Yeshua's ekklesia does not offer daily support, alcoholics and addicts turn to AA for support. AA can teach these people some coping skills and help them develop new habits, but unfortunately, it can also lead them away from Yeshua and eternal life. We must rise to the occasion and offer alcoholics and addicts daily support. Almost every congregation has former alcoholics and addicts in it. These dear brothers and sisters need to start holding daily meetings that offer spiritual, soulish, and physical support for those who still suffer. I hope that Yeshua's ekklesia will do what is right and start supporting the alcoholics and addicts in their struggle. Until this happens, what should the alcoholic or addict do?

If you choose to go to AA for daily support, be careful. Be aware that you are playing with a dangerous snake. This sly snake will try to inject the venom of ecumenism, New Age spirituality, and a false gospel into you. So be on guard, and stay steadfastly submitted to Yeshua and His Word. When you win the battle, leave AA and start a daily meeting in your local assembly so that future alcoholics and addicts will not have to play with a dangerous snake as they struggle to get free. It is my desire to establish *Recovery in Christ* meetings throughout the nation to give Christians the resources and daily support they need to overcome compulsions, obsessions, and addictions. Maybe you could help me fulfill this desire.

[iv] According to Dr. Karl D. Coke, the rabbis say that at age thirteen, Abraham rejected the idols of his father. The rabbis also say that at the age of thirteen, Jacob and Esau went their separate ways, the former to study the Torah and the latter to idol worship. In John 8:56, John says that Abraham rejoiced because he understood that Yah had promised that the Seed would be his offspring. Surely Abraham shared the good news of the Promised Seed with Isaac, and he shared it with Jacob. Thus when Jacob chose to seek Yah at the age of thirteen, he chose to study His teachings and instructions and put his faith in the Promised Seed. Hence, originally, the bar mitzvah was a ceremony in which a boy chose to study the Torah while placing his faith in the Promised Seed, but over the centuries, it became a religious ritual.

Restore! Issue 16, Winter 2000; p. 28, Restoration Foundation, P.O. Box 421218, Atlanta, GA 30342.

[v] In Romans 9, Paul says that Yahweh chooses whom He will show mercy to and whom He will harden. Adam separated man from Yahweh. Man's pride and his drive to be his own elohim to decide between good and evil for himself will not let him submit to Yahweh. The only way that a fallen man can seek Yahweh, submit to Him, and believe His promises is if His Spirit empowers him to do so.

On one hand, Yahweh chose to pour out His grace on Abel, Shem, Japheth, Isaac, and Jacob so that they could seek Him, submit to Him, believe His promises and put their trust in the Promised Seed. On the other hand, Yahweh chose not to pour out His grace on Cain, Ham, Ishmael, and Esau so that they could seek Him, submit to Him, believe His promises, and put their faith in the Promised Seed.

Both Isaac and Ishmael were born with fallen natures, but since Yahweh chose to bring His plan to pass through Isaac, the son of promise, He poured out His grace on him so that he could seek Him, submit to Him, believe His promises, and put his trust in the Promised Seed. However, Yah chose not to pour out His grace on Ishmael. This meant that it was inevitable that his desire to be his own elohim and choose between good and evil would rule him. Hence Ishmael put his trust in the flesh and his own works.

Isaac's ability to believe Yahweh and put his trust in the Spirit to bring the promises to pass was the fruit that Yahweh's election brought forth through the grace it afforded him. Conversely, Ishmael's failure to believe Yahweh and put his trust in the Spirit to bring about the promises was the fruit that his fallen nature produced while separated from the grace that Yah poured out on the elect. Paul says, "So then it is not of him that willeth, nor of him that runneth, but of God that showeth mercy." And, "For whom he did foreknow, he also did predestinate to be conformed to the image of his Son, that he might be the firstborn of many brethren. Moreover whom he did predestinate, them he also called: and whom he called, them he also justified: and whom he justified, them he also glorified" (Rom. 9:16; 8:29–30).

Isaac's faith was the fruit of election, not the root that produced election. Does this negate free will? No, Paul says that Yahweh gives everyone a measure of faith and will save whoever calls upon the name of Yeshua. The mechanism that governs the interaction between Yahweh's election and man's free will is hidden, but this much has been revealed: many are called to salvation, but few are chosen, and Abel, Shem, Isaac, Jacob, and Paul were chosen (Rom. 10:9; 12:3; Matt. 22:14).

[vi] After Adam and Eve fell, the serpent whispered in their ears and told them to gather up fig leaves to make coverings that would hide their sin from Yahweh so that He would fellowship with them. HaSatan took advantage of man's pride and tried to convince him that he could improve himself enough to have a relationship with Yahweh. Essentially, HaSatan inspired man to put together a plan to save himself; that is, HaSatan inspired man to invent religion to improve himself in order to reconcile with Yahweh.

HaSatan's plan was opposed to Yahweh's plan. Yahweh's plan called for man to humble himself and put his faith in Yeshua's righteousness and freely receive His blessings. Hence in every age, HaSatan deceives man into putting a religion together to improve himself so he can have a relationship with Yahweh and earn His blessings. This is what happened with Cain and the people in the land of Nod. This is what happened with Nimrod and the people in Babylon. It is what happened with Ishmael and the people of Israel. It is what happened with Constantine and the Roman Church. It is what happened with Joseph Smith and the people in the Mormon Church. This is what happened with Charles Russell and the people in the Jehovah's Witnesses. It is what happened to Frank Buchman and the people in the Oxford Group. It is what happened with Bill Wilson and the people in Alcoholics Anonymous.

Abram's disobedience caused the Promised Land to be unfruitful. Abram had to turn to the world for provision; that is, he had to go down to Egypt. In Egypt, HaSatan tried to destroy the plan that Yahweh had for Abram's life by corrupting Sarai. Yah stepped in and delivered Sarai so He could keep His promise to Abram. Unfortunately, however, Abram and Sarai came out of Egypt with one of HaSatan's operatives. HaSatan planted an operative in Abram's camp that would give him an inside track to stop Yah from fulfilling His plan. Abram and Sarai came out of Egypt with a beautiful young slave girl named Hagar.

Abram and Sarai waited twenty years for Yahweh to fulfill His promise to give them a son, a great nation and the Seed who would redeem man, restore the earth, and reestablish His kingdom on it. Abram and Sarai got tired and weak, and HaSatan told them to use his operative to bring Yahweh's promise to pass. As Eve had done with Adam, Sarai talked Abram into eating from the Tree of the Knowledge of Good and Evil; that is, she talked him into trusting his senses and logic over Yah's Word. Abram had sex with Hagar, and Ishmael entered the world. Sarai and Abram thought that Ishmael would be the Seed who would build a great nation, redeem man, restore the earth, and reestablish Yahweh's kingdom on it.

In essence, Abram and Sarai thought that they could bring the promised son, the great nation, and the Promised Seed who would redeem man, restore the earth, and reestablish Yahweh's kingdom on it by the works of the flesh; that is, by the works of Abram's penis. The works of the flesh (Abram's penis) seemed to be successful because Ishmael was born. The child grew strong and prospered, and Abram and Sarai were both convinced that he was the promised son. However, when Ishmael was thirteen years old, Yahweh told Abram and Sarai that he was not the promised son. Yahweh renewed His promise and gave Abram and Sarai His Spirit. Yahweh changed their names and told Abram to cut the flesh off the end of his penis, and this became the sign of the covenant of redemption.

Why was circumcision the sign of the covenant? Abram tried to bring the promises forth by the works of his penis, so Yahweh wanted him to cut off the flesh on the end of his penis to remind him that he could not bring redemption, restoration, and the kingdom forth by his works. Every time Abram and his descendants went to the bathroom, their circumcised penises reminded them that their works could not save them, and every time they had sex with their wives, their circumcised penises reminded them that Yah expected them to teach their children that salvation comes by faith through grace and not works.

Circumcision pointed to the fact that Yah would bring forth the Seed who would bring redemption, restoration, and the kingdom forth by His Spirit and not through a man's penis; that is, man's works.

As Yahweh's Spirit implanted Yeshua in Mary's womb without the help of a man's penis, the one that circumcision pointed to and foreshadowed manifested Himself. Yeshua kept the law perfectly, but the Jewish religious rulers turned Him over to the Romans, and they crucified Him. Yahweh's Spirit resurrected Yeshua, and He sent His Spirit to regenerate and live in believers. Yeshua's Spirit circumcises a believer's heart; that is, His Spirit cuts the flesh off the believer's heart so he can obey Him. Circumcision is still the sign of the covenant of redemption, and it still produces the same fruit; that is, obedience to Yahweh.

The sign that Yahweh has redeemed a person is that he obeys His teachings and instructions. Today baptism is the outward sign that the Spirit has circumcised a person's heart, just as physical circumcision was in previous times. However, if a person submits to baptism but does not obey Yahweh's teaching and instructions, the baptism becomes un-baptism (just as disobedience made circumcision un-circumcision), because he did not repent and bow his knee to Yeshua so His Spirit could circumcise his heart. It is no different from what happened to Ishmael. Ishmael submitted to circumcision, but he did not believe Yah and put his faith in His promises, so He did not redeem him.

[vii] The nation of Israel worshiped Yahweh while the other nations worshiped HaSatan, the fallen angels, and demons. The people of the nations (the Gentiles) worshiped many different gods, and whenever they encountered a new god, they would integrate it into their personal pantheon and worship it along with all their other gods. The Gentiles built

temples for their gods and worshiped them by offering animal sacrifices to them to secure their favor. Often the Gentiles strangled the animals, cut their throats, mingled their blood with wine, and drank it. The Gentiles cooked and ate the flesh of the animals in a communal feast at their temples. If there was any meat left, they sold it to the market.

It was normal for parents to abandon infants that they could not afford to raise or offer them to the gods as sacrifices. Some parents gave their infants to priests so that they could raise them to be temple servants. The pagan priests were always on the lookout for infants. A pagan priest would feed and clothe these infants and dedicate them to his god. The children grew up in a temple and were loyal to the priest and the god who "saved" them, and they served him by becoming a temple prostitute. In essence, temple prostitutes were priests or priestesses because they stood between worshipers and their god and united the worshipers to their god in a sexual union. When a worshiper had sex with a temple prostitute, that person became one with the prostitute (who was a priest or priestess) and their god. The Gentiles strangled an animal, offered it to their god, mingled its blood with wine and drank it, ate its flesh, and consummated their union with their god in depraved orgies with the temple prostitutes.

The Pharisees wanted the Gentiles who were coming into their synagogues to prove that they had believed Yahweh and repented from worshiping their pagan gods by submitting to circumcision and keeping the law of Moses. Yah spoke through the Jerusalem Council and decreed that the Gentiles did not have to submit to circumcision or keep the law that He had attached to the written Torah at Sinai.

In the Abrahamic covenant, a circumcised penis was the sign that a man believed Yahweh, repented, and put his faith in the Promised Seed who would come forth by the promise and not by man's works (or by Yahweh's Spirit and not a man's penis) to redeem man, restore the earth, and reestablish the kingdom on it. Yeshua is the Promised Seed; hence circumcision pointed to Him and His finished work.

The council took note of the fact that Yahweh had given the Spirit to the Jews who had submitted to circumcision and kept the law, but He had also given the Spirit to Gentiles who had never submitted to circumcision or kept the law. Yahweh spoke through the council and said that if a Gentile repented and put his faith in Yeshua, then His Spirit would indwell him. Yahweh's Spirit would then circumcise the Gentile's heart, which was the inner reality that the outward sign of circumcision of the penis pointed to. The Gentile's circumcised heart would give him a desire to forsake his former lifestyle and embrace the written Torah, which would show him how to live a blessed life and love Yahweh and his neighbor.

Yeshua's Spirit in a Gentile fulfilled the requirements of circumcision and the law. Thus a Gentile did not have to circumcise his penis or keep the law. A Gentile had to prove that his faith was real by forsaking his former lifestyle and living by a few principles in the Torah *so he could attend the Sabbath services and learn the rest of it.* The council told the

Gentiles to abstain from the pollutions of idols, fornication, things strangled, and blood. In other words, the Gentiles had to forsake everything associated with the worship of pagan gods and turn to Yahweh with their whole heart and learn His ways. This would prove that they had repented and put their faith in Yeshua and that He had circumcised their heart, which is the sign of the covenant. After the Gentiles had professed faith in Yeshua, they submitted to baptism, but this did not prove that they had entered the covenant. The proof that a Gentile had really entered the covenant was a circumcised heart that manifested itself in a changed life and a desire to learn the Torah.

[viii] The apostate sages taught that the Jews represented Isaac and the Gentiles represented Ishmael. These apostates boasted that they (the Jews) would inherit the promises and the Gentiles would not. The apostates said that the Gentiles had to submit to circumcision and follow their rules, regulations, and laws to obtain Jewish legal status (become a Jew). When a Gentile obtained Jewish legal status, then he would inherit the promises. Paul takes their teaching and turns it around on them in order to teach the truth; that is, what the Torah really says.

In Galatians 4, Paul says that Abraham had two sons, Ishmael by a bondwoman and Isaac by a free woman. Paul says that the son who came through the bondwoman had been born by *flesh*, and the son who came through the freewoman had been born by *promise*. In verse 25, Paul says that Hagar (the bondwoman) represents the covenant that Yahweh cut at Mount Sinai "*and answereth to Jerusalem which now is, and is in bondage with her children*". It is important to note that Paul equates Hagar with the Mosaic covenant that the apostate sages in Jerusalem had corrupted, not with the Mosaic covenant itself.

Paul contrasts this perverted version of the Mosaic covenant (the earthly Jerusalem) with the heavenly Jerusalem, which is free from the perversion of the sages and their desire for position, power, wealth, and control. Yahweh cut the covenant of redemption with Abraham, and Abraham knew that he would inherit a city that Yahweh built. Abraham searched for a city whose maker was Yahweh and not man; that is, he searched for the heavenly Jerusalem during his earthly journeys. Therefore, the apostle Paul was contrasting the perverted version of the Mosaic covenant with the Abrahamic covenant.

Gentile commentators say that Paul was contrasting the Mosaic covenant with the new covenant. These people say that the Mosaic covenant held everyone in bondage and that the new covenant sets everyone free from this bondage. These prideful people say the Torah will bring us into bondage if we have anything to do with it, so it is our Christian duty to disregard the Torah. This is absurd. The only Scripture that the first Christians had was the Torah, the Prophets, and the Writings. Do you really think that the apostle Paul would have told Yahweh's people to disregard the only Scripture in existence?

[ix] In the Garden of Eden, Yahweh announced His plan to send the Seed. Yahweh warned that there would be enmity between the Seed of the woman and the seed of the serpent. We see this enmity between Cain and Abel. We see it between the sons of Cain and the sons of Seth. The sons of Seth called upon Yahweh and obeyed His Torah (His teachings and instructions), but the sons of Cain ignored His Torah (His teachings and instructions) and built a city. In other words, the sons of Cain invented a religion that used a political system and an economic system to keep the people of Nod comfortably separated from Yahweh so that they would not repent and put their trust in the Promised Seed.

The sons of Seth fell away from the faith and moved into Cain's city to live with the wicked. The fallen angels mixed their DNA with man's DNA, and man became exceedingly wicked. Yah destroyed man and started over with Noah and his family. After this, we see enmity between Ham and Shem/Japheth. We see it between Nimrod and the righteous remnant of Shem's line. Nimrod used the threat of violence and the promise of peace and prosperity to pull everyone together on the plains of Shinar. Nimrod and his people built the Tower of Babel. Nimrod and his wife put a counterfeit of Yahweh's plan together in which a counterfeit Messiah (anti-Messiah) named Tammuz built a kingdom around this false religion with a political system and economic system that kept people comfortably separated from Yahweh so that they would not repent. In His great mercy, Yahweh confused their speech and scattered these people to the ends of the earth.

Then darkness covered the whole earth. Later Yah turned on the light by calling Abram. Abraham and his sons founded the nation of Israel. Israel was Yah's light that was supposed to shine into the darkness and draw the nations to the light. We see the enmity between Abraham's sons and the Canaanites. We see it between the northern kingdom of Israel and the southern kingdom of Judah. We see it between the apostate sages and the righteous remnant of the ekklesia of Moses. We see it between the apostate sages and Yeshua's ekklesia. We see it between Rome and Yeshua's ekklesia.

The conflict between the seeds fully manifested in the tension between the Roman emperor and Yeshua. The emperors rebuilt the Tower of Babel and reintroduced the religion of Cain with its anti-Messiah. Like Nimrod and Tammuz, the emperor claimed to be the son of God, lord, and great high priest who would bring all the nations of the earth into his great city (Rome) and give them peace and prosperity.

Yeshua is the Son of God, Lord, and Great High Priest who will establish His kingdom on the earth and bring all the nations into His city (the New Jerusalem). Do you see why it would have been dangerous for a person in the Roman Empire to preach Yeshua and His kingdom? The emperors viewed people who encouraged others to believe in their heart that Yeshua was Messiah and to confess Him as Lord as treasonous criminals who were weakening the empire. The people in Rome were afraid to preach the gospel of Yeshua. This prompted the apostle Paul to write, "For I am not ashamed of the gospel." The Roman emperors were anti-Messiahs who were types and shadows of the final anti-Messiah. A person who lived in the Roman Empire had to choose who was going to be his god, lord, and high priest and which kingdom and city he would be loyal to: Rome or the New Jerusalem. The Emperor and the Empire morphed into the Pope and the Roman Catholic Church, and the persecution of the saints continues to this day. Today we face the same choice: will the Pope (Emperor) be our lord and great high priest or will Yeshua, and will we be loyal to Rome (Babylon) or the New Jerusalem. This gives us insight into why the Romans persecuted and killed the saints. It also establishes the proper context for Romans.

The serpent's seed—Cain, Cain's sons, Ham, Nimrod, Tammuz, the leaders of the northern kingdom of Israel, the apostate sages, and the Roman Catholic Church—tried to destroy the woman's seed—Abel, the sons of Seth, Shem, Japheth, Abraham, the leaders of the southern kingdom of Judah, the righteous remnant of the ekklesia of Moses, and Yeshua's Ekklesia. The serpent's seed could not snuff out the woman's seed, however, because Yahweh always preserves a remnant of the woman's seed so that He can keep His promise to Eve. Faces, names, and titles change, but the conflict between the seeds does not.

[x] Early this morning, I received a daily devotional by e-mail from a respected international Christian ministry. The devotional said that in Galatians 4:24, "Paul is saying that the ancient conflict between Abraham's wives, Hagar and Sarah (the mothers of Ishmael and Isaac, respectively), was a spiritual allegory, depicting the conflict between law and grace." I respect this ministry and enjoy their daily e-mails, but unfortunately, this morning's message was in error because it reflects the Gentile mind-set that the Mosaic covenant with its law was the polar opposite of the new covenant with its grace.

The new covenant is a renewed covenant. It is the renewal and the transformation of the Mosaic covenant. The new covenant and the Mosaic covenant are covenants of sanctification. Yahweh designed these covenants to accomplish the same things. Yah cut these covenants to sanctify His people; that is, to turn them away from HaSatan and his kingdom and turn them towards His kingdom. In each covenant, Yah's people blessed themselves or cursed themselves by their actions. In each, Yah forgave and cleansed His people when they disobeyed Him. In each, Yah empowered His people to reach the people in HaSatan's kingdom. So how can these two covenants be polar opposites?

The Mosaic covenant failed to empower people so that they could obey Yahweh and accomplish their mission of reaching the lost. It failed because of man's weakness. Yah put the Mosaic covenant in place as a temporary agent of sanctification that exposed man's weakness (his fallen nature) and pointed him towards the remedy (the Seed). Yah left the Mosaic covenant in place until Yeshua died. Around AD 60, the writer of Hebrews warned that the temple and the Levitical priesthood were passing away; hence the Mosaic covenant as people knew it was passing away. In AD 70, the Romans destroyed the temple, and the priesthood could not function; hence the Mosaic covenant passed into history.

After Yeshua's resurrection, the Holy Spirit transformed the Mosaic covenant into the new covenant. As a person bows his knee to Yeshua, His Spirit baptizes him into His body and puts him to death. Yeshua's Spirit resurrects this person and joins Himself to him; thus the weak link that caused the Mosaic covenant to fail is gone. In the new covenant, Yah blesses His people with all spiritual blessing in Messiah. If Yahweh's people disobey Him, all they have to do is confess their sins and cleanse their conscience. Yah does not curse His people when they disobey Him, but when they disobey Him, they open themselves to the curses. In the new covenant, Yah's Spirit sanctifies us and gives us the ability to obey Him so that we can live a blessed life and reach the people who are still in HaSatan's kingdom.

The new covenant and the Mosaic covenant accomplish the same things, but the new covenant is more effective than the Mosaic covenant because it eliminates man's fallen spiritual nature. The Mosaic covenant does not oppose the new covenant, and they are not polar opposites. Yeshua's Spirit fulfills the law and transforms it into a more usable form to empower us to turn away from HaSatan and turn to Yah to live a blessed life while accomplishing the mission of reaching the lost. There is no conflict between law and grace; grace fulfills the law and reveals the things that Yahweh hid in its shadows.

The presupposition that there was a conflict between law and grace is invalid. The sages were in control of the earthly Jerusalem, and they perverted the covenant that Yahweh cut at Mount Sinai. Thus Hagar represents the sages' religion that gives birth to Ishmaels (children of the flesh). Sarah represents the Abrahamic covenant or the New Jerusalem, which gives birth to Isaacs (children of promise). The conflict was not between law and grace; the conflict was between the sages' religion and Abraham's faith.

[xi] In the older covenants, a person had to believe Yahweh and put his faith in His promises in order to enter the covenant of redemption, and then he had to submit to circumcision, which served as a constant *reminder* that he had to cut off his fleshly desires and obey Yahweh's Spirit and Torah (teachings and instructions). In the new covenant, a person has to believe Yahweh and put his faith in Yeshua in order to enter the covenant of redemption, and then Yeshua circumcises his heart, which *empowers* him to cut off his fleshly desires and obey Yah's Spirit and Torah (teaching and instructions). A person with a circumcised heart will submit to its desires and allow Yahweh to change his life. In both the older covenants and the new covenant, Yah requires His people to submit to circumcision, which is the sign of the covenant.

[xii] In volume 3, I will explain in detail how Yahweh destroys the "body of sin" and re-creates us in the original configuration, and empowers us to recover from our compulsions, obsessions, and addictions. I will walk you through the steps that we have to take in order to break free of the residual effects of the body of sin and live the abundant life. This is the bottom line on recovery: recovery is the process of transitioning from the body of sin

(p. 409) back to the original configuration (p. 408) and learning how to rise above the residual effects of the body of sin and function in the original configuration.

[xiii] Gentile commentators split the Torah into sections by categorizing its commands. They split the Torah's commands into the following categories: moral, ritual, sacrificial, ceremonial, and civil. They say that Yeshua fulfilled the ritual, sacrificial, and ceremonial commandments and released us from them. Therefore, we can ignore the ritual, sacrificial, and ceremonial commands, which include the commands that pertain to Yahweh's feasts, the Sabbath, the dietary guidelines, the cutting or marking of our bodies, and many others. They say that the moral commandments are the only commandments that apply to us. Did Yeshua not fulfill the moral commandments? Yes, Yeshua lived a sinless life, so He fulfilled the moral commandments too. So why did Yeshua not release us from the moral commandments also?

Yahweh is the Father, the Son, and the Holy Spirit, but He is one. Yeshua is the Torah in human flesh. Yeshua is Yahweh in human flesh. Thus the Torah is one. Yahweh did not split His commandments into civil, ritual, sacrificial, ceremonial, and moral categories. Thus we have no right to split His Torah into categories and decide which commandments apply to us and which commandments do not apply to us.

All of Yahweh's commands apply to His people. Yah gave Israel (the Hebrews and Gentiles who came out of Egypt) the Torah, and they said they would obey it. Yah gave the commands to turn His people away from sin and show them how to live the abundant life. He also gave the commands to sanctify His people (set His people apart from the world) so that they could attract the people of the world into His covenants. Most importantly, Yahweh gave the commands so He could forgive His people and cleanse them of their unrighteousness as they failed so that He could have a relationship with them without setting aside His righteousness, because there is no way that He could set His righteousness aside.

Today there is no temple or priesthood, so there are no sacrifices. Moreover, we do not live in an earthly kingdom of Yahweh. Therefore, it is impossible to keep the commandments that pertain to the government of the kingdom (the civil commandments). These commands still apply to us, but it is impossible for us to keep them. This means that Yeshua's Spirit keeps them in us. Yeshua's Spirit establishes the Kingdom in us, and He sets up His Temple in our body. Yeshua's Spirit serves as the High Priest of His Temple, and He sets us apart as priests. In addition, Yeshua was the perfect sacrifice, and so His Spirit fulfills all the sacrificial requirements in us. The commandments that do not pertain to the temple, priesthood, sacrifices, or kingdom government also still apply to us. This means that if it is possible for us to keep one of these commandments, we should keep it because Yahweh gives His commandments to bless and protect us.

Invariably, when a person says that he does not eat anything that Yahweh did not sanctify as food, someone will say, "Well, you are not supposed to trim the edges of your beard, get a tattoo, plant two kinds of seeds in the same field, wear garments with two kinds of fabric, or touch a football either." This is true. The Torah does say these things. Here is the principle: Yahweh knows things that we do not know, and He gives us commands to protect us from things that may or may not be apparent to us. With this in mind, let us look at these seemingly strange and outdated commandments one at a time.

Egyptian priests trimmed the edges of their beards and squared them off for religious purposes. Perhaps these pagan priests did this to attract their gods, propitiate their gods, or for some other reason. Whatever the reason, Yahweh did not want to be associated with this practice, so He told His priests not to trim the edges of their beards. Peter says that we are priests. Therefore, we should not square our beards, if we have them, because Yahweh does not want us to be associated with pagan gods.

Pagan priests also tattooed themselves for religious purposes. Yahweh does not want His people to tattoo themselves because He does not want to be associated with pagan practices. Yahweh could also be trying to protect our health. Moreover, since Yah said that He places a mark on His people and the anti-Messiah places a mark on his people, there may be a spiritual reason behind this commandment.

Dr. William Sudduth wrote *What's Behind the Ink?* In his book, Dr. Sudduth outlines his research into the origins of tattoos and their spiritual ramifications. In his research, Dr. Sudduth found that tattoos originated from bloodletting rituals that served spiritual purposes. His research proves that HaSatan has tricked every culture on earth into giving him worship and glory through tattoos. Cultures were doing this in Moses' day, so Yahweh told His people not to tattoo themselves. When we disobey Yahweh, we glorify HaSatan with our bodies and defile the temple of the Holy Spirit that Yeshua purchased with His own blood. Dr. Sudduth says that tattoos identify us as slaves and invite demons to enslave us.

(If you already have a tattoo, do not condemn yourself or let anyone else condemn you. Simply confess your disobedience as sin, rebuke the demons that you invited into your life, and ask for Yah's protection.)

Recently a group of scientists in Israel studied some wild wheat plants that farmers had never planted with any other crop and compared them to domesticated wheat that farmers had mixed with other crops. The wild wheat was stronger and more disease resistant than the domesticated wheat. So if you want strong, disease-resistant wheat, obey the Torah and never plant it with barley, cotton, or soybeans.

According to Nobel Prize–winning Dr. Otto Heinrich Warburg, everything has an atomic signature frequency. Linen and wool have signature frequencies of five thousand. These atomic signature frequencies promote health and well-being in the human body. However, because of their phase relationship, when we mix linen and wool their frequencies cancel out and can be harmful to the human body. Moreover, when two dissimilar metals touch each other, a tiny electrical current flows through them. Is it possible that a similar atomic phenomenon occurs when we mix fabrics and that it is harmful to our bodies? Yes, it is possible.

Yahweh commands His people not to eat pigs, and He says not to touch their carcasses. Pigs will eat anything, even their own offspring. Pigs are scavengers and garbage collectors. Pigs cannot process the toxins and poisons that they eat, so they build up in their flesh. If we eat pig, we eat the toxins and poisons in them. This puts a toxic load on our bodies and creates inflammation, which results in disease over the long haul. The Torah commands us not to touch the carcass of a pig. Why? Is it possible that some of the toxins and poisons maybe transferred to us transdermally? Yes, it is possible. A football is made out of pigskin, so if you do not want to be transdermally contaminated, do not touch a football.

Yahweh is not a despotic ruler who gives His people commandments for no reason. There is a reason for every commandment. We may not be able to discern the reason, but there is a reason. Thus, if it is possible for us to keep a command, then we should keep it or keep the principle behind it. Remember, if we do not keep the commandments, it will not affect our judicial position, but it will affect our lives.

[xiv] The human spirit flows through the brain to manifest its thoughts, intents, and will on the earth. As the human spirit flows through the brain, it causes neurons to fire. The neurons that fire together wire together and form electrochemical pathways in the brain. The electrochemical pathways in the limbic system (emotional system) interact with the hypothalamus (the brain of the glandular system, or endocrine system) and burn electrochemical pathways in the endocrine system (glandular system) and nervous system. These electrochemical pathways program our brains and bodies to perceive, react, and respond in certain ways and set up homeostatic imbalances that make us crave certain things. When we give our brains and bodies what they want, their systems release powerful neurotransmitters and hormones that make us feel good. Hence these perceptions, reactions, responses, and cravings are self-reinforcing, which means they exert a great deal of control over us, and they are resistant to change.

[xv] The Jerusalem Council issued a decree to the Gentiles who were entering Yeshua's ekklesia. The decree commanded Gentiles not to eat meat from pagan temples in order to demonstrate that they had truly repented from paganism and joined themselves to Yahweh. Much of the meat that the local markets sold came from pagan temples, so when a brother or sister purchased meat from the local market, it troubled the weak Gentiles who had just repented. The weak Gentiles did not want to eat meat because there was a strong possibility that it came from a pagan temple, and abstaining from meat that came from pagan temples demonstrated their repentance; that is, their commitment to Yahweh. So the weak Gentiles ate only vegetables, and they thought that everyone else should eat only vegetables.

[xvi] These verses have nothing to do with Yahweh's instructions in Leviticus that tell His people what animals He permits them to eat and what animals He *forbids* them to eat; that is, the kosher laws. These verses pertain to another set of laws that pertained only to the temple and those who worked in it and visited it: the ritual laws of "pure" and "impure," or "clean" and "unclean."

If a person had a discharge, skin condition, or touched a corpse, he was impure; that is, he was not fit to enter the temple where Yahweh's presence dwelt amongst the holy things (the sanctified things). This did not mean that the person's body was impure or that he had committed a sin; it simply meant that he was in a *state* that was not compatible with Yahweh's presence and His holy things. Once the impure person went through a ritual cleansing, then he was pure and could enter the temple complex.

The Pharisees interpreted the laws of pure and impure and extended them to *everyone in Israel*. The Pharisees said that everyone had to follow their interpretations of the laws of pure and impure at all times. They said that if permitted meat (kosher meat) touched forbidden meat (unkosher meat), then the permitted meat became impure; and if a person ate it, he would be impure. They said if a Gentile touched the meat, then it was impure; and if a person ate it, he would be impure. The Pharisees said that if a Gentile touched a Jew's (a righteous person's) pots or pans, then the pots or pans were impure; and if a Jew (a righteous person) ate with these pots or pans, he would be impure. They also said that if your hands touched a Gentile or something that a Gentile had touched, then your hands were impure; and if you ate without following their hand-washing procedure, you were impure. This meant that you had to go through the cleansing rituals even though you were not a Priest or someone who was planning to enter the temple complex.

What is this system of pure and impure? Well, think of it this way: No one should put a toilet in his kitchen or in a space that connects to it because the act of defecating is not compatible with the act of eating. It is not a sin to put a toilet in your kitchen, but it will hinder your ability to enjoy your meal. In the same way, it was not a sin or a moral trespass when something came out of a person's body to put him in an impure state. It was just that his impure state *prevented him from entering the temple to fulfill his priestly duties or worship Yahweh amongst the holy things*.

The Pharisees said that if a person's body was impure, then he had to submit to the cleansing rituals to purify his body and *be right with Yahweh*. Now, as you will recall, keeping the oral Torah and the halachah affected a person's legal status, which affected his position in the covenant and in the next age. So disobeying the Pharisees' teaching and instructions had grave consequences. The Pharisees' teachings and instructions said that eating kosher food that had become impure was a sin, or a moral trespass, that defiled the body. Therefore, the Pharisees redefined sin and put a heavy burden on the people's backs so they could control their lives.

In Mark 7, Yeshua rebuked the Pharisees for this and told His disciples that nothing that enters into a person's body can defile him (take him out of right standing with Yahweh). Yeshua said that the things that come out of a person's body are what defile him (take him out of right standing with Yahweh). In other words, Yeshua said that sinful words and actions are what defile a person (take him out of right standing with Yahweh).

In the new covenant, Yahweh set up His temple in our body. Yahweh becomes one with our spirit so that He can live in our body with us. Yeshua embodied the cleansing rituals that the law called for. *(This is how He could touch a leper or a dead body and not enter into an impure state. And remember, it was not a sin.)* Yeshua's Spirit lives in us, and He implements the cleansing rituals in us continually. Hence we do not enter a ritually impure state that prohibits us from fellowshiping with Yahweh. This means that all things are pure; that is, nothing that goes into the body or comes out of it can make us impure. Now this does not mean that we can eat the animals that Yah forbids His people to eat. This has nothing to do with the kosher laws. If we eat the things that Yah forbids, we sin, and sin has consequences.

The only thing that can hinder our relationship with Yahweh is rebellion and deliberate disobedience. If we were to go to a pagan temple and eat their sacrifices with the motive of worshiping their gods, this would hinder our fellowship with Yahweh. If we were to knowingly eat meat from pagan temples and did so in front of our weaker brothers without regard for their welfare, this would hinder our fellowship with Yah. If we know that we are not supposed to eat nonkosher foods and we do it anyway, this will hinder our fellowship with Yah. Yahweh weighs the motives behind our actions, not merely our actions.

[xvii] From http://reluctant-messenger.com/didache.htm. [03/2011]

The Didache is, in all probability, the oldest surviving extant piece of noncanonical literature. It is not so much a letter as a handbook for new Christian converts, consisting of instructions derived directly from the teachings of Jesus. The book can be divided into three sections. The first six chapters consist of Christian lessons; the next four give descriptions of the Christian ceremonies, including baptism, fasting and communion; and the last six outline the church organization.

The Didache claims to have been authored by the twelve apostles. While this is unlikely, the work could be a direct result of the first Apostolic Council, c.50 C.E. (Acts 15:28). Similarities to the Apostolic Decree are apparent, and the given structure of the church is quite primitive. Also, the description of the Eucharist (bread and wine) carefully avoids mention of the "body and blood of Christ," obviously being regarded as one of the secret mysteries of early Christianity.

Most scholars agree that the work, in its earliest form, may have circulated as early as the 60's C.E., though additions and modifications may have taken place well into the third century. The work was never officially rejected by the Church, but was excluded from the canon for its lack of literary value.

The complete text of the Didache was discovered in the Codex Hierosolymitanus, though a number of fragments exist, most notably in the Oxyrhynchus Papyri. It was originally composed in Greek, probably within a small community. This is what the Didache says about fasting. "But do not let your fasts be with the hypocrites. For they fast on the second day of the week and on the fifth. But you fast on the fourth day and the day of preparation."

[xviii] In 1 Corinthians 6:12–14, Paul says, "All things are lawful unto me, but all things are not expedient: all things are lawful for me, but I will not be brought under the power of any. Meats for the belly, and the belly for meats: but God shall destroy both it and them. Now the body is not for fornication, but for the Lord; and the Lord for the body. And God hath both raised up the Lord, and will also raise up us by his own power." In 1 Corinthians 10:23, Paul says, "All things are lawful for me, but all things are not expedient: all things are lawful for me, but all things edify not." However, in Matthew 5:17, Yeshua says, "Think not that I am come to destroy the law, or the prophets: I am not come to destroy, but to fulfill."

In Hebrew thought, to destroy the Torah and its law would mean to interpret, explain, and apply it in a way that results in it having little or no impact on our lives so that we could set it aside altogether. This is why Yeshua tells us that He did not come to die to pay our sin debt, rise from the dead to sit at the right hand of the Father, and return in the Spirit to live in us so that we could disregard the Torah (Matt. 5:17).

It looks as if the apostle Paul is at odds with Yeshua! Yeshua says the Torah and its law still apply to us, but Paul says they do not. If Paul is saying that all things are lawful for us, then the Torah and its law lose their impact on our lives. I mean, if all things are lawful for us, then the Torah and its law become irrelevant religious artifacts that Yeshua freed us from through His death, resurrection, ascension, and spiritual indwelling. However, we know that Paul would never contradict or oppose his Lord. So what in the world is Paul trying to communicate to the people in Corinth in 1 Corinthians 6:12–14 and 10:23?

In Dr. Skip Moen's Hebrew word study "Today's Word" for July 28, 2010, he points out that there were no quotation marks in the Greek language and that "All things are lawful for me" are not Paul's words, but a phrase that was used by the people he was correcting. Dr. Moen's view is corroborated by the following theologians: D. A. Carson in the *New Bible Commentary: 21st Century Edition*; W. W. Wiersbe in *Wiersbe's Expository Outlines on the New Testament*; R. B. Hughes and J. C. Laney in the *Tyndale Concise Bible Commentary*;

F. H. Paschall and H. H. Hobbs in *The Teacher's Bible Commentary*; R. L. Pratt, Jr. in the *Holman New Testament Commentary*; John F. Walvoord, Roy B. Zuck, and the Dallas Theological Seminary in *The Bible Knowledge Commentary;* and H. D. M. Spence in *The Pulpit Commentary on First Corinthians.*

Let us look at the historical-cultural context of Paul's statements in 1 Corinthians 6:12–14 and 10:23. The city of Corinth was on a narrow isthmus that was an important crossroad in the ancient world. In the city of Corinth, a person could find goods from any nation on the earth. Moreover, Corinth was a melting pot, so its citizens came from every nation on the earth. Hence the beliefs in this city were extremely diverse, and temples sprang up to accommodate each of these beliefs. Unfortunately, however, this cultivated a spirit of tolerance in the city of Corinth that infected Yeshua's ekklesia.

In the city of Corinth, the pagans held feasts that were religious, political, and social events. Some of Yeshua's disciples who were socialites did not want to seem judgmental or intolerant, so they took part in these feasts. These disciples rejected the religious aspect of these pagan feasts and attended them as political and social events. However, they were eating meat and drinking wine that the pagans had sacrificed and offered to their gods to propitiate them. What is worse, these fleshly disciples were getting drunk and participating in the wild orgies with the satanic temple prostitutes! Conveniently, the disciples who were engaging in these debased activities justified their sinful behavior by coining the following phrases: "All things are lawful for me" and "Meats for the belly, and the belly for meats."

In his letter to the Corinthian believers, Paul was correcting the fleshly people who were using these phrases to justify their sin. However, we do not see this, because there are no quotation marks in the Greek language. Moreover, these two phrases were so well known by Paul's target audience that he did not feel compelled to write something like "you say" in order to identify the phrases as quotations. Consequently, when we read Paul's statement, we get the mistaken idea that he is teaching that Yeshua released us from the written Torah and its law, and we can eat what we want to eat and have sex with whomever we want to have sex with, because, after all, we aren't under the law, but under grace.

Let us take a closer look at what Paul said or, better yet, what he did not say.

The New Living Translation of 1 Corinthians 6:12–14 says, "You say, 'I am allowed to do anything'—but not everything is good for you. And even though 'I am allowed to do anything,' I must not become a slave to anything. You say, 'Food was made for the stomach, and the stomach for food.' (This is true, though someday God will do away with both of them.) But you can't say that our bodies were made for sexual immorality. They were made for the Lord, and the Lord cares about our bodies. And God will raise us from the dead by his power, just as he raised our Lord from the dead."

The NET Bible translates 1 Corinthians 6:12–14 as follows: " 'All things are lawful for me'—but not everything is beneficial. 'All things are lawful for me'—but I will not be controlled by anything. 'Food is for the stomach and the stomach is for food,' but God will do away with both. The body is not for sexual immorality, but for the Lord, and the Lord for the body. Now God indeed raised the Lord and he will raise us by his power."

The Complete Jewish Bible translates 1 Corinthians 6:12–14 as, "You say, 'For me, everything is permitted'? Maybe, but not everything is helpful. 'For me, everything is permitted'? Maybe, but as far as I am concerned, I am not going to let anything gain control over me. 'Food is meant for the stomach and the stomach for food'? Maybe, but God will put an end to both of them. Anyhow, the body is not meant for sexual immorality but for the Lord, and the Lord is for the body. God raised up the Lord, and he will raise us up too by his power."

In these three translations, we can see that the apostle Paul was correcting the people who were using the two popular phrases to justify their behaviors. Essentially, Paul says, "Okay, you say that all things are lawful for you—but I say that all things are not beneficial. You say that all things are lawful for you—but I refuse to be brought into bondage. You say that meats are for the belly, and the belly is for meats—but I say that God will destroy both the belly and the meats."

In Romans 6:15, Paul asks us if we should transgress the Torah and break the law that once bound us to Yah, since we are no longer bound to Him by that law and are not subject to its condemnation and curses, but are bound to Him by the grace that the death, resurrection, ascension, indwelling, and intercession of Yeshua bring. Paul answers this rhetorical question by saying, "God forbid."

Paul goes on to explain why we should obey the Torah and not break the law. In Romans 6:16, Paul says, "Know ye not, that to whomever you yield yourselves servants to obey, his servants you are to whom you obey; whether of sin [transgression of the Torah] unto death [poverty, lack, sickness, disease, addiction, compulsions, obsessions, and physical death] or of obedience [to the Torah] unto righteousness [peace, wholeness, prosperity, health, freedom and a long life]." In Romans 7:12–13, Paul says that the Torah and its law are holy, just, and good, and they reveal the sin that is working to bring about death in us.

In 1 Corinthians 6:12, Paul is saying that Yeshua has set us free from the penalties that the Mosaic law imposed upon saints for violating the Torah. However, if a saint violates the Torah, in the end it will not be beneficial for him or edify him because it will bring him into bondage. In other words, if we sin, we will submit to the bondage of poverty, lack, sickness, disease, addiction, compulsion, obsession, or death. This makes sense when we realize that the Torah is a fence that sets the boundaries we must live in, in order to experience the abundant life, and if we step over the fence and stray into HaSatan's territory, we submit to him and authorize him to bring bondage, destruction, and death into our lives.

In 1 Corinthians 6:13, Paul counters the second phrase. The great philosopher Plato taught that a person should give the body the things that it craves because once it dies and releases the spirit, it will never live again. Other prominent philosophers of that time taught that God would not have given the body desires if He did not intend for them to be fulfilled, and these two lines of reasoning culminated in a philosophy that was summed up by the phrase "meats for the belly, and the belly for meats." On page 451 of his *Jewish New Testament Commentary*, David Stern says that the people who were using these phrases were promoting philosophies that the Gnostic libertines would later systematize.

In *Spirit Wars* (p. 235), Dr. Peter Jones says that the Gnostics believed that the material realm was evil and the spirit realm was good. They also believed that man's body imprisoned his spirit, and when his body died, the spirit won a great victory. The Gnostic libertines were a group of believers who adopted this line of reasoning and said their spirits were hermetically "sealed" by the Holy Spirit, so they could give their bodies what they desired without suffering any spiritual consequences. As Stern points out, the phrase "meats for the belly and the belly for meats" was roughly equivalent to "if it feels good, do it."

In 1 Corinthians 6:13–14, Paul says, in effect, "Okay, you say that meat is for the belly, and the belly is for meat (Yah made the body, and it craves meat; therefore, we should glorify Him by enjoying all meats). But I tell you that God will destroy the belly and the meat it craves and prove that He is sovereign over both man and nature, so we are not indebted to the body and its desires. Yeshua purchased our spirit, soul, and body with His blood, so we are indebted to Him and should follow His Spirit as He leads us to do the things that please Him, which is obeying His Father's commands. I tell you that the body is not for fornication, but for the Lord; and the Lord is for the body. Just as Yahweh has resurrected Yeshua's body, He will also raise our bodies; so do not be deceived by Plato's philosophy, but rather obey Yah."

Paul was not a lawless person, and he did not encourage us to be lawless. To the contrary, in 2 Thessalonians 2:7, Paul warned that the mystery of lawlessness was already at work preparing the way for the lawless one. The lawless one will deceive and destroy those who follow him. Paul encourages us to yield to the promptings of the Holy Spirit as He seeks to restrain us and bring us into obedience to the law of Messiah, which fulfills the intent of the Mosaic law. Paul expects us to be led by the Spirit, which ensures that we do the Father's will and remain safe and secure in the boundaries of the Torah, where we can live the abundant life. Paul is not opposing or canceling Yahweh's dietary guidelines that protect His people from eating scavengers, garbage collectors, and other unbeneficial animals.

Yahweh created everything and said that it was good, but then man rebelled and introduced disorder, corruption, and death into the world. After the fall, the natural order was corrupted. Some of the animals began to eat garbage and the dead, diseased, rotting corpses of men, women, and animals.

As they did, they assimilated death into their flesh because Yahweh did not design their digestive systems to purify and expel the toxins that are in decaying corpses and garbage. If we eat these animals, we will assimilate death into our bodies also.

We see this principle at work in mad cow disease. Yahweh said the cow was fit to eat because the fall did not corrupt its behavior. As He did for all other animals, Yahweh designed cows to eat plants, and for whatever reason, the disorder that fell upon the earth did not corrupt their instincts and cause them to eat rotting flesh. However, man started feeding cows the remains of other cows in the form of meat and bone meal (MBM). Since their digestive systems were not designed to remove the toxins that are found in the MBM, these toxins got into their bloodstream and damaged their brain, causing blindness, loss of muscle control, and death. Then, when men and women ate the flesh of these cows, they developed neurological disorders and died too.

In the sense that Yahweh will not condemn us and put the curses prescribed in the Mosaic law on us for violating the Torah, all things are lawful for us. However, in the end, violating the Torah will not prove to be beneficial or edifying for us. For example, if we violate the Torah's dietary guidelines and eat things that are not food, we will assimilate toxins and poisons into our bodies and open ourselves up to the bondage of sickness and disease, which could lead to financial bondage and premature death.

In sum, Yahweh has crucified us "in Messiah" *and* resurrected us "in Him." The actions and activities of Yeshua's indwelling Spirit, along with His continual intercession for us, are conforming us to His image. Thus we have died to the penalties that Yah prescribed in the Mosaic law for transgressing the Torah. If we eat things that the Torah does not allow, which are not beneficial, edifying, or conducive to the abundant life, Yah will not condemn us and curse us, but we will open ourselves up to HaSatan so that he can.

So, like the Corinthian believers, we can choose to shut one theological eye while examining the Scriptures and see only one dimension of the truth, that "all things are lawful for us," or we can open both theological eyes while examining the Scriptures and see all the dimensions of this important truth.

When we open both theological eyes, we see that technically "all things are lawful for us," because the Mosaic law is no longer our custodian and no longer criminalizes sin and punishes it. However, we prohibit the things the Torah prohibits and allow the things it allows because Yeshua shed His blood for us and sent His Spirit to live in our hearts in order to empower us to obey Him. As we obey Yahweh, we keep the law of Messiah, which is the royal law of love, which fulfills the intent of the Mosaic law.

[xix] In Hebrews 7:12, Yahweh says, "For the priesthood being changed, there is made of necessity a change in the law." In Matthew 5:17–18, Yahweh says, "Think not that I am come to destroy the law, or the prophets: I am not come to destroy, but to fulfill. For verily I say unto you, till heaven and earth pass, one jot or one tittle shall in no wise pass from the law, till all be fulfilled." Is Yahweh confused? No, Yahweh is telling us that the change in the law is not in its content; it is in how He administers it. In the *Complete Jewish Bible*,

David Stern translates Hebrews 7:12 this way: "For if the system of *cohanim* [the priests] is transformed, there must of necessity occur a transformation of Torah."

In the *Jewish New Testament Commentary*, Stern says, "The context makes it overwhelmingly clear that no change or transformation in Torah is envisioned other than in connection with the priesthood and the sacrificial system. The term '*metathesis*' implies retention of the basic structure of Torah, with some of its elements rearranged ('transformed'); it does not imply abrogation of either the Torah as a whole or of the mitzvot not connected with the priesthood and the sacrificial system." Yeshua embodied the priesthood and sacrifices and sent His Spirit to live in us in order to meet the requirements of the law and fulfill its intent in us. This is the change in the law.

xx The word *fulfill* means "to fill full." When Yeshua said He came to fulfill the Torah (and its law), He was saying that He came to fill the Torah (and its law) full of meaning; that is, Yeshua came to reveal the true meaning of the Torah (and its law) by revealing the spirit behind the letter. A person could keep the letter of the Torah and not be right with Yahweh because he was violating the spirit of the Torah.

For example, the Torah says that Yahweh's people were to give Him 10 percent of the plants they grew and animals they raised for food in order to support the temple and its priests. The Pharisees were giving Yah's colaborers 10 percent of everything they grew and raised, right down to the herbs they grew on their windowsills. The Pharisees, however, were not in right standing with Yahweh because they gave their tithes to satisfy their pride and establish their own righteousness, not out of love, mercy, and compassion for Yah's colaborers on earth. The Pharisees obeyed the letter of the law while violating its spirit.

In Yeshua's Sermon on the Mount, He said the letter of the law said it was wrong to commit adultery, but if a man looked at a woman and lusted for her in his heart, he was guilty of adultery. Yeshua was filling the law up to the brim with meaning and revealing the spirit behind the letter (fulfilling the law). Yahweh's system of clean and unclean revealed what was in man's heart and pointed him to the Seed.

The Pharisees, however, believed that they could keep the Torah's dietary guidelines in order to overcome their evil inclination (fallen nature) and transform themselves into Yahweh's image. The Pharisees added their rules, regulations, and laws to the Torah's dietary guidelines in order to ensure that no one violated the Torah, and they figured that their rules would make them more like Yahweh. Once again, the Pharisees' zeal to keep the letter of the law violated the spirit of the law. Yahweh had given His people grains, fruits, vegetables, and animals that they could eat freely and enjoy, but the Pharisees' rules took the joy out of eating and turned it into a religious bondage. Yahweh's system of clean and unclean revealed the fallen nature and its effects on the heart while pointing to the Seed, but the Pharisees used the system of clean and unclean as fig leaves to cover up their fallen nature.

[xxi] In this section, for the sake of clarity, I am going to use the terms that English translations of the Bible use. I am going to use the terms *clean* and *unclean*. Now, technically, the Hebrew word *muttar* represents the kosher laws that permit and forbid different animals. The Hebrew word *tahor* represents the pollution laws that define things as "pure" and "impure" or "clean" and "unclean." The easiest way to communicate the information that I am attempting to convey is to use the terms *clean* and *unclean* consistently instead of bouncing back and forth with *permit* and *forbid*, *pure* and *impure*, which would complicate the discussion and increase the word count of this book.

[xxii] Paul uses the Greek word *broma* in this verse. According to the *Greek Dictionary of the New Testament*, *broma* means "food," specifically, articles allowed or forbidden by Jewish law: meat, victuals. The word comes from a base word that means "to eat." This is important because the word *meat* is misleading. To the modern mind, when we read that demons are lying to us, telling us that we cannot eat certain kinds of meat, we tend to think of pigs and other unclean meats and assume that when some people say we should not eat pigs and other unclean meats, they are trying to deceive us. However, Paul said that demons lied to people by telling them that they could not eat certain kinds of *food*. When Paul wrote the word *food*, he was only referring to those things that Yah had sanctified in the Torah. When a Jew heard the word *food*, he did not think about pigs or other unclean animals because Yahweh had said that pigs and other unclean animals were not fit to eat; that is, they were not food.

Paul is saying that Yahweh created everything and that everything is good, but not everything is fit to eat. In the Torah, Yahweh has told us what animals are fit to eat and what animals are not fit to eat. In other words, in the Torah, Yahweh defined what food was and gave us permission to eat these things freely. Yahweh also commanded us to thank Him after we have eaten and are full so that we remember that He is the giver and sustainer of our lives. No one should tell us that we have to abstain from the *food* that Yahweh has given us to eat, because He has sanctified it in His Word.

[xxiii] In the Age of the Written Torah, the Mosaic law said that *food* could become ritually impure by coming into contact with a person who was ritually impure. Moreover, *food* could become ritually impure by coming in contact with a pot that was ritually impure or by touching an animal that Yahweh said was not fit for food. In sum, Yahweh said that certain animals were fit to eat (food), but these animals (foods) could put priests and visitors to the temple in an impure state if they were mishandled.

Yah sanctified those animals that were consistent with His nature and prohibited those animals that were inconsistent with His nature. Yah's people were not to partake of those animals that were not consistent with His nature or allow them to defile the animals that

He said were consistent with His nature and then attempt to enter into His presence in the temple, because they would defile it.

In our age, Yeshua gives us His nature so that He can establish His temple in our bodies. Hence Yeshua fulfills the ceremonial requirements of the Mosaic law in us. Consequently, we do not have to worry about who has touched our food before we buy it or how someone had handled it or cooked it. Today nothing can make us ceremonially unclean and prevent us from entering into Yah's presence. Yahweh, however, did not change His mind about which animals were fit for food and which animals were not.

This means that no idol, demon, or man could defile the food that Yahweh said was clean and make it unclean; however, if a person did not believe this and was fearful that an idol, demon, or man turned food into something unclean, then for him, the food was unclean (not sanctified). In an absolute sense, Yahweh's Word sanctified all *food*; however, in a relativistic sense, the condition of a person's heart (fearful and unbelieving, or bold in belief) determined whether the *food* was clean for him. Thus Yah's Word and a believing, thankful heart that offers a prayer of thanksgiving to Him for food sanctify it.

[xxiv] Often people try to justify their behaviors that do not line up with the written Torah by saying, "All things are lawful for me, but not all things edify," and "To the pure, all things are pure." In a previous endnote, we discovered that Paul's statement in 1 Corinthians 6:12 does not mean that everything is lawful for us and that as long as it does not bring us into bondage, we can eat anything we want, drink anything we want, and have sex with whomever we choose to have sex with. (See endnote xviii above.)

In Titus 1:15, Paul says, "Unto the pure all things are pure: but unto them that are defiled and unbelieving is nothing pure; but even their mind and conscience is defiled. They profess that they know God; but in works they deny him, being abominable, and disobedient, and unto every good work reprobate." Did Paul mean that since Yeshua becomes one with our spirit and releases us from the custodianship and condemnation of the law, then the Torah's kosher guidelines no longer apply to us, and we are free to live as we wish? If this is what Paul meant in this verse, then he contradicted himself.

In context, Paul was rebuking Judaic Gnostics for their ascetic prohibitions. These people made up rules that prohibited certain behaviors and foods, saying that they rendered those who partook of them impure or unclean. Paul specifically said that these men based their prohibitions on "Jewish fables" and "commandments of men." The Torah is not a Jewish fable or the commandments of men; thus Paul was not referring to the commands that were in the Torah that related to clean (pure) and unclean (impure). Paul was referring to the people who perverted the commands in the Torah for their own profit.

Here is the key to this verse: The Pharisees saw Yeshua sit down to eat without following the sages' rules. The sages said a person had to wash his hands, or else he would defile his clean meat and it would become unclean. If this person ate the "unclean" meat, it would defile him and make him unclean. This "defiled" person could not enter the temple to worship Yah. In Luke 11:41, Yeshua told the Pharisees that all things were clean unto them. What was He saying? Yeshua was saying that what Yah cleansed was clean, and the sages' rules, "Jewish fables," and "commands of men" could not change His decree.

Paul said the same thing that Yeshua did. Paul said that what Yah cleansed was clean, and the Judaic Gnostics' ascetic prohibitions could not change that. However, to the fearful and unbelieving person who had allowed the Judaic Gnostics to defile their conscience, nothing that Yah cleansed was clean.

Paul's reference to the "pure" refers to those whom Yah has shared His nature with in order to purify their heart, enlighten their conscience with His teachings and instructions, and give them the power to walk out their intent. Paul did not say that since Yahweh has made us pure, the Torah no longer applies to us.

From: *Wuest's Word Studies from the Greek New Testament*. (Titus 1:15)

[xxv] People use this concept to justify *dominion theology,* or *kingdom now theology.* This theology says that the church has to take dominion over the earth *so that* Yeshua can return. HaSatan is using this theology to promote the one world religious, political, and economic system of the anti-Messiah.

It was Yah's intent that Adam and Eve establish His kingdom on the earth, but when they fell, it became impossible for them or their offspring to accomplish this task. Adam and Eve's fall created the need for Yeshua and the need for Him to reestablish Yah's kingdom on earth. The Scriptures are a description of how Yah and Yeshua work through the Word and the Spirit to reestablish the kingdom on the earth.

The Scriptures are one continuous, contiguous, progressive revelation of Yah's plan of redemption and restoration. The Scriptures tell us that Yah is implementing His plan in phases. The Tanakh describes the initial phases, and the apostolic writings describe the final phases. The Abrahamic phase is the foundational phase of Yahweh's plan, and the Mosaic phase builds onto the Abrahamic phase. The Messianic phase transforms the materialistic, geocentric mechanisms of the two previous phases into spiritual, universal mechanisms that allow Yah to fulfill His plan without relocating Gentiles to Israel.

The Garden of Eden was Yahweh's kingdom on the earth. Its headquarters was on Mount Moriah. The Garden of Eden prefigured Israel. Adam and Eve were supposed to spread Yah's kingdom (Israel) to the ends of the earth. They failed. Yahweh took His kingdom back to heaven with Him and began offering man citizenship in the heavenly kingdom.

Later Yah birthed Israel and reestablished His kingdom on the earth. The Gentiles who wanted to leave HaSatan's kingdom and enter Yah's kingdom could bow their knee to Him and relocate to Israel. Israel's rulers fell into unbelief and turned their relationship with

Yahweh into a religion, so He said that He would make someone else the stewards of His kingdom.

Yah came to earth to embody Israel and her institutions. Yeshua embodied Israel's institutions and died, resurrected, and sent His Spirit to live in us. Yeshua transformed Israel's earthly institutions into spiritual institutions that no man can lord over or corrupt. This is why the gates of hell will not prevail over Yeshua's ekklesia.

Yeshua's Spirit is in us performing the functions of Israel's institutions and keeping us attached to her righteous remnant. There are believers in every nation, so the commonwealth of Israel covers the earth. Today Yeshua, the King, the Great High Priest, has subjects in every nation, and His kingdom covers the earth. Soon He will return to convert His spiritual kingdom into an earthly one.

When His Father tells Him that it is time, Yeshua will return to reestablish His kingdom on the earth. Now, there will be a kingdom on the earth when Yeshua returns, but it will not be His kingdom. It will be the anti-Messiah's kingdom, and Yeshua will destroy it. Consequently, the only kingdom that men and women are building today is the anti-Messiah's kingdom. Now, I am not saying that the ekklesia should not function as salt and light and slow the decay of society in an attempt to prevent its collapse. We should function as salt and light, but we should not try to force the world to submit to us in order to establish Yeshua's kingdom on the earth. Yeshua will return and establish His kingdom on the earth in person.

CPSIA information can be obtained at www.ICGtesting.com
Printed in the USA
LVOW11s1644170713

343363LV00015B/509/P